CENSORSHIP AND THE IRISH WRITER

Politics, Polemics, and the International Dialectic

Censorship and the Irish Writer: Politics, Polemics, and the International Dialectic

BRAD KENT

UNIVERSITY OF TORONTO PRESS
Toronto Buffalo London

Toronto Buffalo London
utppublishing.com
Printed in Canada

ISBN 9781487567613 (cloth)
ISBN 9781487567637 (EPUB)
ISBN 9781487567620 (PDF)

Library and Archives Canada Cataloguing in Publication

Title: Censorship and the Irish writer : politics, polemics, and the international dialectic / Brad Kent.
Names: Kent, Brad, author.
Description: Includes bibliographical references and index.
Identifiers: Canadiana (print) 20260113964 | Canadiana (ebook) 20260114774 | ISBN 9781487567613 (hardcover) | ISBN 9781487567637 (EPUB) | ISBN 9781487567620 (PDF)
Subjects: LCSH: Censorship—Ireland—History—20th century. | LCSH: Anticensorship activists—Ireland—History—20th century. | LCSH: Authors, Irish—Political activity. | LCSH: Ireland—Intellectual life—20th century. | LCSH: Irish literature—Censorship—History. | LCSH: English literature— Censorship—History. | LCSH: Irish literature—20th century—History and criticism. | LCSH: English literature—Irish authors—History and criticism.
Classification: LCC Z658.I73 K46 2026 | DDC 363.3109415—dc23

Cover design: Heng Wee Tan
Cover image: iStock.com/Gannet77

The manufacturer's authorized representative in the European Union for product safety is Mare Nostrum Group B.V., Doelen 72, 4831 GR Breda, The Netherlands. Email: gpsr@mare-nostrum.co.uk

We wish to acknowledge the land on which the University of Toronto Press operates. This land is the traditional territory of the Wendat, the Anishnaabeg, the Haudenosaunee, the Métis, and the Mississaugas of the Credit First Nation.

This book has been published with the help of a grant from the Federation for the Humanities and Social Sciences, through the Awards to Scholarly Publications Program, using funds provided by the Social Sciences and Humanities Research Council of Canada.

University of Toronto Press acknowledges the financial support of the Government of Canada, the Canada Council for the Arts, and the Ontario Arts Council, an agency of the Government of Ontario, for its publishing activities.

Canada Council for the Arts   Conseil des Arts du Canada

Funded by the Government of Canada   Financé par le gouvernement du Canada

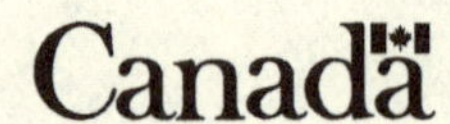

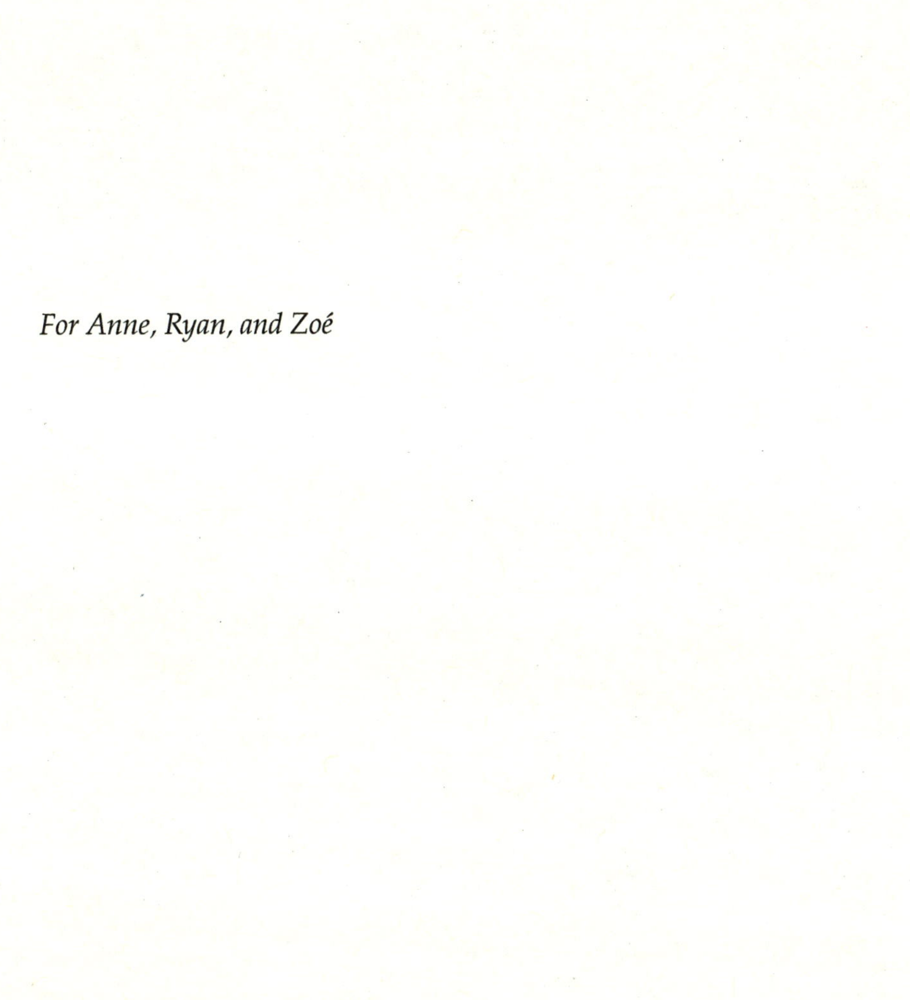

For Anne, Ryan, and Zoé

Table of Contents

Abbreviations

Add. Ms	Additional Manuscript
BL	British Library, London
DDA	Dublin Diocesan Archives
HRC	Harry Ransom Center, University of Texas at Austin
IFCO	Irish Film Classification Office, Dublin
Kew LC	Lord Chamberlain's Papers, The National Archives, Kew, England
KLA	Kilkenny Library Archives
KSC	Knights of St. Columbanus Archives, Dublin
LCP	Lord Chamberlain's Papers, British Library
LCP Corr	Lord Chamberlain's Papers, Correspondence, British Library
NAI	National Archives of Ireland, Dublin
NLI	National Library of Ireland, Dublin
UCD LA	University College Dublin Archives, Michael Tierney Papers
VAMTP	Victoria and Albert Museum Theatre and Performance Archives, London

Acknowledgments

I was fortunate during the research and writing of this book to have been supported by many individuals and organisations. Invaluable funding was provided by the Hobby Family Foundation and C. P. Snow Memorial Fund research fellowships at the Harry Ransom Center, a grant from the Fonds de recherche du Québec – Société et culture, an insight grant from the Social Sciences and Humanities Research Council of Canada, and several travel and research grants from Université Laval. The School of English at Trinity College Dublin hosted me as a visiting professor for a sabbatical leave, during which I conducted some of the research for this book, and the University of Oxford's Brasenose College and St. Catherine's College awarded me visiting fellowships while I was writing the manuscript; I am grateful to the people at all three institutions for their hospitality and the intellectual companionship that they provided. The librarians and archivists at the various places that I worked in were enormously helpful, and I am particularly obliged to Université Laval's *prêt entre bibliothèques* personnel, who over the years have tracked down rare books and secured copies of hard-to-find articles. At University of Toronto Press, Mark Thompson has been an exemplary editor, and I thank him for warmly welcoming this project when I first proposed it and for guiding me through the production process. I would also like to express my gratitude to the editors, journals, and presses that have published my research and allowed me to work through ideas that appear in this book. Three articles in particular form the basis of sections: "Censorship and Immorality: Bernard Shaw's *The Devil's Disciple*" in *Modern Drama* (chapter 2); "The Banning of Bernard Shaw's *The Adventures of the Black Girl in Her Search for God* and the Decline of the Irish Academy of Letters" in *Irish University Review* (chapter 5); and "Shaw, *The Bell*, and Censorship in 1945" in *SHAW: The Annual of Bernard Shaw Studies* (chapter 7).

When I first started considering the issue of censorship, Michael Kenneally, André Lecours, and Ronald Rudin kindly offered me their expertise and advice. Over the years, others have been likewise generous with their friendship, encouragement, and constructive criticism; for this, I would particularly like to thank Guy Beiner, Francesco Cavatorta, Marguérite Corporaal, Sos Eltis, Andrew Hadfield, Allan Hepburn, Margaret Kelleher, Liani Lochner, Jean-Philippe Marcoux, Peter McDonald, James Moran, Chris Morash, Eve Patten, Michel Pharand, Aileen Ruane, Kirsten Shepherd, Lawrence Switzky, Tom Walker, and Jerry White. I'm especially grateful to Leonard Conolly and Nicholas Grene, consummate gentlemen-scholars that I am fortunate to count as mentors and friends. My students have listened to me talk on censorship in lectures and seminars and at times have offered their own comments and perspectives, all of which has helped greatly.

On a more personal level, I'd like to thank my parents for their constant support. I also owe much to Anne, Ryan, and Zoé, who have been faithful fellow travellers; their love, humour, and sense of adventure have long sustained me, and for that, and so much more, I dedicate this book to them.

CENSORSHIP AND THE IRISH WRITER

Introduction

The Contours of Censorship, Politics, Polemics, and the International Dialectic

Having been confronted with a government-imposed censorship of plays for well over a century, dramatists in Britain finally became galvanised in 1907 when yet another of their colleagues had their work banned. The result was a campaign that would last the better part of two years and end in parliament forming a committee to inquire into institutional censorship and the possibility of reform. The movement launched when seventy-one playwrights published a letter of protest in *The Times,* criticising the unfairness of a secretive process that besmirched their good names while denying them the right to defend themselves. This collective energy caused William Archer to fantasise about a more aggressive public demonstration, with playwrights assembling in Trafalgar Square. In his imagining, J. M. Barrie opened the protest by addressing the crowd, and the Savoy Theatre's orchestra played "Rule Britannia," which includes a rousing refrain that insists "Britons never, never, never will be slaves." They then formed a procession headed by Arthur Wing Pinero and Bernard Shaw, who were immediately followed by Edward Garnett and John Galsworthy bearing a red banner with the inscription "Down with the Censor!" Next came W. B. Yeats and Gilbert Murray holding aloft an effigy of the censor and waving a standard blazoned with "Écrasez l'Infâme!"[1]

Here the Irish Shaw and Yeats are imagined as crucial members of the charge being led against institutional censorship in Britain. Alongside them are playwrights from other countries: the Scottish Archer and Barrie, the English Galsworthy, Garnett, and Pinero, and the Australian Murray. As they begin to march, most likely down Whitehall towards Westminster, they do so under slogans in different languages: the English "Down with the Censor!" and the French "Écrasez l'Infâme!" – the latter being Voltaire's entreaty to strike against the autocracy and obscurantism of the Catholic Church. This provides a strong international image, with writers from Australia, England, Ireland, and Scotland drawing upon the inspiration of a renowned French heretic to manifest their discontent and to agitate for greater freedom of expression. In so doing, it highlights how Irish authors contributed to the social and political battles that censorship provoked in other countries. And it foretells how the wider world would come to affect their responses to censorship within Ireland, where they were at times able to rely upon the support of an array of colleagues from elsewhere and at others had to look abroad to build their cases to end the suppression of literature.

While perhaps among the best known, Shaw and Yeats are far from the only Irish writers who have encountered, suffered from, and fought against censorship. The practice has played such a prominent part in the careers of so many that a roll call of those who have struggled with it mirrors the canon of modern Irish literature. Indeed, they compose a significant corpus of great modern literature *tout court*, including such diverse personalities as AE, Samuel Beckett, Lady Augusta Gregory, James Joyce, John McGahern, George Moore, Edna O'Brien, Kate O'Brien, Sean O'Casey, Frank O'Connor, Sean O'Faolain, Liam O'Flaherty, and Lennox Robinson. It is therefore not surprising, given the importance of censorship to literary history and reception, as well as its tendency to provide both farcical events and scandal, that many compelling studies have explored how individual Irish writers have dealt with censorship at various moments in their career.[2] More broadly, literary scholars have examined Irish authors in relation to the censorship of British literature and considered them as part of an Anglophone modernism.[3] In contrast, the study of the censorship of literature in Ireland has been dominated by historians who are more interested in the social and political contexts of literary censorship than aesthetic and philosophical concerns or indeed the writers themselves.[4] Until now, none have teased out a genealogy of the struggles of Irish writers, shown how over time certain reactions and strategies have been employed to differing levels of success, detailed how generations have drawn upon and been buttressed by their elders, and explored how they have adopted, adapted, and rejected the tactics of their forebears to suit their needs, circumstances, and personalities. In so doing, *Censorship and the Irish Writer* breaks with the tendency of censorship studies to restrict themselves to national boundaries by considering the international networks that underpinned these writers' working lives.

By bearing in mind the various ways that Irish writers have been affected by and have in turn attempted to affect censorship, this book is a larger meditation on how and why freedom of expression has been defended and suppressed in Britain and Ireland over the course of almost a century. This examination allows for a greater transnational scope and a longer historical perspective than has been employed in past explorations of the censorship of modernist literature and censorship in Ireland. Indeed, the subject is best understood in an international context because Ireland's censorship laws, crafted shortly after the country's independence, purposely echoed many aspects of British jurisprudence, and the debates that censorship provoked in Ireland sometimes drew upon controversies and arguments in other countries. In turn, when Irish writers fought systems of censorship at home, they often saw these local battles as part of a global war for artistic integrity and freedom of expression. This dual focus on Ireland and elsewhere is an integral part of the experience of many leading modern Irish writers who lived abroad and published with foreign presses. For those who stayed or returned, the national market and their treatment by their fellow Irish citizens and their native government were always primary concerns as they sought to create a freer and more equitable society and to make their livelihoods by their pens. At the same time, they desired to have greater reach and to be read by people around the world, and when Ireland rejected them, they found homes, friends, and work in other countries.

In a study of the effects of censorship on British modernism, Celia Marshik describes "the censorship dialectic" as a process whereby works created in a culture of censorship are inscribed with that very censorship.[5] In many respects, the writers that she examines continued to engage with taboo and obscene subject matter after being confronted with censorship, but they became more sophisticated over time and codified their material in more complex styles and forms. While this book discusses such aesthetic reactions, its focus, as both the title and Archer's fantasy suggest, is rather on the dialectical aspects of the polemical, political, and social responses of Irish writers through an international lens. This is encapsulated most evidently in the various relationships and networks, publishing and reception histories, and physical trajectories of Irish writers. Yet the dialectic also functions in more philosophical terms. Censorious groups and legislation, which, historically, have tended to be national, targeted foreign works to protect societies from external threats. Simultaneously, they cast the internal threats of domestic writers and literature as immoral exponents of cosmopolitanism and alien values. Meanwhile, many banned writers embraced that depiction, considering themselves as part of a broader Republic of Letters and thus not beholden to narrow cultural and political dictates. Instead, they argued that they were potential agents of positive progress, actively seeking inspiration and solidarity in the wider world of literature and appealing to freedom of expression as a universal and essential right that trumps local parochial concerns. The tensions between the conflicting world-views and actions of the censorious and the censored are thus revelatory of what I have termed "the international dialectic of censorship," a phenomenon that will be examined in the chapters that follow.

Censorship and Censors

We must first begin such a study by asking what exactly censorship is. Traditionally, it has been conceived as something that is performed by someone in a position authority, generally a civil servant, judge, religious figure, or elected politician, who is in charge of vetting works and determining their fitness for circulation, staging, viewing, or listening; yet scholars now accept a more elastic definition. While the latest edition of the *Oxford English Dictionary* defines "censorship" as the office or function of an official, it also more capaciously states that a censor is one who judges or criticises.[6] This broader concept, as more recent censorship studies have shown, includes purity movements, presses, publishers, booksellers, theatre producers, journalists, librarians, regular citizens, and even writers and intellectuals who might otherwise be perceived as champions of free speech.[7] The wider scope of these definitions of censor and censorship makes it more difficult to appeal to semantics to deny that censorship has in fact occurred in certain cases, as Sir William Joynson-Hicks, who from 1924 to 1929 was Britain's home secretary, tried to do. Despite having played a significant role in bringing obscene libel charges against presses and publishers, Joynson-Hicks claimed that he was not, in fact, a censor, reasoning that there was no systematic censorship of books in England. "If I understand the word rightly," he argued, censorship "implies a scrutiny by some central authority of the whole output, with a view to a discovery and suppression of such as offend against the standard for the establishment of which censorship is imposed."[8] However, for many people today and even in the 1920s, Joynson-Hicks was indeed a censor.

Such recalibrations of what a censor is have forced scholars to likewise consider multiple kinds of censorship. Even if one hews closely to the classic focus on official forms, there is some variation, with government censorships tending to be either regulative or prohibitive.[9] Regulative censorship is based on surveillance and licensing systems. Examples of this include the Catholic Church, which requires religious officials to obtain the censor's imprimatur before they can publish their work, and the British censorship of plays, which mandated theatres to submit manuscripts for approval before they could be performed. In contrast, prohibitive censorship allows for a work to circulate first, then be tried or banned later. In the United States, plays have long been allowed to be produced and books published without prior permission; if they are considered to fall foul of obscenity laws, they can then be contested in courts of law over their fitness for public consumption. Both Britain and Ireland have long had prohibitive book censorships, although they differ considerably. In Britain, editors and printers can be prosecuted in court for publishing obscene libels and, if found guilty, have fines levied against them or face jail time; in Ireland, because there was for much of its history a relatively insignificant native publishing industry and most books were imported, censorship is post-publication and overseen by a five-member, government-appointed board who determine whether a book should be banned.

The Yugoslav novelist Danilo Kiš, who experienced censorship while living under communist rule, noted two other types that extend from the official variety. The first is what he termed "friendly censorship," which arises when, for example, an "editor (himself a man of letters) suggests that you eliminate such and such a paragraph or stanza from your book for your own good. If he is unable to convince you of his good faith, he will use moral blackmail and confine his fears to your safekeeping – his fate, too, depends upon your willingness to censor yourself, to conceal the censorship from the public."[10] External forms of censorship, whether official or friendly, lead to the second type: self-censorship. Self-censorship, Kiš argued, "means reading your own text through someone else's eyes," which causes you to "become stricter and more suspicious than anyone else could, because you, the author, know what no censor could ever discover – your most secret, unspoken thoughts, which you feel can still be read between the lines."[11] In many ways, this is the end goal of all censorships, no matter what their nature: to affect the thinking of individuals so that they censor themselves, thereby making all external censorship unnecessary.

American lawyers Morris Ernst and Alexander Lindey, who litigated the banning of literature in the United States, including Ernst's successful defence of James Joyce's *Ulysses* in 1933, also noted "personal censorship" as a significant force, but from a less negative standpoint.[12] Personal censorship is essentially one's conscious decision not to read a particular author or to boycott someone, something, some institution, or some country because of one's tastes, values, and beliefs. Unlike the other forms of censorship mentioned above, this is based on personal choice and requires no coercion. In many regards, this is as much a freedom as the freedom of speech because it suggests that we should not be forced to read certain works or adhere to certain ideas in much the same way as we should not be prevented from expressing ourselves through the works we create, read, listen to, and watch. This is relevant to the distinction between censorship and selection, which is particularly important for librarians, presses, bookstores, theatres, and even individuals in general.[13] Whereas censorship implies a conscious decision to not purchase or to withdraw from circulation a certain book or author for a particular reason, selection is not a negative act. Selection is instead determined by such factors as budgetary constraints, the interests of an institution's patrons, limits on one's leisure time, and shelf space.[14] At the end of the day, one has to prioritise and live within one's means. For example, a theatre might wish to mount productions of any number of plays, but they must narrow the choices down according to such matters as potential commercial interest, the size and type of their company of actors, whether a play is still in copyright and performance rights have to be paid, its perceived quality, and the desired coherence or variety when programming a season. In this sense, a play's themes or political, religious, economic, and sexual viewpoints might not be factors in deciding if it will be produced. In certain contexts, one therefore has to tread lightly in making claims about whether or not censorship has in fact occurred.

As for official censorship, we can trace its creation to Rome in the third century BCE, when a functionary was first appointed as censor and was charged with the dual task of registering Rome's citizens and supervising public morals.[15] The register that they oversaw is known today as the census, which shares etymological roots with *censor*. As the censor's duty was to determine one's belonging and status in the eyes of the state, when someone was censored, they did not share the same rights as their neighbours, and they were, at least metaphorically, cast out of the tribe. In this sense, the international dialectic of censorship is ingrained in the origins of the practice: some citizens are embraced by censors, while others are rendered alien. Certainly, many Irish writers felt like outcasts upon being censored both at home and abroad. Because of the moral role of the censor, the message was, effectively, that these writers did not share the same morality as their fellow citizens and thus were considered pariahs and outlaws.

At the same time, we must be aware that there is a slippery understanding of morality. While the terms *moral* and *immoral* are often conflated with *good* and *evil*, morality is instead best understood as that which is customary among a people and represents the shared collective values of the majority. In censorship debates, there is often a positioning of parties between those who see morality as holding together the social fabric and needing to be protected, and those who deem morality to be outdated and in need of being challenged and modernised. Censorship and morality are therefore imbricated. Indeed, that which is banned is that which contravenes and threatens morality because immorality proposes a counter set of values to supplant the dominant morality. For some people, this is the allure of censored writers: they are perceived by authorities as criminals, radicals, and rebels who could overturn the current order.

As we will see, those in positions of power and those who seek to maintain morality often label banned writers not only as evil, immoral, criminal, and radical, but also as lewd, immodest, impure, blasphemous, lascivious, filthy, disgusting, indecent, and obscene. These last two terms are particularly important in censorship legislation, the modern origins of which are found in England's Obscene Publications Act of 1857, which effectively codified the censorship of literature, and the precedent-setting Cockburn ruling of 1868, which provided the legal definition of obscenity as that which tends to deprave and corrupt. As the *Oxford English Dictionary* attests, scholars have debated the etymological origins of "obscene." For some, it derives from the Latin *caenum*, meaning mud or filth, while for others it derives from *scaena*, meaning the setting of a play.[16] In combining the two, we might conclude that the obscene offends by performing a filthy act in public and censorship is therefore justified as preventing such acts from being read, seen, or heard, and thus protecting the community from being negatively affected. However, there is very little consensus on such essential matters as how exactly filthy literature is defined, what it means to deprave or to corrupt someone, who that perceived audience would be, how someone's corruption or depravity could be traced to a particular work over other factors, or how many people would have to be corrupted or depraved to justify censorship. Writing in 1930, the year after the Irish government passed the Censorship of Publications Act and in the wake of a few highly publicised obscenity trials in England, Bernard Causton and G. Gordon Young argued that the result of such legal uncertainty was that all books were judged according to "the lowest common denominator of character."[17] That is, acceptable, moral literature would be determined by what was considered fit for children or people who were deemed to be easily influenced. In the end, Alec Craig argues, slack legal definitions led to many arbitrary judgments that "proved a fruitful source of injustice to individuals and damage to science, literature and society."[18]

One of the difficulties for many modern writers was that while sex and sexuality were increasingly considered acceptable subjects of discussion in public, authorities held literature to higher standards. In Western countries, censorship has had a changing focus since the Middle Ages. For the Catholic Church, censorship was directed at heresy and blasphemy, meaning ideas that ran counter to religious doctrine. With the rise of modern empires and nation-states in the 1600s and 1700s, the focus then turned to political censorship and especially the espousal of democracy and republicanism that threatened the feudal and monarchical order. At times, religious and political censorship were intertwined, as evidenced in the treatment of Spinoza in the Netherlands of the late seventeenth century and the Encyclopaedists in Enlightenment-era France.[19] From the mid-nineteenth century onwards, there was then a shift in censorship towards a focus on sex and sexuality. Again, this is a broad tendency that is helpful for conceptualising general historical changes and should not be considered a hard and fast rule. The rise of democracy, capitalism, socialism, communism, and fascism, for example, gave cause for political censorship; indeed, in polities whose dominant ideologies conflicted with them, they were often associated with sexual immorality to highlight their perversion and their threat to the nation.

In many respects, this is why writers sought to distance themselves from charges of pornography despite engaging with the obscene. After writing *Lady Chatterley's Lover*, D. H. Lawrence published *Pornography and Obscenity*, a pamphlet in which he sought to differentiate the two terms. For Lawrence, sex appeal, or that which is often defined as obscene, is perfectly normal. In contrast, "Pornography is the attempt to insult sex, to do dirt on it." This, he said, was "unpardonable."[20] Sounding like a high-minded puritan, Lawrence suggested that pornographical people were filth-mongers, charging them with conflating "the sex flow and the excremental flow."[21] James Joyce differed in his approach, using Stephen Dedalus in *A Portrait of the Artist as a Young Man* to distinguish between works of art that have sexual subjects and those that seek to titillate. For Dedalus, improper art is kinetic in that it provokes desire (a move towards the object) or loathing (a move away from the object). In contrast, proper art causes one to behold, to contemplate, and to admire; by so doing, it arrests the mind and raises it above desire and loathing.[22] Allison Pease refers to writers like Lawrence and Joyce as engaging in the aesthetics of obscenity, which "is a mode of sexual representation that, while potentially affecting the sensual interests of its readers, does not, as opposed to pornography, seek sexual arousal as its main purpose."[23] Unlike Lawrence and Joyce, Pease admits that the aesthetics of the obscene can still elicit sexual interest, but she is careful to emphasize that the work's assertion of form "holds off the collapse into the pornographic."[24] While Pease's formulation is helpful for discussing works that are more readily identifiable as high modernist in their experimentalism, as we will see, many of the censorship battles that were waged over the almost hundred years covered by this book were contested over naturalism and realism, both of which have been traditionally sidelined in modernist studies despite posing the more direct threat to dominant moralities. Harry M. Clor's distinction between pornographers as those "concerned with arousing and indulging the sexual fantasies of readers" and serious realist authors that depicted sex as those "concerned with telling the truth as they understand it" is therefore useful for better understanding distinctions that many censors failed or refused to make and that authors, intellectuals, and lawyers employed to defend a range of writing.[25]

Politics

The challenges posed by censorship become particularly acute in democracies where government is, by definition, of and for the people. Who are the people represented by the censorship and who are the people negatively affected by it? And how many of each are there? In certain forms, censorship can be a manifestation of Ernest Renan's famous response to the question "What is a nation?": it is "a daily plebiscite."[26] That is, just as the idea of the nation requires public support, so censorship depends upon such support to maintain its legitimacy. Once it deviates too much from public opinion, it becomes susceptible to reform or wholesale abolition.

In all democracies, there are tensions between competing rights, which differ from public opinion in that rights are legally enshrined. How these tensions are negotiated determines to what extent a democracy is liberal or conservative. Broadly speaking, liberal democracies are more focused on individual rights while conservative democracies are more focused on collective rights. A liberal democracy tolerates individuals who might be regarded as countercultural or who openly challenge the dominant morality in favour of other values and morals, which implies that there should be less censorship.[27] However, this does not mean that there should be total freedom. John Stuart Mill, the great philosopher of Victorian liberalism, insisted that "the individual is not accountable for his actions," but only "in so far as these concern the interests of no person but himself. . . . [F]or such actions as are prejudicial to the interests of others, the individual is accountable, and may be subjected to social or to legal punishment, if society is of the opinion that the one or the other is requisite for its protection."[28] In contradistinction, polities that prioritise the collective over the individual are by definition less tolerant of deviance and therefore would be prone to have more censorship and be more conservative.[29] In democracies, there is thus a conflict, often a healthy one, between the claims of the individual and the collective that can provoke any combination of debate, retrenchment, and shifts in morality. As an expression of values, censorship becomes a flashpoint for these instances of questioning and hardening of positions.

As the history in this book traces, there was in Britain and Ireland a general movement from conservative to liberal democracy. Yet the countries did not move at the same speeds in this transition, and at times they oscillated between the two poles, although not necessarily simultaneously or in the same direction. Britain of the Victorian era and the early twentieth century is often regarded as politically and culturally conservative: social values were religiously puritan, the class system was still by and large intact, the empire enjoyed its golden age, the social welfare state had yet to see the light of day, and women and some men did not have the right to vote, thereby making it both a conservative *and* a partial democracy, refusing certain rights based on one's gender, class, or country of origin. The Bloomsbury writer Clive Bell offered one of the more damning pictures of Britain in these years, asserting that it was "one of the least free countries in the world." Citing a plethora of parliamentary acts that restricted individual liberties, including those pertaining to alcohol, gambling, and literature, he concluded that a British subject in 1923 was "at least as much a slave as he was under Cromwell and his colonels."[30] However much he might have been exaggerating for rhetorical effect, he rightly noted the relative lack of freedom of fellow citizens compared to the freedom that people in other countries enjoyed, noting that the French could attend plays by Henrik Ibsen and Bernard Shaw and read books by Honoré de Balzac and D. H. Lawrence that he could not. He referred to the overseers and supporters of censorship as "The Enemies of Freedom," as they sought to impose their will on others and maintain a conservative society.[31] Just as censors and puritans demonised banned writers, Bell illustrated the common countermove to demonise those who sought to limit personal rights.

In contrast to the Britain of these years, and despite its colonial relationship, Ireland represented a relative beacon of real and hoped-for liberty. As we will see, the Abbey Theatre was modelled on the continental and British independent theatre movements, which freed it from commercial demands and allowed it to stage plays that were considered aesthetic and nationalist rather than strictly popular. When the

Lord Chamberlain refused to licence Shaw's *The Shewing-up of Blanco Posnet* in Britain, the Abbey gave it an unlicensed production, in the process challenging British mores and authority. Politically, while suffragettes fought for their rights, the Proclamation of the Irish Republic, which was drafted by the leaders of the 1916 Easter Rising, addressed Irishmen and Irishwomen alike. Most famously, it guaranteed "religious and civil liberty, equal rights and equal opportunities to all its citizens" and declared "its resolve to pursue the happiness and prosperity of the whole nation and of all its parts . . . oblivious of the differences carefully fostered by an alien government."[32] Yet in pre-independence Ireland, there were also more conservative elements afoot and in positions of power.

Indeed, pre-independence Ireland looks most liberal when it is compared with Ireland in the half century following independence. Post-independence Ireland, the period from 1922 to the 1960s, was a conservative democracy buoyed by insularity. This was due to several factors, including trade wars and protectionist policies; the robust Irish-Ireland movement that advocated for all things Irish by promoting the Irish language, national chauvinism, and a xenophobic world-view; and the dominance of the Catholic Church over so much of Irish life. This conservativism attracted a great deal of criticism from both within and beyond Ireland's borders. While Irish writers, as we will see, were vocal about Ireland's closed society, its most renowned international critic at the time was the American anti-Catholic polemicist Paul Blanshard, who had previously published the bestselling *American Freedom and Catholic Power* and *Communism, Democracy, and Catholic Power*. Writing in 1953, when Ireland's censorship was in its most zealous period, Blanshard charged that the country was more devoutly Catholic than even fascist Portugal and Spain, being "the only modern democracy with no divorce, no legal birth control, and no comprehensive public-school system."[33] So aligned were the Church and state that he referred to Ireland as "The Clerical Republic."[34]

Meanwhile, other commentators insisted that the relationship between church and state was positive. In his defence of the Catholic viewpoint of censorship, the Jesuit priest Harold Gardiner argued that because the goal of society is the common good, authority, which governs society, should be respected and loved.[35] When authority is not respected, it must coerce. While he admitted that unbounded coercion could lead to injustice and tyranny, benevolent authority coerced "as a means to prevent the frustration of the common good."[36] Yet Gardiner did not suggest what methods or mechanisms should be crafted to prevent authority from sliding into tyranny – mainly because this would suggest that power needs to be kept in check. In Orwellian terms, he instead argued that coercion can lead to greater freedom because coercing those who fail to follow society's rules or abide by its norms and mores works towards the greater good. As for the Catholic Church, Gardiner maintained that "by reason of its divine mandate" it "has not only the right but the *duty* of safeguarding the faith and morals of its subjects."[37]

Although apologists have downplayed the abuses of the Church and state in Ireland in preserving a conservative democracy that preyed on its most vulnerable and the detrimental impact that censorship had on Irish writers, the bulk of historical studies and government reports published in the twenty-first century flat out contradict them.[38] Similarly, regardless of the quality of their scholarship, many earlier histories of twentieth-century Ireland have become terribly dated, in part because of their lack of archival access and foreknowledge of such reports, in part because of their methodologies, and in part because of their inability to grasp, from both theoretical and practical standpoints, how religious capital and values functioned in Ireland. J. H. Whyte, for example, surveyed cases in which the church hierarchy was consulted, publicly protested, or imposed itself in the political sphere and calculated that this only amounted to a paltry average of once per year, thereby representing involvement in only a small fraction of legislation and thus minimal political influence.[39] However, the sociologist Tom Inglis has insisted that such statistics hide more than they reveal about church-state relations because they fail to account for how Catholic politicians, who formed the majority of those in the Irish parliament, had internalised the church's teachings.[40] Indeed, as Fearghal McGarry argues, clerical power in Ireland was "demonstrated not by clashes between church and state but by their absence; the acceptance of the Catholic hierarchy's authority across the political spectrum explained the failure of one of the most ostentatiously Catholic states in Europe to produce a Catholic political party."[41] As Catholicism was the dominant religion in Ireland, many people sought religious capital, which enabled them "to attain the symbolic power of the Church" and accrue social, political, and economic capital.[42] Moreover, the Church controlled healthcare and schools, meaning that it had a monopoly of power over sexual knowledge and the education of future generations. Andrew F. Comyn, who was appointed to the Censorship of Publications Board in 1956, suggested that "the aim of the schools appeared to be to produce a safe man who led a good life and asked no questions; a sort of Catholic 'Yes-man.'"[43] While post-independence Ireland was not a theocratic state, it was thus a theocratic society.[44]

At no time did the power of Catholicism in Ireland become so evident and as consolidated as the week-long 1932 International Eucharistic Congress, at which the hundreds of thousands of attendees participated in the expression of "a faithful adherence to Roman orthodoxy *and* an indigenous Irish Catholic identity" that was overseen by religious and political officials.[45] Writing in 1954, the diplomat and future politician Conor Cruise O'Brien remarked that in Ireland, "Church and State exist in harmony as inexpugnable bastions of the family."[46] Even in the 1970s, when this book ends with a shift towards a more liberal society in Ireland, 78 per cent of all respondents to a survey said that they would like to see their son become a priest and believed that priests were better than lay people, and 86.5 per cent argued that should a conflict arise between the Church and the state, the Church should have authority because, as a divine institution, it is infallible.[47] Given that the Church demanded its followers to adhere to its doctrines, Anthony Keating has argued that in post-independence Ireland, Irish Catholicism was "deeply conservative and authoritarian, with an overstated pessimism regarding the people of Ireland's ability to withstand foreign vice without the application of rigid clerical discipline."[48]

The result of the collusion between church and state and the primacy of religious capital was that post-independence Ireland became far more of a conservative democracy than Victorian Britain. Most concretely, it created what James M. Smith has called an "architecture of containment" that illegally incarcerated and maltreated Irish citizens on an industrial scale.[49] In such institutions as the Magdalen laundries, women who were considered sexual deviants, mainly for being promiscuous or having children out of wedlock, were extrajudicially confined, ruthlessly exploited for their physical labour, and subjected to all manner of horrific abuse.[50] The architecture of containment was further expressed in the government's censorship legislation and spread into such varieties of informal censorship as social exclusion, bullying, censure, boycotting, and protesting. In this sense, censorship in Ireland, as in many other polities, worked in both directions – bottom-up and top-down – with each side granting the other agency and legitimacy. This censoriousness was so prevalent that it extended to authorities censoring themselves. Most notorious in this regard was the fate of the Carrigan Report (1931), which detailed the findings of a government-appointed committee to inquire into juvenile prostitution. The report showed an alarming increase in the number of sex offences against those under sixteen years of age and a horrendous tendency of authorities to not prosecute guilty parties.[51] So scandalous was the report that the government suppressed it, believing that it damaged exceptionalist claims of the nation's morality as a Catholic country and would undermine faith in public authorities.[52] In such circumstances, the children were multiply victimised: in the first instance, they were abused; in the second instance, they did not have recourse to justice, protection, and adequate health services; in the third instance, their truth was expunged from the official record; and in the fourth instance, their experiences did not lead to reforms that could protect future victims. This was in many ways the pattern of censorship: a stymieing of reality in order to maintain an idealistic image of society and thus the status quo. In turn, this allowed authorities to engage in the international dialectic of censorship, to point their fingers beyond their borders and to locate immorality and perversion in foreign influences. They also blamed Irish writers who lived abroad, who were more cosmopolitan in their outlook, and who published in other countries and enjoyed popularity in those markets. As John A. Murphy has commented, censorship in Ireland is xenophobic, expressing "a moral and cultural Sinn Féinism which requires a self-sufficiency in ideas and in literature, as well as in political status and the economy."[53]

In this way, the architects and guardians of conservative Ireland attempted to curtail and deny the influence of Irish writers and intellectuals. Bishops in their Lenten pastorals and priests in their sermons demonised the literati. In one particularly trenchant polemic, the Catholic writer Aodh de Blácam noted how a Portuguese friend informed him that while the country was prospering under the fascist dictatorship of António de Oliveira Salazar, the only demographic that complained was the intelligentsia: "One might know that they would be discontented. The cynic and destroyer always are."[54] Closer to home, he denounced how the "heresiarch Shaw" and others of his kind had downplayed the effects of their impropriety.[55] The Jesuit priest Patrick J. Gannon similarly mocked the raging of intellectuals against Irish censorship laws, and in particular how, on one occasion, "From England the redoubtable G. B. Shaw intervened with a contribution which had not even the dialectical acumen or seasoning of humour rarely absent from his iconoclastic pages."[56] Oftentimes unwilling to take the polemics of censored writers and intellectuals seriously, conservatives simply ridiculed them. Coming from those who wielded religious capital, the attacks did much to undermine the cultural, social, and political capital of more liberal thinkers. While some personalities like Shaw rose to the challenge of such attacks and continued to write and organise against conservative morality, the effect that they had was at times detrimental to frank discussion of taboo and controversial subjects. For example, when referring to the banning of Kate O'Brien's novel *The Land of Spices*

(1941) for a single sentence in which the protagonist's father is discreetly described as having been discovered in a homosexual embrace, the formerly censored writers Benedict Kiely and John Broderick, speaking almost fifty years later, were reduced to circumscription, respectively noting that the character "was having, you know the thing, just a line and a half" and that the book "was banned for just one phrase; you know the one. Ridiculous."[57] If even those who are among society's most individualistic and articulate censor themselves and are reduced to allusions, ellipses, and silences, then the architecture of containment has achieved significant success towards ensuring its survival.[58]

As Michel Foucault famously put it, "power produces knowledge," "power and knowledge directly imply one another," and "there is no power relation without the correlative constitution of a field of knowledge."[59] Because censorship controls knowledge, power is needed to wield it, whether this comes from institutional affiliation, one's position within society, or the backing of a vocal body of people who are motivated to act. Indeed, Gardiner admits that the coercive nature of censorship exemplifies "the exercise of control."[60] Dr. Cornelius Lucey, the chair of philosophy and political theory at St. Patrick's College Maynooth and later the archbishop of Cork, openly stated this in 1937: "There is something seductive about the written word. Those who read it come almost unconsciously to make its ideas and its outlook their own. Only if they find one writer contradicting another do they exercise anything like judgment on it. Hence whoever can control the reading matter in a community can control, too, the minds and emotions of the citizens."[61] Such rationale emphasized the need for the Church to maintain its control of the Irish education system not only to determine *what* future generations would read, but also *how* they would read and, in turn, how they would think. As opposed to developing critical, independent citizens, the emphasis was rather placed on rote learning and the regurgitation of orthodox views. In this context, the censored writer is defined as a criminal, an enemy of the people who undermines society. In all polities, censorship is a punishment for having committed a crime, although such further measures as fines, imprisonment, enforced exile, torture, and execution can also be levied. Yet the target of the punishment, Foucault notes, is not simply the criminal, the one who has been found guilty; above all, he argues, punishment is directed at "the potentially guilty" as a warning based on "the representation of public morality."[62] Censorship therefore not only functions as a way of educating banned writers and possibly bringing them back into the fold but also, more importantly, as a way of instructing other writers as to what is acceptable so that they do not produce immoral work. More broadly, it is directed at all people to apprise them of the norms and mores of their society.

In this sense, censorship becomes imbricated in the nation-building and citizen-formation process. This is especially true in a newly independent country such as Ireland that introduced censorship legislation to distinguish itself from Britain and to keep out unwanted foreign influences to ensure that morality was univocal and unbendingly static rather than multivocal and flexible. Judith Butler thus asserts that censorship makes "certain citizens possible and others impossible" by achieving "cultural control over their own representation and narrativization."[63] In effect, censorship allows a state to neuter challenges to its legitimacy and to build and enforce consensus.[64]

Although censorship punishes, warns, controls, and silences, it also publicises both itself and that which it censors. This is positive from the censor's point of view as it allows people to see where power is situated and who wields it, thereby reinforcing that power. Foucault underlines this didactic function, claiming that "punishments must be a school" and "an ever-open book" because a "secret punishment is a punishment half wasted."[65] Yet the paradox of censorship is that while it publicises the crime, labels the criminal, warns others against committing the same offences, and tells people how they should act, think, and feel, the banned idea, book, or person is given a heightened sense of importance. Going back to the lesson of the Garden of Eden, the forbidden fruit is difficult to resist. By drawing attention to the immoral, censorship can simultaneously make that immorality both less and more attractive. In return, by being branded an outlaw, the censored writer might not be ashamed and repentant, but rather be proud of their newfound status, seeing it as a sign of their independence and refusal to kowtow. Their notoriety can also transform them into a celebrity of sorts and lead to increased readership and wealth. Such an unashamed writer tends to resist more openly by participating in polemics and public meetings, and organising people towards safeguarding and augmenting freedoms of speech. In this way, censorship, rather than proving to be a punishment, can in some cases become more of a reward by granting the writer greater power and forms of capital and an incentive for others to follow their lead.

Pedigrees of Censorship Arguments

Just as we might speak of liberal and conservative democracies, we could consider censorship arguments in similarly broad terms. For all intents and purposes, conservative arguments in favour of censorship can be traced back to Plato's *Republic*, which proposes to welcome some authors, but ban others to protect the integrity of society and its citizens. Focusing first on children as an audience, Plato emphasizes the role that censorship has in supplementing education so that the young do not "take into their own minds opinions for the most part contrary to those we shall think it desirable for them to hold when they are grown up."[66] In this way, the republic would ensure its stability by avoiding the introduction of competing values and moral systems while indoctrinating future generations. Blasphemy was of particular concern, Plato believing that Homer and Hesiod had written unfavourably of the gods. As a result, society should "bury them in silence." If their tales were to be retold, the retelling should only occur before "a very small audience ... admitted under pledge of secrecy."[67] To ensure that such writing was avoided in the future, Plato proposed a law that all writers and speakers would have to abide by the notion that "God is not the cause of all things, but only of the good."[68] Allied with this concern, he desired to ban any tales that represented rulers as corrupt or greedy so as to preserve idealist views of authority as benevolent. Plato also targeted allegorical works because many people, especially children, would not be able to decode them properly. Other negative tendencies in writing, such as provoking the fear of death, should be avoided in favour of stories that promote desirable values, such as courage. This would ensure that people act in accordance with the commands of authorities, such as by soldiering bravely into battle and not avoiding war. Most importantly, then, Plato believed that storytelling should be circumscribed because it had the power to influence and mould people and thus either transform society or help maintain the status quo.

Not surprisingly then, Irish writers did not turn to Plato for inspiration in their struggles with censorship. Instead, they often cited the seventeenth-century English Puritan writer John Milton and his pamphlet *Areopagitica* as most representative of their viewpoints and to bolster their claims. Written in 1644, *Areopagitica* denounced the government's licensing order of the previous year, which mandated that authors acquire a licence to publish their work. Under the auspices of this regulation, Milton's tracts advocating divorce were suppressed because they were deemed to promote sexual libertinism. The new law, Milton argued, would discourage learning and prevent truth from circulating, would cause people to stop exercising their reason and intelligence, and would prevent future discoveries and innovations.[69] The result of such censorship would therefore be "a perpetual childhood of prescription," in effect infantilizing citizens.[70] Milton reasoned that to kill a human was to kill a reasonable creature that was made in God's image, but to destroy "a good book" was to kill reason itself, for "a good book is the precious life blood of a master-spirit, embalmed and treasured up on purpose to a life beyond life."[71] Yet Milton never did define what determines a book's goodness, thereby leaving the term open for interpretation.

In making his appeal, Milton referred to Galileo Galilei, whose argument in favour of the heliocentric model of the universe, which proposed that the earth revolves around the sun, led to him being placed under lifetime house arrest and his theory being suppressed by the Catholic Church. This was because Galileo's findings ran counter to the Church's geocentric model, which insisted that the universe revolved around the earth.[72] By gesturing to Galileo, Milton suggested that the licensing law would cause England to suffer "incredible loss," becoming worse than an enemy who stops up their ports to prevent the traffic of goods as "it hinders and retards the importation of our richest merchandise, truth."[73] Instead, England, which had "proclaimed and sounded forth the first tidings of reformation to all of Europe," should cultivate "faithful labourers to make a knowing people, a nation of prophets, of sages and of worthies."[74] In this way, *Areopagitica* not only argues for greater freedoms of speech, but also posits that England had returned to the world the truth and reason of ancient Greece by casting off the tyranny and oppression of the Catholic Church; yet the rulers were attempting to resuscitate tyranny and oppression through the licensing act. In many respects, this echoes the complaint of Irish writers, who noted that once the country had achieved independence from Britain, legislators then passed censorship laws to curtail their newfound freedom.

Despite their differences, Plato and Milton had a shared belief in the power of stories to shape individuals and society, which is fundamental in both conservative and liberal perspectives of censorship. However, as opposed to fearing change, the liberal by and large embraces it to usher in positive progress. While the conservative is worried about collective cohesion, the liberal is focused on the liberty of individuals to express themselves. Yet there are two grades of liberalism: collectivistic and autonomistic. The former is achieved through the modern state and admits the need for some cohesion, whereas the latter is the result of the state's diminished role and considers the individual more sacrosanct, thereby making it more radical and situating it towards the extreme end of the conservative-liberal spectrum. Collectivistic liberalism, which was embraced by the majority of political and social reformers and Irish writers covered in this study, dominated much of the debates, while the autonomistic liberal viewpoint was only a fringe element. Because it is not as radical with regard to individual liberty, collectivistic liberalism accepts the need for some forms of censorship and cohesion, although it insists that these be more tolerant of opposing value systems as well as less stringent and punitive than under conservatism. Meanwhile, autonomistic liberalism is far more absolute in insisting on freedoms of speech, no matter how potentially asocial, hate-filled, and destructive that speech might be.

The classic collectivistic liberal view of censorship was theorised by John Stuart Mill in his essay *On Liberty*, written in 1854 and published in 1859. Mill's concern was not with liberty of the will, but rather civil and social liberty and in particular "the nature and limits of the power which can be legitimately exercised by society over the individual."[75] To avoid abuses of those in power and to increase the liberty of individuals, Western societies had over the course of the previous centuries curbed the liberties of rulers. Liberty, Mill reasoned, had therefore been achieved through two complementary movements: obtaining political rights for individuals and establishing constitutional checks to prevent authoritarian interference. According to Mill, the goal for democratic societies was to find a balance between individual independence and social control. In most cases, censorship was not warranted because without allowing for dissent and unorthodox opinions, we cannot be certain that the measures, rules, and customs that we follow are necessarily the best. By testing them against discordant ideas, a society should adopt or adapt new approaches and concepts, in part or in whole, or become more certain of the rightness of their established practices and opinions.

Aside from governmental power, Mill was concerned with the potential for a collective authoritarianism and tighter democratically imposed social controls, arguing that it was society's duty to find the limit of "the legitimate interference of collective opinion with individual independence: and to find that limit, and maintain it against encroachment, is as indispensable to a good condition of human affairs, as protection against political despotism."[76] There thus have to be checks on informal, social censorship and the ability of the majority and public opinion, which Mill memorably labelled "collective mediocrity," to unjustly impose its will on individuals and minorities.[77] Social intolerance, he admitted, "kills no one, roots out no opinions"; however, it provokes the sort of self-censorship that Kiš described by inducing people to "disguise" their opinions or "to abstain from any active effort for their diffusion." The "price paid for this sort of intellectual pacification," Mill argued, "is the sacrifice of the entire moral courage of the human mind."[78] Of particular concern for him were "Persons of genius." While these people have always been a small minority, he insisted that for them to grow and survive, they require "an *atmosphere* of freedom" as they are "*more* individual than other people – less capable, consequently, of fitting themselves, without hurtful compression, into any of the smaller moulds which society provides in order to save its members the trouble of forming their own character."[79] At the same time, Mill favoured individual freedom to express discontent in the form of personal censorship, that is, to assert one's ability to express distaste with and to stand aloof from someone, but, he insisted, we should not "make his life uncomfortable."[80] On the whole, he pleaded for tolerance because "unless we are willing to adopt the logic of persecutors, and to say that we may persecute others because we are right, and that they must not persecute others because they are wrong, we must be aware of admitting a principle of which we should resent as a gross injustice the application to ourselves."[81] In this regard, censorship is narcissistic, with the censor convinced of the rightness and superiority of their morality and then imposing that morality on others. As we will see, Irish writers were threatened by forceful community censorship that at times could be even more insidious than government censorship, leading to a detrimental impact on their ability to make their livelihoods and to express themselves. This is precisely why Bernard Shaw argued that "Toleration and liberty have no sense or use except as toleration of opinions that are considered damnable, and liberty to do what seems wrong."[82] Such freedoms, the liberal viewpoint insists, should be promoted and safeguarded both for individuals and for the health of the agora.

The German social scientist Jürgen Habermas has shown that the modern agora, or public sphere, was largely the result of the modernisation of European economic relations. Habermas traces its origins to England in the latter part of the seventeenth century, with the growth of markets and trade bringing the spread of news and information. This led to the formation of an educated class of professionals who were able to communicate and speak against the ruling powers and to make a case for their own interests and rights. Informally, this freer culture became institutionalised in the coffee houses and salons of England and France, and while it began with literary interests, it gradually became more political in nature. This trend reveals how "critical debate ignited by works of literature and art" essentially paved the way for "economic and political disputes."[83] Writers and intellectuals then published their debates and ideas in periodicals to circulate them more widely. As Habermas notes of the end of the seventeenth century, "The elimination of the institution of censorship marked a new stage in the development of the public sphere. It made the influx of rational-critical arguments into the press possible and allowed the latter to evolve into an instrument with whose aid political decisions could be brought before the forum of the public."[84] By the end of the nineteenth century, W. T. Stead, one of England's leading newspaper editors, remarked on how new technologies had led to the growth of the public sphere: "The telegraph and the printing-press have converted Great Britain into a vast agora, or assembly of the whole community, in which the discussion of affairs of State is carried on from day to day in the hearing of the whole people."[85] This is what free speech theorists refer to as the "marketplace of ideas," the agora in which thoughts – and works of art – should be allowed to circulate and compete.[86] In *On Liberty*, Mill maintains that with a vigorously free public sphere, truth will win out in the end. In retrospect, with the preponderance of misinformation and conspiracy theories becoming ever more menacing to the survival of truth in the digital age, it is a rather quaint belief that truth will necessarily conquer falsehood through reason and recognition.

Mill, however, was not wholly in favour of an unregulated marketplace of ideas. Indeed, in *On Liberty*, he attends carefully to articulating a harm principle, which defines what should be regulated and banned in order to ensure that the safety of society and individuals is not threatened. In effect, "the sole end" for which people "are warranted, individually or collectively, in interfering with the liberty of action of any of their number, is self-protection."[87] In determining what constitutes harm, Mill insists that feelings be excluded, as "there is no parity between the feeling of a person for his own opinion, and the feeling of another who is offended at his holding it; no more than between the desire of a thief to take a purse, and the desire of the right owner to keep it."[88] Such limitations as exist against hate speech, which includes the advocacy of genocide, slander, which unjustly destroys one's reputation, or copyright infringement, which steals creators' intellectual property and affects their ability to make a livelihood, are concrete examples of the Millian harm principle codified into law.[89] How conservative or liberal a democracy is can be determined, in part, by how that polity defines harm: the more conservative a society is, the broader its definition of harm will be, and thus more cases will fall under the parameters of censorship, whereas the more liberal a society is, the narrower its definition of harm will be, and, in theory, fewer subjects and cases will be censored.

Typologies of Censorship Rhetoric

These conflicting viewpoints are encapsulated in the rhetorical strategies that have been implemented wherever and whenever censorship has been an issue. Most strikingly, people from either camp raise the same subjects, but espouse opposite attitudes regarding them. It is helpful to understand pro-censorship arguments and the censorship mentality first as they have in many respects determined anti-censorship arguments, which tend to be made in response to suppression or threats of suppression.

The most common pro-censorship rhetorical strategy is to appeal to *public health*. Society is understood to need guardianship to maintain or to restore its health, while certain ideas and forms of literature are cast as unhealthy. Typical adjectives used to smear such ideas and literature include *poison*, *sewage*, *filth*, *pollutant*, *contaminant*, and *trash*. In the period that this study covers, public health had become an increasing concern, with rapidly expanding cities and inadequate infrastructure leading to squalor that in turn caused regular outbreaks of disease.[90] Pro-censorship advocates tapped into this concern, publishing essays with titles like *Moral Poison in Modern Fiction* and "Poison in the Wells."[91] Such polemicists regularly speak of censored and even all modern literature as toxins and sewage that need to be prevented from infecting the body politic. In this sense, they appear to be compassionately acting out of concern for the moral and physical health of their fellow citizens to ensure that society will survive.[92]

This polemical concern for public health is closely related to a number of other strategies, most notably *national security* and *national exceptionalism*. By appealing to the nation, polemicists focus on identity and a sense of belonging while depicting the nation as pure and in danger of being flooded with foreign ideas and literature. This is symptomatic of the international dialectic, with even native writers being disparaged for having lived elsewhere or being in allegiance to moral standards and literary forms from other polities. In Britain, this often took the form of Francophobia. In Ireland, France was also demonised, but the main focus was Britain. Irish writers who were banned or considered dangerous were slandered as being tainted with foreign morals or being crassly concerned with money made in other markets as opposed to Ireland and its well-being. In this way, the nation becomes exceptionalist: it is pure or needs to have its purity restored, and censorship is proposed to be the bulwark that will protect the country from the filthy tide approaching its shores. Censorship thus becomes a cultural and ideological border, built to keep out alien influences and to ensure that the dominant belief system remains undisturbed.

The pro-censorship mentality is often a form of *paternalism*, and thus it tends to raise the cry of *virginibus puerisque* (for maidens and youth). Because children are not mentally and morally developed to the point where they can make informed decisions about what they read, hear, and watch, society must censor for them. Girls figure more often than boys in such rhetoric, with many polemicists alluding to their purity and the danger of them being led astray. This sexism is evident in some pro-censorship arguments where women are likewise lumped in with children as needing censorship's protection. In this sense, the censor is a manly defender of hearth and home and has a duty to his family and society in general. This is reflected in the fact that the vast majority of public censors – government appointees, church leaders, journalists, polemicists, and purity movement founders – have been men.

Associated with this paternalism is *classism*. In some debates, pro-censorship advocates raise the spectre of the undereducated masses reading immoral works and even imply that the lower classes are somehow more predisposed to immorality than the middle and upper classes. Just as many censors tend to be men, they also overwhelmingly come from society's higher ranks and are inclined to have preconceived, negative conceptions of those from the lower rungs. As censorship helps to maintain the status quo, it therefore props up the class system. As a result, snobbery has factored into many decisions not to ban certain works. In Britain and Ireland, if a book was published at a high cost as opposed to being readily accessible in a paperback edition, it was generally looked upon with more tolerance. Similarly, when books were published in foreign languages, they were left untouched, but their translations into the English vernacular rendered them more accessible to the masses and thus prone to be censored.

Alongside appeals to public health, the labelling of books and ideas as good or evil based upon their perceived *morality* or *immorality* is a typical gesture of pro-censorship arguments. As already noted, being deemed "immoral" was the kiss of death for many a writer, but it could also provide them a boost towards popularity. Again, the pro-censorship viewpoint is that society and its morality is somehow under threat. Immorality thereby becomes a catchword for all literature and ideas that differ in some respect from mainstream society's cherished values. Often depicted as causing degeneration and degradation, immorality must be stamped out for civilisation to survive.

If immorality poses such a threat, then the writer who is deemed immoral is *othered*, labelled a deviant, a criminal, in ill-health, morbid, and a pervert. They must therefore be punished and can thus be held up to public mockery, have their works banned, and be boycotted. There are some such arguments that consider the writer or speaker as being beyond the pale, as incapable of reformation, while others view them as wayward souls who only need to be guided along the path of righteousness towards salvation.

Because censorship provides a barrier between the moral and the immoral, the appeal to a *slippery slope* becomes important to maintaining distinctions. If an exception were to be made, if there were some slackening in deciding what should or should not be banned, or if some reform that could weaken censorship were to be imposed, the thinking is that there would follow an inevitable slide into a morass of immorality and degradation. In this sense, censorship keeps the moral ground beneath our feet from shifting and prevents us from losing our moral bearings.

While anti-censorship arguments tend to be liberal in nature, they still have a strong sense of the collective. As in pro-censorship polemics, one of the most common anti-censorship rhetorical techniques is an appeal to public health. However, as opposed to new ideas and literature being threatening to the body politic, they are considered as helping it. In some instances, they can inoculate like a vaccination: by being subjected to new ideas in small doses, people adapt to them and can thereafter live without fear of being harmed. Countering pro-censorship appeals to public health, anti-censorship campaigners point out that while sewage openly festering in the streets can demonstrably lead to illness and death, the same has not been proven to occur through reading, listening to, or watching works deemed immoral. Moreover, there is a cart-before-the-horse aspect to the anti-censorship arguments: if society wishes to have cleaner literature, then society needs to cleanse itself as art merely reflects life. As we will see, this was particularly the reasoning of the naturalists and many realists.

Similarly, while national exceptionalism and national purity arguments in favour of censorship claim that the practice protects public health, anti-censorship campaigners tend to view such nationalism as a logical extension of *xenophobia* and *racism*. The thinking goes that when society closes itself off to outside influences, it stagnates and eventually collapses into ruin because it fails to respond to current circumstances while the rest of the world advances. This is the counterargument of the international dialectic. Greater exposure to ideas and literature from elsewhere does not mean unthinking adoption; rather, potentially adapting them to local conditions can help society to progress and then, in turn, to spread that knowledge and art to other countries. In this way, the nation will become healthier, come into its glory, and be a beacon in the world.

Instead of protecting the country from other polities and cultures, anti-censorship polemicists tend to call for *greater education of the masses*. Censorship takes decision-making away from the individual and places it firmly in the hands of a knowing authority. In Britain and

Ireland, with the passage of successive education bills in the nineteenth century and the concomitant rise in literacy rates, there was a genuine concern by many pro-censorship campaigners that more people could read who lacked the mental, moral, and ethical faculties to critically engage with the material. As a result, they would be too susceptible to and influenced by what they read, and what they read, it was feared, was often indiscriminately immoral. Anti-censorship crusaders countered by stating that rather than revealing a need for greater censorship, the situation instead demonstrated that better education was required so that people could make informed decisions for themselves. Furthermore, they argued that those who were more educated should not be penalised by having their right to access certain works denied simply because of the perceived inadequacies of other people.

Anti-censorship arguments claimed that if the censor was therefore paternalistic, censorship was essentially institutionalised *infantilisation*. Because, under a censorship regime, decisions are made by others as to the fitness of books and ideas to circulate in society, individuals are forced into a child-like state of irresponsibility. Ridding society of censorship would thus uphold the crux of liberalism: responsibility and freedom of the individual to decide and act for themselves. As an extension of this personal responsibility, anti-censorship campaigners assert that virtue must be exercised. In the Garden of Eden, God prohibited the forbidden fruit, but Adam and Eve were still able to taste it. He had, in effect, tested their morality and they failed. People need temptation to resist because this in part defines our own moral and ethical systems. Free will, another important concept in liberalism, is therefore paramount as people must be able to exercise it with some regularity and not be treated as though they are in a perpetual child-like state of impulsivity. Moreover, anti-censorship campaigners would tend to argue that people should not be denied the taste of the forbidden fruit so that they can have the knowledge of good and evil and thereby make better informed decisions themselves.

Just as the moral and immoral are important in censorship campaigns, so *morality* and *immorality* become integral in anti-censorship polemic, but from a radically different angle. While in the former the two become bywords for good and evil, in the latter they are understood as that which is accepted by the majority and that which is accepted by a minority. In this sense, custom, not rightness, defines morality. Therefore, morality needs to be tested by immorality to discern its fitness. Best practices as they are currently known could be found to be less desirable or effective than other ways of doing things. Because morality is defined by the dominant and generally largest group of people in a society, appeals to morality are linked to Mill's notion of the tyranny of majority. Censorship is thus considered to impede progress and maintain the status quo, and in doing so it punishes those who differ from the norm.

Given that censorship prevents innovation, anti-censorship campaigners appeal to a *catalogue of martyrs*. These martyrs are often historical figures who suffered for their heterodox views through censorship and other forms of punishment, but who many people in later years would accept as being right or moral. Three of the most common martyrs evoked by anti-censorship crusaders are Socrates, who was tried and executed for corrupting the youth of Athens through his teachings; Jesus, who was tried by a Jewish judicial body for acting and preaching against the faith and was crucified for those crimes; and, as we have already seen, Galileo, who was put under house arrest by the Catholic Church for proposing a heliocentric model of the universe. Despite the various forms of censorship that such martyrs suffered, their views were essential to the development of religious, ethical, political, philosophical, and scientific thought, just as writers have been censored through the years only to have their works later considered masterpieces.

While some art receives due recognition well after it is made, other works achieve classic status relatively quickly. Despite the fact that some aspects of these works might conflict with later moral developments, they are often allowed to circulate and are openly venerated because they are ingrained in the culture and widely recognised for their importance. This apparent hypocrisy is at the heart of *the classics* argument. When more contemporary works are considered to be too immoral, anti-censorship crusaders most commonly hold up the Bible and Shakespeare as having problematic passages. Should they be subjected to the same standards, then the Bible and Shakespeare would not be read, considered sacrosanct, or performed on the stages of the world. There is a considerable amount of sex, violence, and generally immoral behaviour depicted in both, yet because they are established classics, they are permitted. In banning more recent works, the censorship could, in effect, be snuffing out a prospective Shakespeare or a book as potentially world changing as the Bible.

Anti-censorship arguments can also turn the tables on the censor by claiming that they are the one who is perverse, in effect *attacking the censor*. This is based on the understanding that sometimes the best defence is a good offence. At times, Titus 1:15 is cited to support this view: "Unto the pure all things are pure: but unto them that are defiled and unbelieving is nothing pure." In this sense, the prurience of the censor means that they are in fact sex obsessed. Others go further: as we will see, both George Moore and Bernard Shaw published brutally frank personal attacks on their censors. In so doing, the focus is shifted from the banned work and writer to the incompetence and perversion of the censor, thereby forcing the debate onto whether a more reasonable person should fill the position or even whether the position and practice should be entirely abolished.

A variation of attacking the censor is to *point out both questionable bans and deeply immoral works that are not banned*. These cases are not necessarily liminal in nature, intended to probe the cultural and moral borders of censorship, although they can do that. Rather, anti-censorship crusaders use them to illustrate the inherent difficulty of censoring works based on qualitative measures that are adjudged by normal, fallible humans who are not only driven by their own and the law's biases, but are also guided at times by whim or given to moments of severity. By raising such points, the polemicist seeks to undermine public confidence in the law and the censor and to persuade those in power that the institution needs massive reform or complete abolition.

When censorship is wielded by an authority with no opportunity for defence or appeal, anti-censorship campaigners often argue in favour of *the importance of due process*. As we will see, this was the case with Britain's censorship of plays and Ireland's censorship of publications. In Britain, playwrights had to submit their work for pre-production approval, at which time they were told that it could be performed in public as is, that it could be performed in public with required amendments and within strict parameters, or that it could not be performed in public. As anti-censorship campaigners argued, writers in such circumstances had fewer rights than fraudsters, murderers, and rapists because they were denied their rights to appear in court, to defend themselves and their works, and to appeal unfavourable decisions. Consequently, many people complained that writers were held to higher standards than others, including public speakers who were allowed to say whatever they wished without first having their speeches vetted. This situation was inherently unjust as all citizens were not treated equally before the eyes of the law.

Thus far, "anti-censorship" has been used without discussing some of the nuances covered by that umbrella term. While some people were absolutists, the majority of writers covered in this study were not so radical in their writings, public statements, and personal beliefs. They were anti-censorship with regard to the specific forms of censorship mentioned in the preceding paragraph, but they were not in favour of full liberty to print and perform whatever one wished. In this respect, they were against the way that censorship was practised, but they were not against the principle of censorship. This *moderate position* made their claims appear more reasonable, highlighting the need to curb certain topics or forms of culture and to allow others. Indeed, Jonathan Dollimore has argued that "an effective opposition has to recognize that in principle" literature and art "*may* harm."[93] The common line, taken by those like Lawrence and Joyce, was to distinguish between art and pornography, praising and defending the former while denouncing the latter. As we have seen, this was aligned with another strategy, which was to *make a special case for art*, suggesting that it should not be circumscribed in the same way as other modes that indulged in the obscene and the indecent.

Moral Panics and Social Organisation

At heart, the need to censor arises from a perceived threat. If this perceived threat is deemed considerable, then it can provoke fear and anger that in turn give rise to panic. When this panic becomes widely felt or is stoked in a sufficiently large number of people who become motivated to act, the result is a moral panic. The impulse of moral panics is to defend society from the perceived threat, but, more than that, it seeks to assert and impose morality. In so doing, the group heading a moral panic lays claim to the dominant and legitimate morality and reaffirms its power to define what is good and evil, moral and immoral, and permissible and impermissible. At times, they can feed into larger culture wars and seek to demonise and marginalise other groups to diminish their threat to morality, but they can also promote legislation and official actions to control the perceived threat. This is laid bare in the description of the British Obscene Publications Act and the Cockburn ruling as sweeping aside the law to "make room for hysteria" and Samuel Beckett's charge that Ireland's Censorship of Publications Act was "panic legislation."[94] In surveying contemporary movements that led to moral panics, Mill noted that they "cause the public to be more disposed than at former periods to prescribe general rules of conduct, and endeavour to make everyone conform to the same standard. ... Its ideal of character is to be without any marked character; to maim by compression, like a Chinese lady's foot, every part of human nature which stands out prominently, and tends to make the person markedly dissimilar in outline to commonplace humanity."[95] In general, then, moral panics are conservative in nature and are thus despised by liberals as they seek to warp and deform individuals to conform to another's desired standards.

The South African sociologist Stanley Cohen, whose work has dominated the field of moral panic studies for over half a century, posits that such movements are inclined to focus on seven types of social phenomena and identities: young, violent, working-class males; school violence, bullying, and shootouts; drugs and drug addicts; child abuse, paedophiles, and satanic rituals; the media's reporting on sex and violence; welfare cheats and single mothers; and refugees and asylum seekers.[96] Many of these are marginalised groups, targeted by the moral majority for their potential to disrupt the status quo and cause society's degeneration. As Cohen has argued, there is often a disproportionality in moral panics as they tend to exaggerate the number of cases, the strength of the threat, and the damage that it could inflict. However, he warns against those who would judge too harshly moral panics and the restrictions that follow in their wake, arguing that we must not assume that a moral panic is more of a menace to society's well-being than giving free rein to its targets. "Only with a prior commitment to 'external' goals such as social justice, human rights or equality," he insists, "can we evaluate any one moral panic or judge it as more specious than another."[97]

Cohen points out that, fundamentally, "moral panics are condensed political struggles to control the means of cultural production." Therefore, by studying moral panics we can "identify and conceptualize the lines of power in any society, the ways we are manipulated into taking some things too seriously and other things not seriously enough."[98] This is best demonstrated in the labelling of the aforementioned social phenomena and identities as deviant. As established earlier, censorship was no different, with writers branded as immoral. With regard to labelling, a series of questions arise: Who or what is being labelled? At what point in time? Who is doing the labelling? Why might they be labelling these phenomena or groups of people? And what is the broader historical, social, political, and cultural context? Deviants generally have the label imposed upon them. At times, they might refuse it, but at others they might embrace or appropriate it.[99] This was certainly the case for banned Irish writers, who could individually or collectively react in either way, depending upon the circumstances and the personalities involved.

Social movements that push for greater or continued censorship share many of the attributes of moral panics. Yet writers significantly differ from the groups that Cohen studied. For one, Cohen's groups, and in particular the youth gangs he focuses on, are closely associated social and geographical groups that tend to be readily identifiable by visual markers, such as their types of dress and haircuts. In contrast, writers are more solitary and diverse by nature, and they are also more individually identifiable through name and facial recognition and the style of their writing, leading to the common use of such adjectives as *Shavian*, *Yeatsian*, *Joycean*, and *Beckettian*. Because they are known entities, the media and organisations have to work harder to cast them in a particular light. In some cases, writers might, like Shaw, already be perceived by large segments of society as deviant or at least controversial, and they could be depicted differently according to the case at hand, as occurred with Yeats when he was sometimes positioned as a good nationalist, and at others as a bad one. For writers such as Joyce and Edna O'Brien, the authorities and the press demonised them early on in their careers, allowing them to be labelled as deviant much more easily. There are also significant class and educational differences between writers and the youth delinquents that Cohen studies. Moreover, writers tend to have important networks in the media and among other well-spoken public figures who can defend them and, just as importantly, publish their self-defences. Indeed, Irish writers routinely had access to the leading papers in Britain and Ireland as well as other outlets that were more ideologically inclined to accept their works and frame coverage of events in their favour. They also had the inherent eloquence of their profession to plead their cases even if censorship lacked due process. As we will see, this did not always persuade others to help instigate reforms towards greater freedoms of expression or change public opinion, but they had considerably more agency and articulateness than Cohen's deviants.

There are, therefore, two types of social organisation that tend to consolidate around censorship. The first is formed by those who support censorship and drive moral panics. In Britain, these included the Society for the Suppression of Vice (SSV) and the National Vigilance Association (NVA), the former founded in 1802 to target such purveyors of indecency as importers and shopkeepers with the aim of prosecuting them, the latter founded by W. T. Stead and William Alexander Coote in 1885 to reinvigorate the work of the SSV.[100] Similar groups formed much later in Ireland, including the Catholic Truth Society in 1899, the Irish Vigilance Association in 1911, and the Knights of St. Columbanus in 1915. Meanwhile, the Catholic hierarchy and their clergy impelled Catholic Action and lay groups to protest. As we will see, all of these organisations were instrumental in creating moral panics around the issue of immoral literature and in instigating censorship debates, prosecutions, and legislation.

The second type of social organisation is formed by those who are against how censorship is practised, if not also against censorship in principle. The history of Irish writers in this respect is somewhat ambivalent. At times, they curiously failed to coalesce in any meaningful way. At others, they founded organisations and led movements to promote the reform or the dismantling of censorship, some of them even lobbying politicians behind the scenes. These groups could be as informally associated as the 1907–9 campaign to reform the British censorship of plays, or they could be as formally instituted as the Irish Academy of Letters and Irish PEN. In later years, Irish writers joined intellectuals, lawyers, journalists, and politicians to found broader organisations that robustly defended freedoms of speech, including the Irish Association for Civil Liberty and the Censorship Reform Society. Each of these groups had different levels of success and remained as forces for different lengths of time, often puttering out because they had failed to make the desired impact, because of the departure of significant figures, or because their objectives had been achieved.

Surveying essays by and interviews with censored Irish writers, Julia Carlson concludes that the most serious consequences of censorship were the fostering of "the ignorance and provincialism of the Irish people and the intellectual and moral alienation of Irish writers."[101] Indeed, some three decades after her debut novel, *The Country Girls* (1960), was banned, Edna O'Brien, one of the more courageous and combative figures in the history of censorship, recalled receiving absolutely no support from her family, who were as ashamed as she was for having "done something awful." To make matters worse, she received anonymous letters decrying "sewerage and all that innuendo."[102] While she was already living abroad in Britain, her shame was so strong that she considered moving to Australia.

However, as O'Brien's cofounding of the Censorship Reform Society attests, she and others fought back with considerable gusto. Refusing to be cowed, Irish writers have a long lineage of combativeness, beginning with George Moore and Bernard Shaw and moving forward to W. B. Yeats, AE, Sean O'Faolain, and O'Brien.[103] While they formed social organisations, they also collectively produced an important body of anti-censorship writing – including prefaces, pamphlets, letters to editors, essays, newspaper articles, petitions, and manifestoes – gave interviews, and eagerly participated in public debates. This study traces a history and a genealogy of these forms of the censorship dialectic to show that while censorship did indeed negatively affect the creative writing of Irish authors and in some ways impeded their influence on society, it also had productive and positive effects, not only on the development of modernist forms and styles, but also on increasing the writers' importance and creating an aura around them that, while negative in many respects, also enhanced their popularity and helped them to create and to cultivate public personas that they turned to their advantage. Indeed, there were moments in which Irish writers purposely inflamed moral panics. While censorship was detrimental to writers and society, it thus also became instrumental in the making of reputations.

Similarly, while there is a temptation to see the history of Irish writers and censorship in Whiggish terms of an ever-increasing liberalism leading to greater freedoms of speech, the reality is rather more tidal or pendulous in nature. There is an ebb and flow, a back and forth, between periods of greater liberty and periods of greater suppression, and between moments of success and moments of failure. Admittedly, there is more freedom of expression for writers at the end of this study than there is at the beginning and in the middle. Yet while it is important to remind ourselves of this general tendency, it is equally important to pay attention to the subtler movements throughout time, to grasp the smaller struggles that contribute to the larger. In the end, the broader history of censorship and this more focused study of the experiences of Irish writers testify to the rightness of the adage that liberty must be fought for every day. That struggle is essential to every democracy, wherein multiple forces, ideologies, and demographics wrestle for control.

Censorship and the Irish Writer covers a broad period, from the final decades of the nineteenth century, when governmental censorships and purity movements in Britain and Ireland were created, enjoyed widescale support, and held considerable power, to the latter half of the twentieth century, when governmental censorships were dismantled or considerably liberalised and purity movements began to lose their sway. It therefore pulls up short of the technological revolution of the digital age, which significantly changed literary, political, and social landscapes. Yet the writers that this book covers did much to usher in change, too. Indeed, without them, freedom of expression in both Britain and Ireland would not have remained such an important and contested right.

The International Dialectic of Censorship

Censorship and the Irish Writer endeavours to add to and challenge our understanding of censorship and, in particular, Irish writers' engagement with the practice. While it discusses at length the many political, social, cultural, and philosophical issues that have been outlined thus far, with its focus on Britain, Ireland, and the larger world of literature in which Irish writers circulated, its ethos and perspective are driven by articulating and illustrating the international dialectic of censorship. Granted, this is part of a wider global shift that has occurred in Irish studies in the twenty-first century. Historians, for example, have led the way in developing the concept of a Green Atlantic, arguing that Irish history needs to be understood in an international context.[104] In so doing, and in casting their nets even more widely across the globe, they have considered the ways in which the Irish have affected the trajectory of other polities. In literary studies, scholars have likewise increasingly considered Ireland as part of a world system, from detailing writers' engagements with foreign peoples, cultures, and aesthetics to describing how their own works have circulated abroad.[105] Similarly, researchers have begun to grasp how Irish literature has engaged with the newer generations of immigrants that have settled in the country since it joined the European Union and became an economic success.[106]

In censorship studies, though, the tendency is to maintain the emphasis on the national, mainly because censorship is encoded and practised according to local, often national, laws. As the office of the Roman censor attests, a censor's dual duty is to determine what belongs to a given polity and to supervise morality. In this sense, we could extrapolate that that which is censored does not adhere to and thus cannot belong to the body politic. There is therefore an international dimension to the theoretical underpinning of how censorship functions. Censored works and writers are, in effect, deemed foreign. Often, they are depicted as cosmopolitan, a negative trait in the eyes of the censor, generally because of the cultural miscegenation and otherness associated with the term. Indeed, *cosmopolitan* necessarily points to diversity and elsewhere against the narrower claims of the local community. Typically, then, censors see threats as emanating from works and people beyond their borders and thus use censorship as a *cordon sanitaire* erected to maintain national purity and cohesion. The national writer is thus a greater threat because they represent what happens when the local encounters the more universal, pointing to the possibilities of what the local might become if it is not protected.

Yet, somewhat contradictorily, governments frequently look abroad for inspiration from other polities and groups to assess how they have managed censorship to control the direction of national culture and society. When in the 1920s Ireland began to consider what form its censorship of literature would take, it looked at legislation in several countries. Such internationalism took on another shape in Geneva when, from 12 September 1923 to 31 March 1924, the League of Nations held the International Convention for the Suppression of the Circulation of and Traffic in Obscene Publications. Most European countries participated, as did a handful of governments from the Caribbean and Latin America. As the name of the conference suggests, countries were concerned with the spread of obscene publications and, feeling powerless against what was entering their borders from elsewhere, began to cooperate towards thwarting such material. Thus, even those who were most concerned with how to prevent the foreign invasion of immorality and other literary norms and cultures were guided by a form of internationalism.

As for the writers, internationalism often both informed their perspectives and was a soothing balm when national governments or populations turned against them. While pro-censorship arguments cast banned national writers as being polluted by alien influences, such writers have historically been proud about those same foreign models, alluding to them in their work, adopting their aesthetics, adapting their themes, and praising them in letters, essays, and interviews. For them, the mind should not be hindered by national boundaries or local considerations; rather, they should be free to integrate into their own work what they have experienced or read from elsewhere. This exaltation of writers from other polities thus puts them at risk of running afoul of the dominant national norms and mores that inform censorship. In some ways, they take succour in the international, feeling part of a Republic of Letters that will lead the charge for a new morality in aesthetics as well as in society. Even their catalogue of martyrs to the cause, notably Socrates, Jesus, and Galileo, is taken from other peoples. When Irish writers do point to their compatriots as victims of censorship, they most commonly cite those of global standing, such as the early Nobel laureates Yeats and Shaw, as well as the influential Moore and Joyce. As they charge, by remaining closed to ideas and peoples from beyond the country's frontiers and by demonising the eminent among them, national insularism leads to stasis, regression, and the downfall of the nation. By being part of the larger current of world affairs, the nation becomes healthier, allowing for renewal, growth, and evolution. This, for many banned writers, is the crux of the international dialectic.

More importantly, Irish writers have often understood that individual censorship battles, whether in Ireland or in other polities, are part of a larger global war that is waged for freedom of expression. In international law, freedom of expression was recognised as a basic human right during the latter part of the history that this book covers. For many Irish writers, like their colleagues from elsewhere, freedom of expression is a value that knows no boundaries, a universal right that should be fiercely protected and will, theoretically, lead to social, political, and cultural progress. As such, freedom of expression, within certain Millian limits, supersedes local parochial demands. This belief has led Irish writers to found and join international organisations that promote literature and defend freedom of expression. It has also resulted in them campaigning to support writers who are nationals of and banned in other countries. When they have been censored themselves, Irish writers have similarly turned abroad for support from colleagues, publishers, presses, editors, and theatres that value freedom of expression and would produce and circulate their work. Moreover, we must recall that Irish writers were not only banned in Ireland, but also in other countries, where they sometimes led the charge for reform. Indeed, Irish writers have made their cases against censorship both at home and abroad, in part to air their grievances, in part to find an audience, in part to battle different systems of censorship, and in part to embarrass their homeland in the hope that doing so might provoke reform.

Using Irish writers as a case study, this book seeks to illustrate and explain the many facets of this international dialectic of censorship. Making use of previously unearthed archival materials, it provides a compelling account of how Irish writers have both resisted and failed to resist censorship through politics, polemics, and social organisation. At times, episodes appear to be merely local or national in importance, but, ultimately, they all contribute to a fascinating history of international scope.

Chapter One

Setting the Template: George Moore and the Public Face of Resistance

To better understand how Irish writers responded to and were affected by censorship, it is important to turn back to the earliest of Irish modernists: George Moore. Allison Pease and Celia Marshik have demonstrated that the relationship that high modernists like James Joyce and Virginia Woolf had with obscenity and censorship was preceded by such mid-Victorian writers as Algernon Charles Swinburne and Dante Gabriel Rossetti, whose experiences set the templates for later struggles, rebellion, and aesthetic innovation.[1] Irish critics have similarly recognised that going further back than 1900 is necessary for contextualising and better understanding literature produced in the twentieth century. Declan Kiberd's *Inventing Ireland*, for one, begins its examination of "the literature of the modern nation" with the *fin de siècle* authors Oscar Wilde, Bernard Shaw, and Somerville and Ross, and *The Oxford Handbook of Modern Irish Theatre* opens with chapters devoted to exploring nineteenth-century legacies.[2] The same cannot be said, however, of how scholars have examined censorship through the lens of Irish studies: Joan FitzPatrick Dean's work on theatre censorship in Ireland is focused on the twentieth century; Peter Martin's history of censorship in the first two decades of independence only gestures as far back as 1911 to the founding of the Irish Vigilance Association; and Michael Adams's seminal study of the political and legal history of literary censorship in Ireland takes only the post-independence period as its remit.[3] By casting back to such earlier figures as Moore, we can see how what occurs in a particular context is often rooted in an earlier, although not temporally neat, periodisation. Moreover, by considering the wider international contexts of such writers, we can better discern how complex phenomena occur in different polities and how national trajectories are often affected by what goes on beyond as much as within a country's borders. In the case of Ireland, many of whose writers have lived, worked, published, staged their works, and found success abroad, international contexts are especially important in this regard.

George Moore is key to this study not only because he was "the pet bugaboo" of Victorian England or the first modern Irish writer to be confronted with censorship, but also because he provided at once a positive and a negative model to his successors.[4] When censorship threatened him, Moore refused to shy away from battle, asserting his right to freedom of expression. He was pugnacious in the press, and his public persona provided the prototype for many writers. If we were only to consider how he served as a model through his polemics, he would be important, but Moore went further, seeking substantial material and social reforms in his struggles that eventually led to significant changes in how the publishing industry was structured, how libraries served their patrons, and how people were able to access literature. Indeed, more than perhaps any other nineteenth-century writer, Moore was responsible for promoting and affecting freedom of expression in Britain. As this chapter will illustrate, the Irish Moore, who looked to the French novelist Émile Zola for inspiration and fought vigorously against forms of suppression in Britain, provides a compelling example of how the international dialectic of censorship functions.

The Context of Moore's First Novel

The international aspects of Moore's struggles with censorship began even before he wrote a word of his first novel. Born into the landlord class in County Mayo in 1852, he moved to Paris to become an artist after inheriting the family estate. The French capital offered a bubbling cauldron of aesthetic experimentation, and Moore was quick to insinuate himself in avant-garde circles. The impressionist Édouard Manet, who painted a famous portrait of Moore, referred to the Irishman as "*le plus parisien de tous les anglais.*"[5] In a letter to his compatriot John Eglinton, Moore wrote: "We were born it is true, in Ireland, but my cradle was rocked in the Nouvelle Athènes."[6] While in Paris he failed to make his mark as a visual artist, but he made a number of important contacts, including Stéphane Mallarmé, Ivan Turgenev, and, especially crucial for Moore when he turned to writing in the early 1880s, Émile Zola. By this time, he admitted that he wished to be "*un ricochet de Zola en Angleterre*" – an echo of Zola in England.[7]

This was a daring claim to be made by a young and unproven writer when French literature was a byword for all that was immoral, indecent, and obscene.[8] In many ways, what the French literati experienced in the mid-nineteenth century would befall their English and Irish colleagues in later decades, notably with regard to the ways in which lines were drawn around how reality was depicted and what could and could not be said. Their scandalous reputation was the result of the challenge that French writers – notably Gustav Flaubert, Charles Baudelaire, Guy de Maupassant, and Zola – offered the reading public and their subsequent prosecutions by French authorities. In the first such case, Flaubert's *Madame Bovary* was taken to court in 1857 over obscene libel charges. Although Flaubert is known as an aesthetic stylist, prosecutors fixed on what they deemed to be his realistic portrayal of French provincial life, arguing that his book's "obvious anti-idealist agenda was demonstrably antagonistic to the aesthetic and (therefore) moral status quo."[9] While the tribunal found Flaubert not guilty, it insisted that the "proper" role of literature is to "beautify and enhance the spirit by elevating the intelligence and purifying morals rather than to inspire disgust for vice by offering a portrait of the disorder that may exist in society."[10] This would set a precedent for a great deal of what would follow in France, Britain, and Ireland: the authorities determined that literature should have a spiritually uplifting effect, and therefore it should not probe or depict anything that challenges people's ideas or values or causes them to question the ways in which their society is structured. Literature should be edifying, and, if it is not, the fault is the author's.

The second major test came later in 1857 with the prosecution of Baudelaire's *Les fleurs du mal*, a verse collection with notoriously vivid descriptions of body parts and functions. The case was made that Baudelaire threatened French society by menacing women and children, two demographics that had been and would continue to be gestured towards as being susceptible to immorality and needing protection by authorities. In response, Baudelaire argued that his work should not be perceived in relation to its audience, but evaluated on its aesthetic merits. As he claimed in the preface of the second edition: "This book was not written for my wives, my daughters, or my sisters; nor for my neighbour's wives, daughters, or sisters. I leave that task to those interested in confusing virtuous acts with beautiful language."[11] Baudelaire was ambivalent to the charge of corrupting women and children because this was not his aim. As such, he refused to be subjected to this standard as a litmus test for whether his writing should be banned. In this sense, there were two imagined audiences: the authorities perceived a *general audience*, one that included those they considered the most susceptible members of society; and the writer perceived *no specific audience* and rejected any attempts to judge his works by their *potential* to negatively influence people. As with Flaubert's case, the terms of this argument over audience – one that infantilises women and feminises children as less critical than a manly reader – have been echoed throughout the history of censorship trials and polemics.

Zola likewise embraced less idealistic forms by creating the hyper-realistic "naturalism." There was a need, Zola argued, to diagnose society through a scientific, proto-sociological approach. In this regard, he argued, "The environment must determine the character"; that is, for naturalists, people did not necessarily act of their own accord, but rather in ways that were shaped by their socio-economic reality, familial and communal culture, and genetic predisposition.[12] It was a distinctly utilitarian view of art that was meant to reflect contemporary society and in so doing serve a social need. He thus differed from his predecessors in suggesting that his work was not merely aesthetic, but was propelled by an impetus towards moral and structural reforms.

While Moore's first novel was more satirical than naturalistic, one might argue that, despite their differences in tone, the genres are similar in their objectives as they seek to instigate change. Published in 1883, *A Modern Lover* lampoons the contemporary art and literary scene of London; it is a sort of roman-à-clef that recounts the rise of Lewis Seymour, which is due more to his good looks and social skills than his middling talent. In one scene, a modern novelist who is a rather thinly disguised Thomas Hardy is asked why he always tackles "unpleasant subjects"; he responds in Zola-esque terms: "We do not always choose what you call unpleasant subjects, but we try to go to the roots of things, and, the basis of life being material and not spiritual, the analyst inevitably finds himself, sooner or later, handling what this sentimental age calls coarse." Indeed, he likens the modern novel to "the moral dissecting room" and suggests that it provides a "contemporary history, an exact and complete reproduction of social surroundings of the age we live in."[13] It would turn out to be a prescient exchange.

In England at this time, there was no statutory body to which books could be referred for examination and possible banning. However, as we will see in a moment, publications were prosecuted in the courts for obscenity. Less formally, private circulating libraries, which existed because there were very few taxpayer-funded public libraries at the time, enacted an effective unofficial censorship. For a nominal annual fee, people could borrow books through a vast network of such libraries, the two biggest chains being Mudie's and W. H. Smith. Literacy rates rose significantly in the late nineteenth century with the expansion of the educational system, due in large part to successive parliamentary acts beginning in 1870 that rendered school mandatory until age thirteen. At the same time, despite mean increases in wages and purchasing power, books remained unaffordable for most people, which made the prospect of borrowing a more attractive option. A great deal of this was due to the market being dominated by the costly triple-decker novel and the immense influence that the circulating libraries wielded over the publishing industry.

The triple-decker – or three-volume – novel became standard in the early nineteenth century. Previously, novels could be anywhere from two to seven volumes, but it was Sir Walter Scott who popularised the triple-decker by publishing in the format.[14] Circulating libraries liked that it was expensive to produce, which meant that most people had to become members if they wished to read novels. Indeed, a triple-decker tended to be sold for a prohibitive thirty-one shillings and sixpence, while Mudie's most popular membership cost a subscriber one guinea (twenty-one shillings) per year and allowed them to borrow an unlimited number of volumes.[15] With very few exceptions, writers were obliged to publish triple-deckers, effectively forcing them to conform to length requirements. This led to padding and the addition of storylines, which some felt compromised their artistry.[16] Most popular were romance and adventure; didacticism and traditional morality were imperative; and, almost without exception, virtue had to triumph and wrongdoers had to pay for their sins. The circulating libraries' advance readers vetted books and recommended or advised against purchases; they thereby dictated publishing practices through their ordering, in large part because they were the major source of revenue in the field. This financial clout led to them exerting "a material, intellectual and moral dictatorship."[17] In response, publishers issued five hundred copies of a novel in three volumes. Only if the reception was good would they then make one-volume editions. Not all publishers were poorer for this situation: in addition to profiting from their own sales, a number of them owned stocks in circulating libraries. When Mudie's went public in 1864, for example, publishers immediately bought half of the shares.[18] In the end, there was little incentive for publishers to buck a system that guaranteed them profits.

Aside from their advanced readers and lending rates, the circulating libraries relied heavily on the comments of their membership to gauge what was popular and acceptable. Because of the time that was required for someone to read a novel, "a notable portion of its readers" was found "among the idle females of the middle-classes whose view of life was narrow."[19] This dominant and demanding demographic further restricted writers. Moreover, the fact that the Victorian family tended to read their books aloud meant that children, and especially young girls, came to be the standard by which morality was determined.[20] This "young girl" standard effectively combined the gender and age biases that were raised against Baudelaire.

In this way, Charles Edward Mudie and William Henry Smith came to enforce the puritanical Victorian moral code. Smith believed that his mission was to provide "sound literature," an outlook that his competitor shared.[21] Mudie defended himself from those who raised freedom of expression arguments by claiming that he was too timid to take on such battles. As a businessperson, he had to consider commercial demands, from which stemmed his rights and freedoms to serve his clients as he wished; moreover, he had the right to stock only those volumes that he considered moral.[22] If people did not like it, they were free to found or patronise a competing circulating library that catered to more risqué tastes. He had long been clear that his was a *select* circulating library, one advertisement running: "C. E. Mudie is again under the necessity of reminding the Subscribers to his Library, that while he desires to give the widest possible circulation to every work of acknowledged merit or general interest in HISTORY, BIOGRAPHY, RELIGION, PHILOSPHY, TRAVEL, and the *higher* class of FICTION, he reserves the right of *selection*."[23]

The problem for people who wished to access more daring works was that the circulating libraries commanded the marketplace, thereby impacting both the business and the aesthetic sides of publishing until well into the 1930s.[24] This is why Mudie's advertisement drew some ire, one writer noting that his library "exercises so prodigious an influence on literature that the principles on which it is conducted are a matter of public interest"; he had, in effect, become "the dictator of literature."[25] The only alternative to Smith's and Mudie's in the late Victorian and Edwardian periods were the public Carnegie libraries. These were founded in cities all over the world – although largely in the United States, Canada, Ireland, and Great Britain – by the munificence of the American industrialist and philanthropist Andrew Carnegie. However, the first of these were only established in 1883, the year in which Moore published *A Modern Lover*, and thus they had yet to affect the marketplace. In the first decades, the readership of these new libraries was generally composed of the lower-middle and "respectable" working classes, but the moral standards of the Carnegie libraries were similarly guided by patrician restriction as their governing boards consisted of politicians and the clergy.[26]

While the paternalism and relative puritanism of libraries in this period offered somewhat of a bulwark against shifts in the publishing industry, they could not hold back certain trends. From 1814 to

1846, religious books accounted for 20.3 per cent of all books published and fiction only 16.2 per cent, while from 1870 to 1919, religious books slipped to 15.5 per cent and fiction rose to 23.3 per cent.[27] For 1880 to 1889, the decade that saw the debut of Moore as a novelist and Zola translated into English, religious works only accounted for 14.9 per cent of all books published, while 26 per cent were fiction; indeed, the market share of fiction rose steadily each year to a height of 31.6 per cent in 1889.[28] The decrease in religious books and the corresponding increase in fiction could be interpreted on one level as a move in society towards more secular forms of reading, although the religious, didactic, and moral tenor of fiction varied widely. The need to control reading could therefore be understood as motivated by two main concerns: the emergence of a large reading public that did not come from the social class of society's leaders and were thus held in patrician suspicion; and the rise in popularity of fiction, which had to be vetted for its morality, over religious publications. This was the context in which Moore began his career as a novelist.

The Censorship of *A Modern Lover*

From the outset, Willam Tinsley, Moore's publisher for *A Modern Lover*, had some trepidations over the book. Tinsley had found massive success with *Moonstone* (1868), Wilkie Collins's bestselling detective novel, and books by other major writers of the period, including Sheridan Le Fanu, G. A. Henty, and Ouida. He was adept at spotting talent, having taken on a young Thomas Hardy when others would not, but this risk led to financial losses on *Desperate Remedies* (1871), *Under the Greenwood Tree* (1872), and *A Pair of Blue Eyes* (1873). Despite the lucrative revenues some of his titles generated, Tinsley was known as a poor businessperson who failed to exploit what he had.[29] His relationship with Moore both supports and challenges this view.

Upon meeting Tinsley, Moore boasted that he had been living in France and had learned from the French school of novelists. When he mentioned that his manuscript was titled *A Modern Lover*, Tinsley admitted that the daring name would likely attract many readers, but he feared that the libraries might not approve of it. After hearing Moore describe his book, Tinsley said that it was "a risky story, but all depends upon the treatment."[30] In the end, Tinsley only agreed to publish it by first getting Moore to commit to paying for up to forty pounds of debt should the libraries not buy enough copies to cover his costs.[31]

Moore might have been courting controversy with the title of *A Modern Lover*, but the book was glowingly reviewed in some of the day's leading periodicals. *The Spectator*, for one, said that "there is no trace" of "moral good-for-nothingness." Moore wrote in the "plain prose" of realism, yet, "unlike the tone of the 'naturalistic' writers (for whom we suspect Mr. Moore of an admiration much to be deplored)," he "does not offend." The reviewer differentiated Moore from the naturalism of Zola and "the hogs of his sty" in his sensitive rendering of the scene in which Gwynnie Lloyd consents to be a model for the artist Lewis Seymour when he threatens to commit suicide. The passage is treated with "strength, truth, delicacy, and pathos" as well as "skill and beauty," not sensationalistic voyeurism. Gwynnie's selflessness, coupled with her pained reaction upon seeing her naked painted form, shows her decency; Seymour's selfishness is exposed to readers, who watch him exploit people on his ascension in the London art world.[32]

Mudie's purchased fifty copies of *A Modern Lover* without any apparent concern about its morality.[33] However, after receiving complaints from two female readers, Mudie refused to circulate the novel. The women had taken umbrage with the very scene that *The Spectator* had praised for its delicacy. If anything, Gwynnie's shyness, her ensuing shame, and her flight from Seymour's life immediately thereafter make her story more of a conservative cautionary tale than an enticement to depravity. But Mudie was a businessperson, and he did not consider it in his interest to contradict his clients. Moore challenged him in person, claiming that that Mudie was "acting in defiance of the opinion of the press." He then vowed to circumvent Mudie by finding a publisher who would issue his next book in one volume at a reasonable price so that he could "appeal direct to the public."[34] For Moore, the problem remained that he was on the hook for the forty pounds he had promised to Tinsley should the book not sell, but fortune favoured him when the fully insured warehouse holding Tinsley's stock was incinerated by fire.[35]

Mudie's censorship had been informal and silent, surreptitiously undertaken behind the scenes. Moore's threat eventually exposed this insidious censorship to the public, but it was a massive gamble: he had no guarantee that his next book would be as good as his first, he lacked the connections to be well-supported in his fight, and he could not be certain of how the public would react to the issues of censorship and freedom of expression. He was fortunate because inheriting his family's estate allowed him to weather the economic effects of not adhering to the governing dictates of the publishing industry that demanded that he sheepishly acquiesce to the circulating libraries. Being financially independent, he was therefore relatively free to lead the charge for aesthetic, material, moral, and economic reforms to the novel. Yet to go about such reforms, Moore was dependent on others in one major respect: he had to find a willing publisher. As luck would have it, he found two such men: W. T. Stead and Henry Vizetelly.

Moore's first step was to make the polemical case for freedom of expression to prepare the ground for the reception of his fiction. He became convinced to act following a visit with Zola in April 1884, when the master encouraged the disciple to rebel against the circulating libraries by publicly denouncing their pernicious effects on the development of literature.[36] Meanwhile, Moore stumbled upon an unlikely partner in the Congregationalist W. T. Stead. As Low Church Protestants, Congregationalists advocated puritanism, including proscribing alcohol and promiscuous sexuality, but they were also prominent in such radical movements as abolitionism, Chartism, and suffragettism. Stead viewed the press as a tool for moral reform along Congregationalist lines. This was particularly evident during his editorship of the *Pall Mall Gazette*, one of London's leading newspapers, from 1883 to 1889. Under his guidance, the *Pall Mall Gazette* pioneered both investigative journalism and sensationalist reporting. Stead also contributed to the development of the New Journalism, a term coined by Matthew Arnold in 1887 to deride Stead's style.[37] The New Journalism rendered newspaper writing more personal, less neutral. It consisted of editorialising and commentary based on observations, research, and fact, but it also ushered in gossip reporting and instigated such formal innovations as shorter paragraphs and articles, more spacing to increase readability, and the inclusion of accompanying illustrations, maps, and diagrams. Moreover, with the advent of by-lines, writers could cultivate personalities, just as the newspapers in which they wrote had their proper characters and ideological leanings.

Stead referred to such writing as "the future of journalism": "everything depends upon the individual – the person. Impersonal journalism is effete. To influence men you must be a man, not a mock-uttering oracle." This was true for the writer, but it was especially true of a good editor, who could be "the most potent among all those whose counsels guide the holders of our Imperial sceptre."[38] For Stead, the press was the truest form of government, being more in touch with people than an MP; after all, the public casts their vote daily on a newspaper by purchasing or refusing to purchase it, while an MP generally holds office for some years between elections.[39] Into the ear of the capable editor, he suggested, "are poured the cries, the protests, the complaints of men who suffer wrong, and it is his mission to present them daily before the conscience of mankind."[40]

Given this conception of the newspaper, Stead's large-circulation daily was an ideal vehicle for Moore in his quest to appeal to – and perhaps even shape – public opinion. However, in his attempt to reform how literature was produced, received, and treated, Moore and Stead made for an odd couple. Indeed, while both men advocated reform, Moore was hoping to liberalise literature while Stead sought to curb the more sexually audacious material of the time.

Recognising the value of a good scandal, and seeing in Moore the sort of personality that was representative of the New Journalism, Stead published Moore's "A New Censorship of Literature" on 10 December 1884.[41] In it, Moore complained that circulating libraries forbade any discussion of religion and morals because of the sensitivities of young girls and widows. For such people, "political questions have no interest, and it is by this final amputation that humanity becomes headless, trunkless, limbless, and is converted into the pulseless, non-vertebrate, jelly-fish sort of thing which, securely packed in tin-cornered boxes, is sent from the London depot and scattered through the drawing-rooms of the United Kingdom."[42] Moore then related how his publisher had informed him that although *A Modern Lover* had been a critical success, it was a commercial failure because Mudie, whom he referred to as Mr. X, refused to circulate copies in his libraries unless a patron specifically requested it, simply because of the complaints of "two ladies from the country." Having exposed Mudie's tactics, Moore made a plea for freedom of expression, but he was equally focused on using the occasion to trumpet his forthcoming novel, *A Mummer's Wife*. The new book, he noted, would be published in an affordable one-volume edition, emphasizing the links between economics and individual rights. At the same time, he posited himself as a martyr for the cause. Unshackled as he would be from the obligation to cater to the whims of the circulating libraries and their matron readers, he concluded:

> I shall now, therefore, for the future enjoy the liberty of speech granted to the journalist, the historian, and the biographer, rights unfortunately in the present day denied to the novelist. Whether others will follow my example, whether others will see as I see that the literary battle of our time lies not between the romantic and realistic schools of fiction, but for freedom from the illiterate censorship of a librarian, the next few years will most assuredly decide. I do not fear for the result. My only regret is that a higher name than mine has not undertaken to wave the flag of Liberalism and to denounce and to break with a commercial arrangement that makes of the English novel a kind of advanced school-book, a sort of guide to marriage and the drawing-room.[43]

In wondering whether people would follow him, Moore essentially begged others to join his liberal cause for less restricted trade and more social, political, and aesthetic tolerance.

As one might expect, some people did not agree. One person opined: "Why should we have thrust on us books that neither profit nor divert, merely that a morbid-minded man may have the money on which to batten and nourish his unwholesome imaginings?"[44] The rhetorical question illustrates two common pro-censorship arguments. First, the writer is depicted as almost vampiric. A novel written by such a monstrous individual must likewise be a manifestation of sickness and criminality, and so its circulation must be prevented. Literature is therefore understood to be something that should be wholesome, catering, in effect, to spiritual and moral well-being, while harmful books essentially poison the body politic and thus threaten public health. Second, such morbidity is maintained through economics. In salaciously writing of taboos, the author only seeks to line their own pockets. This argument is actually twofold: it melds the threat of people writing for the basest instincts with the notion that such writing leads to wealth and further perversion. This is the filth argument, which is an offshoot of the public health argument. In its simplest form, filthy minds create filthy literature, which generates filthy lucre and propagates more filthy minds.

Meanwhile, some of Moore's colleagues published their support for him. However, as he had feared, none of the more recognised writers of the day came to his defence. Instead, those who sided with him were his exact contemporaries. Only in their early thirties and perhaps casting into the future of their fledging careers, these writers were concerned with the direction of literature. Robert Langstaff de Havilland, for one, attested that he had suffered the same fate with the libraries: two people complained about his novel *Enslaved* (1884), which resulted in its withdrawal from circulation. De Havilland's testimony was important for giving credence to Moore's account and for revealing the resignation that most people had with the system. Indeed, he believed that it would take many writers combined with brute force to overcome the obstacles that they faced in their struggles for freedom of expression. The problem, he noted, was those who "are ever on the watch for a chance of posing as paragons; it flatters their vanity and lends them a certain reputation for uprightness in their little circle." In contrast, he argued that the English public "may be relied upon to condemn a novel if it be unhealthy"; therefore, "let them at least have the chance of judging for themselves."[45] It was a plea for liberal tolerance: people should not impose their tastes and opinions on others as others have the right to make their own informed decisions.

George Gissing was similarly supportive of Moore, having also suffered from censorship when one publisher turned down *Mrs Grundy's*

Enemies (1882) because they felt that it would not please the ordinary reader at Mudie's; his next book, *The Unclassed* (1884), was rejected by another publisher because they thought it "unwholesome."[46] In affording Moore the opportunity to explain "the practical position of an English novelist who studies life," Gissing argued that the *Pall Mall Gazette* had "performed an essential service ... to the cause of art." The implication was that Anglophone writers, especially those who found favour with British matrons and the patriarchs of the library committees, had not been studying life, but rather had been depicting ideals and embodying the dominant values. These novelists, he said, feared damaging "their popularity, and consequently their income." The result was that English novels were "miserable stuff." "Let novelists be true to their artistic conscience," he implored, "and the public taste will come round."[47] In effect, if artists had more freedom, they would shape public taste and values would follow suit. This is the very tension that has figured in censorship debates throughout time and across geopolitical frontiers. On the one side are the writers who advance a liberal progressive view that by being tolerant of innovative forms and challenging content, new mores and norms will be adopted that will lead to a better society. On the other side are the censors and moral guardians who advance the conservative view that accepting innovative forms and challenging content will lead to the destruction of society's moral and social fabric.

As the debate played out in the pages of the *Pall Mall Gazette*, Moore was busy completing his sophomore novel, *A Mummer's Wife*. However, because Tinsley published according to the market and was not interested in bucking the system, Moore sought a press that was willing to take more risks. In stepped Henry Vizetelly.

After working several years in Berlin and Paris as correspondent for the *Illustrated London News*, Vizetelly wrote a number of his own books and translated Marius Topin's *L'homme au masque de fer* into English as *The Man with the Iron Mask* (1870). During his time abroad, he became enamoured with continental literature and, in 1884, after his return to London, he founded a press to translate the day's leading works. Vizetelly recognised that the increasingly literate market was ripe for exploitation as its tastes had not yet been formed, and he believed that the best way to make headway was to produce affordable one-volume editions. At this time, English readers only had access to poor American translations of Zola or had to read him in the original French.[48] Seeing an opportunity in the market and seeking to share his love of French literature, Vizetelly published Zola's *L'Assommoir*. Moore began the translation, but as he was busy with writing his own novel, the task soon fell to Vizetelly's son Ernest, who would go on to translate a number of Zola's books. Vizetelly soon tapped others to work for him, such as Eleanor Marx-Aveling, Karl Marx's daughter, who translated Flaubert's *Madame Bovary* in 1886. The English volumes of Tolstoy and Dostoevsky that soon followed were among the first to appear in English. In many ways, Vizetelly was the ideal publisher for Moore in that he was willing to issue novels in one-volume editions at reasonable prices, which would circumvent the tyranny of the circulating libraries. Just as importantly, by publishing Russian and French literary lions of the late nineteenth century, Vizetelly paved the way for Moore, whose naturalist writing would indigenise continental forms and contribute to changing the direction of Anglophone prose. In so doing, Moore's novels would be read not in isolation as an Anglophone anomaly, but as part of a broader, contemporary European movement.

Ever the disciple, Moore had learned from Zola to design a novel to break into uncharted subject matter and to provoke interest in his work with advance articles in the press that taught readers how to receive it.[49] Just as Zola challenged society in writing about coal miners' desperate lives and working conditions in *Germinal*, in *A Mummer's Wife* Moore wrote a scandalous tale about a woman who leaves her husband to join her lover's touring theatre troupe. Moore's article in the *Pall Mall Gazette* was therefore not only a high-minded call for freedom of expression, tolerance, and a reformed book trade, but was also intended to create advance publicity for his forthcoming work and to be an Anglophone manifesto for naturalism.

The problem for Moore was that even though he did not mention Mudie by name in his article, he had told him in person that he would challenge his business model. Moreover, Moore's heroine Kate Ede is driven to leave her husband for a travelling actor-manager in part because she constantly reads the sort of sentimental romances that were in demand by the middle-class matron readers of the circulating libraries. Moore thus insinuates that her immorality – both her adultery and her brutally detailed fatal slide into alcoholism – is caused by idealist literature. The result was inevitable: both Mudie's and W. H. Smith refused to purchase *A Mummer's Wife*, in effect banning it from their readers. Unsurprisingly, Mudie's banned two of Moore's other novels, *A Drama in Muslin* (1886), also published by Vizetelly, and *Confessions of a Young Man* (1888), which recounts Mudie's censorship.[50] Fortunately for Moore, the implications of the libraries' ban of *A Mummer's Wife* were offset by the book's affordability: the first edition, which was marketed at the popular price of six shillings, sold out in six weeks, and the novel was issued in six further printings over the next four years.[51]

With a hint of regret at having missed an opportunity to create a real stir, Moore later immodestly claimed that he would have become "a Dreyfus case" if he had not been able to sell *A Mummer's Wife*.[52]

Moore and Freedom of Expression

Moore's reaction to being censored was understandably swift and, coupled with his letter in the *Pall Mall Gazette*, set the template for how writers would respond to a variety of censorships. Taking his cue from John Milton's *Areopagitica*, he wrote a polemical treatise on censorship that Vizetelly published in pamphlet form and sold for only three pence. It was, again, a crude exercise in marketing as much as a defence of higher principles as the final page included an advertisement for *A Mummer's Wife* that was accompanied by quotes from favourable reviews. Yet the quotes were not only selected for their praise of Moore and his skill; they also provided a guide for the potential reader of his book on how to approach its naturalist form.

The title of the pamphlet – *Literature at Nurse, or Circulating Morals* – is crisp and witty. As with his article, Moore links authorities who act as censors to a milking mother, at once feminising them and alluding to the parental control they inappropriately wield over other adults. Literature is similarly kept in its infancy as opposed to growing and maturing. The libraries police morals, circulating only those works that they deem acceptable. Now freed from the publisher-librarian cabal, Moore revealed the truth behind the rather poorly kept secret that the Mr. X whose libraries had banned his books was indeed Mudie. Relating the entirety of the case, including the positive press reviews, his meeting with Mudie, and the rationale he was given for his book's withdrawal from circulation, Moore undertook a wholesale attack on the system. As we will see, multiple elements of his rhetorical strategy would be replicated later by other writers, including personally attacking the censor; itemising examples of questionable works that had not been censored; noting the effects of censorship on literature and society; alluding to the immorality of great works; claiming that literature can contribute to public health; and issuing pleas for tolerance and freedom of expression.

The most shocking aspect of Moore's pamphlet is its personal attack on the censor. Indeed, it includes one of the greatest and most intemperate rants against a censor that can be found:

> [A]lthough I am willing to laugh at you, Mr. Mudie, to speak candidly, I hate you; and I love and am proud of my hate of you. It is the best thing

> about me. I hate you because you dare question the sacred right of the artist to obey the impulses of his temperament; I hate you because you are the great purveyor of the worthless, the false and the commonplace; I hate you because you are a fetter about the ankles of those who would press forward towards the light of truth; I hate you because you feel not the spirit of scientific inquiry that is bearing our age along; I hate you because you pander to the intellectual sloth of to-day; I hate you because you would mould all ideas to fit the narrow limits in which your own turn; I hate you because you impede the free development of our literature.[53]

The censor is a "fetter," thereby inhibiting the artist and preventing progress. Compared to the artist, who seeks the truth, Mudie, as a censor, purveys false ideals. These are important sets of related dichotomies that are often used by those who make the case for freedom of expression: artist/censor, real/ideal, truth/falsehood. Notably, Moore revealed the furtive censorship and gave it a public face in Mudie; the visceral hatred that Moore felt towards Mudie, coupled with his depiction of himself as high-minded and Mudie as backwards, directed the public to feel the same. Knowing that there was censorship in terms of which books were being published, purchased, and circulated by the libraries induced considerable professional and economic anxiety in the prospective writer, and later being the focus of such censorship only intensified matters. By personalising his attack, Moore not only took aim at Mudie's profit margins, but also at his reputation. Just as the artist and his work are rendered objects of disgust through censorship, the censor here is not simply held up to ridicule; he is rendered an object of disgust in turn.

Censors are inevitably judged not only by what they censor, but also by what they do not. To dispel the illusion that he was somehow indecent or obscene, Moore outlined the plot of *A Mummer's Wife* followed by detailed summaries of three books that were currently in circulation at Mudie's: Mrs. Campbell Praed's *Nadine*, W. H. Mallock's *A Romance of the Nineteenth Century*, and Robert Buchanan's *Foxglove Manor*. All three of these, he noted, had highly wrought plots with plenty of scandal. The titular character of *Nadine* commits adultery and tries to cover it up when her lover dies by dragging his corpse from her room; she later abandons her baby and moves to the continent, where she marries a Russian prince. Mallock similarly tells of adulterous relationships. Meanwhile, Buchanan's book simply "reeks of the pulpit and the alcove," featuring a parson who uses his religion to seduce his congregation but is thwarted in the end. Two of Ouida's novels – *Puck*, about a courtesan and her many lovers, and *Moths*, about "a dissolute adventuress" who sells her daughter to a lover – were likewise available on Mudie's shelves.[54] Moore wondered how Mudie could allow such books in his libraries if he had banned his. The question was raised as much for Mudie as it was for Moore's audience. In so doing, Moore revealed the indiscriminate nature of censorship.

Returning to the metaphor of his title, Moore examined not only the effects of censorship on literature, but also on the wider society: "Instead of being allowed to fight, with and amid, the thoughts and aspirations of men, literature is now rocked to an ignoble rest in the motherly arms of the librarian. That of which he approves is fed with gold; that from which he turns the breast dies like a vagrant's child; while in and out of his voluminous skirts run a motley and monstrous progeny, a callow, a whining, a puking brood of bastard bantlings, a race of Aztecs that disgrace the intelligence of the English nation."[55] Because censorship intervenes in the marketplace of ideas, it impacts the intellectual development of the people. While the censor attempts to protect, the people who are the focus of that care are harmed, becoming deformed and incapable of independent thought. In this sense, Moore furthered an evolutionary argument: for him, censorship leads to degeneration (becoming as savage as Aztecs), while freedom of expression leads to social progress (the glory of the English nation) because ideas are considered and tested. The evolutionary argument that Moore espoused is thus similar to the conservative outlook that he railed against elsewhere, a considerably racialised and indeed racist view that depicts humanity and Western civilisation (England) as pure and suggests that censoring new ideas has the potential to cause society's decline (becoming the equivalent of Aztecs).

Moore also made the anti-censorship argument that were the same standards applied across time, we would be deprived of the classics, going so far as to claim that "three-fourths of our libraries would have to be condemned as immoral publications."[56] Similarly, he appealed to the public health argument, which posits that literature reveals society's ills and in so doing allows us to understand what needs to be reformed. "To analyze," he said, "you must have a subject; a religious or sensual passion is as necessary to the realistic novelist as a disease to the physician. The dissection of a healthy subject would not, as a rule, prove interesting."[57] In asserting freedom of expression and rejecting the young-girl standard in literature, Moore wisely couched his argument as a moderate point of view, which was a tack that many after him would imitate of necessity. "I would not have it supposed," he said, that "I am of opinion that literature can be glorified in the Temples of Venus. Were the freedom of speech I ask for to lead to this, we should have done no more than to have substituted one evil for another. There is a middle course, and I think it is this – to write as grown-up men and women talk of life's passions and duties."[58] Yet knowing that Mudie and other like-minded entrepreneurs justified their censorship on business principles, Moore ended not through more rhetorical flourish, but by imploring people to boycott the circulating libraries until they ended their moral dictatorship.

Alongside of Moore's polemical assault, Vizetelly continued to publish Zola's novels. Following *L'Assommoir*, he issued translations of *Nana*, *Germinal*, and *Pot-Bouille*, the latter appearing as *Piping Hot!* The opening pages of the 1887 edition of *Piping Hot!* included a two-page advertisement for Moore's *A Mummer's Wife* that featured a subtitle identical to that of *Piping Hot!* – *"A Realistic Novel"* – thereby inviting readers to link together the two men and their works. Vizetelly also recognised the marketing power of censorship, the advertisement indicating that Moore's novel had "been placed in the Index Expurgatorius of the Select Circulating Libraries of Messrs. Mudie and W. H. Smith." If censorship seeks to keep something out of the public sphere, Vizetelly understood that it could also be used to drum up business, using the psychology of Satan in praising the forbidden fruit.

Importantly, Moore also provided a preface for Zola's novel. From this point on, prefaces formed another weapon in the arsenal of anti-censorship campaigners. These paratexts introduce the audience to the book, in effect guiding them on how to receive it. While articles, pamphlets, and manifestos are all important to the cause, the preface is more direct in that it both accompanies and precedes the book.[59] In writing the preface for Zola's novel, Moore also effectively presented himself as Zola's Anglophone interpreter. Both men would thrive on the notoriety that they brought to one another.

Moore's preface covered many of the arguments outlined above, but he began more closely to his subject by depicting Zola as a colossus who struggled against the ignorant opinions of the masses. Furthermore, Moore adulated Zola's artistry, from his sentence structure to his telescopic vision of society that provides both broad views and unflinching, intimate portraits. For Moore, Zola was "a great epic poet," "the Homer of modern life."[60] He considered *Piping Hot!*, which details the sordid lives of the inhabitants of a Parisian apartment building, a "terrible satire on the 'bourgeoisie'" and claimed that it ranked with the works of Juvenal, Voltaire, Pope, and Swift.[61] Zola – and, through association, Moore – was thus given canonical status, in effect rendering him unassailable because the classics are touchstones in the development of civilisation. Yet Moore gave his argument a grander note, announcing that "the great literary battle of our day is not to be fought for either realism or romanticism, but for freedom of speech."[62] In this, he was prescient once again.

The Rise of the National Vigilance Association and Moral Panic

Matters came to a boil with Vizetelly's publication of Zola's *La Terre*. Translated by his son Ernest and sold as *The Soil*, the uncompromising novel recounts the story of the peasants of the Beauce whose greed for the earth leads to divisive fights between generations of families.[63] The constant thieving, conniving, legal machinations, abuse, rape, incest, and murder are all cast as perverse outcomes of their avarice and the base means by which they acquire land. Ernest later admitted that in his translation of *La Terre*, he had toned down much of Zola's material. This is evident in a comparative reading of just the first two chapters of Zola's original and Vizetelly's 1888 edition. At the outset, we are introduced to Hyacinthe, a drunken poacher and wastrel who has a talent to audibly break wind on command, which he does for the always-appreciative local audience. Vizetelly excised all mention of this "infirmity" and Hyacinthe's outrageous nickname – Jesus Christ. He feared that such blasphemous and earthy humour would have given "offence to people who no longer read Sterne, and who knew little or nothing of Rabelais."[64] Following considerable outcry in France over the publication of *La Terre* in 1887, Henry Vizetelly went over Ernest's proofs to ensure that it would not offend *too much* as both men desired to garner Zola renown in England, but they recognised the potential limits of freedom of expression. Yet they did not have to concern themselves with the censorship of the circulating libraries as they were now poised to bypass them through their cheap one-volume editions. In the years before Moore and Vizetelly came along, there were few major censorship debates in England regarding the book trade as everything was controlled through back-door channels. However, by circumventing the informal censorship of the libraries, the Vizetellys and Moore set themselves on a collision course with authorities that would change the way that literature was thereafter treated.

Like most people in London, the Vizetellys would have recognised at the time that the context had considerably shifted. Moore's article in the *Pall Mall Gazette* appeared in December 1884, *A Mummer's Wife* in early 1885, and *Literature at Nurse* in the months that followed. That summer, W. T. Stead, Moore's former editor, instigated a massive moral panic. Beginning on 6 July 1885, Stead published a series in the *Pall Mall Gazette* entitled "The Maiden Tribute of Modern Babylon" to expose the nasty underbelly of prostitution. Noting that more than fifty thousand plied the trade in London, from those working street corners to those housed in brothels, Stead mercilessly detailed the living and working conditions of these women with the eye of a naturalist writer. Most scandalously, Stead recounted how he was able to purchase a thirteen-year-old virgin for five pounds.[65] This caused church representatives from across the country to give vigorous sermons on the subjects of virtue and moral duty. It was the first example of how investigative journalism could not only reflect but also shape society.

Indeed, "The Maiden Tribute of Modern Babylon" prompted parliament to readdress the stalled Criminal Law Amendment Bill, which was to raise the age of consent from thirteen to sixteen. Outraged citizens pressured the government to pass the amended legislation. One of the prominent agitators was William Alexander Coote, who argued that the only way to "remove the vice was to demonstrate, and get public opinion to demand equal justice to all."[66] The culmination of this activity was a march, led by Coote, that wound through the city to Hyde Park.[67] Between 200,000 and 250,000 people were estimated to have participated. Later that week, a number of these same people met "to consider the best means of suppressing gutter literature," the result being the establishment of the National Vigilance Association (NVA). As a high-ranking member of the NVA, Coote proposed that people cooperate to stamp out obscene writing.[68] With Coote at the helm, the NVA would become a more open and aggressive force for social purity than the circulating libraries.

In advance of the Hyde Park rally, Stead had been in talks with Coote and Bramwell Booth, the son of the Salvation Army's founder, to establish what soon became the NVA. Stead wrote the organisation's statutes and hired Coote as its secretary.[69] He was also a staunch and active member, sitting on a number of their committees, including those devoted to literature and parliamentary and municipal affairs.[70] From the time of its founding, Stead was therefore more than happy to give the NVA ample coverage, and he and Coote worked in coordinated fashion. Beginning in 1886, Coote employed retired police officers as private detectives and had a network of "fanatical informers" supply intelligence on the presence of obscene literature. Public opinion, partly shaped by Stead through the *Pall Mall Gazette*, led to London's chief commissioner instructing police officers to enforce the law against indecent publications. There was a corresponding explosion of arrests for such crimes, from eight in 1885 to fifty-four in 1886.[71]

As secretary of the NVA, Coote led protests against Vizetelly for his publication of "pernicious" literature, with Stead duly supporting the crusade.[72] The latter contacted Vizetelly in March 1888 to inquire into the sales figures of his French novels. Of the 240 titles that Vizetelly published at the time, only 30 were from the French realist school, including works by Zola, Flaubert, the brothers Goncourt, and Guy de Maupassant.[73] Vizetelly candidly admitted that he had sold "considerably more than a million" copies of Émile Gaboriau's and Fortuné Du Boisgobey's detective novels and still sold two hundred thousand per year. Meanwhile, *Nana* was the bestseller among Zola's titles with almost one hundred thousand shifted. "We reckon it a bad week," Vizetelly remarked, "when the sale of our Zola translations falls below a thousand volumes."[74] No mention was made of Moore or other Anglophone writers that Vizetelly published. Stead's line of questioning suggested that Vizetelly was a threat not because of his entire catalogue, but because degraded French forms and values were invading and menacing English society. This became a recurrent theme in censorship controversies. Censorship and social purity movements are guided in part by a sense of national security, hence the names of various organisations, such as the *National* Vigilance Association, that are founded in response to a perceived influx of obscene and indecent foreign literature. This is the pro-censorship aspect of the international dialectic, in which the national is posited as pure in contradistinction to immoral foreign writers and those who promote them.

Matters took a turn for the worse for Vizetelly when Liberal politician Samuel Smith, an active member of the social purity movement, raised in parliament the issue of Vizetelly's sales of French literature. On 8 May 1888, he proposed a motion stating "That this House deplores the rapid spread of demoralizing literature in this country, and is of opinion that the law against obscene publications and indecent pictures and prints should be vigorously enforced, and, if necessary, strengthened."[75] As for Zola's novels, Smith referred to them as "dirt and horror pure and simple."[76] He implored his colleagues to consider "what such literature had done for France. It overspread that country like a torrent, and its poison was destroying the whole national life."[77] If England were not careful, it too would be destroyed. The problem, he suggested, was that England already had a mechanism to ensure its survival, but had yet to use it properly. Officials, he beseeched, should prosecute purveyors of indecency under the terms of the Obscene Publications Act.[78] Henry Matthews, the home secretary, agreed, adding that unlike classic literature, which was written with no evil purpose, the authors of their own time wrote "with the object of directing attention to the foulest passions of which human nature was capable, and to depict them in the most attractive forms." This was part of a "calculated" effort "to do great harm to the moral health of the country."[79] With unanimous support, Smith's motion passed.

The effects of this institutional ballast to the social purity movement were immense. The NVA immediately began to raise funds to prosecute Vizetelly under the terms of the Obscene Publications Act.[80] Three decades earlier, in a parliamentary debate on 11 May 1857, the same year of Flaubert's and Baudelaire's trials, Liberal politician Lord Campbell, at the time Britain's chief justice, announced to his colleagues that he "had learned with horror and alarm that a sale of poison more deadly than prussic acid, strichnine [*sic*], or arsenic – the sale of obscene publications and indecent books – was openly going on."[81] Once again, literature was understood in terms of public health, in this case contributing not merely to the ills of society, but to its potential death. Campbell thus introduced a bill, which was passed that summer. Troublingly, the resultant Obscene Publications Act did not define the term *obscene*. It took until 1868 to rectify this situation, when Sir Alexander Cockburn, Campbell's successor as chief justice, rendered a decision in a case against Benjamin Hicklin, who had distributed an anti-papist book of scandalous excerpts purportedly taken from Catholic confessionals. Cockburn wrote that "the test of obscenity is" whether it would "deprave and corrupt those whose minds are open to such immoral influences and into whose hands a publication of this sort may fall."[82] Lawyers Morris Ernst and William Seagle later declared: "With this utterance sanity was swept away, and Victorian literary prudery and the law made to coincide. Or rather law was swept aside to make room for hysteria." Any book would now be open to prosecution. "A literary reign of terror had been instituted," Ernst and Seagle concluded.[83] It would, however, take social purity campaigners two decades before they would wield this weapon to bludgeon writers and their publishers.[84] As we will see in subsequent chapters, the legislation and legal decision would also shape the future of post-independence Irish censorship law and the direction of Irish literature.

Having raised enough funds, the NVA launched the first legal challenge against literature and freedom of artistic expression in Britain. Vizetelly appeared in court on 10 August 1888 to answer for having published three obscene works: *The Soil*, *Nana*, and *Piping Hot!* As the latter included Moore's preface, he and his work would be implicitly tried. Herbert Henry Asquith, the future Liberal Prime Minister from 1908 to 1916, prosecuted the case. The presiding magistrate considered *La Terre* to be the worst of the lot and determined that Vizetelly could be tried for obscene libel on it alone.[85] Unfortunately for Vizetelly, his counsel was terribly unprepared, admitting to the court that he had not read much of this sort of literature while supposing that there was worse out there. The magistrate sided with Asquith, sending the case to the Central Criminal Court.

Meanwhile, Vizetelly and Moore took their case to the public. Produced on Moore's advice and with his assistance, Vizetelly published a lengthy booklet with an equally lengthy title: *Extracts Principally from English Classics: Showing That the Legal Suppression of M. Zola's Novels Would Logically Involve the Bowdlerizing of Some of the Greatest Works in English Literature.*[86] Vizetelly sent it to Sir A. K. Stephenson, the solicitor to the treasury, hoping that it would convince him to stop the prosecution. In his letter to Stephenson, he noted that the hundreds of quotations from the classics were "far more objectionable" than any in his translations of Zola. He found it odd that so many who were involved in the temperance movement, like countless members of the NVA, could be against the writer of *L'Assommoir*, which details the seedy and tragic lives of those inflicted with alcoholism. "Is life as it really exists," he conjectured, "with the vice and degradation current among the lower classes, and the greed, the selfishness, and the veiled sensuality prevalent in the classes above – to be in future ignored by the novelist who, in the case of M. Zola, really holds the historian's pen?"[87] The letter, published in Stead's *Pall Mall Gazette,* made an implicit link between the public service of Stead's revelation of juvenile prostitution three years previously and the horrors revealed in Zola's novels: both men were social reformers working in different genres. However, Vizetelly's letter included prescient warnings that were cut – effectively censored – from the version published in Stead's newspaper: "Time we are told brings round its revenges, and the books burnt by the common hangman in one age come to be honoured in the next"; in the end, Zola's novels, in "spite of their admitted coarseness, will take rank as classics among the productions of the great writers of the past."[88]

For his part, Moore published an article, "A Plea for a Literary Censorship." He was not concerned with whether the books in question were "of an indecent character." Instead, he doubted the fitness of "twelve London shopkeepers" to render a decision on "difficult questions in art and morals." On the one side, he said that the defence would inevitably, like Vizetelly, "lecture them on the tradition of English literature," illustrated with choice passages from Shakespeare, Sterne, and Byron, and suggest that a guilty verdict would "inflict irreparable injury on art." On the other side, the prosecution would select juicy excerpts from Zola and suggest that a guilty verdict would "protect their wives and daughters from contamination." Meanwhile, the newspapers would "be filled with columns of the most objectionable matter," people would focus "on the uncleanest aspect of an unsavoury discussion," and the result would be that *La Terre* would become a bestseller. He noted that the members of the NVA thereby "propagate that which it exists to suppress." The result would be "very black" for both morality and art, with neither the better for all the fuss.

Oddly, Moore's solution was for less freedom in the publishing sphere; he proposed that they should develop a test "whereby the legal and moral right of way of a book may be determined." There already existed a pre-performance censorship of plays under the auspices of the Lord Chamberlain, so why should they not have a literary censorship that would mitigate against the informal censorship of libraries and ensure that tawdry matters would not be published? He insisted on "the absolute and inalienable right of the artist to write as he pleases," but "now, when literature is menaced on one side by ignorant jurors, on the other by ignorant librarians, it behoves someone to cry Halt. The ideal artistic state is of course uncurtailed liberty; but since this cannot be, it is better for art to be restrained by artists than to be trampled on by tradespeople." Moore naively believed that there could exist an "enlightened censorship." Such an institution, he suggested, would be composed of "any three leading men of letters."[89] It was a bold move, but one that purity movement members might have found to be akin to a jury of thieves, rapists, and murderers determining the guilt of fellow criminals.

Simultaneously with this article, Moore published the autofictional *Confessions of a Young Man*. Importantly, he did not go through Vizetelly, rather publishing it with Swan Sonnenschein. In recounting Mudie's banning of *A Modern Lover*, Moore wrote: "Human nature has from the earliest time shown a liking for dirty stories; dirty stories have formed a substantial part of every literature." He asserted that such stories were therefore "inherent in the human animal. Call it a disease if you will – an incurable disease – which, if it is driven inwards, will break out in an unexpected quarter in a new form and with redoubled virulence."[90] In this sense, he and Zola were doing society a service. He could thus conclude: "I am ashamed of nothing I have done especially my sins."[91] It was an important declaration: he would not be badgered into abandoning his beliefs, and he held that he had acted with moral intent.

Meanwhile, Vizetelly's case had changed from one instigated by a private body, the NVA, to one being led by the public prosecutor.[92] On 31 October 1888, despite Vizetelly's tactics and Moore's article, a jury charged the former with publishing obscene libels. Relying upon the Cockburn ruling, the question was "whether the tendency of the work was to corrupt and deprave the minds of those who are open to such influences and into whose hands it would fall." That older works had not been indicted was irrelevant: they were not on trial and their existence did not justify obscenity. Sir Edward Clarke, the solicitor-general who led the Crown's case, would later make a second mark on literary history when he represented Oscar Wilde in his case against the Marquess of Queensbury for criminal libel and defended Wilde when he was subsequently tried for homosexual practices. In *La Terre*, Clarke said, he had identified twenty-one passages, some running for several pages, "such as no writer with pure motives ever put into a literary work." Indeed, he did not believe that "there was ever gathered together between two covers so much bestial obscenity" and considered it "a filthy book from end to end."[93] When the jurors protested having to hear the passages, Clarke said he would gladly stop the moment that they would agree to charge the book as obscene. Witnessing this, Vizetelly pled guilty and promised to cease publication of Zola's works. Addressing Vizetelly, the judge said that he did not believe that he had published the books to deprave people and he shared Clarke's desire not to see Vizetelly imprisoned; the result was a hundred pound fine.

To ensure that the trial's implications remained in the public eye, Coote and the NVA published a booklet entitled *Pernicious Literature* in January 1889. It featured the court transcripts and press clippings and opened with a statement by Coote that drew attention to the particular harm that such literature posed. He focused on men's responsibility to propose a paternal censorship and tied this to the future of the nation, with the booklet intended to "sound a note of alarm, and rouse the manhood of England to action in relation to the growth of this evil, which is to-day a menace to our religious, social and national life."[94]

Following the trial, with the family company facing financial ruin, Ernest Vizetelly excised and rewrote passages of the other Zola novels for which his father had templates and set about printing these heavily bowdlerised volumes.[95] Meanwhile, Coote and the NVA kept busy: working with Scotland Yard detectives, they raided several properties and seized some five thousand photographs.[96] By that spring, they turned their attention back to Vizetelly and his expurgated Zola translations. On 30 May 1889, Vizetelly was tried for and again found guilty of committing obscene libel. This time, with little left in his coffers, he was sent to Holloway Gaol for three months. Booksellers sent a deputation to Coote, asking him to go through their stock and inform them what they may not sell. One trade publication distanced itself from Vizetelly, stating that his list was "not one which excites our entire admiration" and that his translations were "dubious additions to our current literature"; and yet they sympathised that he had to fight by himself over such a large question as freedom of expression.[97] Coote, however, believed that Vizetelly got what he deserved for having flooded the nation with "foreign filth" and "polluted" the country's youth.[98] For his part, Vizetelly's son Ernest drew up a petition signed by over a hundred authors protesting against his father's harsh treatment. These included Thomas Hardy, Ouida, John Addington Symonds, Leslie Stephen, George du Maurier, Robert Buchanan, H. Rider Haggard, William Archer, Henry Irving, and Henry Arthur Jones, as well as the Irish Moore, Sheridan Le Fanu, Frank Harris, and T. P. O'Connor.[99] Perhaps inevitably given his history and his relationship with Vizetelly, the press attributed the petition to George Moore.[100]

Fallout

Vizetelly was released from prison at the end of August 1889 and died on 1 January 1894. The trials and his convictions took a severe toll on him, Moore later writing that he had "always looked upon Henry Vizetelly's death as a judicial murder" and wondering "if the members of the Vigilant Society [sic] ever work in their beds asking themselves if they were murderers."[101] Moore was understandably angry at what Rachel Potter has called the "prowling prudes" of the purity movements.[102] Yet Moore and Vizetelly were responsible in part for provoking the prowling prudes to begin their moral panic. They had revealed and challenged the censorship of the circulating libraries, helping to instigate revolutionary reforms to the publishing trade by issuing affordable one-volume editions to the public. This change essentially caused the NVA and like-minded groups to petition the courts to suppress literature that they felt countered their morality.

Another unforeseen and unwanted outcome was that most publishers and editors came to fear prosecution. Audacious writers had to find the few publishers who dared to push the boundaries of modern literature and morality or go elsewhere, such as to France, where the book trade was not subjected to British law, thereby illustrating another aspect of the international dialectic of censorship. This resonated in the careers of many of the canonical modernist writers, beginning with Thomas Hardy's difficulties in publishing *Tess of the d'Urbervilles* and *Jude the Obscure*, through to D. H. Lawrence, James Joyce, Radclyffe Hall, and Henry Miller, and even as late as the mid-twentieth century with Vladimir Nabokov and J. P. Donleavy. The lesson of the Vizetelly trials was that writers had to adapt to the prejudices of publishers and editors, who were themselves conditioned by pressures from the purity movement and the threat of legal action. The result was that while

British and Irish literatures became increasingly frank, it took them decades to achieve the explicitness associated with French realism and naturalism. As for Zola, *La Terre* was circulated freely in Britain in French editions. In 1894, it was again translated into English alongside five of Zola's other novels – *L'Assommoir, La Curée, Germinal, Nana,* and *Pot-Bouille*. Yet as this series was privately published for the Lutetian Society's members at a very high cost (twenty-one guineas for the set of six), the NVA did not bother themselves with it, and there was no prosecution.[103] The discrepancy in the treatment was clear: Zola in cheap English editions was vulgar and threatened the masses, but in French or in expensive translated volumes, his works were permissible as they catered to the higher social classes.

Of the controversy involving Mudie's, Adrien Frazier submits that Moore's public handling of it through his articles in the press launched his literary career.[104] Even more broadly, Moore created a template for modern writers in an age of increasing media coverage and literacy rates: they should use censorship to manufacture publicity and to bring the spotlight on them by revealing the censorship of their works, in a way touting and justifying their own scandalous and shocking writing. That is, they should not hide from being labelled indecent or obscene, but broadcast that label. At the same time, as his "A Plea for a Literary Censorship" attests, Moore was wise enough to distance himself from being in favour of complete literary freedom and to present himself as an ethical and moral artist who sought some middle ground. In doing so, he gave himself an air of respectability while flaunting his literary bona fides and making a case for greater tolerance for literature. In the end, naturalism was brought to the Anglophone world via three men: the French Zola, his Irish disciple Moore, and his English publisher of Italian origins Vizetelly. The making of modern literature in Britain and its relationship with censorship was therefore an international affair with an Irish writer firmly at its core.

This coming together of artists and editors attests to the international dialectic of censorship. Indeed, Moore looked abroad for his models, saw the aesthetic experiments in French painting and literature as something that could inspire English art and writing, promoted these artists in Britain, and adopted their modes in his own work. The response was that censors and purity campaigners, in denouncing the tide of foreign filth that threatened to poison the populace and ruin civilisation, acted to suppress this literature and demonise those who wrote and supported it. This speaks to the significance of the National Vigilance Association, which sought to maintain morality in the country, exorcise any immoral elements from it, and prevent the infiltration of immorality from abroad. On the one hand, censorship was considered a measure that would protect the country, its most vulnerable citizens, and the national culture. On the other hand, it was perceived as something that stymied freedom of expression, the circulation of new art and ways of seeing the world, and cultural stimulation and rejuvenation. For those against censorship, the suppressed foreign artistic modes were seen as innovative and having the potential to provoke positive aesthetic and social reform.

One of the lessons to be learned from these experiences was how the lack of a concerted collective effort at times hindered the fight for freedom of expression. Some of Moore's colleagues published letters of support for him, and one should not underestimate what this might have cost them, potentially making them targets for the NVA and causing their works to be blacklisted at the circulating libraries. Furthermore, many writers signed the petition drafted by Ernest Vizetelly to protest the law's harsh treatment of his father. In this, they were joined by a loose coalition of actors, newspaper editors, and other public figures. However, these efforts never coalesced into meaningful resistance to sway public opinion and ramp up political and social pressure to protect freedom of expression for writers and publishers. Despite this apparent failure, the actions of these people represented an important series of first steps. As for Moore, when he was faced with censorship, his ability to concretely effect material and structural change to the publishing industry was radical and his combative public persona was to prove influential for how writers would defend themselves, their profession, and their art. Ultimately, though, the task of rallying and organising people to make political and legal change would fall to his compatriot Bernard Shaw.

Chapter Two

Evolving Tactics: Bernard Shaw, Relentless Antagonism, and Organised Resistance

For the next two decades, when the focus of censorship switched from the novel to the theatre, a similar scene played out with another Irish writer at its centre. Bernard Shaw would adopt a number of Moore's tactics, but he also developed new weapons in the fight for freedom of expression and social reform. This stemmed in part from their different situations, for while Moore, alongside Vizetelly, largely fought a lonesome battle against censorious forces, Shaw was part of a community of artists, which helped writers to shoulder the load. As a result, they refused to give in to public opinion, government inertia, and powerful commercial forces. This concerted effort, piecemeal though it may have been at times, was driven by three major factors. First, theatre brings together many disparate individuals to mount a cohesive production, so most of the people involved were already used to collaboration and compromise towards a larger objective. Second, Shaw acted as a politicised leader, which was a natural role for one who spearheaded the Fabian Society – one of London's most influential socialist associations – as its most engaging and tireless lecturer and pamphleteer. And third, writers and artists were in these decades, like trade unions across the Western world, collectivising to further their professional interests, as evidenced in the founding of the Society of Authors in 1884.

In addition to the more collective resistance of writers that will become evident in this chapter, there is a development of the international dialectic of censorship in Shaw's experiences that was not present in Moore's travails. Just as Moore looked abroad to Émile Zola for his aesthetic model, Shaw's playwrighting, especially at the outset of his career, was inspired by the Norwegian Henrik Ibsen's formal innovations and socially provocative theatre. Similarly, while Moore and Vizetelly would challenge and ultimately transform the economic model of novel publishing in their struggles with censorship, so Shaw and his colleagues would simultaneously fight against the commercial theatres and institutional censorship by participating in the independent theatre movement, founding their own companies, and producing their own shows. However, unlike Moore's and Vizetelly's experiences, the independent theatre movement was a wider European phenomenon in which dramatists, actors, directors, and artists inspired and collaborated with one another, toured countries beyond their own, performed the works of daring and groundbreaking contemporary playwrights from other cultures, and established new modes of production that their colleagues elsewhere adopted. Such work led to aesthetic experimentations and social, economic, and political challenges to the existing order across the continent. The result would be direct confrontation with official and unofficial censors.

At the time of the Vizetelly trials, Shaw was still a few years away from writing his first play and had laboured as a budding author in relative obscurity since completing his first novel in 1879. Of the five novels that he had written, four were serialised in socialist papers and three of them were not issued in book form until the twentieth century, when Shaw's celebrity made them a profitable venture and his views had become less shocking to British morality. The exceptions, *Cashel Byron's Profession* and *An Unsocial Socialist*, were published, respectively, by the Modern Press in 1886 and Swan Sonnenschein in 1887. William Swan Sonnenschein was a rare bird, a radical who also published Karl Marx and, during Vizetelly's difficulties, Moore's *Parnell and His Island* (1887) and *Confessions of a Young Man*. As Elizabeth Carolyn Miller notes, in the 1880s, Shaw was considered "*the* preeminent socialist novelist."[1] Given the cultural context and the power of the circulating libraries, his avant-garde politics and unconventional stories represented too much risk to most publishers' bottom lines.

It is therefore only natural that Shaw, the Fabian Socialist and writer of advanced novels, would be drawn to Vizetelly's trials, representing as they did a concomitant challenge to conservative aesthetic forms, the dominant morality, and the economics of publishing. Two days after the verdict in the first trial, Shaw, writing in *The Star*, attempted to recalibrate the issues at stake. He lamented: "I wish that *The Star*, as a Radical paper, would try to educate jurymen in the principles of liberty of speech and of the Press, instead of discussing whether M. Zola has the charm, the humor, the style which redeem the works of Rabelais, Chaucer, and Boccaccio."[2] The issue was therefore not whether Zola could be proven to have written only as frankly as others before him had, but "whether a writer may or may not expose to society its own wickedness." Indeed, "whilst that most venomous of all social pests, the rich man's son, sows his wild oats, we are not to tell on him on pain of fine and confiscation. One can only wonder at the state of mind of the persons who believe that such conditions as these will purify and elevate literature." For one as reform-minded as Shaw, the freedom to point out society's ills was an essential right and even a responsibility that the writer had towards his fellow citizens. While he was concerned with freedom of speech in general terms, it was through his activities in the theatre that the subject of censorship affected him most closely.

The Shelley and Ibsen Controversies

British theatre censorship had existed in various forms going back to the Master of the Revels, who in Tudor times was charged with licensing plays for performance. From the Restoration until the early eighteenth century, the theatre had relatively free rein, despite fears that it could foment revolutionary fervour. By the 1720s, satires had become particularly popular, with a growing shift in focus from human frailties to public misdeeds, moving from general calls for reform in behaviour to the ridicule and critique of specific politicians. Leading the charge was Henry Fielding, who mercilessly depicted the corruption of Prime Minister Robert Walpole in a series of scathing satires, five of which were produced in 1736 and 1737 alone.[3] Worried that the stage was affecting public opinion, the government presented legislation that became the Licensing Act of 1737. Under the new law, plays had to obtain permission from the Lord Chamberlain, a high-ranking member of the monarch's household, before they could be publicly performed. To alleviate the Lord Chamberlain's work, an "examiner of plays" was hired to read each manuscript submitted and to recommend passing, cutting, or banning it, with a licence granted or refused accordingly.[4] This process stood in place until censorship was repealed in 1968. However, the institution changed certain of its practices over time. In addition to proscribing the portrayal of politicians and the monarchy, examiners of plays and Lords Chamberlain gradually developed a long list of prohibited subjects. These included blasphemy, religiously sensitive subjects, and clergymen cast in a poor light; depictions of foreign people that could negatively affect relations with other countries; certain revolutionary figures, such as Robert Emmett, for much of the nineteenth century; the romanticisation of criminality; sex and nudity; and incest, homosexuality, and sexual disease. As studies have shown, the censorship was consistently motivated by the unwavering belief of those in authority that to control society, one had to control the theatre.[5]

While Moore and Vizetelly dealt with the circulating libraries controversy, another front in the war against censorship opened in the theatre, but from a rather unlikely source: the Shelley Society. Devoted to the radical Romantic poet Percy Bysshe Shelley, the Shelley Society was founded at a meeting on 10 March 1886. Among the five hundred people packed into University College London's Botany Theatre were Shaw, the playwright Henry Arthur Jones, and the Irish poet John Todhunter.[6] Platform speakers attested to the need to study and promote Shelley and to issue reprints of his work. Frederick J. Furnivall, the Shelley Society's founder and an editor of the *Oxford English Dictionary*, noted that one of their objectives was to stage *The Cenci* (1819), Shelley's horror-incest play about the ruthless and diabolical Count Cenci. However, he noted that the Lord Chamberlain had refused to licence a performance.[7]

In late 1885, Furnivall had approached Edward Pigott, the Lord Chamberlain's examiner of plays from 1874 until his death in 1895, about the possibility of staging Shelley's work. Pigott recognised that *The Cenci* "is a literary masterpiece, and from the first line of it to the last there is not an impure word or thought." This recognition of the play's aesthetic value shows some enlightenment on Pigott's part, but it is rather hard to square it with his opinion that "all the genius in the world cannot make a play of which <u>incest</u> is the central motive."[8] As Furnivall was an acquaintance of Pigott's, he personally visited him the next month to discuss the matter.[9] Once he was convinced that he could not obtain a licence to stage the play publicly, Furnivall struck upon the idea to hold a private, members-only performance, which would place the performance outside of the jurisdiction of the Lord Chamberlain. To this end, Furnivall secured the Grand Theatre in Islington, with both him and the theatre's manager assuring Pigott and other officials that absolutely no admission would be charged.[10]

There had been rumours of a possible performance of *The Cenci* for some time. As early as August 1885, the actress Alma Murray had made it known to journalists that she would like to tackle the role of Beatrice.[11] It was no surprise, then, that she immediately accepted when the society, which she had helped to cofound, offered it to her.[12] Murray's name and the whispers of scandal based on the Lord Chamberlain's refusal to licence the play helped with publicity, but the society was not willing to leave matters to chance. To this end, it appointed Shaw as press officer, charging him to ensure that the performance was widely reported and to distribute tickets for the 7 May show.[13] In slightly over a month, the generated buzz drove membership from 144 at the first meeting to almost double that by the second.[14]

Although Pigott had hoped that attendance would remain relatively modest at 1,500, the society claimed that there was "a very crowded and enthusiastic house, composed of over 2,400 members and their friends."[15] For its part, the press was highly critical of the production. While most reviewers admitted the literary aspects of the play, they justifiably questioned its dramatic qualities. They also condemned it as irredeemably immoral, referring to the subject of incest in circumlocutionary terms, a form of censorship itself that ensured it remained hidden from the public. Evoking the patriarchal concerns of all censors, the *Daily Telegraph* was one of many papers that questioned the presence in the audience of so many young ladies, charging that "it was their fault, or that of their husbands, fathers, and brothers, if they were shocked."[16]

Almost a month after the show, Shaw published a review of it. Instead of focusing on Shelley's aesthetics or the performance of the actors, he rather noted the context and mode of production, detailing how the Shelley Society had to circumvent the Lord Chamberlain to produce the play and how he refused to sell tickets to avoid it becoming a public performance. A licence, he explained, was not granted "on the ground that the performance of such a play would deprave the public." However, he wryly added, "So far, the anticipated depravation of the public seems not to have come off; for the conduct of the nation has not perceptibly altered for the worse." He concluded by hoping that the censorship would soon be "extinct."[17]

As we will see, this event set the twofold template for Shaw's career: first, align himself with a contentious literary lion and in so doing trumpet his own iconoclasm; and second, use that writer to push for some measure of socio-political reform. Censorship provided the occasion for controversy, which Shaw relished for the debate it engendered and for its potential to usher in broader change. This is not to suggest that Shaw's championing of embattled writers was merely based on egotism and political utilitarianism. Indeed, he firmly believed in the virtues of these artists. In the case of Shelley, he continued to attend and to give lectures at the meetings of the Shelley Society for the next six years, and he consistently noted his indebtedness to the poet throughout his career.[18]

The next big battle in British theatre censorship was to feature another Shavian idol with Shaw again leading the charge. From the outset, British reception of Henrik Ibsen was tied to the Irishman. The socialist monthly *To-day* serialised Shaw's *An Unsocial Socialist* from March to December 1884; immediately after, Ibsen's *Ghosts* appeared from January to March 1885, followed by Shaw's *Cashel Byron's Profession* from April 1885 to March 1886. Ibsen's most important English-language translator in the 1880s and 1890s was the critic William Archer, who in 1885 secured Shaw his first paid job as a journalist and co-wrote early drafts of Shaw's first play, *Widowers' Houses* (1892).[19] And in late 1885, Shaw played Krogstad in a salon reading of Ibsen's *A Doll's House*, with Karl Marx's daughter Eleanor playing the role of Nora.[20]

Beginning in 1890, Archer published a five-volume English-language edition of Ibsen's drama.[21] That summer, the Fabian Society held a series of talks on "Socialism in Contemporary Literature." Among the speakers were William Morris on Gothic architecture, Sergius Stepniak on Russian fiction, Sydney Olivier on Zola, and Shaw on Ibsen. There is thus a clear indication of how intellectuals saw a link between Zola and Ibsen in that their work had the potential to provoke social change. In his talk, Shaw openly stated that Ibsen "is not a socialist."[22] However, he claimed that, like the Fabians, Ibsen saw the necessity to challenge society and the ideals upon which it was founded. In doing so, Shaw argued that Ibsen was a realist who pointed out society's evils, beginning with the restraints placed upon the individual to ensure conformity and maintain the status quo. This, he stressed, was Ibsen's importance for socialists.[23]

Once again, change in British culture came via the continent. Although in 1887 he was an unknown employee of the French gas company, André Antoine quickly became the inspiration for radical change in European theatre when he created the Théâtre Libre – the Free Theatre – in Paris.[24] This was the year after the Shelley Society had produced its members-only performance, and Antoine ran his theatre along the same lines. Over the course of the theatre's seven-year run, Antoine produced several non-commercial playwrights who came to form the canon of modern drama, among them Ibsen, August Strindberg, Leo Tolstoy, Ivan Turgenev, Gerhart Hauptmann, Eugène Brieux, and Auguste Villiers de l'Isle-Adam. In 1889, the Théâtre Libre went on tour to London, where it produced Léon Hennique's *La mort du duc d'Enghien* and *Jacques Damour*, the latter adapted from Zola's novella of the same name. The *Evening Telegraph* typified the hostility of the national press in warning its readers that Antoine's company had been founded to produce "a class of naturalistic plays, which no manager of a respectable theatre would touch, so to speak, with a long pole."[25] Rather than being repelled, J. T. Grein, who had recently immigrated to England from the Netherlands, was inspired to found a British Théâtre Libre that would provide "a theatre free from the shackles of the censor, free from the fetters of convention, unhampered by financial considerations."[26] Only weeks earlier, a new theatre in Berlin – the Freie Bühne, or Free Stage – was launched along similar lines with a production of Ibsen's *Ghosts*.[27]

Ibsen and Zola were proving to be the litmus tests for what was considered acceptable in European culture, with moralists condemning them, censors banning them, and progressives and the avant-garde embracing them. As the Théâtre Libre and the Freie Bühne attested, it was necessary for managers and directors to foster a devoted cohort of artists to make quality performances feasible and to cultivate dedicated audiences to subsidise the venture. In this respect, they had to go beyond the one-off production of the Shelley Society. At the outset of 1891, George Moore contributed to the cause with the publication of *Impressions and Opinions*, which featured three essays directly related to what Grein had proposed. The first was a reprint of Moore's review of the Théâtre Libre's 1890 production of *Ghosts*, which concluded: "Why have we not a Théâtre Libre? Surely there should be no difficulty in finding a thousand persons interested in art and letters willing to subscribe five pounds a year for twelve representations of twelve interesting plays."[28] The second provided a brief history of the Théâtre Libre itself, and the third, entitled "On the Necessity of an English Théâtre Libre," made an extended plea for a non-commercial, private theatre in London. He admitted that there were no good contemporary English plays, but he suggested that they might be written should a space be provided where they could be produced. However, he insisted that, just as Antoine produced a mix of French and foreign plays, they should produce good new English plays in conjunction with the best drama that the continent had to offer, once again demonstrating the international dialectic in which foreign literature would help to strike a blow against national censorship.[29]

In February 1891, Grein, Moore, Shaw, and Archer were among those who founded the Independent Theatre Society (ITS), with Ibsen's *Ghosts* slated to be their first production the next month. Following Moore's concept of a London Théâtre Libre, the ITS promised plays by Bjørnstjerne Bjørnson, Strindberg, Tolstoy, Théodore de Banville, Edmond Goncourt, and original plays by Moore, William Wilde, Cecil Raleigh, and C. W. Jarvis.[30] While the list of foreign-based playwrights attests to the earnestness of the venture, the domestic playwrights they proposed have hardly stood the test of time, revealing the task that the ITS faced in cultivating and supporting homegrown talent to fulfil its mandate.

Even before *Ghosts* was performed, the production caused considerable concern, with newspapers warning that English society had been infected with the onslaught of "Ibsenility," a blend of atheism and socialism meant to fight "against the conventionality of our society, against our religion, and our constitutionalism."[31] For its production of *Ghosts*, the ITS had secured the Royalty Theatre in Soho. Fearing that her licence for other productions would be put at risk, Kate Santley, the Royalty's manager, wrote to the Lord Chamberlain, explaining that she had only rented her premises because the ITS had promised that it would be a private performance and added that she was "most anxious to do whatever you desire in the matter."[32] For his part, Pigott considered Ibsen to be "a Realistic Writer after the manner of Zola." He understood the threat that Ibsen posed, noting that the play, were it to be submitted, "would certainly not be licensed." However, because the performance was private, the authorities had "no power to interfere."[33]

There were links between Shelley's *The Cenci* and Ibsen's *Ghosts* that went deeper than their modes of production. In both, destruction is wrought by egocentric patriarchs. Yet whereas in *The Cenci* a bloodthirsty and incestuous patriarch tramps the boards, in *Ghosts* the drama extends from how people deal with the horrors that the deceased Captain Alving has left as his legacy. A serial adulterer whose flings have been kept secret by his wife and the local pastor, Captain Alving has passed on syphilis to his son Oswald. When others learn of Oswald's love for Regina, the Alvings' maid, it is revealed that she is his half sister, sired by his father and one of his lovers. Broken by the loss of Regina and facing a degenerative future as he descends into idiocy, Oswald pleads with his mother to assist with his suicide, the play ending with her struggling with the decision to euthanise him.

Given the frank treatment of such controversial subject matter, it is unsurprising that the ITS's production of *Ghosts* provoked a moral panic. Reviewers were reduced to censoring themselves by once again employing circumlocution and innuendo, so horrible and unspeakable was the play's theme. Some suggested that to have staged it before an audience that included women was among the worst of crimes and charged that those who attended lacked shame. *The Era* considered the play "foul and filthy." "Ibsenity," they charged, "looks very much like obscenity."[34] The reviewer in the *Gentlewoman* called Ibsen a "gloomy sort of ghoul, bent on groping for horrors by night." And writing in the *Daily Telegraph*, Clement Scott memorably referred to *Ghosts* as "An open drain; a loathsome sore unbandaged; a dirty act done publicly; a lazar-house with all its doors and windows open."[35] Filth, disgust, disease, shamelessness, repugnance, abhorrence, horror: the lexicon of the reviews attests to the link that is understood to exist between the theatre and public morality and, correspondingly, the potential damage that the play could inflict upon British society.

Such reactions immediately provoked Shaw to rework as a book the lecture that he had given on Ibsen. By 15 August 1891, *The Quintessence of Ibsenism* was published.[36] Shaw's study opens with a direct attack on those who supported the censorship. Ibsen, he said, was greeted in England with the same hostility that Shelley met in his day, for, like Shelley, Ibsen was a "pioneer," "a gentle humanitarian," and "an unnatural corruptor of public morals and family life."[37] In this respect, Shaw claimed that such men as Ibsen and Shelley – and by extension himself – were realists, while critics like Scott were idealists. For Shaw, society is composed of units of 1000 people, wherein 700 are philistines who are fine with life as it is. Meanwhile, 299 are dissatisfied with the status quo, but not willing to change matters by reforming society, they create illusions or ideals to mask reality and thus are idealists. The problem is that the idealists do not keep their ideals private, but seek to impose them upon others. This leads to idealism, which forces individuals to accept that "standard moral conduct" is "absolutely valid under all circumstances," while "contrary conduct or any advocacy of it" is "discountenanced and punished as immoral."[38] The remaining individual is the realist, a pioneer "like Shelley and Ibsen" who is the one person "strong enough to face the truth." In denouncing ideals and pointing to reality, the realist terrifies idealists, which drives them to persecute him: "They will crucify him, burn him, violate their own ideals of family affection by taking his children away from him, ostracize him, brand him as immoral, profligate, filthy, and appeal against him to the despised Philistines, specially idealized for the occasion as Society."[39] And, of course, they will ban his works.

Like Mill, then, Shaw argued that the tyranny of the majority works against advancement, expunging new ideas from society and thereby ensuring conformity and society's downfall because of its inability to progress and to adapt to new contexts. In denouncing the "detestable censorship" of plays, he claimed that society must abolish it and establish "Free Art in the sense in which we speak of Free Trade." The problem was that the idealists supported its maintenance because they regarded "Art as a department of original sin. To them the theatre is an unmixed evil, and every restriction on it a gain to the cause of righteousness."[40] With the press owned by wealthy older men, Shaw understood that critics had to toe the line drawn by their masters or risk unemployment. In so doing, they failed to live up to the "courage of their profession," and thus realists – the Zolas, Moores, Shelleys, Ibsens, and Shaws of the world – were censored and slandered as filthy, disgusting, and immoral.[41]

With growing challenges from the avant-garde, the government formed a joint select committee to inquire into the functioning and continued relevance of the censorship. Yet the committee, which sat from 28 March to 25 May 1892, was mainly charged with determining whether the licensing of plays should be extended from the theatres to cover music halls and variety shows. The range of witnesses to appear before it ran the gamut of society, including lawyers, architects, politicians, theatre managers, actors, a police officer, a fire chief, theatre critics, the comptroller of the Lord Chamberlain's office, and the examiner of plays. It is a comprehensive list, but it is noteworthy that not one playwright gave evidence.[42]

The testimony given by the examiner of plays provided a direct window into the mind of the censor by betraying the need to control. Pigott insisted that censorship maintained "public order and decency" as well as "public morality," and it was thus "expedient" that it exist.[43] Most tellingly, he testified to the censor's wish to remain invisible, to seem less involved than he actually was in interfering with plays. He freely admitted that he often circumvented official channels, confidentially negotiating with theatre managers and playwrights. In this regard, the censorship was even more insidious than many in the abolitionist movement had feared: not only had the censors refused licences, which were at least on the official record, but they had gone through secretive networks to prevent plays from being staged as they were written. Unfazed by such concerns, the committee's report proposed maintaining the status quo and the censorship continued unabated.

The Arrival of Shaw as a Force

In his testimony, Pigott betrayed some enjoyment in the failure of the ITS to nurture native talent, with "one of their own promoters" telling him that "they cannot get a play written for them for love or money."[44] However, a few months later, on 9 December 1892, the ITS launched Shaw as a playwright with a performance of *Widowers' Houses* at the Royalty Theatre. It was the birth of the greatest Anglophone playwright since Shakespeare, the Irish writer midwifed by the English Shelley, the Norwegian Ibsen, the Scottish Archer, the Dutch Grein, and the independent theatre movement that had begun with the French André Antoine. In a further reflection of the international dialectic, like Moore and the evolution of the modern novel in English, the development of modern English theatre was to have an Irishman firmly at its centre, surrounded by a constellation of global figures who mixed new artistic forms and progressive politics while they struggled against a censorious culture.

For its part, the ITS was hindered by lacking a permanent home and the wariness of theatre managers to rent them their premises for fear of falling foul of the Lord Chamberlain. Before Shaw's play, the ITS produced an adaptation of Zola's *Thérèse Raquin* on 9 October 1891, a double bill of Théodore de Banville's *The Kiss* and Edvard Brandes's *The Visit* on 4 March 1892, and W. G. van Nouhuys's *The Goldfish* on 8 July 1892.[45] As the dates attest, it was hardly a steady attack on mainstream theatre culture. Moreover, its effect on the censorship was perhaps counter to the abolitionist cause, with such private performances functioning as relief valves for criticism by allowing a potentially scandalous work to be performed once or twice before a limited audience of cultural elites. Yet this should not minimise the ITS's importance as "the bulwark of the English modernist movement" until its eventual demise in 1898.[46] It had created a space, although, granted, a mobile and unstable one, to nurture talent and to produce challenging contemporary works from the continent.

Shaw had similar objectives when in 1895 he was hired by his compatriot Frank Harris to write theatre criticism for the *Saturday Review*. Never one to be shy of self-promotion, he trumpeted his reviews as "a siege laid to the theatre of the XIXth Century by an author who had to cut his own way into it at the point of the pen, and throw some of its defenders into the moat."[47] One of his first articles was a review of the publication of William Heinemann's *The First Step*, which had been denied a licence by the Lord Chamberlain. Shaw used the occasion to excoriate the censorship as an "insane institution" and to defend Heinemann's play from the implication that in being refused a permit it was somehow indecent.[48] Moreover, he accused Pigott of having licensed "intentional and gross indecencies."[49] He again attacked Pigott for this laxness in another review.[50] In both of these articles, Shaw alluded, as he would in later writings, to the prevalence of adultery, bigamy, sexual assault, and other such topics on the stage, which were apparently acceptable as long as they were treated in a farcical or melodramatic manner, but not if they appeared in a play that showed that they had tragic consequences.[51]

When Pigott died the next month, Shaw devoted his entire article to discussing the censorship of theatre and Pigott's legacy. Entitled "The Late Censor," it appeared to be an obituary. It is that, but it is perhaps one of the finest examples of what we might term a modern obituary, in the sense of what Jahan Ramazani has defined as the modern elegy.[52] While an elegy is a poem of mourning that praises the dead and comforts the bereaved, a modern elegy rejoices in death, attacks the deceased, the self, or the addressee, and refuses to console; a modern obituary does much the same. Most notably, Shaw condemned Pigott, calling him "a walking compendium of vulgar insular prejudice, who ... had at last brought himself to a pitch of incompetence." Moreover,

Shaw declared that Pigott's "official career in relation to the higher drama was one long folly and panic, in which the only thing definitely discernable in a welter of intellectual confusion was his conception of the English people rushing towards an abyss of national degeneration in morals and manners, and only held back on the edge of the precipice by the grasp of his strong hand."[53] It was the greatest and most shocking public assault on a censor since Moore's declaration of his hatred for Mudie.

At the beginning of April, Shaw took aim at another notorious censor: William Alexander Coote, who was still the secretary of the National Vigilance Association. Coote had taken exception to a touring cinema production and denounced the films as "shameful" and "the ideal form of indecency," causing Shaw to joke that he supposed Coote found them to be "an ideally desirable form of indecency."[54] Unsurprisingly, Shaw charged Coote with "being in artistic matters a most intensely stupid man, and on sexual questions something of a monomaniac."[55] He had caught on to an important strategy that he would employ throughout his career, applying Moore's tactic of heaping scorn, mockery, and disgust onto censors. Shaw, though, went further, deflecting the criticism of banned artists onto those who banned them, thereby making the competence and motives of censors, not authors, the focus of debate.

While his polemics attacked censors, his plays gave censors the occasion to strike back. In the spring of 1893, Shaw followed up on the promise of *Widowers' Houses* with *The Philanderer*, which proudly wore the influence of his Norwegian idol with its two middle acts set in a fictional Ibsen club. On 20 August, Shaw began composing his third play, *Mrs Warren's Profession*, which he completed on 2 November.[56] One of the most controversial plays in the annals of theatre history, *Mrs Warren's Profession* is an unforgiving examination of prostitution. The titular character rises from poverty by selling her body and eventually becoming co-owner of a chain of brothels on the continent, revealing that she did so not out of some predilection for vice or evil, as some might have it, but because it was one of the only professions in which a woman could improve her economic circumstances. The play implicates the audience in perpetuating such social evils, and ends with Kitty Warren daring them to stop her – with the implication being that the only way to do so is to pay women liveable wages for safe, regular work. On 12 December 1893, Shaw offered *Mrs Warren's Profession* to the ITS, although he waited until 13 February 1895 to read it to Grein and others, less than three weeks after the publication of his "obituary" of Pigott.[57] A year later, Shaw believed that there was "no question" of its production.[58]

By 1898, the ITS had run its course and in its stead rose the Incorporated Stage Society. Founded in 1899, the Stage Society was a noncommercial theatre company with three objectives similar to those of its predecessor: to discover new British playwrights; to produce classical and contemporary foreign plays; and to produce plays that had been refused licences.[59] Within ten years, it would produce thirty-seven "local" and twenty-five foreign plays, yet another testament to the international dialectic. Its first season began with the premiere of Shaw's *You Never Can Tell* on 26 November 1899, followed by performances of Sydney Olivier's *Mrs Maxwell's Marriage*, Ibsen's *The League of Youth*, Fiona Macleod's *The House of Usna*, Maurice Maeterlinck's *Interior* and *The Death of Tintagiles*, Gerhart Hauptmann's *The Coming of Peace*, and Shaw's *Candida*. With plays bookending the first season, Shaw was announced as the most important Anglophone writer for the literary theatre. The next season the Stage Society produced an equally eclectic mix of foreign and British plays, but its third season got off to a late start. Instead of beginning in November, as they had the first two years, it took them until January to produce their first show. This was not the result of indolence but was rather because they had no place to call their own and thus needed to rent a theatre. Yet welcoming managers were in short supply. Indeed, thirteen theatres, three hotels, and two music halls were among those who refused to hire out their premises.[60] The reason: the play was *Mrs Warren's Profession*. As Shaw surmised, the "sole obstacle to the performance" was the censor's "intimidation" and "absolutely autocratic power" that could "ruin any West End manager who offends him."[61]

In fact, Shaw had submitted *Mrs Warren's Profession* to George Redford, the examiner of plays, in March 1898. His application has to be one of the oddest in the history of censorship, admitting to Redford "the impossibility of anyone dividing with me the responsibility for such a play."[62] He simply asked Redford if he would indicate the offending passages. Redford refused, stating that "it is not for me to attempt any 'dramatic expurgation' with the blue pencil." The onus was instead on Shaw "to submit ... a licensable play."[63] Shaw thus rewrote it, changing Mrs. Warren's profession from a prostitute to a thief and excising any hint of incest that had arisen in questions of who was the father of Vivie, Mrs. Warren's daughter.[64] This vandalised version was licensed, allowing Shaw to retain performance copyright of his play when it was published in its original form. However, the original version was still banned from British stages.

When the press caught wind of the Stage Society's efforts to produce *Mrs Warren's Profession*, they instigated yet another moral panic. The

Pall Mall Gazette led the charge, warning playgoers that they would be subjected to a "moral miasma" and wondering whether they would be "fascinated by Mr. Shaw's genius in proving that black is whiter than white, provided that an economic standard can be established."[65] Likewise, the *Daily Telegraph* feared "an hysterical outcry such as greeted the staging of *Ghosts*."[66] Meanwhile, the play's notoriety impacted casting, with actresses who had been approached to play Kitty concerned with the material and the effects that playing the role might have on their career. Mrs. Theodore Wright, the first actress to whom Shaw proposed the role, refused when he read it to her, considering it "a play that ought not to have been written."[67] For her part, Fanny Brough objected to being involved in "the so-called wicked play"; however, she "energetically and enthusiastically" consented to participate once she had read the script for herself.[68]

Despite the play's reputation, the Stage Society secured the Lyric Theatre for performances on 5 and 6 January 1902. As with *The Cenci* and *Ghosts*, critics denounced Shaw's play while remaining incapable of even mentioning that it was about prostitution and raised the possibility of incest. The reviewer for *The Globe* would not "define the nature of the piece lest he should outrage the susceptibilities" of his readers.[69] The *Daily Graphic* declared that the subject was "unmentionable."[70] The *St. James's Gazette* likewise vaguely referred to the play's "disgusting theme," which was "[g]rossly unsuitable for stage treatment before a mixed audience." Indeed, the critic claimed that "the play is wholly evil" as it contained "one of the boldest and most specious defences of an immoral life for poor women that has ever been written"; they also hoped that the Stage Society would "eschew dramatic garbage in the future."[71]

Shaw quickly went on the attack. That same month, he penned a preface, which he published in a stand-alone edition of *Mrs Warren's Profession*. Shaw's response opened with a spirited defence of his play, which he noted draws "attention to the truth that prostitution is caused, not by female depravity and male licentiousness, but simply by underpaying, undervaluing, and overworking women so shamefully that the poorest of them are forced to resort to prostitution to keep body and soul together." However, he admitted that he had endangered his career. As the Lord Chamberlain, who "has despotic ... power over our theatres," had effectively banned his play, Shaw saw himself as "branded by implication, to my great damage, as an unscrupulous and blackguardly author." Yet the injury to society was greater, as the true nature of prostitution was "more effectually masked than ever."[72]

Shaw referred to his preface as "The Author's Apology," but it is no more of an expression of regret than is the *Apology* of Socrates, the

Greek philosopher using the occasion of his trial for impiety and corrupting youth to accuse the men of Athens of being misled by their ignorance of truth and wisdom and their preference for honours and wealth.[73] This position is due, rather, to the term's etymological roots in *apologia*, which means a defence of or a justification for one's opinions.[74] Shaw thus argued that his play exposed prostitution as part of capitalism's systemic exploitation. In his fight against prostitution as a social evil, he noted that he was actually in line with the "sterner moralists" of the NVA. As he considered that "fine art is the subtlest, the most seductive, the most effective instrument of moral propaganda in the world," he wrote plays that would offer an alternative to the status quo. In this way, he hoped to "persuade even London to take its conscience and its brains with it when it goes to the theatre, instead of leaving them at home with its prayer-book."[75]

Having defended his play as both ethical and good in intention, Shaw turned to attacking the examiner of plays for keeping such works from the stage while licensing those that rendered prostitution glamorous. Prostitutes regularly walked the boards, but only as long as they died of consumption, committed suicide offstage, or were rejected by others. The effect of this was that young women would be attracted to luxurious living while understanding that the superficial endings were "mere pious forms ... to save the Censor's face." Shaw thus refused to be silenced, promising that he could not "be starved into making my play a standing advertisement of the attractive side of Mrs Warren's business."[76] To illustrate his point on the censorship's tendency to permit lascivious works, and to ridicule it as a supposedly moral force, Shaw outlined the plots of two licensed plays, similarly to how Moore had summarised risqué books on Mudie's shelves. In the first play, a prince feigns to ravish his new bride's chambermaid in order to be discovered and have the marriage annulled, but the servant enjoys his passion. In the second, a man attempts to rape a woman, but when she faints, he leaves, yet she, believing that the worst has happened, becomes attracted to him and they marry in the end. Shaw argued that the reason for the apparent hypocrisy in banning his play and in licensing these others was that the latter relied on "coarse humors and the physical fascination of sex" and thus complied with the requirements of the censorship, "whereas plays in which these humors and fascinations are discarded, and the social problems created by sex seriously faced and dealt with ... are suppressed."[77] That is, the censorship would allow melodramatic and comedic treatments of sex that left the status quo intact, but it would not countenance more tragic and philosophical treatments that impelled structural reform.

Seeing that the press supported the censorship, Shaw also castigated reviewers. He claimed that many of them were "intellectually baffled" by *Mrs Warren's Profession* and noted how they had disparaged it because the issues it discusses should not be mentioned before women.[78] Yet Shaw rejected such pretence to chivalry: the play was written for women, and it was mainly through the determination of women that it was produced. Moreover, while critics had wanted Shaw to heap scorn on Mrs. Warren and have her shoulder the responsibility for prostitution, he refused to do so, instead aiming "to throw that guilt on the British public itself."[79] He emphasized that "it is quite natural and *right* for Mrs Warren to choose what is, according to her lights, the least immoral alternative," but that "it is none the less infamous of society to offer such alternatives. For the alternatives offered are not morality and immorality, but two sorts of immorality."[80] In this sense, Shaw posited himself as the realist who pulled away the masks of idealism, with theatre reviewers and the censorship promoting a false image of society as virtuous and threatened by such villains as Mrs. Warren and Shaw.

While Shaw railed against the theatre censorship, this was but one of many forces that sought to prevent new thought from instigating social advances. "All censorships exist to prevent anyone from challenging current conceptions and existing institutions," he argued. "All progress is initiated by challenging current conceptions, and executed by supplanting existing institutions. Consequently the first condition of progress is the removal of censorships.'[81] Shaw's preface was concerned with the specificities surrounding his own play, but he used these to engage with larger philosophical issues. As a Fabian Socialist pamphleteer and lecturer, for Shaw a preface was not so much a manner to introduce a play as it was a forum for provoking social and political reform. When he was censored, it was thus the logical medium in which to mount a spirited defence of both his play and himself and a concomitant appeal for why censorship should be abolished and freedom of expression expanded and protected.

Censorship in the New Century

In addition to the Stage Society, a new crop of independent theatres began to make their marks in the early twentieth century. In 1904, Ireland's Abbey Theatre was founded in Dublin by W. B. Yeats and Lady Augusta Gregory, and that same year, Harley Granville-Barker teamed up with J. E. Vedrenne to found a new company at London's Court Theatre. Just as the Abbey was to circumvent commercial demands to produce a new drama that would represent Irish experiences, the Court was to provide literary drama with a solid brick-and-mortar home. With Shaw's plays receiving 701 of the 988 performances in Granville-Barker's three-year run at the Court, it became a de facto Shaw repertory theatre. However, like the ITS and the Stage Society, the Court sought other new dramatists, producing plays by St. John Hankin, Robert Harcourt, Yeats, John Masefield, Elizabeth Robins, and Granville-Barker himself, as well as Gilbert Murray's translations of classic Greek drama and the work of leading contemporary European dramatists, including Hauptmann, Maeterlinck, and Arthur Schnitzler.[82]

The effect of the Barker-Vedrenne Court seasons were profound on Shaw's career. With his plays performed so often in London and produced with high standards of directing and acting, he was increasingly considered the most important living English-language dramatist. In the opening months of the 1904 season, the sitting prime minister, Arthur Balfour, and several other members of parliament attended the Court on more than one occasion to watch Shaw's *John Bull's Other Island*, which astutely dissects the Irish question and neoliberal economic colonialism. Shaw's reputation as the day's fashionable playwright was cemented when, during a Royal Command Performance of the play, King Edward VII reportedly laughed so hard that he broke his chair. In addition, Shaw wrote in this period several of modern drama's masterpieces, including *Man and Superman* and *Major Barbara*, both of which premiered at the Court in 1905.

Despite his newfound success, Shaw remained attuned to the effects of censorship on the development of theatre. On 29 June 1907, he published an article in *The Academy*, entitled "The Solution to the Censorship Problem," that rehashed much of what he had written elsewhere; yet it was important for maintaining attention on the Lord Chamberlain's office. Just as he had attacked Pigott, Shaw noted that Redford was equally over his head in his capacity as examiner of plays and accused him of "gross laxness." Taking a typically paradoxical approach, instead of reproaching Redford "for refusing to license Mrs Warren's Profession ... I ask him how he can defend his licence for Man and Superman, The Philanderer, Candida, and even the innocently popular You Never Can Tell. There is not one of my plays that is not boiling over with sedition, blasphemy, and even impropriety."[83] If Redford were conscientious, Shaw argued, he would also ban from the stage such dramatists as Arthur Wing Pinero, John Galsworthy, J. M. Barrie, Masefield, Hankin, and Granville-Barker. However, Redford could not do so, for if he were to abolish the drama wholesale, he would crush the theatre. In the end, Shaw proposed that, like in the United States, the stage should be regulated by the rule of law, and if a play were to breach it, then it should be duly prosecuted in an open courtroom. Within a week, Redford struck back in what would become the first salvo of a two-year battle for control of the stage. This battle would be further notable for featuring several figures who decades later would be central in the struggle between censors and writers in Ireland, including Edward Garnett, Hugh Law, Galsworthy, and Shaw himself.

On 5 July 1907, Redford sent a letter marked "Private" to Edward Garnett indicating that he found it "painful" to decline recommending a licence for Garnett's play *The Breaking Point*.[84] He had first approached the theatre manager and asked him "privately" to withdraw it, yet as the manager had persisted, Redford had no choice but to ban the play. Better known as one of the keenest editors in British publishing history, Garnett nurtured the talents of Joseph Conrad, W. Somerset Maugham, Ford Madox Ford, D. H. Lawrence, and T. E. Lawrence, as well as such Irish writers as Liam O'Flaherty and Sean O'Faolain. Eventually, prodded by his friend Galsworthy and inspired by Granville-Barker's seasons at the Court, Garnett turned his hand to writing drama.[85] When his first play was rejected, he looked to Shaw and Archer for support.

Shaw suggested that they organise a resistance against the censorship, which was a novel and potent approach for writers.[86] Archer agreed, claiming that the play would be "an excellent place on which to fight the Censor. There is not the ghost of a legitimate objection to it." He proposed to "stigmatize with some severity Redford's method of writing private letters suggesting the withdrawal of a play, instead of frankly vetoing it. This is simply a pitiful dodge to evade responsibility."[87] That September, Garnett published his play with three discursive texts: a combative preface in the Shavian mould; a call for the formation of "a society for the defence of intellectual drama"; and, in imitation of both Moore and Shaw, an open letter to the censor.[88]

Shortly thereafter, word came down that Granville-Barker's most recent play, *Waste*, was also refused a licence. Granville-Barker had an idea that it would be banned, recounting as it does the relationship between a young woman, who dies when she obtains an illegal abortion, and her politician lover, who, distraught over this loss and with his professional future destroyed as a result of the scandal, commits suicide. Recognising that censorship thrived on silencing dissent, Granville-Barker granted *The Globe* an interview in which he drew a link between *Waste* and *Mrs Warren's Profession*, noting that while dramatists might allude to or make light of certain topics, they were not permitted to treat them seriously. His duty, as he saw it, was to speak to the press because "we want public opinion informed in this fight for a theatre freed from the fetters of an unconstitutional office."[89] Like Garnett and Shaw, he published his banned play so that the public could decide whether it was indecent. Meanwhile, *The Breaking Point* had become a bestseller.[90]

Even before *Waste* was banned, Galsworthy and Archer drafted a letter that they sent to leading writers. Published in *The Times* on 29 October, it was signed by seventy-one prominent British and Irish authors, including Barrie, Conrad, W.S. Gilbert, Hankin, Harcourt, Thomas Hardy, Laurence Housman, Henry James, Henry Arthur Jones, Masefield, Maugham, George Meredith, Gilbert Murray, Pinero, Elizabeth Robins, Alfred Sutro, Algernon Swinburne, Arthur Symons, J. M. Synge, H. G. Wells, Yeats, and Israel Zangwill, as well as the banned Granville-Barker, Garnett, and Shaw. The letter noted the old bugbears: authors had no mechanism of appeal against the censor's decisions, their good names were publicly maligned when their plays were refused licences, and theatre should be subjected to the same laws as other forms of art.[91]

Perhaps the letter's most important effect was not on public opinion, but rather in galvanising writers. Granville-Barker collaborated with the Stage Society to produce his play that November, Shaw securing the Imperial Theatre only because it was slated for demolition.[92] Shaw emphasized the necessity of staging *Waste* as soon as possible: if they did not hit back at Redford, he would be emboldened to refuse more licences.[93] Seeking to maintain interest in the subject, Shaw published a letter in *The Nation*. Explaining how the censorship operated, he noted the taboos on religion, sex, abortion, incest, and venereal disease, which ensured that such subjects could not be treated seriously, thereby stunting the progress of society. Once again, the only way forward was to abolish the censorship.[94]

Following the publication of the protest letter in *The Times*, the government determined that the best way to defuse the situation was to welcome a deputation of playwrights to meet with Prime Minister Henry Campbell-Bannerman. However, Campbell-Bannerman suffered a severe heart attack, and the meeting was postponed. The playwrights' deputation was to include Barrie, Galsworthy, and Murray.[95] Although they tried to recruit Shaw, he oddly opted not to join them when they later met with Herbert Gladstone, the home secretary. Over the following months, the government delayed action, hoping that the will to reform would fade.[96] To maintain momentum, the Stage Society produced Garnett's *The Breaking Point* on 5 and 6 April 1908. Unlike *Waste*, it was considered by critics of all stripes to be dull and lacking in dramatic skill.[97] It was only of interest, they claimed, because it had been censored.

Between the government's stalling and the poor quality of *The Breaking Point*, the abolitionists' energy began to flag. Fortunately, though, they counted among their ranks Robert Harcourt, who was both an accomplished playwright and a Liberal MP. On 17 December, Harcourt proposed a bill to abolish the censorship.[98] The motion was placed on the backburner when the House recessed for the Christmas holidays, but Harcourt was patient, introducing a private member's bill on 22 April 1909.[99] While the government tried to block it, Harcourt's bill instead wound up being undone by circumstances, with what became known as the People's Budget of 1909, which would impose higher taxes on Britain's wealthiest to pay for new social welfare programmes, taking priority.[100] Seeing his colleague stymied, Shaw jumped into action once again over the course of a summer that would cement his reputation as the leader of literary drama and the main proponent of freedom of expression. As with Moore, an Irish writer would head the charge against censorship in modern Britain.

Shaw Takes the Reins

At the outset of 1909, Shaw began work on a new play that was calculated to provoke the censorship. *The Shewing-up of Blanco Posnet*, which he completed that March, tells the tale of a rogue on the American Western frontier. A fast liver and a faster talker, Blanco is caught for having stolen the sheriff's horse and brought back to town to face mob justice at the hands of the "Vigilance Committee." It is not difficult to see Blanco as an analogy for the censored playwright in Britain: having committed a purported crime, Blanco is quickly tried before a kangaroo court with no method of appeal. Consistent with all melodramas, however, Blanco is saved by the last-minute appearance of the mother whose son he tried to help while he was on the run. The objection of the censor was to the play's repeated blasphemy.[101] Knowing that such material was interdicted, Shaw had quickly written a one-act play chockfull of it, hoping to bait Redford and to maintain the debate on theatre censorship.

Upon receiving the manuscript and recognising that the proposed production represented potential controversy, Redford sought the Lord Chamberlain's advice. Redford was convinced that Shaw would not consent to change a word, which would lead to the production shutting down and Shaw starting a press campaign. The Lord Chamberlain suggested that Redford try to persuade the theatre manager to make requested changes and so avoid scandal.[102] Redford thus contacted the manager of His Majesty's Theatre, Sir Herbert Beerbohm Tree, to ask him if he could get Shaw to revise his play. Tree approached Shaw, but to no avail.[103] Faced with Shaw's intransigence, the Lord Chamberlain banned the play.[104]

As Redford had feared, Shaw used the occasion to renew the campaign for abolition. He immediately issued a statement to the press, charging that he had suffered "injury" and "insult" in having his play refused a licence. However, the true cost would be for the younger playwrights, who, unlike himself, could not afford "to lose the price of months of arduous labour and be blacklisted by managers as dangerous."[105] The lesson for them was to write light-hearted farces and not more serious-minded literary drama.

This episode became part of a broader effort that coalesced around the Irishman, who served as the chief promoter of abolition. Harcourt asked Prime Minister Herbert Henry Asquith whether the government had given further thought to the bill that he had proposed and said that he would press the issue no further, in exchange for the government establishing a select committee to examine the censorship and to hear evidence. The Prime Minister admitted that "the time has come for some such inquiry."[106] Asquith, the same man who had so forcefully prosecuted Vizetelly twenty years earlier, now opened the door to reviewing how censorship functioned in Britain. But as the committee had yet to be struck, the pressure had to be maintained.

Shaw thus continued his press campaign with a series of letters to *The Times* throughout the spring and summer of 1909. In explaining to readers how the censorship functioned, he revealed that he had lost money; yet unlike any other worker who suffers financially because he is libelled, a playwright had no recourse. The tactic here was to present himself as a tradesperson who had been victimised by the law and yet lacked a mechanism of legal appeal.[107] The letter provoked contrary responses – including one from Redford himself – as well as Shaw's gleeful retorts.[108] Hoping to mobilise even more people, Shaw publicly lectured on the censorship of plays at a meeting of the Poets' Club.[109]

Just before *The Shewing-up of Blanco Posnet* was banned, Shaw wrote another one-act play that appears equally calculated to provoke the censor. Just as *Blanco Posnet* was condemned for blasphemy, *Press Cuttings* breached the oldest rule of the censorship by depicting a living politician on stage. The two main protagonists of Shaw's play are Mitchener, the secretary of state for war, and Balsquith, the prime minister, the latter an amalgam of Balfour and Asquith, and the former a characterisation of Lord Kitchener. The play satirises these politicians, but it is more pointedly a farce of anti-suffragette views, with Balsquith entering the play in drag because, with female protestors calling for his head, he fears for his safety. In mid-June, as Harcourt and Shaw pressured the government, the play went into rehearsals. Upon reading the script, Redford requested that the theatre manager amend it because he could not licence a play that held "the Premier up to ridicule."[110]

As expected, Shaw refused to compromise and seized the occasion to make the case public through *The Times*. He argued that his characters were no worse than the caricatures of living personalities that were regularly represented in Christmas pantomimes and political cartoons.[111] He also gave an interview to *The Observer* to make the point again that a great deal of what had been licensed was no better than what had been banned. Recounting J. M. Barrie's "Punch and Judy," a sketch licensed by Redford, Shaw noted how it satirised him as "Superman," which he found "confessedly humorous," as well as Balfour and his fellow liberal politician Joseph Chamberlain, both of whose public utterances were included in the script. In being able to laugh at a satire of himself, Shaw implied that only those who were thin-skinned or hypocritical demanded protection. Such hypocrisy, Shaw said, was why "I have devoted myself to the destruction of the Lord Chamberlain."[112] While Redford understood Shaw's threat, he appears to have underestimated him. Indeed, Redford missed that *Press Cuttings* is set on April the first. In his war against censorship, Shaw was out to make fools of the authorities, and they had fallen into his trap by banning the play.

The combination of Harcourt's persistence in parliament and Shaw's press campaign led to the establishment of a parliamentary committee to inquire into the censorship of the theatre.[113] The committee was composed of ten members, including five peers and five commoners. The latter group consisted of Harcourt (Liberal), Hugh Law (Irish Nationalist), Lieutenant-Colonel Lockwood (Conservative), Alfred Mason (Liberal), and Herbert Samuel (Liberal). Open hearings were held over twelve days from 29 July to 24 September, and those who testified included Redford, theatre managers, critics, and playwrights. The inclusion of playwrights was a marked difference from the 1892 committee proceedings when not one testified and William Archer was the sole witness against the censorship. Archer appeared once again, as did several individuals prominent in the abolitionist movement, including Shaw, Barrie, Galsworthy, Granville-Barker, W. S. Gilbert, Housman, Gilbert Murray, Pinero, and Cecil Raleigh. A few of the people who were involved, notably Shaw, Law, and Galsworthy, would later have some bearing on the struggles for freedom of expression in post-independence Ireland.

The testimonies reflected definite schisms between the professions. Theatre managers supported the censorship because the licensing system protected them from liability, which thereby ensured the smooth functioning of their business. In contrast, the playwrights believed that the system smothered the vitality of the theatre. In his appearance before the committee, Galsworthy testified that the censorship had discouraged him from broaching certain subjects on stage that he could write freely of in his prose works. He also read letters that he had solicited from Thomas Hardy, Henry James, H. G. Wells, and Arnold Bennett, all saying that they, too, had been deterred from writing plays. The effect of the censorship on the development of English theatre was evident, he claimed, in the very fact that if one were to survey the list of dramatic authors of the nineteenth century, there was not one name in the same class as those in the realms of fiction, poetry, and *belles lettres*.[114]

As soon as he was informed of the committee's formation, Shaw began writing a statement that he came to consider his *Areopagitica*, although he believed that it would "supersede Milton."[115] Before his appearance, he sent copies to his colleagues in the Dramatists' Club, imploring them to fight the censorship.[116] When Shaw testified on 30 July, he submitted his statement on the precedent of Henry Irving having had his statement accepted as evidence by the 1892 committee. The chair immediately cleared the room. Once people were reconvened, he simply noted that the committee had decided not to accept Shaw's evidence, although it had been a split decision, with Harcourt and Law in the minority.[117] The difference between the decisions in 1892 and 1909 perhaps lay in the fact that Irving's statement had been in favour of the censorship, while Shaw's was against it. Yet it would garner a wider audience when Shaw published it as a part of the preface to *The Shewing-up of Blanco Posnet* in 1911. The irony appears to have eluded the committee that they censored Shaw's statement from appearing as evidence in an inquiry into censorship.

Running over eleven thousand words, Shaw's statement covered four of the more common arguments against the current system. First, there was a fundamental hypocrisy in allowing for a free press while subjecting the theatre to pre-censorship. He rejected the argument that the gathering of people in a public space made controlling the stage essential because of safety issues. As Shaw asserted in his testimony, several political meetings and rallies that he had attended had ended in riots, but society recognised the liberty to assemble and to speak in public. Second, like his colleagues, Shaw testified that the censorship had deterred him from writing certain plays. For example, while he had long desired to dramatize the life of Muhammad, Shaw had refrained from doing so because he knew that its potential effects on British foreign relations would result in it being banned, the Lord

Chamberlain mindful to not offend the sensitivities of the Ottoman government and the millions of Muslims in the British Empire. Third, Shaw criticised the censorship's consideration of plays based not on their subjects, but on their approach to those subjects, which allowed for a light-hearted treatment of adultery but banned a serious treatment of it. And fourth, he noted the system's further hypocrisy in its consideration of when plays had been written and first produced. For example, while Ibsen's *Ghosts* was banned in part for its treatment of incest, Shakespeare's *Hamlet*, which likewise addresses the subject, was permitted on London stages because it was performed well before the 1737 Licensing Act. This same provision allowed for productions of ribald Restoration drama while curbing sexual frankness in more contemporary works.

Ever the provocateur, Shaw took matters even further by making a case for immorality and openly labelling himself immoral. When Sidney Webb, Shaw's close friend and Fabian colleague, read the statement's draft, he warned Shaw against taking this tack. Webb feared that the effect on public opinion would be disastrous.[118] However, Shaw ignored Webb's advice. "I am not an ordinary playwright in general practice," he claimed to the committee. "I am a specialist in immoral and heretical plays."[119] Holding that "current morality as to economic and sexual relations" was "disastrously wrong" and regarding "certain doctrines of the Christian religion as understood in England today with abhorrence," he admitted: "I write plays with the deliberate object of converting the nation to my opinions in these matters."[120] The problem, said Shaw, was that society misunderstood the true meaning of "immoral" and "moral": "Whatever is contrary to established manners and customs is immoral. An immoral act or doctrine is not necessarily a sinful one: on the contrary, every advance in thought and conduct is by definition immoral until it has converted the majority."[121] It is for this reason, he argued, that "immorality should be protected jealously against the attacks of those who have no standard except the standard of custom, and who regard any attack on custom – that is, on morals – as an attack on society, on religion, and on virtue."[122] Shaw contended that morality therefore did not need censorship to protect it: it was safeguarded by laws against obscenity, blasphemy, libel, and treason. As we have seen in the treatment of literary drama and naturalist fiction, the national press, purity movements, government officials, the judiciary, and mainstream audiences were all guardians of morality. Shaw considered public opinion in particular to have an "enormous weight," as it could enforce "social ostracism which is stronger than all the statutes."[123] The result, he said, was that it is rather immorality that needs protection and morality that needs restraint, because morality "is responsible for many persecutions and many martyrdoms."[124]

Shaw had a lifelong fascination with martyrs, from Jesus Christ, who was the protagonist of Shaw's unfinished first play, to Dick Dudgeon of *The Devil's Disciple* and the eponymous heroine of *Saint Joan*. This is also evinced in his defences of Oscar Wilde and the rebels of the 1916 Easter Rising in Ireland. In his statement to the committee, he noted Carl Linnaeus, Charles Darwin, Thomas Henry Huxley, Thomas Carlyle, John Ruskin, and Samuel Butler as "at present condemned by the Greek and Roman Catholic censorships," yet their writings were important in establishing scientific truths.[125] A censorship of conduct would effectively wipe out immorality in the social and political spheres. Such measures would have suppressed George Washington and anti-colonial struggles, Martin Luther and the Reformation, Galileo and the heliocentric model of the universe, and the blasphemies of Jesus and Muhammad.

The solution, he posited, was tolerance and liberty. And the true measure of tolerance and liberty, he argued, was "toleration of opinions that are considered damnable, and liberty to do what seems wrong."[126] Shaw contended that countries that were the most tolerant and free were those that flourished, while those that were the least tolerant and free were those that stagnated and declined. In Shaw's terms, a person, a behaviour, or an idea is not always immoral. With shifts in peoples' belief systems and cultures, shifts in the definition of morality follow. The immoral is not, according to Shaw, inevitably worse, wrong, or inherently evil; that which is immoral simply has yet to be accepted by a significant proportion of the community. All reform, because it challenges the status quo and revises thought, was at one time immoral. Therefore, because progress depends upon reform, it depends upon immorality. Without the presence of the immoral, society would fall to ruin. As proof, Shaw suggested that we look no further than Spain: it had once dominated all of Europe, but the Inquisition's attempt to extinguish heresy relegated it to a third-rate political power by effectively destroying native intellectualism.[127]

As literary drama was a theatre of problems and ideas, Shaw's plays and those he had championed had to be permitted on the stage. Yes, such works would contribute to a contentious culture in which people disagreed and were sometimes offended. However, according to Millian liberal free-speech theory, open discussion in the public sphere should lead to the acceptance of truth, the reformation of broken systems, and the ability to respond to problems more effectively and efficiently. This is precisely the utilitarian rationale behind naturalism: showing how people have been determined by their environment affords a better understanding of the social conditions and forces that shape individuals as well as groups. With this diagnosis in hand, the thinking goes, people should be impelled to improve society. Shaw emphasized this sense of the artist's role and the need to rid society of censorship. Comparing the work of the author with that of the medical professional, he said: "It is no more possible for me to do my work honestly as a playwright without giving pain than it is for a dentist. The nation's morals are like its teeth: the more decayed they are the more it hurts to touch them. Prevent dentists and dramatists from giving pain, and not only will our morals become as carious as our teeth, but toothache and the plagues that follow neglected morality will presently cause more agony than all the dentists and dramatists at their worst have caused since the world began."[128]

Not surprisingly, Shaw was miffed at his statement being refused by the committee. Indeed, the decision reflects that the inquiry was not about reform but was rather about giving the appearance of the democratic process taking place. That he had printed the statement at his own cost because he had been informed that it would be entered into evidence was further proof for him that the committee had been rigged to humiliate him for daring to attack officialdom.

Following his appearance, Shaw wrote a private letter appealing to Herbert Samuel to include his statement in the evidence, but Samuel had to accept the decision of the majority.[129] Recognising this, Shaw published a letter in *The Times* outlining his case that the committee should accept his statement as it was in keeping with the precedent of the 1892 inquiry.[130] If he had hoped to sway the committee, his actions had the opposite effect. When proceedings opened on 5 August, Shaw, who had been invited to continue giving testimony, was summarily dismissed before he could speak. The official position was that he had already presented his views.[131] Although the committee had planned to return to him the copies of his statement with a show of disdain, Shaw noted that Hugh Law, "being an Irishman, with an Irishman's sense of how to behave like a gallant gentleman on occasion, was determined to be able to assure me that nothing should induce him to give up my statement or prevent him from obtaining and cherishing as many copies as possible."[132] Yet Shaw was "deeply offended" by the others, for he argued that in accepting public service, they had no right to act in such a manner.[133]

Shortly thereafter, he was to get a measure of revenge. While she was in England earlier that June, Lady Gregory spent some time with Shaw. On the last occasion that they met, he gave her a copy of *Blanco*

Posnet and, a little afterwards, offered it to the Abbey.[134] His intent was to exploit the loophole that set Dublin outside of the Lord Chamberlain's jurisdiction, while the city was close enough that the British press would be able to attend. With Yeats's support, Lady Gregory accepted Shaw's offer, believing that it would "show up the hypocrisy of the British Censor."[135] The truth of the matter was that she was not interested in fighting for the cause of freedom as much as ensuring the Abbey's future by restoring its financial health. Indeed, with their patent due to expire the next year, they needed £5000 to keep afloat.[136] By staging a banned play by a leading Irish playwright, they could drum up a considerable audience.

Matters then took a decidedly negative turn. Once they caught wind of the venture, the British authorities at Dublin Castle – the seat of British colonial administration in Ireland – moved to suppress it. Over the course of August, there were considerable negotiations between Lady Gregory and British administrators and debate in the Irish and British press. With the opposition from colonial authorities, *Blanco Posnet*, despite having no Irish characters and not being set in the country, was heartily embraced by nationalists. They understood that the crisis entailed the right of the Irish to determine what plays would be shown at their national theatre for an Irish audience. Thus, the play once again became a conduit for freedom of expression. Although the authorities repeatedly threatened the Abbey, Lady Gregory recognised that she had public opinion behind her and accordingly went ahead with the production on 25 August. Wisely, the government opted not to intervene.[137] Following the performance on opening night, Lady Gregory wrote to Shaw: "The shouts are still in our ears! Never was such a victory."[138]

Meanwhile, reviewers were baffled at the play having been censored. *The Times* suggested that critics were unanimous on one point: "The play is perfectly innocuous."[139] Shaw crowed that the "defeat of the Censorship was as complete as anything human can be."[140] Despite the authorities' efforts to prejudice people, the public reception demonstrated that the censorship was an anachronism. Once again, it took an independent theatre to provide a platform for literary drama and freedom of expression. That it was in this case an Irish theatre, with Irish directors and actors producing a play by an Irish writer in the face of official opposition from British authorities, further illustrates the importance of considering the censorship of Irish writers and literature in a broader narrative not confined to the country's borders. Indeed, the production was the outcome of a larger movement that also entailed the impassioned work and organisation of British writers, actors, managers, and publishers, and thereby attests to the necessity of seeing these matters as part of an international network and phenomenon.

A few months later, the parliamentary committee published its report. Despite Shaw's attempts to influence public opinion and to pressure the committee, most of the mechanisms of censorship would remain in place, although there were two notable exceptions. The first was that the Lord Chamberlain could now consult a council of advisors following a negative report from his examiner of plays to ascertain whether the play in question should be licensed, expurgated, or banned. The second was that theatre managers were no longer obliged to apply for a licence; however, if the play were deemed obscene or indecent, they would be liable and the attorney general could prohibit the performance of the play for up to ten years.[141] The censorship of plays continued to function in this slightly reformed manner until it was finally abolished in 1968, unable by then to maintain control of the theatre in an era of civil rights and rapidly changing social, cultural, and political mores. In the almost six decades between, there were gradual allowances for such shifts in society, but the institution proved too archaic to survive.

From Moore to Shaw

As the initial chapters illustrate, two Irish writers – George Moore and Bernard Shaw – were at the fore of developing modernist aesthetics, challenging norms and mores, combating censorship, and defending freedom of expression in Britain. As the early careers of the Irishmen attest, there is a need to consider Irish and British literary histories as further conjoined to broader European, if not global, movements. On the surface, there is nothing particularly Irish about Moore's *A Modern Lover* or *A Mummer's Wife*, but then, despite their English settings, some people might claim that there is nothing particularly English about them either. Moore was a proud disciple of Zola, and his early works were inspired by his master; in this sense, they were French books written in English. However, coming from an Anglo-Irish line, Moore was perhaps less apt to be devoted to English tradition and more open to other modes. The same could be said for Shaw in his promotion of the Norwegian Ibsen and his adoption of the Socratic play of ideas as his dominant mode. Their works led censors, purity movements, and conservative critics to repeatedly issue public health warnings that foreign writers carried a contagion that threatened the national culture and could harm otherwise fit citizens. Zola's novels and Ibsen's theatre had to be stopped. But the two Irishmen embraced these artists and fought for cultural forms that contributed to a larger drive for progressive political and social transformation.

It was inevitable that meaningful change would take considerable time and effort. In addition to the conservatism of British society, Moore and Shaw found themselves aligned against institutions that had held literature in check, most notably the circulating libraries, the publishing industry, the press, the commercial theatres, and the Lord Chamberlain. The quarter century of struggles they encountered places censorship at the very heart of the shift towards an Anglo-modernist aesthetic. As has always been the case, censorship was an indicator of what was and was not acceptable in society. And because so many Irish writers in this period wrote for British audiences and were published by British presses, British censorship therefore played a central role in the development of a national Irish canon. This legacy would last well beyond the years in which Ireland was a part of the United Kingdom. As later chapters will show, British jurisprudence would importantly inform censorship legislation in Ireland and affect the reception and circulation of Irish writers in their own country.

While the Irishmen both deserve places among those who have fought against censorship, significant differences in the cases of Moore and Shaw merit further consideration. Comparing the two campaigns, Moore's was distinctly solitary. A part of this stems from the more isolated nature of novel publishing: manuscripts pass from an author to a publisher and printer, but there are few other intermediaries. Furthermore, once a novel is published, it tends to be read in seclusion, either by someone alone or within the confines of the family home. A play, however, passes from an author to a theatre manager, director, actors, scenographers, and costume designers, and it is performed, one hopes, before hundreds of people at a time. Perhaps, then, novelists were not as drawn to organised protest as theatre practitioners because the latter, naturally more collective, had an organic community in place. Indeed, collaboration towards a shared objective is the essence of theatre. Yet the differences were considerably deeper. Moore was writing at a time in which British letters were still timid, while Zola had Balzac, Flaubert, and Baudelaire before him. Meanwhile, although the Shelley Society gave the first major blow to theatre censorship, this was never more than a one-off venture. It was rather in the 1890s, once people had become inspired by the work of André Antoine and the Théâtre Libre, that a recognised movement began, which is considerably earlier than Celia Marshik's assessment that a broad coalition against the censorship only formed in the first decade of the twentieth century.[142] Moore, though, was essentially on his own with Vizetelly. The two men received little support in the pages of the press, the Society of Authors was still in its infancy and did not offer any help, and no serious campaign emerged to defend the embattled publisher or to support circumventing the monopoly of the circulating libraries and the tyranny of the triple-decker novel. Without such moral and material backing, they alone faced the coordinated efforts of the press and the purity movement to discredit and ruin them.

Shaw was thus fortunate to find himself at the cusp of a changing context. When the Independent Theatre Society was founded in 1891, there were no major literary dramatists in London to supply works. It began with plays from abroad, but Shaw and others soon arrived on the scene, responding to the new conditions. It is therefore no surprise that when the 1892 parliamentary committee inquired into theatre censorship, the only voice in favour of abolition was William Archer, a critic, while when the 1909 committee sat, many important dramatists readily made the case for a free stage. In the quarter century that covers the censorship struggles of Moore and Shaw, writers had become aware that a concerted and combined effort was needed to create the conditions for greater freedom of expression.

Meanwhile, there developed a broader acceptance of the more radical art that had appeared as threatening when Moore published his first novels. The ITS broke the ice by creating an artistic body that would foster, promote, and produce literary drama, but it lacked a building of its own and as such was at the mercy of applying to theatre managers to use their facilities when they were not otherwise booked with lucrative shows. In the first decade of the twentieth century, with the advent of the Court Theatre, the Abbey Theatre, Manchester's Gaiety Theatre, and the Glasgow Repertory Theatre, literary drama had solid foundations. The economic viability of these places demonstrated that there was a large and growing audience for new art that went well beyond the elite of the metropolis. If there was a material link between the cases of Moore and Shaw, it was perhaps in this: while Moore's abolitionist crusade led to new approaches to producing the novel and ushered in innovative publishing practices and forms, Shaw's led to new ways of producing theatre. Their censorship battles thereby had significant impact on formal invention, social and political content, and modes of production.

In this sense, despite the different contexts and genres in which they struggled against censorship, the cases of Moore and Shaw reveal several commonalities. In addition to leading the charge towards the radical shifts noted above, the two Irishmen stand out from their contemporaries in their sheer audacity and pugnaciousness. At heart, censorship is a form of punishment. The author or speaker is told that what they have written or said is unacceptable, and they are sanctioned accordingly. While neither of them was fined, imprisoned, tortured, banished, or killed, Moore and Shaw suffered pecuniary losses, and in the case of the former's first novel, had fate not intervened and had the warehouse stocking copies not burned, he would have been financially ruined. Moreover, the banning of their works essentially labelled them as filth mongers and purveyors of perversion, and, as they and their colleagues protested, they had no recourse to appeal or to defend themselves in court. This was, effectively, a form of legalised slander and libel. Yet both Irishmen refused to be silenced. Indeed, Shaw was the public face of the abolitionist movement throughout his unrelenting campaign, appearing before the parliamentary committee, but also granting interviews and writing articles, letters to editors, prefaces, and plays specifically intended to provoke the censor. In so doing, he provided a great deal of energy to the movement and became a lodestar for freedom of expression.

Although he failed to rally writers in the same way, Moore was equally forceful in his public statements. He dared to confront Mudie in person when he was a little-known writer and followed this with an absolutely scathing public pronouncement of his unmitigated hatred for the man. Moore fought against the stigmatisation of being labelled an indecent writer by turning the prudish Mudie into an object of disgust and scorn. If a further objective of censorship is to serve as a deterrent, punishing an errant author or an indecent work as a warning to others, then Moore's tactic was rather to make himself into the heroic rebel. In this way, he was an important precursor for Shaw, who also fought relentlessly. Similarly to Moore, Shaw publicly ridiculed those who censored, like Pigott and Redford, and such purity movement leaders as Coote, who were instrumental in both supporting the official censorship and turning public opinion against writers. Perhaps the best example of this was his taunting of Anthony Comstock, the head of the New York Society for the Suppression of Vice, by coining the derogatory term "Comstockery" to refer to overzealous, prudish activism.[143] Yet Shaw surpassed others by revelling in the notoriety that censorship had thrust upon him and trumpeting his immorality. In so doing, he challenged the philosophical underpinnings of censorship, emphasizing that he was not immoral in an evil sense, but rather in the sense of holding opinions that were not the norm. By abolishing censorship, he could broadcast his opinions and thereby convert others to his point of view, with the intent of making his immorality become the new morality.

Such controversial strategies were typical of Shaw. If censorship sought to forbid the fruit, he understood how he could play temptation to his advantage. There is a natural, perhaps perverse, attraction for what has been denied us. Shaw held some dangerous fascination as both that which had been forbidden and that which tempted people towards the forbidden. Furthermore, as a journalist and a notable socialist pamphleteer, he knew the economics of the publishing trade: controversy sold papers. And controversy had the additional benefit of augmenting his notoriety and celebrity. Shaw thus used the press as much as it used him. By taking his case to an establishment paper like *The Times,* he addressed a wide audience and gave his protests the veneer of respectability. He returned the favour in noting how, following his parliamentary testimony, he "transferred the scene of action to the columns of The Times, which did yeoman's service to the public on this, as on many other occasions, by treating the question as a public one."[144] Shaw viewed the agora, the marketplace of ideas, as an essential public good. It was for this that he praised *The Times* and so steadfastly argued for the abolition of theatre censorship.

Although the term "abolition" is used and Shaw and his colleagues repeatedly referred to their cause as "abolitionist," we should not confuse this with an absolutist liberal or libertarian perspective. There was no writer involved in the campaign who argued that there should be unrestrained free speech. Rather, they argued for doing away with the obligation to obtain a licence to produce their work in public. Such demands on playwrights, they maintained, were undemocratic as no profession was subjected to the same requirements. Novels and newspapers could be published without first subjecting them to licensing laws of the sort that Milton had railed against in *Areopagitica.* Meanwhile, platform speeches and pulpit sermons were delivered to large numbers of people, and they were not subjected to pre-performance censorship, despite the fact that some, as Shaw attested, had led to riots. Playwrights thus sought to be treated the same as other professionals, to be judged post-performance on whether their plays were indecent or obscene. If they were thus charged, then they should have the right to defend themselves and to appeal. What they might have pointed out was that, when published, not one of the plays prohibited in this period was prosecuted under the terms of the Obscene Publications Act.

In the end, the tyranny of the circulating libraries and the triple-decker novel was not overcome through campaigns and pamphleteering, but rather by the market. Despite dramatists mounting a coordinated effort, even the most optimistic person had to admit that the reforms to theatre censorship were modest. One lesson was that time and broader social shifts would cause change. This was certainly the case in the second decade of the twentieth century. Ibsen's *Ghosts* received a licence in 1917, for example, as part of the campaign against the increased prevalence of venereal disease caused by soldiers on leave.[145] Until the abolition of censorship in 1968, when the institution could no longer be sustained in a radically more liberal society, writers offered no resistance organised along the lines of that from 1907 to 1909. However, as we will see in later chapters, several of the people who played important roles in that campaign, including Shaw, Garnett, Galsworthy, and Law, would come to affect the struggles for freedom of expression in Ireland two decades later when the government established its own censorship of literature. Although in very different ways, these men would serve as models for a generation of Irish writers who were but children at the time of the 1907–9 campaign. Importantly, a few of the lessons would be lost, and new contexts, mechanisms of censorship, and personalities meant that some of the strategies and outcomes would necessarily be different. Indeed, censorship takes on different forms in different times and in different polities. Yet as a practice it essentially operates in similar ways despite such differences, seeking to curb or eliminate forms, ideas, and people from the public sphere, to control not just messages but the people behind the message and those who are its intended audience. Moreover, there are a limited number of tactics available to opponents. Because of this, there would also be many similarities between the censorship struggles faced by Moore and Shaw in Victorian and Edwardian Britain and those that Irish writers would later face in Ireland.

The effect that British censorship had on Irish literature is a further component of the international dialectic. This mirrors the effect that Irish writers had on British censorship and freedom of expression, which was due in part to the prominence, antagonism, and ethical and aesthetic imperatives of Irish writers at the time, coupled with the fact that many of them lived in Britain, which was their main market. Such internationalism was augmented by the fact that Irish writers were inspired by literature from elsewhere: just as Moore turned to Zola, Shaw turned to Ibsen, both of whom became bugbears for censorship advocates and heroic martyrs for anti-censorship campaigners. Similarly, when Shaw and his colleagues sought to challenge the censorship and economics of commercial British theatres, they looked to the continent for the models of Paris and Berlin. With Irish writers being important participants in the independent theatre movement, it is no surprise that its ethos came to inform the founding of the Abbey, Ireland's national theatre. As the succeeding chapters will continue to show, such global contexts and dynamics must be accounted for to better understand the relationship between Irish writers and censorship.

Chapter Three

The Scene Shifts to Ireland: James Joyce, Brinsley MacNamara, and Lennox Robinson

Towards the end of the 1907–9 censorship campaign, the focus of Irish writers transferred from Britain to Ireland with the Abbey's production of Shaw's *The Shewing-up of Blanco Posnet*. In this case, Irish writers coalesced to thwart British authorities, aligning artists' demands for freedom of expression and the cause of nationalists. With the status quo having been maintained in Britain by the censorship of plays and the Obscene Publications Act of 1857, Ireland was positioned to become a beacon for a more liberal society. Yet there were many forces afoot in Ireland that would ensure that the country would be just as constraining an environment for writers.

The censorship struggles of James Joyce, Brinsley MacNamara, and Lennox Robinson attest to how Irish writers continued to view their personal battles, in these cases waged mainly in Ireland, as part of the larger international fight for freedom of expression. While the accounts share some similarities with the experiences of Moore and Shaw, we see in them some new forms. Joyce is particularly interesting for how he illustrates Danilo Kiš's notion of "friendly censorship," wherein an editor suggests certain excisions because they claim that they care about how publishing the work could negatively affect the writer's livelihood, reputation, and well-being. Moreover, although Moore and Shaw faced the economic consequences of being censored, we see in MacNamara's case how the wrath of the censorious can have an economic and indeed physical impact on those close to writers. For Robinson, censorship would lead to a loss of employment and social ostracism; as collateral damage, it also nearly resulted in the collapse of a major international scheme for funding the country's public libraries.

Just as England had the National Vigilance Association (NVA), Ireland had the Irish Vigilance Association (IVA), which would instigate the country's first concerted efforts of grassroots censorship. A quarter of a century after the foundation of the NVA, a Limerick group calling itself the Vigilance Committee formed on 5 October 1911, with members brought together by a concern over an "ever-growing evil – the evil of immoral literature." In an illustration of the international dialectic of censorship, they believed that Ireland had been besieged by a foreign wave of menacing literature that could cause "the destruction of our distinctive national spirit. It means more, as it will break down the noble moral standards which have brought happiness to Ireland when nothing else could have done so. The lessons of history, and the works of economists are clear in their teaching that when the moral standards of a country are lowered, social ruin and domestic unhappiness increase." Such literature, they avowed, would lead to murder, suicide, depravity, and insanity. Indeed, marrying this national exceptionalism to a public health argument, they believed that "these evils merit as much attention as the microbes of phthisis."[1] They argued that only censorship could maintain the nation's well-being and assure its future.

The work in Limerick caught the attention of likeminded people in Dublin, who met to form a local chapter and thereby nationalise the crusade into what would become the IVA.[2] At one meeting in Limerick, a priest appealed to all people to inform the committee of any immoral publications and then gave "a splendid lecture of the evils of bad literature" that pointed out "the great havoc it had wrought in England and in the Continent."[3] The underlying anxiety was that unlike those other places, Ireland had yet to be corrupted by such literature, but it was only a matter of time before it would be swamped should they not protect themselves. The IVA would wage an aggressive public campaign in the following years, as well as privately appeal to bookstore owners to not sell immoral literature.[4] However, its energies were soon siphoned off by the onslaught of World War I and the national independence movement.

Founded in 1899, the Catholic Truth Society of Ireland (CTSI) took a different tack. As opposed to focusing on evil literature, the CTSI created its own press, Veritas, to publish and promote Catholic literature.[5] Indeed, Veritas essentially flooded the market with inexpensive pamphlets that emphasized Catholic doctrine. This led Cardinal D'Alton to assert that the CTSI provided "an antidote of the anti-Christian literature coming to our shores in increasing quantity."[6] With the emphatic support of priests and bishops across the country and His Eminence Cardinal Logue, the CTSI quickly became the lodestar for moral Irish culture. On 6 June 1900, a little over six months after it was founded, the CTSI released its first twenty-five titles; by 22 September, 250,000 copies had been sold, and by the end of 1903, the CTSI had published another 139 titles. A little over a decade later in 1914, the CTSI's most popular work, Father F. E. O'Loughlin's *The Life of Our Lord* (1901), sold its millionth copy.[7] For a country of just over four million people, these are astounding figures.

Like the IVA, the CTSI was shaken by World War I. The conflict had deleterious effects on its finances and membership, the former worsened by the Easter Rising of 1916. Located in the city centre at 2 Lower Abbey Street, its headquarters was damaged and printing plates and pamphlet stocks were ruined by the shelling from nearby battles. It suffered further setbacks due to the increased cost of paper during wartime, which rendered the production of affordable pamphlets all but impossible. However, the appointment of Frank O'Reilly as secretary and manager in May 1918 brought about a renaissance. Under his guidance, the organisation sorted out its finances and modestly raised the price of its pamphlets, which the public returned to purchasing at pre-war numbers.[8] As we will see, because of O'Reilly's work, the CTSI was well-placed to become a force for the pro-censorship movement.

While presses and printers continued to censor manuscripts based upon the potential of their being prosecuted under the terms of the Obscene Publications Act, individuals and loosely formed coalitions, as well as associations like the IVA and CTSI, would further threaten writers' freedom of expression. The links between such groups and the Catholic hierarchy being so strong and the power of the Catholic Church in Ireland being so dominant, Irish writers would face massive odds in their struggles to combat censorship. In so doing, the younger generation would emulate the strategies of their predecessors Moore and Shaw, but they would also fail to learn and apply important lessons that arose from those earlier battles. As this chapter will show, some Irish writers responded to censorship through aesthetic means, but by not publicly engaging with censors and by not collectively organising themselves, they would have no discernible impact upon the direction of freedom of expression in their country.

At the same time, Joyce, MacNamara, and Robinson would, in various ways, cannily attempt to avoid censorship and its effects by turning to international networks. When a press in one polity effectively censored their works by refusing to publish them on moral grounds, they turned to presses elsewhere. In many respects, this would mirror Shaw's collaboration with Lady Gregory and Yeats to produce *The Shewing-up of Blanco Posnet* in Ireland when the Lord Chamberlain banned the play in Britain. However, this aspect of the international dialectic of censorship is given greater force in the cases of Joyce, MacNamara, and Robinson as the censors were Irish. As opposed to the previous chapters, in which Irish writers were censored by British authorities and thus perhaps rather less problematically othered and alienated from the public, when Irish writers were banned in Ireland, they essentially became estranged from their compatriots and home country. As this and the succeeding chapters will show, while such practices seek to ensure the purity and health of the nation, they thus create a crisis of belonging for those who are censored, sending some into exile and preventing them from actively participating in the public sphere.[9]

James Joyce: The Individualist

Largely due to the 1921 prosecution of the editors of the *Little Review* for publishing excerpts of *Ulysses* and a New York judge's decision in 1933 that the novel was not obscene, James Joyce has become the symbol for the censorship struggles of the Irish writer. However, his first and less celebrated encounters with the practice occurred as early as 1906, when he dealt with printers and editors while attempting to publish *Dubliners*. The repeated demands for him to revise passages, change words, and omit entire stories led to Joyce's own nine-year odyssey and his final rejection of Ireland, which was cemented by his refusal to return to its shores.

Initially hoping to publish with a respected London-based press to increase his visibility and to avoid being associated with the provincialism of his homeland, Joyce approached Grant Richards. Richards, who founded his eponymous publishing house in 1897, made a name by publishing the work of Bernard Shaw, including the stand-alone volume of *Mrs Warren's Profession* that marked the Stage Society's controversial production in January 1902 and that featured Shaw's anti-censorship preface.[10] In 1901, Richards also established the World's Classics series, which Oxford University Press would purchase four years later.

Joyce contacted Richards in October 1905, hoping to interest him in his manuscript. "I do not think that any writer has yet presented Dublin to the world," he wrote, despite it being "a capital of Europe for thousands of years" and "the second city of the British Empire." He also pointed out that he had seen several books on Irish subjects and so thought that "people might be willing to pay for the special odour of corruption which, I hope, floats over my stories."[11] Richards responded that while "books about Ireland do not sell," he and others who had read Joyce's manuscript had "admired it so much" that they decided to publish it.[12]

Despite such initial interest, Richards quickly lost his enthusiasm. He informed Joyce that the printer to whom he had sent the book had refused to print it because he objected to the story "Two Gallants," in which one man boasts to another how he has seduced a woman. Richards asked Joyce either "to suppress it, or, better, to modify it in such a way as to enable it to pass."[13] Joyce was understandably furious, responding that Richards had already accepted the book and adding that the "printer's opinion of it does not interest me in the least."[14] Unsurprisingly, he would not countenance the printer's other demands to alter some passages of "Counterparts" and to excise the word *bloody* from "Grace."

Richards did his best to pacify Joyce. He explained that he did not care what the printer thought, but that if the printer took that view of the book, it was likely that the booksellers, libraries, and a good portion of the public would, too. Exemplifying Kiš's notion of friendly censorship, he counselled Joyce: "You have told me frankly that you look to your future being helped by your literary work. The best way of retarding that result will most certainly be to persist in the publishing of stories which – I speak commercially, not artistically – will get you a name for doing work which most people will regret." In this respect, publishing the book without ridding it of scandalous language and material would negatively affect its "commercial possibilities" and "our business generally."[15] Indeed, Richards was in "precarious financial" straits.[16] He was thus motivated by the fear that an attack on Joyce's book would negatively affect the sales of his other titles.[17] Although he was sympathetic with Joyce, desired to publish good literature, and understood, having published *Mrs Warren's Profession*, that censorship might drive business, as we saw in the case of Vizetelly, doing so could be disastrous, as under the terms of the Obscene Publications Act, publishers and printers were held liable for their books. Richards's caution was thus motivated by very real financial and legal dangers.

At first, it appeared that neither side would budge. Joyce continued to protest, raising the spectre of his countryman in denouncing Richards's trepidation by asking him whether a mid-Victorian publisher "would not have rejected a book by George Moore or Thomas Hardy?"[18] He then turned to the larger issue at stake and his stupefaction that such concerns should be considered in England: "Is it possible that at this age of the world in the country which the ingenuous Latins are fond of calling 'the home of liberty' ... that I cannot write the phrase 'she changed the position of her legs often'? To invoke the name of Areopagitica in this connection would be to render the artist as absurd as the printer."[19] Yet he did not stop there, invoking not only Moore and Milton but also

Zola, telling Richards that he would not be prosecuted for publishing *Dubliners*: "The worst that will happen, I suppose, is that some critic will allude to me as the 'Irish Zola'!"[20] Moreover, Joyce was adamant that the passages that he refused to alter were "the points which rivet the book together. If I eliminate them what becomes of the chapter of the moral history of my country? I fight to retain them because I believe that in composing my chapter of moral history in exactly the way I have composed it I have taken the first step towards the spiritual liberation of my country."[21] While Joyce's battles were thus local and personal in nature, he saw that they had implications for the nation and, in evoking Milton, Moore, and Zola, considered them to be part of a larger global war for freedom of expression waged by writers across historical periods and thus exemplary of the international dialectic of censorship.

However, tired of the fight and wishing to have his work published, Joyce began revising the stories, immodestly warning Richards that by forcing him to do so, "you will retard the course of civilization in Ireland by preventing the Irish people from having one good look at themselves in my nicely polished looking glass."[22] By October 1906, Joyce wrote to say that the censorship fiasco had had a negative effect on his creativity and that he was now unable to complete the novel that would eventually become *A Portrait of the Artist as a Young Man*.[23] Later that month, Richards returned *Dubliners* to Joyce, saying that while he understood that Joyce believed they had treated him badly, he was convinced that he would later come to see that they had acted in his interest.[24]

Despite his reluctance to publish with a provincial press, after several more London-based editors rejected his manuscript, Joyce turned to Ireland. Founded in Dublin in 1905, Maunsel was financed by the author Joseph Maunsell Hone, with its day-to-day operations overseen by the journalist Stephen Gwynn and George Roberts, a co-founder of the Irish National Theatre Society. Given that most renowned Irish writers already had contracts with London presses that offered better terms, distribution, and marketing, Maunsel had to concentrate on cultivating the next generation. Due to Roberts's connections in the theatre world and Maunsel's focus on literature of the Irish revival, the press had the support of Yeats, Lady Gregory, and J. M. Synge. This led to the publication of Synge's *The Playboy of the Western World* in 1907 and, following his death in 1909, his collected works.[25] Maunsel thus appeared to be the ideal publisher for Joyce's book: *Dubliners* was set in Ireland and authored by a promising local talent, and they had already published Synge's *Playboy*, which, with its provocative subject matter and language, had caused riots in Dublin during its first run in 1907.[26] In the spring of 1909, Joyce signed a contract with Roberts to publish *Dubliners*, but the next year he ran into familiar difficulties when Roberts said that he would only publish it if Joyce agreed to cut the story "Ivy Day in the Committee Room."[27] Roberts protracted the situation by making increasingly onerous demands. Eventually, Joyce had had enough and decided to take his case to the people.

Joyce's sortie was akin to the strategy that both Moore and Shaw had employed: rendering public the secretive work of the censor to allow the general population to scrutinise the practice and to shame the censor. Joyce had been in Dublin to witness *The Shewing-up of Blanco Posnet* firsthand as a corresponding reviewer for *Il Piccolo della Sera*. Like others in the press corps, he considered Shaw's play to be "innocuous" and wondered "why on earth the work was intercepted by the censor."[28] Yet he had taken note of Shaw's struggles. Thus, as with Moore and Shaw, Joyce recognised that he had to argue his case through the press, prompting what Richard Ellmann refers to as "one of Joyce's most outlandish moves in the dispute."[29]

On 17 August 1911, a full two years after he had signed his contract with Roberts, Joyce sent a letter to several newspapers, although only two published it: *Sinn Féin* and, with a controversial passage omitted, Belfast's *Northern Whig*. His intent was to throw "some light on the present conditions of authorship in England and Ireland." Recounting his prolonged attempt to publish *Dubliners* with Richards, Joyce noted how he agreed to Maunsel's demand to tweak a passage in "Ivy Day in the Committee Room" in which one character believes that Edward VII thought of his mother, Queen Victoria, as "*The old one*," and refers to the king as "just an ordinary knockabout like you and me. He's fond of his glass of grog and he's a bit of a rake, perhaps, and he's a good sportsman." However, when further pressed "to omit the passage or to change it radically," Joyce declined to do so.[30] Hone later surmised that Roberts had demanded that "Ivy Day in the Committee Room" be excised because he did not wish to insult Lady Aberdeen, the Lord Lieutenant of Ireland's wife, who had published several tracts with Maunsel pertaining to her anti-tuberculosis campaign and who had been a longtime ally of social purity movements.[31] In light of this, the omission of the story would have been economic censorship to ensure that Roberts did not run afoul of one of his more lucrative customers. Yet Roberts denied that this was the case.[32] Joyce's eventual solution was to add "a prefatory note," but the press refused and in response he gave Maunsel permission to publish with whatever changes they wished.[33]

Like Moore and Shaw before him, Joyce was not only risking his reputation in taking his argument to the public, but also his potential to make a living as an artist. Moore had attacked the timid publishers and puritanical libraries, while Shaw insulted the censorship of plays and its bureaucrats, as well as theatre managers for colluding with the system. These were hardly conducive to them getting a foothold in the field, yet their pugnacity and persuasive arguments drew people to their side. Joyce similarly attacked the press with whom he was currently negotiating the publication of *Dubliners*. He might have hoped that in doing so he could sway Roberts either through his own arguments or through social pressure had the public and other writers coalesced behind him. Yet Joyce had not contacted other artists. As he lived abroad, he lacked the on-the-ground networking in which both Moore and Shaw engaged. In the end, it appears that his public letter and his inability to garner widespread support sunk his cause.

By the summer of 1912, Joyce, having returned to Ireland, tried to find an amicable resolution. On 18 August, a full three years after he had signed the contract with Maunsel, he had a heated two-hour meeting with Roberts, who now demanded the omission of "An Encounter" as well as further deletions from "Ivy Day in the Committee Room."[34] Exasperated, Joyce contacted George Lidwell, a solicitor and family friend. Lidwell warned Joyce that Roberts would not be his only concern as "there is at present in existence in this city a Vigilance Committee whose object is to seek out and suppress all writing of immoral tendencies."[35] Indeed, from 1911 to 1913, which were "peak years" for the IVA and other social purity movements, "some small shops were subjected to crowds of several hundred protesters, windows were defaced and broken, and publications were confiscated and even burned at public demonstrations."[36] The month before Joyce returned to Ireland, a crowd of twenty thousand showed up at Dublin's Mansion House in support of the suppression of immoral literature while inside a meeting on the subject was held by several dignitaries, including the mayor and Lord Aberdeen. The mayor remarked that from that time, "the war cry would go around that an upheaval was taking place in Ireland's capital against the pernicious literature and immoral photographs that had been rampant within it and other cities," and read a telegram from the Pope who gave his blessing to their cause. The IVA then reported that "the movement for the suppression of infidel and immoral newspapers and periodicals had not been inaugurated a moment too soon" and appealed for the public's help to rid the country of such material. For his part, Lord Aberdeen praised those who combatted the "abominable iniquity ... of debasing books or pictures."[37]

Lidwell further warned Joyce that if the IVA drew the attention of the authorities to the final paragraphs of "An Encounter," in which an old lecher approaches two boys, masturbates, and fetishistically speaks of whipping children, it was "likely they would yield to the pressure of this body and prosecute." He thus advised Joyce to "delete or entirely alter the paragraphs in question."[38] However, Lidwell wrote again to say that the passages "are not likely to be taken serious notice of by the Advisors of the Crown," and thus he did not believe that "a conviction could be easily obtained."[39] Joyce forwarded this second letter to Roberts, but, wishing to simply "end this interminable discord," he agreed to omit "An Encounter" from *Dubliners*. Yet he demanded that the collection have a prefatory note: "*The scheme of the book, as framed by me includes a story entitled An Encounter which stands between the first and second stories in this edition.*"[40] Joyce hoped that the bowdlerised version would be warmly received and thus induce Roberts to include the story in subsequent editions.

Meanwhile, Roberts's lawyers found "the book to abound in risks of action of libel."[41] No longer were the events and language of Joyce's stories in question. The issue was now that in Joyce's adherence to capturing the essence and veracity of Dublin, he had made too many references to local people and businesses. All of these, as Roberts's attorneys informed him, were potential grounds for libel should those named take offence. Therefore, Roberts argued, it was not he but Joyce who was in breach of contract, and thus Joyce should pay Maunsel to cover the costs they had incurred thus far.[42]

Within days, Joyce left Ireland for the last time in his life. While this situation was not the sole factor, it played no small role in his permanent exile. Incredibly, however, he continued both to pursue publication of his book with Maunsel and to attack Roberts. On 15 September, back in Trieste, Italy, Joyce printed his broadside "Gas from a Burner," a satirical poem written from Roberts's perspective and in which the imaginary Roberts claims he defends his country from the immorality of its writers. Having received Joyce's manuscript, he says:

I printed it all to the very last word
But by the mercy of the Lord
The darkness of my mind was rent
And I saw the writer's foul intent.
But I owe a duty to Ireland:
I held her honour in my hand,
This lovely land that always sent
Her writers and artists to banishment.[43]

As for Joyce himself, the broadside version of Roberts protests that he wrote

> of Dublin, dirty and dear,
> In a manner no blackamoor printer could bear.
> Shite and onions! Do you think I'll print
> The name of the Wellington Monument,
> Sydney Parade and Sandymount tram,
> Downes's cakeshop and Williams's jam?
> . . . .
> No, ladies, my press shall have no share in
> So gross a libel on Stepmother Erin.[44]

Joyce published the poem on the continent, beyond the jurisdiction of British authorities, then sent it to his brother Charles in Dublin for general circulation.[45]

"Gas from a Burner" is a rollicking jibe at Roberts for having wasted so much of Joyce's time and for not having the courage to publish *Dubliners*. Yet it was perhaps facile to attack a man who would have been at risk of prosecution when Joyce, as the writer and living in exile, was safely out of harm's way. Joyce lamented to Yeats that while Roberts had agreed to sell him the books for thirty pounds, the printer refused to hand over the thousand copies and instead "broke up the type and burned the whole first edition."[46] He begged Yeats to "do me a great service" and "intervene" with publishers. This would, he hoped, be of "some service also to the literature of our country."[47]

After he was rejected by several more presses, Joyce sent Richards the manuscript, hoping that he might change his mind. He now suggested publishing *Dubliners* with a preface, which was a reproduction of the letter he had sent to newspapers followed by an update on all that had since transpired. Ezra Pound published the proposed preface in the 15 January 1914 issue of *The Egoist*.[48] Like Moore and Shaw, then, Joyce attempted to affect the reception of his book. Indeed, he suggested to Richards, who had now agreed to publish *Dubliners*, that including his account of the book's publishing difficulties, or in the very least a "sensational" account of its burning, "might help to push the sale."[49] In the end, there was no need to worry about the book possibly attracting censors as *Dubliners* was not prosecuted and reviewers were mild in their criticism.[50]

While Joyce would be confronted with censorship again in the years to come, he became more reclusive. From the time that the *Little Review*, a small American literary magazine, started serially publishing episodes of *Ulysses* in 1918, Joyce's book encountered all sorts of censors, including those who supported it. Margaret Anderson, the *Little Review*'s editor, expurgated passages, as did Pound, who served as the European-based editor. Anderson's edits were undertaken to avoid the wrath of authorities while Pound suggested to Joyce that he had made aesthetic emendations; however, Paul Vanderham argues that Pound's changes were "little more than thinly disguised religious objections to Joyce's tendency to subvert hierarchies cherished by Pound, especially that which separates the erotic and excremental aspects of human sexuality."[51] Clare Hutton similarly notes in cataloguing Pound's deletions that they highlight his "prudery."[52] Despite such excisions, the United States postal service seized and burned the January 1920 edition of the magazine because they detected obscenity in the third part of the Cyclops episode.[53] Margaret Anderson said that each of the four times they received a notice from the post office that a copy of the *Little Review* had been destroyed, "It was like a burning at the stake."[54] Things came to a head later that summer when the authorities confiscated the issue featuring the Nausicaa episode, which describes Leopold Bloom masturbating as he watches Gerty MacDowell tease him in the distance with a view of her knickers. Although Lidwell had warned Joyce of the activities of the IVA, Joyce could not have foreseen interference from the New York Society for the Suppression of Vice, which led the charge to prosecute Anderson and her co-editor, Jane Heap.

The trial of Anderson and Heap focused on the immorality and obscenity of Joyce's book. While the prosecution argued that it would corrupt young women, the defence demurred, contending that it caused readers to recoil from vice. In the end, Anderson and Heap lost their case, were fined fifty dollars each, and could no longer publish instalments of *Ulysses*. Joyce's novel was similarly banned in England, Canada, and Australia.[55] To publish it, Joyce had to resort to the Parisian bookstore owner Sylvia Beach, who created her own imprint for the occasion.

Unlike his involvement with *Dubliners*, Joyce fought no battles over the censorship of *Ulysses*. One could assume that he had given up the cause after the years of frustration and the toll that it had had on his ability to complete *A Portrait of the Artist as a Young Man*. Perhaps he felt that his attention and energies were better spent on creating art and leaving the battles to others who were more adept at fighting than he was. Or his passivity was simply the final manifestation of his refusal to engage with society, the incarnation of the aloof artist that Stephen Dedalus seeks to become in *Portrait*. Yet while he did not enter the fray in either the legal or the polemical fields, Joyce responded to the censorship by incorporating elements of it in *Ulysses*: the 1920–1 trial informed the trial scene of the Circe episode, and the Ithaca episode is infused with legalistic language. Moreover, Joyce considered the book's final chapter, the Penelope episode, to be "probably more obscene than any preceding episode."[56] As several leading critics have concluded based on their examination of manuscript revisions, Joyce reacted to censorship by referring to it in *Ulysses* and intentionally ramping up the book's obscenity.[57] Thus, while he no longer engaged in polemics, he made the case for freedom of expression through his aesthetics. In this sense, he reclaimed the creativity that censorship had robbed from him. Like Shaw with his censor-baiting plays *The Shewing-up of Blanco Posnet* and *Press Cuttings*, incorporating censorship in his fiction afforded Joyce some measure of revenge.

However, while he began with the same polemical strategy as Moore and Shaw, Joyce's own attempts to combat censorship were considerably less effective. Joyce fought the censors head-on in dealing frankly with both Richards and Roberts and for some time resisted revising his work to become less offensive and therefore less likely to be prosecuted. Moreover, he made his struggles public by publishing a letter to the editor in newspapers and circulating a satirical broadside to protest his treatment by Roberts. Yet none of these outlets had anywhere near the same influence as *The Times*, in which Shaw published his many letters, or the reach of Shaw's and Moore's pamphlets. Moreover, Joyce mainly worked on his own from abroad, lacking the social networks that Shaw exploited. By the time that Joyce finally contacted Yeats, he had spent six painful years being rejected by publishers. Yet as his later experiences with *Ulysses* attest, even those who championed his work believed that the only way to circumvent censorship was to censor it themselves.

Brinsley MacNamara: Social and Economic Censorship

At the heart of Maunsel's trepidation about publishing *Dubliners* was the potential twofold reaction of government prosecution for obscenity and public charges of libel, although neither came to pass when the book was published in England. When Maunsel published Brinsley MacNamara's first novel, the roman-à-clef *The Valley of the Squinting Windows* (1918), MacNamara and his family encountered censorship of another order. Most of the cases of censorship we have seen thus far were top-down, with authorities and businesspeople controlling freedom of expression and justifying such measures by saying that they did not wish to offend consumers or to deprave and corrupt citizens. Had there been a censorship of plays that extended to Dublin, it is possible that *The Playboy of the Western World* might not have been performed at the Abbey Theatre in 1907 and that the weeks of unrest and public debate would have been avoided. The reaction of the public to MacNamara's novel provides the opportunity to consider what happens when, in the absence of a top-down censorship, a form of grassroots censorship erupts.

MacNamara's *The Valley of the Squinting Windows* is such a savage satire of smalltown Irish life and the public's reaction to it was so violent that its title has become a byname for the gossipy narrow-mindedness of rural Ireland. When his hometown quickly saw through the conceit that Garradrimna was no fictional locale, but rather readily identifiable as Delvin, County Westmeath, the reaction against the author and his family was swift and brutal. One of the ironies of the case is that MacNamara, whose birth name was John Weldon, attempted to protect himself by not only renaming the town, but also by publishing under a nom de plume.

The book's reception in the press might have indicated the furore that awaited it. The *Freeman's Journal* titled their review "Romantic Ireland's Dead and Gone" and linked MacNamara with Joyce as writers ushering in a younger generation's claim to the realist novel as the dominant Irish genre.[58] In a thoughtful assessment, the *Irish Independent* said that "the reader may dislike the occasional touches of realism or manifestations here and there of a deep-rooted bitterness on the author's part towards some of his characters," but suggested that they "can only lay the book aside with the feeling that here is yet another young writer likely to leave his mark on Irish literature." The "apparent purpose" of the novel, the reviewer concluded, was "to accomplish a merciless exposure of the petty jealousies and suspicions, the consuming curiosity regarding one another's private concerns, the vicious exultation in any item of local scandal which enter too largely into village life in Ireland."[59] MacNamara's talent was in how adeptly he pulled back the curtains to reveal the people behind the squinting windows.

However, many people in Westmeath were not so urbane and detached. MacNamara's identity was well enough known that the local press referred to the author of *The Valley of the Squinting Windows* as "John J. Weldon (Brinsley MacNamara)" and even associated his father, James Weldon, with the book.[60] A group of Delvin's citizens, upset with the "facile writer" who had satirised them through thinly veiled characterisations, took matters into their own hands.[61] On 28 May 1918, crowds of people gathered to listen to the book being read aloud and delighted in teasing one another about how they were portrayed. This quickly ended when one group of ladies came upon the description of the postmistress steaming open letters for her own amusement. At about the same time in a local pub, the owner became ashamed while reading it for customers when he stumbled upon characters who resembled him and his wife. The publican then offered free drinks and urged those assembled to take action.[62] Around three dozen men then marched up the street to a store where the two Weldons were believed to be.[63] While the son had already left, the father was confronted by the mob and told to quit Delvin. When he refused, people screamed "Pull him out!" and then dragged him into the street. Just as he was about to be beaten, a police officer intervened, allowing Weldon to run into the building and flee through the back door.[64] The officer later testified that a man in the crowd said that Weldon "should be strung up like a fox for the hounds."[65] One person claimed that Weldon had provoked the attackers by trying to assault them with a stick, apparently not interpreting Weldon's actions as self-defence when confronted by a lynch mob.[66] The officer further stated that at one point the crowd threatened to rush the store and that he had to put his hand on his holster, telling them that they had either to get back or to "take the consequences."[67] Unable to wreak vengeance on the Weldons, the crowd descended to the market square where they burned a copy of the book.[68] They then walked to a club a few miles away where the son was supposed to have gone, but, having been forewarned by a friend, MacNamara had already escaped.[69]

There was a general belief that the son was not the only one working under the nom de plume, with people suspecting that the father had co-written it. The day after the father and son had been targeted by the mob, around sixty people stormed the school in Ballinvalley and demanded that James Weldon resign as teacher. When he refused to go, the men told his assistant and the seven pupils who were in attendance to leave. There would have been more children, but many had bolted when they saw the approaching mob.[70] By all accounts, the crowd was so indignant that, once again, only the arrival of the police saved Weldon from injury.[71] Thereafter, both Weldon and the school were placed under police protection.[72]

Unsatisfied, the mob marched to the presbytery and demanded that Father Tuite, the parish priest, do something. Tuite walked to the school and tried to fire Weldon, but Weldon told him that, according to regulations, only the bishop could do so; the priest responded by giving him three months' notice.[73] When Weldon approached Tuite the following day to plead his case, the priest told him that it would be better for him if his son were not to live with him. By the end of the week, the school was closed, but it was reopened on the following Monday after Tuite told his parish that they should end their protests because they had acted inappropriately. Ten pupils returned on the first day, and after a fortnight the students numbered thirty. However, some townspeople visited families to demand that they stop sending their children to the school, picketed roads, prevented children from getting to class, and organised to drive children to schools further away.[74] When these tactics failed to have the desired effects, locals threatened Weldon that if he did not resign his position, his son would be kidnapped and exiled from Westmeath. Towards the end of June, a deputation of around sixty people demanded at a town meeting that the councillors withdraw Delvin children from the Ballinvalley school.[75] Meanwhile, some people met to ascertain if they could prosecute MacNamara and Maunsel for libel, although one newspaper, showing some savvy, warned them that should they do so they would only bring fame to the author and the book and ridicule on the townspeople.[76] In the end, they agreed not to sue MacNamara and his father in return for Weldon signing a statement that he had nothing to do with the writing of the book.[77] A year later, the locals were informed that they were still being mocked in Dublin for imitating their depiction in the very book they were protesting.[78] Indeed, they were incredibly oblivious to the irony of the situation.

With such publicity, Maunsel was well placed to profit. However, they had only printed a thousand copies, whereas two thousand was a normal first run for them. When the anger became manifest in Delvin, instead of issuing more copies and marketing the book as having created a scandal, Maunsel withdrew it and made no further attempt to advertise it.[79] Roberts and his lawyers had had misgivings about *Dubliners* because they suspected that they would be open to libel charges. In this later case, the identification of Delvin's citizens with characterisations in *The Valley of the Squinting Windows* and the consideration of some locals to sue for libel suggested that Maunsel had acted prudently with Joyce's book. Indeed, by using the names of real people and businesses in his stories, Joyce would have caused them to run a greater risk. Despite – or because of – the scandal, Maunsel stuck with MacNamara, publishing his novel *The Clanking of Chains* in 1920.

For the American edition of *The Valley of the Squinting Windows*, MacNamara wrote a preface, but it was distinctly unShavian: running a relatively meagre five pages, it contextualised and sympathised with the Irish reaction rather than attacking those who had burned the book and threatened him and his father. MacNamara opened by discussing the works of five prominent nineteenth-century Irish novelists:

Charles Kickham, William Carleton, Charles Lever, Samuel Lover, and Gerald Griffin. While Moore and Joyce referred to themselves as Irish Zolas, MacNamara rather regretted that Carleton, like Kickham, was prevented from becoming "the Irish Balzac" because of his sentimentalism.[80] For their part, Lever and Lover laughed at the comic Irish peasant, and Griffin failed to inject his farmers with any spiritual energy. All five of them simply created stereotypes, working with "such exact opposites as saints and sinners, heroes and *omadhanns*, earnest passionate men and *broths of bhoys*. And somehow between them, between those who wrote to degrade us and those who have idealized us, the real Irishman did not come to be set down. From its fiction, reality was absent, as from most other aspects of Irish life."[81] Just as Joyce sought to hold the mirror up to the people of Dublin, MacNamara sought to do so to the people of rural Ireland. However, instead of turning to Joyce for inspiration, MacNamara looked to the Irish theatre. He praised the Abbey and its playwrights for performing "plays dealing with subjects which no Irish novelist, thinking of a public, would have dreamt of handling," and he was amazed that their works had somehow been accepted throughout the country.

He recounted for his American readers how the people of Delvin had "burned my book after the best medieval fashion and resorted to acts of healthy violence."[82] For MacNamara, realism had the same effect on people as Zola and Moore believed naturalism did and Shaw claimed of his and Ibsen's theatre: it jarred them from ideals and got them to see the world anew. Yet he was considerably premature in his declarations of how realism would now be received in Ireland. He claimed that "A change had come, by miraculous coincidence, upon the soul of Ireland. It was not afraid of realism now, – for it had faced the tragic reality of the travail which comes before a healthy national consciousness can be born. No longer would the realist be described in his own country as merely a morbid scoundrel or an enemy of the Irish people."[83]

MacNamara's preface thus adopts several of the common polemical strategies that we have seen. He depicts his art as that of the present and, importantly, the future, breaking off from the tired traditions of the past. Those traditions, steeped in sentimentality and idealism, caused society to revolt against his novel, but he believed that his work had now awakened the people from their slumber. The censorship and violence to which he and his father had been subjected were merely the final convulsions of idealism attempting to stymie reality and progress. Like Shaw, then, his work and its reception become a case for the importance of allowing for immorality. One of his shortcomings was that while Moore, Shaw, and Joyce made their cases in the countries in which they were confronted by censorship, MacNamara published his preface in the United States.

Delvin, however, was not finished with his father. Following the initial boycott and the mob's storming of the Ballinvalley school, most of the pupils had returned by the end of June. Yet when the Weldons attempted to purchase basic goods, local store owners refused them service. One neighbour took pity and bought things for them; under cover of night, the Weldon children would run between the houses to bring food home. After a while, the neighbour was found out, and they, too, were refused service.[84] Even when James Weldon's mother died, no one loaned or rented him a car to attend her funeral.[85] In the autumn, school attendance nosedived. From 1919 to 1921, enrolment fluctuated between eighteen and twenty students on average; in 1922, it fell drastically to thirteen.[86] This was a far cry from the forty-three students who had attended the school before the book was published.[87] Because the pay of schoolteachers was aligned with attendance figures, and their salaries in turn determined their pensions, this represented not only social censorship, but also a significant threat to James Weldon's livelihood. With the numbers having stabilised at these lower figures, on 1 January 1923 his annual salary was dropped by a massive £161, which would result in a £72 loss to his annual pension.[88] Feeling that there had been a conspiracy, Weldon sued his persecutors.

The case was held in Dublin from 5 to 8 December 1923 and was covered by newspapers across the country. Journalists were drawn by a fantastic tale that involved a celebrated writer made more fantastic by his father suing community leaders for £4000 in damages. The defendants were Father Tuite and several local farmers and tradesmen.[89] Weldon suing a priest was a remarkable event considering the power and spiritual authority of the Catholic Church over the Irish people at the time, especially given that he was a schoolteacher and the Church managed the national schools, yet it attests to how desperate and righteous he felt.

The court heard evidence establishing the events of 28 May 1918 and of the days and weeks that followed. When a police officer recounted that the mob had demanded that Weldon resign and apologise, the presiding judge was taken aback, asking, "Apologise for what, Serjeant; for having a son?"[90] Meanwhile, the counsel for the defence offered that the only sympathetic character in the book was the old schoolmaster, while all of the others – the priest, farmers, traders, and teachers – were "held up to ridicule and contempt."[91] The townspeople were provoked by potentially libellous depictions and the perverse portrayal of the parish priest as flirtatious. Moreover, the defence attorney and some of the witnesses accused Weldon of having beaten boys, which Weldon flatly denied; the implication was that there was no boycott, but that parents had stopped sending their children to the school because Weldon had been abusive.[92] One witness told of how two of the defendants threatened him with not being able to use their land for pasturage if he continued to send his younger brother to the school.[93] Another man testified that he was ordered to join the mob that descended on the school on 29 May, but that he felt bad about it and slipped away as soon as he could.[94]

The judge was antagonistic to witnesses for the defence. As his comment above indicates, he abhorred that the sins of the son were being visited on the father. He also found the reasoning of some of the mob participants difficult to fathom. One man said that he had simply been maintaining a grudge against Weldon that his father had had with him. However, he stopped participating in the protest because he felt that the other protestors did not support him enough in his own troubles. To this, the judge concluded: "I wonder is there much worse said about the people of Delvin in the book than you have said now."[95]

The counsel for the defence argued that there was no question of a parent's right to select the school for their child, "and just as one person was entitled to do that, so were 20 or 22 entitled to do it."[96] Furthermore, as one witness pointed out, the reason for the fallen attendance could be attributed to the closing of the local workhouse and the police barracks. For his part, Father Tuite testified that he had tried to bring peace by placating the people after they had stormed the school. He had "never supported a boycott" and, like the judge, felt that it was unjust that Weldon was being tormented for what his son had written.[97] As the defence wryly noted, it appeared that the only person who had gained anything from the events that unfolded was MacNamara, for he had received "an advertisement that had secured for him, probably for all time, a position that would take him from the obscurity from which he might not otherwise have emerged."[98] In the end, the defence argued that there was no conspiracy against the plaintiff, but that "there was an epidemic of indignation against the schoolmaster."[99]

Weldon's lawyer countered that in his forty years of service as a teacher, "there had never been a scratch against him," that his character and abilities were good enough for Father Tuite to hire him for the Ballinvalley school in 1904, and that he had enjoyed cordial relations with his fellow citizens until the events of 28 May. Given this situation, what followed meant that the defendants were solely motivated by the book and that a conspiracy had been hatched. The intensity of their anger and irrationality was demonstrated by the fact that the police had to protect Weldon. As for Father Tuite, he never expressed his disapproval of the people behaving in an unruly and unfair manner.[100] The lawyer concluded: "If this sort of thing was allowed to go on there would be no real social life in Ireland."[101]

In the end, the jury failed to agree on a verdict, meaning that Weldon's case had come to naught. A little over a month later, a group of writers, headed by Yeats, AE, and Oliver St. John Gogarty, set up a subscription fund to help Weldon launch an appeal. They had done so, they claimed, because the case affected "the entire community."[102] Advertising in the *Irish Statesman*, they sought to attract to their cause Ireland's liberal intelligentsia and cultural elite. A. E. Malone also sent private letters to people instructing them that an appeal would help Weldon to obtain reparations, but it would also defend "a vital principle of cultured society – freedom of thought and speech. Through the father in this case, it is sought to enfetter the son and should it be successful, a deadly blow will be dealt to artistic freedom."[103]

Weldon never did appeal. Seeing his position in the community as untenable, he resigned. Shortly thereafter, he had a heart attack that left him severely weakened, and he eventually moved to County Wicklow. Within days of the new headmaster taking up his position at the Ballinvalley school, enrolment jumped to forty and by June it was forty-nine.[104] Meanwhile, MacNamara took a Joycean tack by continuing to satirise the town in his next novel. Curiously, while his American publisher issued it under the title *In Clay and in Bronze* (1920) and his usual monicker Brinsley MacNamara, his London publisher, Eveleigh Nash, rather followed in the steps of Maunsel, attempting to avoid as opposed to profit from scandal by issuing it under the title *The Irishman* and using a new pseudonym, Oliver Blyth.[105]

While the appeal fund set up for Weldon framed the cause as one of freedom of expression, to a certain extent many of those who boycotted the Ballinvalley school were merely exercising their own freedom of expression. In not sending their children, they were showing that they disagreed with the book that Weldon's son had written and that they did not wish to be associated with it. Where they hindered their case was in forcing people to join the boycott through social and economic pressure and by preventing passage to the school and issuing threats of violence. Such threats are in fact abuses of freedom of expression in that they direct harm at an individual. This, then, is the philosophical point on which the case turned: were they justified in exercising their freedoms, or did their freedoms, directed collectively, hinder the ability of others to exercise their freedoms, such as the freedom to make a living or to make their own choice whether to join the boycott? With regard to freedom of expression for writers, the lesson was that if people did not like what they wrote, the community would impose social and economic censorship on both them and their families.

One of the defining aspects of the case, especially given what we have seen of Moore and Shaw, is that Irish writers failed to coalesce around MacNamara and his father until it was too late. There was no media campaign to enlighten the public on the freedoms of expression that were at stake. The press had given extensive coverage to both the events of May 1918 and the trial of December 1923, but writers did not intervene in the public sphere at either moment. When they finally set up their appeal fund, James Weldon had become a broken man. For his part, while MacNamara, like Moore and Shaw before him, published a preface recounting the treatment that he and his father had suffered at the hands of the townspeople of Delvin, he did nothing to sustain such polemics. Instead, he reacted very much as Joyce had to censorship, failing to coalesce Irish writers around his cause and preferring to respond to the social and economic censorship of both him and his father by directing more satire at Delvin. Indeed, just as Joyce approached Yeats late in the day to intervene with publishers on his behalf, so Yeats was recruited to MacNamara's case well after the scandal had passed.

Lennox Robinson, *To-Morrow*, and the Carnegie Libraries

In 1924, a new monthly, *To-Morrow*, was founded by the twenty-two-year-old writer Francis Stuart and the twenty-year-old artist Cecil Salkeld as a venue for adventurous literature and progressive thought. For the first issue that August, they solicited short stories by Lennox Robinson and Liam O'Flaherty; W. B. Yeats's poem "Leda and the Swan"; contributions from the younger generation of poets, including Joseph Campbell and F. R. Higgins; an essay on the German philosopher Jacob Böehme by Stuart and another on the principles of painting by Salkeld; and a book review of O'Flaherty's *The Black Soul*. As Robinson later recalled, they were "brilliant contributions but all were on rather audacious lines."[106] Such audacity would cause the editors and Robinson to run into significant difficulties that would echo the cases of Joyce and MacNamara and foretell what awaited writers in a newly independent Ireland.

Three of the works included in the first issue of *To-Morrow* hinge on overt sexuality. Yeats's renowned sonnet vividly recounts the rape of Leda at the hands of Zeus, who comes to her in the form of a swan, and the destruction of one era and the beginning of another. In Liam O'Flaherty's "A Red Petticoat," an impoverished, starving widow with four children blackmails Mrs. Murtagh, a store owner, into giving her six months' worth of provisions in return for not telling others that Mrs. Murtagh has been having an affair with the local tailor. Robinson's "The Madonna of Slieve Dun" was likewise provocative, focusing on Mary Creedon, a young virgin who, returning home late one night, is raped and impregnated by a drunken tramp. Because she faints and is naive in the extreme, Mary fails to understand what has happened to her and comes to believe that she is the virgin mother to a Jesus-figure who will be born on Christmas day. While the people of town mock her at first, they come to be gentler in her presence as they witness her piety and certainty. The story concludes with the birth of a daughter and Mary's death, then leaps forward to a pub in Cork where a tramp, who has just related the tale to fellow revellers, is celebrated as a rogue for his exploits.

Although all three works were daring for their depictions of sex, it was Robinson's story that became the focal point of the ensuing controversy. For his part, Robinson claimed not to have envisioned its scandalous potential. However, when he first offered it to an English weekly in 1911, the editor told him that although it was one of the best stories he had ever read, he was returning it because he feared that it would offend readers. A decade later, Robinson published it in *Vanity Fair* and, apparently, not a single reader complained.[107] When Stuart approached him about contributing to his new monthly, Robinson gave him "The Madonna of Slieve Dun." Although a major New York magazine might not have received complaints, it is difficult to imagine that the editors of *To-Morrow* did not consider the possibility that the three incendiary works might provoke puritanical elements in Irish society. Indeed, George Yeats, wife of W. B. Yeats, claimed that the Talbot Press had refused to publish "The Madonna of Slieve Dun" in a collection of Robinson's stories and that *The Nation* had rejected it because the editors found it "indecent."[108] She regretted that her husband's poem would now be tainted by association.

The controversy began with a Dublin press that refused to print the monthly with Robinson's story included. It then became public when the editors announced in the *Irish Statesman* that they were "compelled to look outside Ireland for printers who will not interfere with the contents of a paper published in the interests of the Arts."[109] The editors were evidently using the controversy to attract more readers and drum up sales. Robinson added fuel to the fire, lamenting in the *Irish Statesman* that Ireland was infested with "bad art, bad politics, bad religion." Stuart and Salkeld, he said, "believe in the immortality of the soul, they are certain that it is the absence of this belief that makes possible bad bishops, bad politicians, bad artists." Moreover, "The story was written in good faith and in Christian faith – it is now stigmatized as blasphemous and indecent."[110] When the first issue was in production, the editors announced that the success of the journal would "depend largely on whether it is denounced with sufficient savagery" and doubted "whether it is impish enough to arouse violent antagonisms. It really requires a great deal of art to stick a needle into the national being so that it sits up and howls."[111] For the editors of a nascent periodical that sought to stir things up, they could not have hoped for better advance publicity, but they failed to reckon with the force of the backlash.

What followed came to be known as "the Carnegie row." As noted earlier, the Carnegie libraries scheme was a transnational philanthropic project established in 1883 and financed by the American industrialist Andrew Carnegie. The effects of it were massive, and it contributed in no small part to the downfall of the private circulating libraries. After only two decades of operations, it funded the building of over 2000 public libraries in Europe and North America. While in 1880 there were only 48 public libraries in the United Kingdom, by 1909 there were 522, of which 295, or 56.5 per cent, had received grants from the Carnegie Trust. Similarly, while in 1896 there were 971 public libraries in the United States, by 1923 there were 3873, of which 1408, or 36.4 per cent, had received Carnegie grants.[112]

The Carnegie Trust was likewise generous in Ireland. Between 1897 and 1913, it granted over £170,000 to build 80 libraries across the country, and in 1919, it financed projects in 81 per cent of Irish towns that had rate-supported public libraries.[113] In 1915, the Carnegie trustees appointed Robinson to the position of organising librarian for Ireland.[114] In this role, he was responsible for financing local councils that wished to found, refurbish, or stock libraries. Over the years, he hired several capable young librarians who would go on to shape Irish culture, including Frank O'Connor, Hubert Butler, and Thomas MacGreevy.[115] While the potential furore of *To-Morrow* fumed in the waiting, Robinson plugged ahead with his work for the Carnegie libraries.

At this time, the Carnegie trustees in Ireland were John Henry Bernard, the Church of Ireland's former archbishop of Dublin and the current provost of Trinity Collee Dublin; Thomas A. Finlay, a Jesuit priest, co-founder of the Irish Agricultural Organisation Society (IAOS), and chair of political economy at University College Dublin; Thomas Lyster, a librarian at the National Library; James Wilkinson, the librarian of the Carnegie Library in Cork; Desmond O'Brien, president of the Royal Hibernian Association; Thomas O'Donnell, a former Irish Parliamentary Party MP; Lionel Smith-Gordon, the librarian of the Irish

Co-operative Organisation Society (the successor of the IAOS); AE; Lady Gregory; and, as secretary and treasurer, Robinson. While most members were respected librarians or well-known artists, the first two, although they also held important educational positions, represented the power of religious capital in post-independence Ireland. Indeed, many of the country's oversight committees responsible for education and the arts included bishops, priests, reverends, and pastors. For the Carnegie libraries, most local Irish committees were chaired by parish priests and, it has been suggested, were influenced by the IVA.[116] In many cases, priests oversaw the selection and purchase of books, and they purged the works they deemed immoral and obscene.[117] It was also not uncommon to keep books under lock and key and only allow them to be borrowed upon request.[118] This religious control of the Carnegie libraries was to cause no end of difficulty for both the functioning of them in Ireland and Robinson's career.

By mid-September, W. B. Yeats noted that *To-Morrow* had "caused a great sensation." Having caught wind that the government was considering its suppression, he met with Ernest Blythe, Ireland's minister for finance. Blythe confirmed the rumour but said that William T. Cosgrave, Ireland's president of the executive council (which under the 1937 Constitution would become the taoiseach, or prime minister), "had really thought of doing so, not because of anything said in it, but because some man, a German who is anti-Church, has written saying Lennox Robinson's idea of the foundation of Christianity in his story is probably the right one." Cosgrave apparently feared that Robinson was "trying to pervert the nation."[119] He thus sent the story to Kevin O'Higgins, the minister for justice, who refused to prosecute, saying that doing so "would merely represent the moral attitude of a certain people, and place, and time."[120]

While Cosgrave decided not to act, the Carnegie committee was thrown into disarray when Father Finlay resigned in protest of Robinson. Before the resignation, Lady Gregory had only been thinking of the potential fallout affecting her beloved Abbey Theatre, seeing as Yeats and Robinson, both directors of the Abbey, had published sexually charged material, but she now came to realise that the library scheme and its effects on Irish culture were at stake. She met with AE, who told her that he did not think that the story was particularly good, but he did not wish to fight two churches on the matter, as now Bernard was also furious about the publication. Robinson had intimated to AE that he had been considering resigning from his position with the libraries as it was interfering with his other work; AE and Lady Gregory hoped that if he resigned, Finlay would rejoin and the problem would simply dissipate. The committee then drafted a letter asking Finlay to reconsider, adding that they found that the *publication* of the story, and not the story itself, was unfortunate and deplorable.[121] This did not placate Finlay, leading Bernard to resign in solidarity. Faced with these resignations, Lady Gregory argued that they should "reduce the mass of worthless novels from the libraries," fearing that book selection would now be scrutinised and that they had to ensure that they were above reproach.[122] Here, then, the desire was not to make a case for freedom of expression and thought, with the resigned members allowed to refuse being affiliated with Robinson, who they perceived to be an immoral writer, and the other members believing that all sides had the right to express themselves. Instead, they sought to ensure the morality of the libraries. However, before they could enact any policy, the trust dismissed the entire committee and Robinson was fired from his position. Furthermore, as Lady Gregory had feared, the Abbey Theatre suffered when the Carnegie Trust soon thereafter refused it a £5000 grant that had seemed a certainty before the scandal erupted.[123]

For its part, the Carnegie Trust sought to ensure its legitimacy and morality in the eyes of the people. Even after the mass dismissals, at a meeting to ascertain if they should establish a library scheme for County Offaly, three priests submitted letters "expressing disapproval of the project." One "said that the scheme should not be accepted unless the books to be circulated were chosen by a local committee" and "took strong exception" to the works of Robinson and Yeats. Another said he wanted "nothing to do with a Carnegie Library. ... They are storehouses of wretched novels and semi-pagan stuff of the same cultural level as penny illustrated papers from England, which, I am sorry to say, our people buy and smoke like opium, with the same narcotic effects on their brains and better life."[124] In Ireland, such public health arguments coupled with statements of national purity would be repeated throughout the years. Meanwhile, Robinson became a byword for blasphemy.[125] Later, he recounted how the experience "was inexpressively painful to me. It alienated many of my Catholic friends and with some the breach will never be healed."[126] Now scarred, he wished it all to be "forgotten."[127]

As for the new monthly, the effects of the controversy were immediately felt. It published its second issue in September 1924, featuring more poems by Higgins and a continuation of Salkeld's essay on the principles of painting, as well as a piece by Arthur Symons on the French painter Honoré Daumier, stories by Iseult and Francis Stuart, and a meditation on the tendencies of young Irish poets. Running only six pages, *To-Morrow* did not advertise its contributors, unlike in the first issue where they broadcast them just below the masthead. There could have been need for reticence this time around, but the fact of the matter was that the paper was struggling to attract bigger names and people were not supporting it. Controversy, in this case, had a deleterious effect, with *To-Morrow* folding after only two issues.

In the wake of the Carnegie row, Robinson moved outside of the city, leasing a house in Dalkey. While this could be interpreted as a fashionable retirement to a coastal suburb, he leaves the impression that as he felt morally and emotionally withdrawn from society, there only remained his physical removal. His expression of the pain of the experience reveals that he was profoundly traumatised. Relationships lay in ruin, he was branded immoral and blasphemous by Ireland's moral arbiters, he had lost his job, and he had narrowly escaped being prosecuted by his government. These were and remain some of the very real social, economic, legal, and political effects of censorship. In a closely knit society like post-independence Ireland, they could be felt even more acutely than what Irish writers had previously suffered in Britain.

It was understandable that the Carnegie Trust decided to cleanse itself of the committee to remain a viable operation in Ireland. In the wake of the scandal, Ambrose Coleman, a well-known Irish Dominican friar and author, published a position paper on how the clergy should approach the Carnegie libraries. Appearing in the *Irish Ecclesiastical Record*, an influential journal read widely by the Catholic hierarchy and parish priests, Coleman's article noted that while Carnegie's largesse had been a generous windfall for Ireland, book selection should be grassroots in nature, handled by the local committees that were headed by bishops and parish priests. While he denigrated the Irish peasant as uncultured and harbouring a powerful hatred of books and learning, he warned priests that they had to beware of town-based readers and provincial intellectuals. These people insistently demanded "ordinary up-to-date English fiction, and they sometimes ask for certain books by name that the librarian could not conscientiously procure for them."[128] He suggested that it would be unfair to saddle tax-paying peasants with the costs of purchasing and maintaining such books for a minority of people. Therefore, he argued, "If the Carnegie Trust is to inspire confidence as regards its good intentions it should look well to the class of persons it appoints to control its work in Ireland. A great deal hinges on the *personnel* of the central executive, and the members must be above all suspicion. The Irish people cannot be expected to submit to influence and control exercised by writers belonging to the neo-pagan Dublin school of literature."[129] He suggested that after a two- or three-year period of accepting Carnegie's money to build their infrastructure and stock their shelves, county councils should cut all ties with the trust so that they could "carry on the same work absolutely independent of foreign or alien influence and dictation."[130] Doing so would allow local committees to focus on supplying their libraries with books written by good Catholics, thereby allowing the Irish, and in particular their priests, to control reading and to dictate their own culture. In this sense, Coleman encapsulated the censor's viewpoint of the international dialectic, harbouring fears of foreign, immoral literature and values contaminating a pure Ireland.

Meanwhile, several of the librarians that Robinson had hired felt betrayed by the scandal, and this sense of betrayal would impact how they and others of their generation would confront censorship in the coming years. In the immediate aftermath, Frank O'Connor, born Michael O'Donovan, decided to employ his pseudonym to create "a loophole against the sort of mistake Lennox Robinson had made when he published his silly little story under his own name."[131] However, as he was later censored on more than one occasion and his real identity was common knowledge, he was about as safe as Brinsley MacNamara before him, although he never suffered the same job loss as Robinson or faced the same violence as MacNamara and his father. Hubert Butler simply lamented the inevitability of Irish writers bringing "calamity on the libraries ... when they collided with piety and prudery."[132] Looking back on the controversy, Robert Tobin remarks that it was "a major defeat for the liberal intelligentsia at the hands of majority opinion" and that while Robinson's dismissal "was a high price to pay for the exercise of free speech, arguably the price itself testified to the urgency of paying it."[133] It was indeed urgent, as the latitudes of freedom of expression had yet to be established in the newly independent Ireland.

The Shift to Ireland

While Ireland appeared to be protective of writers' freedom of expression in the case of *The Shewing-up of Blanco Posnet*, the decade and a half following that production revealed that Irish writers would face in their homeland many of the same challenges as they had in Britain. Although the censorship of plays was not a determining force in Ireland, there existed different forms of censorship. For editors and printers, the hesitancy to publish daring new works arose from a combination of factors, including the threat of being prosecuted for libel or obscenity, the personal morality of the people involved, and the fear of economic sanctions through the potential loss of clients. Moreover, with the rise of grassroots organisations like the IVA and the CTSI, writers were confronted with puritans ready to lodge complaints against their work. As the cases involving Joyce, MacNamara, and Robinson show, it was a struggle for writers to defend their work, their livelihoods, and even their selves in the face of tenacious, hostile opposition and extrajudicial punishment. They also reveal that controversy in the realm of freedom of expression can lead to the breakdown of social order, infringe upon individuals' other rights, and provoke very severe social and economic censorship for not only writers, but their families as well. In Foucauldian terms, the lessons were communicated to future writers as a warning. Benedict Kiely recalled that MacNamara's name became "a household two-words ... for horror"; in fact, when a local priest discovered that Kiely was embarking on a literary career, he told him that he should not disgrace his county like MacNamara did.[134]

When considering the experiences of these three writers and their predecessors Moore and Shaw, it becomes evident that Irish writers failed to adequately learn lessons from the past. Moore and Shaw were particularly adept at rhetoric, and they ensured that their polemics circulated as widely and as often as possible. Joyce and MacNamara applied some of the same rhetorical techniques, but they wrote shorter and fewer pieces that were less aggressive and persuasive. Instead, they responded through their art, but in doing so they were not as immediate, and therefore they lost the momentum to have an impact on the direction of their society when the public's attention was attracted by scandal. Unlike Moore and Shaw, all three of the younger writers also failed to organise resistance in a meaningful way. As such, their struggles remained personal, which further led to their inability to have an impact on the public sphere. Despite these failings, Joyce and MacNamara recognised that although they fought local battles, they remained part of a larger historical and international war waged by writers in favour of freedom of expression. Yet as we will see in the next chapter, the trio's failure to organise in a timely and forceful manner would be the hallmark of Irish writers in the first decade following the country's independence, and it would have a disastrous effect upon freedom of expression and the direction and place of literature in Ireland for years to come.

Furthermore, this chapter introduces aspects of the international dialectic of censorship that Moore's and Shaw's experiences did not reveal. For one, Irish writers used international networks to evade censorship and its effects. While Joyce preferred to publish in England, when English presses were wary about his writing, he turned to Ireland. And when Irish presses showed similar reticence, he turned back to Grant Richards in England. Later, when working on what would become *Ulysses*, Joyce published excerpts in the United States, and, when the book was finished, he was forced to publish it with Sylvia Beach in Paris as no press in the Anglophone world would touch it for fear of prosecution. MacNamara similarly experienced difficulties publishing in Ireland when Maunsel only printed half of its usual run for the first edition of *The Valley of the Squinting Windows*. Moreover, Maunsel refused to print more copies and to use the controversy to drive sales. MacNamara then wrote a preface for the American edition of his novel, which, even though it was tame in recounting the scandal, would have piqued the curiosity of bookstore browsers. Similarly, when *To-Morrow* ran into difficulty with Irish printers, who declined to help publish Robinson's story because they considered it obscene and blasphemous, the editors hired an English printer. Although the three cases have distinct differences, they attest to how Irish writers used international networks, editors, printers, and publishers. In this sense, conservatism and censorship in one polity can drive the writer to look abroad to find sympathetic professionals who are more liberal, more profit-driven, or more devoted to aesthetics to help them maintain their freedom of expression and their ability to live by their pen.

At the same time, some of the printers and publishers might not have recognised their refusal to print or publish the works as a form of censorship. Rather, they might have determined that their refusal was an expression of their individual right to avoid being implicated in something that ran counter to their ethics or morality and that it protected them from negative economic and legal consequences. Yet the norms and mores that they expressed in their decisions to turn down these writers cannot be considered as wholly separate from the dominant norms and mores of the national culture. Indeed, as the prosecution of the editors of the *Little Review* in New York, the lynch mob in Delvin, and the firing of Robinson and the Irish Carnegie trustees demonstrate, the refusal of the printers and publishers often aligned with the majority and the official position with regard to the fitness of these works to circulate within their local or national borders.

If we go back to the origins of the first office of censor in ancient Rome, we see that Cato not only oversaw the census, but also determined the morality of the people to be counted as citizens. In this sense, the censor determines who does or does not belong to the local or the national body politic. Partly in recognition of the impossibility of living as an artist in Ireland, Joyce would go into exile, becoming an unallied cosmopolitan on the continent. The case of MacNamara, in which the locals in Delvin threatened to kidnap him and to drive him from the community, illustrates the danger of censorship in its more extreme forms and the need for the artist to live in more tolerant, salubrious surroundings. The main difference between the cases of Joyce, MacNamara, and Robinson and those of Moore and Shaw is that while the latter were Irishmen who sought to impose themselves, their morality, and continental aesthetics on British culture and were censored for doing so, the former were censored by their own countrymen. Indeed, the Irish Moore and Shaw were, despite the alignment of Ireland and Britain under the auspices of the United Kingdom, foreigners in Britain, so there was no implication of them being excluded by their native culture. For Joyce, MacNamara, and Robinson, however, the censorship that they experienced, their loss of employment, and the threats that they received in Ireland were punishments for transgressing and thus undermining the norms and mores of the nation to which they belonged. Censorship thereby renders the censored national subjects strangers in their own land and consolidates the notion of a cohesive and coherent national culture.

As we have seen throughout the three chapters thus far, ensuring the purity of the nation is a constant concern in censorship discourse. Ambrose Coleman's statement that libraries in Ireland should be free from "foreign alien influence" attests to such anxieties. That he was a priest, as were many of the founders and leaders of the CTSI and the IVA, testifies to the close association in Ireland between nationalism, Catholicism, and censorship. This nexus was increasingly evident as the country gained political independence, passed its own censorship legislation, and oversaw institutions devoted to determining the suitability of literature and other arts in Ireland. As we will see, this was a product of specific nationalist attempts to Hibernicise or de-anglicise Ireland and thus rid it of external influences, a position that envisions all that is Irish as necessarily good and desirable and all that is not as suspicious and potentially subversive of the nation-building project. With the shift in the next chapter to post-independence Ireland and the gradual establishment of institutional censorship, the paradoxical role that Britain will play as both bugbear and model will illustrate yet another aspect of the international dialectic of censorship.

Chapter Four

A Made-in-Ireland Censorship: Polemics and Institutional Formation

The Irish Free State was established on 6 December 1922, one year to the day from when the Anglo-Irish Treaty was signed by delegates of both the British and the provisional Irish governments. As with so many countries that have emerged from periods of anti-colonial activity, there was a great deal of hope for the future of an independent Ireland. This was particularly true of Irish writers, who had long been at the fore of nationalist movements. In the late nineteenth century, antiquarians and folklorists, including Lady Gregory, W. B. Yeats, and Douglas Hyde, collected the stories of the peasantry and the myths of ancient Ireland. In 1892, Yeats, Charles Gavan Duffy, and T. W. Rolleston founded the Irish Literary Society to promote literature written on Irish subjects, and in 1899, Yeats, Lady Gregory, George Moore, and Edward Martyn established the Irish Literary Theatre, which would form the basis of the Abbey Theatre in 1904. Many writers also participated in the armed struggle, including Patrick Pearse and Thomas MacDonagh, who were executed as rebel leaders in the wake of the Easter Rising in 1916. Similarly, a younger generation of writers, among them Frank O'Connor, Peadar O'Donnell, Sean O'Faolain, and Liam O'Flaherty, were actively involved in the Anglo-Irish War of 1919–21 and later the Civil War of 1922–3. Having invested so much energy in contributing towards the nationalist awakening and Ireland's independence, writers justifiably felt that they had an interest in the form that the country would take following independence. Freedom for them meant, in part, freedom to express themselves by their pens. However, many of them would become disillusioned with how they and their art were regarded and treated by their fellow citizens.

As its first piece of legislation, the Dáil (the Irish equivalent of the House of Commons) enacted the Constitution of the Irish Free State. Under Article 73, all laws that were currently in force in the Free State continued to be in effect, provided that they were not inconsistent with other articles in the Constitution, until they were either repealed or amended by the Oireachtas (the bicameral Irish parliament). Two weeks later, on 20 December 1922, the Dáil passed the Adoption of Enactments Act, which reiterated Article 73 of the Constitution in officially adopting British law as it had extended to Ireland prior to independence. The most important of these laws with regard to censorship was the Obscene Publications Act, along with the jurisprudence of the Hicklin test, which defined the obscene as that which tends to deprave and corrupt. The structure of British governance and forms of censorship in Ireland therefore remained largely unchanged immediately after independence, save for the fact that those who now enforced the law were Irish. In this regard, the international dialectic of censorship is manifested in how one country borrows from another's laws in drafting its own, despite its desire to distinguish itself as an independent and distinct polity. As we will see, this dialectic becomes further evident in the way Ireland's legislation was directly informed by contemporary British obscenity trials. As for Irish writers, they would demonstrate a spirited if ineffectual resistance to censorship as they engaged in polemics both at home and abroad.

The Precedent of Cinema

While the censorship of literature would cause far greater controversy throughout the years, the government first targeted the cinema when it introduced the Censorship of Films Bill on 3 May 1923. Speaking in the Dáil, Kevin O'Higgins, the minister for justice, argued that the measure for a nation-wide censorship was unanimously supported.[1] The legislation, O'Higgins admitted, was provoked by a deputation of members "representing various bodies interested in the moral welfare of the people."[2] Among these were representatives from the Irish Vigilance Association (IVA), the Priests' Social Guild, the Catholic Church, the Protestant Episcopalian Church, and the Presbyterian Church, which constituted a cross-section of the major religions in Ireland and demonstrated that the initiative was not only driven by Catholics. Kevin Rockett has convincingly argued that the cinema was the initial focus of these groups because of the relative ease with which it could be controlled when compared to literature. As films were screened in public, fewer copies were brought into the country than were potentially offending publications. Moreover, the newness of the medium made it more susceptible to control as reading habits were by this time already well formed and the prominence of the literary arts in the national struggle for independence further bestowed upon them the political and social capital that film lacked. Accordingly, the legislation was meant to be the first step in institutionalising other forms of censorship.[3]

One of the first deputies to speak on the matter was William Magennis, a professor of metaphysics at University College Dublin who would figure prominently in censorship debates in the following decades. First as a TD (Teachta Dála, the Irish equivalent of an MP) and later as a senator, he argued passionately for the principles of censorship and against liberal reformers. As a testament to his interest in the subject and the esteem in which he was held by authorities, he would later sit as the chair of the Censorship of Films Appeal Board from February 1924 to April 1929 and as a member of the Censorship of Publications Board from 1933 until his death in March 1946. According to Magennis, the necessity of censorship stemmed from the Irish people's lack of sophistication:

> [I]f the community were properly educated there would be no necessity for a censorship. But we are not in an ideal community – very far from it – and people, especially the rising generation, require to be protected from an environment that is certainly not conducive to good morals, and they require to be saved from themselves. There has been no education in this country of a primary sort that would enable those who constitute the main part of an audience at a kinematograph theatre to discriminate judiciously between what, while it is attractive and admirable as a piece of photography, is seductive and prejudicial to a proper life and to a proper outlook upon life.[4]

In addition to reflecting the paternal role of the censor, Magennis expressed nationalist anxieties, believing that as the Irish people had yet to be instructed through state-run schools that would ideally teach critical thinking and inculcate Irish values, there was a pressing need to institute censorship. He emphasized this in stating the distinct relationship between censorship and citizenship, demonstrating at the outset of the debates the role that censorship was to have in constructing a national populace and imaginary. This was of primary interest in Ireland following the divisive revolutionary period: censorship was conceived as a means of coalescing the country by enforcing a narrower, more cohesive morality that was exemplified in "a proper life" and "a proper outlook upon life."

The bill ran its course with near unanimity and was passed as the Censorship of Films Act on 16 July 1923. The new law established a sole paid film censor with an appeal board of nine members who worked under the jurisdiction of the minister for home affairs. Cinemas across the country now had to apply for licences to show films, and if they were charged with screening banned films, or parts of films that had been cut by the film censor, they faced fines and the threat of not being able to renew their licence. The film censor was granted the power to ban and cut films if they considered them "indecent, obscene or blasphemous or because the exhibition thereof in public would tend to inculcate principles contrary to public morality or would be otherwise subversive of public morality."[5] Because of the Hicklin case, there was no need to define the terms *obscene* and *indecent*. Yet what represented public morality, how this was to be interpreted, what its principles might be, and how something might pose a subversive threat to it were left unresolved. As a result, the role of the film censor was highly subjective. It was therefore necessary to fill the position with a person of high moral standards who had the ability to understand and critically analyse not only the narrative, but also the visual images and potential audience of a wide variety of motion pictures.

Over the course of the next two years, the censorship of films ran relatively smoothly. However, certain inadequacies in the original legislation became apparent and on 3 April 1925, O'Higgins presented the Censorship of Films (Amendment) Bill.[6] The purpose of the amending legislation was to take into account advertisements for the cinema, the fear being that too many of these were risqué. After the original act was passed, O'Higgins said that he was surprised to receive letters from clergymen and priests over the types of films being shown. Yet, he noted:

> Inquiry in many cases showed that the opinions were being formed from the advertising posters that were being exhibited in connection with these pictures, the fact being that the scenes depicted on the posters in most cases did not occur at all in the actually exhibited films, and in some few cases were scenes that had been deleted by the Censor in the performance of his functions. Posters of this kind found their way into practically every town and into a great many villages in the country, and, as I am informed, did considerable harm.[7]

What exactly that harm was and how it was measured was not indicated. Regardless of such concerns, under the new legislation, which was enacted on 27 June 1925, the film censor had to approve promotional posters for films before they could be displayed.

The Censorship of Films Acts of 1923 and 1925 institutionalised the practice of in camera censorship in Ireland. Under the new laws, censorship became a secretive process wherein the reasoning that informed decisions was not rendered public, and, unlike court cases, there was no allowance for the accused to mount a defence. During the debates in 1925, Bryan Cooper, an independent TD, suggested that while he was against such legislation in both principle and theory, he supported it because it was "a logical sequel" to what had already been passed.[8] The onus was therefore placed upon precedent. Indeed, no voice was raised for reform of the original act, and it was deemed that censorship had to be necessarily more stringent rather than more relaxed. Now that censorship was enshrined in Irish law, other media could be likewise subjected to government control.

The Case for Literary Censorship

From the outset of 1925, there was a movement afoot to target literature. It began in earnest when the *Irish Ecclesiastical Record* published an important article by R. S. Devane that argued in favour of legal remedies to combat indecent literature. Devane, a priest from Limerick who had been involved with the IVA since its inception, insisted that the government draft censorship legislation informed by Irish norms and mores. As a member of the executive of the Priests' Social Guild, he had been part of a deputation that had recently met with Kevin O'Higgins.[9] Although he admitted in his article that during the meeting he and his colleagues asked O'Higgins to draft a bill, Devane failed to mention that O'Higgins had suggested that Devane write the article to help create an atmosphere that would facilitate legislation.[10] As was the case in Delvin, a censorship conspiracy was hatched; however, here it remained out of the public eye.

In arguing that censorship should be nationalised to account for the cultural and moral differences of the Irish people, Devane proposed four legal remedies. The first was that legislators should develop broader and more comprehensive definitions of obscenity and indecency. This was important as the Irish, Devane claimed, were a pious people with strict religious values. As an offshoot of those values, his second legal remedy was that the Irish should declare contraception and "race suicide" literature as obscene and ban the sale of anything that would assist with birth control or abortion.[11] The third remedy struck directly at literature, with Devane suggesting that a blacklist of obscene publications should be produced and updated regularly. Noting the published lists of banned books in Canada, Britain, the United States, and France, he praised Canada in particular for banning nine of Guy de Maupassant's works. Indeed, the country was "not squeamish in its methods of dealing with the 'Art for Art's sake' humbug, when carried too far; even Balzac himself did not escape the sacrilegious hands of these Canadian literary iconoclasts!"[12] He allowed that perhaps Ireland should not be as comprehensive as Canada, but insisted that it should adopt "practical means of dealing with immoral or grossly offensive books or magazines, which will save us from the necessity of prosecutions, and the consequent publicity."[13] In addition to adhering to different values, the Irish censorship that Devane proposed would, unlike the trials in Britain, be in camera and thus skirt due process by avoiding the courts. Therefore, just as Irish writers considered their struggles with censorship through an international perspective and sought help from colleagues in other countries, Irish censors cast abroad for models. As for the final remedy, which stemmed from the three others and was pertinent to the revisions to the censorship of films, he argued that advertisements should also be subjected to the legislation. In conclusion, Devane claimed that for these four remedies to be adopted through legislation, there must be a resolute organisation of religious groups to pressure the government to act.[14] Such action, he said, adopting the parental guise of the censor, would protect "our youth from corruption by a debased press that mistakes license for liberty."[15]

Soon thereafter, a special subcommittee of the Catholic Truth Society of Ireland (CTSI) was organised to assess censorship legislation in other countries and to suggest how it might be effected in Ireland, thereby forming "a new offensive movement on behalf of morality."[16] That summer, the subcommittee reported its findings to the CTSI executive and sent copies of a draft bill to the Catholic hierarchy for its approval.[17] Bishops then visited O'Higgins to discuss such legislation in January 1926, just after the passage of the second Censorship of Films Act. Suggesting that the control of film should be a step towards the control of print media, *The Leader* informed its readers that the "new censorship of movie pictures is now in operation and we hope it will work satisfactorily. What about some sort of censorship on imported dirty papers[?] ... Why not forbid their entry into the State altogether?"[18] As a nationalist paper, *The Leader* was particularly focused in its attacks on indecent literature crossing the border from England and threatening Irish morality. Confronted by government inaction, it pleaded with the IVA to remedy the situation.[19] Furthermore, it called for the youth of Ireland to join the IVA and the CTSI to help establish greater Irish freedom from alien influences, hoping that efforts would result in a "new literary school." This new literature would be in accordance with Catholic values and present Irish life in a way that would, reflecting their allegiance to the doctrine of idealism, "raise us, brighten us, and make us proud once more of our country."[20]

These cases for a censorship based on Catholic, nationalist values were given considerable support by the eruption of controversy when the Abbey Theatre staged Sean O'Casey's *The Plough and the Stars* in February 1926. While his first two plays, *The Shadow of a Gunman* (1923) and *Juno and the Paycock* (1924), had been wildly successful, the situation had recently changed at the Abbey, with the government granting it an £850 annual subsidy. This gave the theatre considerable freedom to produce plays by making commercial concerns less of a factor in staging and selection, but it came with a quid pro quo that the government would now appoint a member to the Abbey's board of directors. Although ostensibly chosen as a financial guardian, George O'Brien "quickly assumed the role of censor."[21] Upon reading *The Plough and the Stars*, O'Brien was convinced that it would be successful, but worried that there were elements of it that "would seriously offend the audience" and thus believed "that it must be amended."[22] Of particular concern was a suggestive love scene between Jack and Nora Clitheroe, the prostitute Rosie Redmond's overt sexuality, and the curse words and "salty phrases" peppered throughout the play.[23] Yeats agreed that the love scene was "most objectionable," telling O'Brien that they would attend to revising it in rehearsals, but he and the other directors defended Rosie and the pub scene as they juxtapose the characters' squalor against the idealist, nationalist discourse of the Voice, the character whose lines, audibly spoken offstage, were taken directly from the writings of Patrick Pearse.[24] Fearing a showdown, Lady Gregory believed that her and Yeats's position was "clear": "If we have to choose between the subsidy and our freedom, it is our freedom we choose." She reminded O'Brien that "there was no condition attached to the subsidy" and that "there was no word at all about his being a censor."[25]

Despite these behind-the-scenes concerns, *The Plough and the Stars* premiered with no controversy and to much acclaim on 8 February 1926, with advanced bookings breaking Abbey records.[26] Among the Dublin glitterati in attendance were the writers F. R. Higgins, Liam O'Flaherty, Lennox Robinson, A. E. Malone, Oliver St. John Gogarty, and Yeats, the politicians Ernest Blythe and Kevin O'Higgins, and Chief Justice Hugh Kennedy. Despite qualms about the pub scene, it was "longly applauded," and the entire play was followed with "feverish interest," ending with the players repeatedly called back and O'Casey appearing on stage to an ovation.[27] Yet during the intermission, James Montgomery, Ireland's official film censor, confided that he was glad to be off duty, and while Yeats had wined and dined Blythe, Kennedy, and O'Higgins beforehand, accompanied them to the show, and introduced them to the actors, neither of the latter two liked the play.[28] Such misgivings by leading government officials suggested that although the public welcomed the newest play by the country's hottest dramatist, authorities harboured reservations that boded ill for freedom of expression.

On the fourth night, several women who had lost men in the Easter Rising sat in the audience. Among them were the widow of Tom Clarke, Pearse's mother, Kevin Barry's sister, and the notable feminist Hanna Sheehy-Skeffington, whose husband Francis had been wrongly executed. They had come to protest the pub scene, believing that the appearance of the nationalist tricolour flag in a pub and Rosie cavorting with men about to engage in the Rising was a desecration. When the curtain lifted on the second act, "pandemonium" broke out as the women "shouted, booed and sang," "shocking epithets" were hurled at the actress playing Rosie, and nationalists sang "The Soldiers Song" from the balcony.[29] In response, others cheered and applauded to support the players, the noise from both parties drowning out the dialogue and forcing the actors to end the scene in dumb show. By the third act, the audience cracked under the tension, leading people to charge the stage. One man hit an actress, and as he turned on another, an actor stepped in and punched the man, sending him flying into the wings. For her part, Sheehy-Skeffington scolded the actors, telling them that if they were real men, they would refuse to play their parts, and that they only had to sing "God Save the King" to complete their treason.[30] During the scuffle, Yeats pushed to the front of the stage. Drawing a parallel with the riots provoked by J. M. Synge's *The Playboy of the Western World*, he scolded the audience: "Is this going to be a recurring celebration of Irish genius? Synge first, and then O'Casey! The news of the happenings of the last few minutes here will flash from country to country. Dublin has once more rocked the cradle of a reputation. From such a scene in this theatre went forth the fame of Synge. Equally the fame of O'Casey is born here tonight. This is his apotheosis."[31] Police were then called in to clear the theatre of the protestors and restore order.

Shortly thereafter, gunmen showed up at one of the actors' homes to kidnap him, but he was thankfully out at the time. This led to the Abbey keeping the players in the green room between the Saturday matinee and evening performances.[32] When they sought to revive the play a couple of months later, a group of "anti-Casey republicans" threatened to blow up the theatre; Yeats and Robinson ensured that they were equipped with fire extinguishers, but decided against informing the others to prevent the production from being kiboshed and a more general panic from ensuing.[33] O'Casey, however, revelled in the notoriety and success. In his own account of the events, he cast Yeats as "an aged Cuchullain in his hero-rage," "confronting all those who cursed and cried out shame and vengeance on the theatre, as he conjured up a vision for them of O'Casey on a cloud ... rising upwards to Olympus to get from the waiting gods and goddesses a triumphant apotheosis for a work well done in the name of Ireland and of art."[34] In the end, the widely reported protests led to O'Casey, his play, and the Abbey gaining in celebrity and reaping the financial rewards of the controversy.

In the weeks that followed, O'Casey and Sheehy-Skeffington debated in the pages of the national press. Sheehy-Skeffington, who, as we will see, would become instrumental in anti-censorship campaigns, protested against freedom of speech in this case. Yet she was careful to emphasize that her protest was not "directed to the moral aspect of the play. It was on national grounds solely, voicing a passionate indignation against the outrage of a drama staged in a supposedly national theatre, which held up to derision and obloquy the men and women of Easter Week." She charged that O'Casey's realism was the sort "that would paint not only the wart on Cromwell's nose, but that would add carbuncles and running sores in a reaction against idealization," and that only in Ireland "could a State-subsidised theatre presume on popular patience to the extent of making a mockery and a byword of a revolutionary movement on which the present structure claims to stand." Yet she was adamant that she was not calling for official intervention, stating that "The only censorship that is justified is the free censorship of popular opinion."[35]

In response, O'Casey said that, having spoken with some of the republican women protestors, he had discovered "that the National tocsin of alarm was sounded because some of the tinsel of sham was shaken from the body of truth." To their objection to the tricolour appearing in a public house because one had supposedly never been in such a place, he noted how he had seen it "painted on a lavatory," "flown from some of the worst slums in Dublin," and "thrust from a window of a she-been." As for the charge that his play dimmed the memory of the rebel martyrs by showing men who fought with fear, he countered that had they not been afraid, "what is the use of sounding forth their praises? If they knew no fear, then the fight of Easter Week was an easy thing, and those who participated deserve to be forgotten in a day, rather than to be remembered for ever." As politicians were able to express themselves freely, he insisted, "I claim the liberty in Drama that they enjoy on the platform (and how they do enjoy it!), and am prepared to fight for it."[36]

Following the incidents of the opening week and the exchanges in the national press, a public debate between them was scheduled, with throngs of people filling Dublin's Mills Hall to overflowing capacity. For the most part, O'Casey and Sheehy-Skeffington simply rehashed what they had already said in their letters to the press, but the occasion allowed others to join in the fray. In the end, the meeting was a peaceful and orderly affair held "in the best of good humour" with each participant "taking or receiving hard hits in their turn."[37] As good-humoured as he might have been, O'Casey left Ireland for good shortly afterwards, now seeing that Cathleen ni Houlihan "could be a bitch at times."[38] Joan FitzPatrick Dean has argued that the backroom battle over *The Plough and the Stars* between Lady Gregory, Yeats, and Robinson on one side and O'Brien on the other helped to ensure that Ireland did not enact a theatre censorship.[39] However, the incident underlined the links between censorship, Catholic morality, and nationalism that would inform the debates on literary censorship in Ireland and, more importantly in the years that would follow, how that censorship would be exercised.

The Committee on Evil Literature

While the theatre was spared, literature became the new target for censorship. On 12 February 1926, the day after the riot at the Abbey over *The Plough and the Stars*, with the ground prepared by the Catholic press, religious sodalities, and the passage of the second Censorship of Films Act, O'Higgins, who had seen and disapproved of O'Casey's play earlier that week, appointed a five-member Committee on Evil Literature (CEL) "to consider and report whether it is necessary or advisable in the interest of public morality to extend the existing powers of the State to prohibit or restrict the sale and circulation of printed matter."[40] The CEL was composed of Robert Donovan (professor of English literature at University College Dublin), William Edward Thrift (professor of physics at Trinity College Dublin, and an independent TD), Father James Dempsey, the Reverend T. Sinclair Stevenson, and Thomas J. O'Connell (a member of the Irish National Teachers' Organisation). In a demonstration of pluralism as it was understood in the early years of post-independence Ireland, two of the members were Protestant and three were Catholic; in keeping with the tradition of censorship being a patriarchal institution, all were male; and reflecting the didactic and moral imperatives of censorship, three were educators and two were religious leaders.

Soon after its formation, the CEL issued an invitation for the public to submit "a summary of the evidence and recommendations which they proposed to offer."[41] Several groups, including the Marian Sodalities of Ireland; the Irish Retail Newsagents', Booksellers' and Stationers' Association; the Catholic Writers' Guild; and the Garda Síochána (the Irish national police force), sent representatives or submitted statements. In addition, special invitations were sent to Father Devane and a number of religious organisations, meaning that censorship was a foregone conclusion; it was only a matter of determining whether the status quo would be maintained or the government would create a more restrictive institution. The opportunity to stand before the CEL was thus interpreted as an occasion to affect the way the institution would function, and not as a means to challenge its establishment. Indeed, that Father Devane was the sole individual contacted to give testimony provides further ballast to the claim that he and O'Higgins worked in conjunction to establish in Ireland an institutional censorship of literature.

In advance of their appearance, the IVA submitted a summary of evidence related to publications in Ireland. Formed to combat evil literature, the IVA, despite asking Dublin newsagents "to sign a pledge against stocking or selling objectionable papers," had little success because "the lure of gain overcame" any "sense of righteousness." They argued that the futility of their campaign proved the necessity of establishing an institutional censorship with the authority and power to enforce the law, especially as "the evil literature problem (which is prima facie a moral one) ... is more pressing than ever."[42]

Representing the Irish National Teachers' Organisation (INTO) at the CEL's hearings on 21 April 1926, W. B. Joyce, who was heavily involved with the IVA and later became a member of the Censorship of Publications Board, echoed the sentiments of the IVA on the necessity of censorship. Joyce argued that the current law was ineffective and that the Judicial Proceedings Bill, which was then being discussed in Westminster and was later enacted to render it unlawful to publish "indecent medical, surgical or physiological details" that emerged from reporting on legal proceedings and were "calculated to injure public morals," did not go far enough.[43] He also praised Sir William Joynson-Hicks, the British home secretary, but noted that Joynson-Hicks did not have the mechanisms at his disposal to properly tackle indecent literature. While Joyce thought that birth control literature should be banned outright and that "authors like Balzac and Rabelais" were dangerous, the greatest threat was modern writers. "Compared with these," he said, "Rabelais is to my mind an innocent. ... There are of course some bad Irish writers of whom Joyce is the worst."[44] Whereas the classics might discuss or introduce matters pertaining to sex, he considered them more discreet as they guided readers to act appropriately in their own lives. Modern writers, in contrast, "exaggerate the sex interest and set it before the other phases of life."[45]

At one point during Joyce's appearance, the matter of better educating the public was suggested as perhaps the best preventative measure against evil literature. Cultured people, Thrift noted, tended to pass over this class of publication. As a teacher, Joyce admitted that education was important; however, he argued, young people did not have sophisticated discriminating powers. Yet later in his appearance he testified that as a teacher he had never found a student in possession of an objectionable book.[46] This suggests a number of possibilities pertaining to evil literature in Ireland: one, the booksellers and librarians were in fact doing their jobs properly by not letting evil literature get into the hands of youths; two, the presence and threat of evil literature in Ireland had been greatly exaggerated; three, youths did in fact have the necessary discriminating powers Joyce claimed they lacked; four, youths were smart enough to keep such literature hidden away from authority figures; or five, some combination of the four. However, he insisted that "we cannot wait for the spread of culture" because "immoral reading is not confined to the uneducated." Culture, then, was appealed to in the sense of a high, national culture distinct from the popular culture of the masses. As with Magennis in the debates on film censorship, Joyce illustrated the anxiety inherent in the nation-building of a newly independent country. Legislation was needed for the people, it was argued, "to prevent temptation being thrown in their way." No challenges to this rationale were offered by the members of the CEL, and at no point did they raise the importance of free will, thereby suggesting that they shared the same beliefs.

The one group that posed somewhat of a challenge to the structure of institutionalised censorship was the Catholic Writers' Guild. Representing the guild, Padraig de Burca questioned the need for a secretive censorship board. Instead, he argued, cases should be tried before a jury, as this was the right of all people charged with criminal acts. The CEL concluded that de Burca therefore respected "that remnant of the British Constitution" in Ireland, implying that he somehow valued British law more than a law of Irish making. De Burca defended himself from this charge, stating, "I would rely on a jury of my countrymen." While the existing censorship law was borrowed from British law, which had been legislated in part by Irish members of Parliament, it would be locally interpreted according to the norms and mores of Irish people. This is both the benefit and the frustration of the relative nature of the term *obscene*. The CEL, however, attacked what its members viewed as a challenge to institutional censorship. Donovan, for example, asked de Burca if he did not "fear that one of the twelve would be lacking in moral rectitude." Likewise, Thrift claimed "that a great deal of the public confidence in juries has been shaken by the history of jury action in Ireland."[47] De Burca rejected these points by noting that citizens took the risk of one member of a jury lacking in moral rectitude every day and that he did not feel that the public confidence in juries had been shaken for it. In fact, the nature of Donovan's and Thrift's questions suggests that it was *their* confidence in juries that had been shaken and that they sought to control outcomes. The CEL therefore all but pronounced that a parental, top-down censorship must be established to act in the interests of the Irish people, who were not equipped to determine what they themselves should read.

Unsurprisingly, when the CEL published its final report on 28 December 1926, it concluded that the existing laws were inadequate.[48] This was supported by the testimony given by almost all of the people who appeared before the inquiry as well as a statement of evidence provided by the Gardaí.[49] In addition to the witnesses, the CEL considered legislation in Britain, Canada, the United States, France, Australia, New Zealand, and South Africa. The greatest concerns were summarised as the ineffectiveness of the laws arising from interpretations of the terms *indecent* and *obscene,* and the wide circulation of immoral publications and birth control literature. According to the CEL, the main challenge arose from the fact that only the most "grossly obscene" cases were prosecuted and charged, while magistrates and prosecutors tended to be laxer "in cases of a less obvious character."[50] The charge was thus that the law was not harsh enough on those who propagated obscene and indecent publications. However, the system was considered faulty not merely in its laws, but also in its guiding philosophy by presuming that a charged party was considered innocent until proven guilty. The report suggested that it was rather more appropriate to treat those who were indicted as guilty until proven innocent. This lack of balance was once again the product of whom the CEL had testify before it, who composed the CEL, and whose evidence it chose to include in its decision and report.

While much of the focus was on contraceptive "propaganda," the CEL also discussed its views of literary censorship. It noted that some witnesses would only offer readers Bowdler's edition of Shakespeare, while others claimed that "nobody" would be so "ridiculous" as to ban Shakespeare and the classics.[51] The schism, they reasoned, was directly tied to people's assumptions of the potential readers, some envisioning young girls and youths, others envisioning "persons of mature minds."[52] The CEL warned that the state should not be so narrow as to focus on an imagined readership of young girls for what is permissible. Yet they charged that "many contemporary writers exercise a licence much less controlled by concern for the accepted moral standards than did their predecessors. In their choice of subject and in the mode of treatment there are far less reserve and reticence than there were formerly observed."[53] The focus on young readers and recent literature reveals the tension between an old-guard conservative morality and a new-guard counter-morality in competition for the souls of the next generation. This was precisely the same tension that had been evident in the censorship struggles of earlier decades, as we have seen with George Moore and Bernard Shaw. With the switch from Britain to a newly independent Ireland, such concerns appear more pressing because they are intermingled with the nation-building process and the direction and shape that morality will have in forming citizens.

The CEL made several recommendations towards establishing institutional censorship in Ireland. The first and perhaps most important among them was for broader legal interpretation of the terms *indecent* and *obscene* that would make banning evil literature significantly easier. To assist with the work, a censorship board should be created "consisting of from nine to twelve persons, representative of the religious, educational and literary or artistic interests" of the country, who would suggest bans to the minister for justice.[54] Morality would thus be established by people from a range of backgrounds. The report was clear that censorship "should not extend to questions of a political or economic kind," but how this was to be regulated and ensured was not addressed.[55] Birth-control literature, it suggested, should not be banned outright, although its circulation should be tightly controlled and restricted to authorised persons only, meaning mainly those in the medical professions. It also asked that greater powers be granted to the Gardaí so that they had the right to obtain warrants and enter premises where indecent publications were kept with the intent to sell them. Finally, it sought to extend powers to the customs authorities to block the importation of banned publications and the postal authorities to refuse delivery of indecent publications.

Although Irish writers failed to present a case for artistic licence and freedom of expression, the *Irish Statesman*, under the editorship of AE, was vocal in its opposition to a strenuous censorship. In the time between the CEL's sittings and the publication of the report, the paper underlined its moderate position in admitting that "there is evil literature," while warning that the "history of censorships in Europe has recorded the suppression of much fine literature."[56] To this end, it said that the report, and any legislation drafted in its wake, should be judged by the scope it granted the censorship and "the precision with which what is evil is defined," and concluded by doubting whether any country that had attempted "to make its people virtuous by legislation" had "any perceptible results."[57]

When the report was published in February 1927, the *Irish Statesman* applauded the censorship of base and salacious crime reporting, but lamented that literature was considered through the same lens. "The greatest masters of literature have always claimed freedom to deal with any aspect of life," it pronounced, "and we owe to that unfrightened intelligence, that penetrating vision, and all-exploring genius unforgettable wisdom about human nature."[58] It was not literature but rather narrow-minded groups who sought to censor literature that constituted the greater danger. As evidence, AE pointed to the crippling of English drama by the censorship of theatre, while in Ireland, where there was no censorship of plays, "we produced the most dramatic literature in Europe."[59] Censorship only made writers timid by impinging upon creativity and shackling the soul. "You cannot make literature out of undiluted sweetness," he added, "any more than you can have light in a picture without equal and contrasted shade."[60] The virtue of the soul was rather to stand between darkness and light and make its choice. While the *Irish Statesman* offered these comments for legislators to consider alongside the report, neither AE nor such high-profile kindred spirits as Yeats submitted a statement of evidence to or gave testimony before the CEL. Their policy of waiting to see the tenor of the report before commenting on the issue was an abdication of duty, and it is odd that they considered their polemical writings to carry more weight than their possible involvement in the process. They had intervened too late, and the template for a literary censorship in Ireland was already set.

Introducing the Censorship of Literature

A year after the CEL published its report, Catholic organisations began to worry that legislation would not be tabled. Frank O'Reilly, the secretary of the CTSI, wrote to William T. Cosgrave asking whether he would use his influence as the head of government to introduce a law to address censorship.[61] A few months later, the IVA similarly inquired as to whether such action was forthcoming.[62] Cosgrave advised the groups to be circumspect and reassured them that work was progressing, but that legislation takes time to draft.[63]

While these initiatives were important indicators of the mood in religious quarters, the first renewed campaign for the censorship of evil literature can be traced to an article that appeared in the February

1928 issue of the *Irish Rosary*, a periodical that was edited by Dominicans and belonged to the IVA.[64] Written under the title "The Modern Sex Novelists," the author praised James Douglas, a Northern Irishman who had recently published in the London-based *Daily Express* an invective against the spectral image of the pervert-writer in calling for a rigorous censorship. Douglas was "reviled by the literary intelligentsia and many of his Fleet Street colleagues."[65] Rather colourfully, Ezra Pound once told the Cumann na nGaedheal politician Desmond FitzGerald that Ireland should ban "the writings of that abysmal shit James Douglas" and hoped that he might soon be "decapitated."[66] Yet Douglas was "revered around [England's] breakfast tables as a torch-bearer of propriety and good sense."[67] Building on Douglas's work and blending the public health argument with the paternal duty of censors, the *Irish Rosary* claimed that "some of the most filthy and notorious of sex novelists belong to the Irish pagan clique" and "that many Irish women and girls borrow the novels of these salacious writers from the circulating libraries, and gloat over them at home."[68] As evidenced in the testimony given before the CEL, the problem of indecent literature was not solely found in foreign countries, with Irish writers apportioned responsibility for immoral writing and for posing a threat to the country's female population. The article thus highlights a significant aspect of the international dialectic of censorship, with the *Irish Rosary* using a Northern Irishman's article, published in England, to create a moral panic and thus instigate censorship legislation in Ireland. As the journal's name, *Irish Rosary*, attests, Ireland and Catholicism were often conflated, and those who did not exhibit Catholic morality were necessarily cast as others, even if they were putatively of the tribe.

The *Irish Rosary* continued its appeal for censorship with an article by Robert Kirkwood, who noted that the dangers of immoral literature were being tackled by the work of the CTSI. However, he admitted that despite their indefatigable efforts, the problem persisted because of the sheer number of publications. The real issue, he claimed, was not overtly filthy papers, but the more subtle literature, such as "new books and plays that tried to inculcate false systems of philosophy, false ideas of morality and false teachings of science."[69] As with many crusaders against modern literature, he targeted realist writers in particular. Such writers "would have us believe that there was no need to stem the tide of Evil Literature, because life in Catholic Ireland was every bit as that portrayed in this self-same Evil Literature."[70] Evil literature was thus understood to be as much a product of Ireland as it was of England or France or any other country, with no nation holding a monopoly on obscenity. Echoing the debates surrounding the struggles of Joyce,

MacNamara, and Robinson in the preceding decade, Kirkwood suggested that the danger of the Irish artist was that they portrayed Irish life in a wholly negative light, leading the reading public to have negative views of the nation. As such, the images of the realist artist were as false as the images of the romantic writer. Therefore, he concluded, "He deserves to go – and speedily. He is undermining the defence."[71] Although realist and romantic writers were similarly charged with presenting false images of Ireland, it was only the realist that must be cast out because they undermined the defence and weakened the spirit of the nation. Like a diseased tumour that infects the body politic, the realist must be removed so that they do not spread their harmful ideas to other parts, thereby causing irreversible damage and perhaps even destroying society. Such thinking had led, in part, to the exile of Moore, Shaw, Joyce, and O'Casey, the near kidnapping of MacNamara, and the firing of Robinson.

There was therefore discernible relief in the Catholic press when, on 19 July 1928, James Fitzgerald-Kenney, the minister for justice, introduced the Censorship of Publications Bill.[72] When it resumed in October after the summer recess, the Dáil debated the proposed legislation over the course of three days. Foremost among the changes that the bill enacted on the CEL's recommendations was the composition of the Censorship Board. Believing that a large censorship board would slow the machinery and that having only one censor would place an unfair burden upon an individual, the government proposed a committee of five members.[73] In examining publications, the Censorship Board was asked to keep in mind that it was assessing the property of a publisher and a writer. It then had to balance this in consideration with the "duty to the public to see that demoralising and degrading literature" would not circulate in the country.[74] However, Fitzgerald-Kenney provided an important instructive caveat: "A book can be fairly condemned only when in its whole course it makes for evil, when its tenor is bad, when in some important part of it, it is indecent. It must not be condemned if it has here and there one or two exceptional passages."[75] As such, the Censorship Board had to "exercise a judicial discretion."[76] The most significant guiding principle in the bill was that *obscene* and *indecent* were narrowly defined as being tied to notions of "sexual morality" and "sexual perversion."[77]

Although some members of Fianna Fáil voiced concern over the wording of the bill, they wholly endorsed the principle of censorship and the measures that the legislation represented. Most notable among these supporters were P. J. Ruttledge, who later took over as minister for justice and thereby became responsible for censorship, and Éamon de Valera, the future taoiseach (Irish prime minister).[78] Seán Lemass, another future taoiseach, offered the only criticism of the government, but it was merely to lament that it had "been too slow and cautious in introducing a measure of this kind."[79]

Yet there were some meaningful voices of dissent. Professor Michael Tierney, a Cumann na nGaedheal senator who represented the National University, was concerned with the possible advent of an overly zealous censorship that banned books too easily and indiscriminately, fearing that Ireland would make itself a laughingstock. His scepticism of the censorship was well enough known in advance that R. S. Devane wrote to him insisting that "real literature lies in no danger whatsoever from the passage of the Bill into law."[80] Devane also sent him copies of his pro-censorship articles, including the one in the *Irish Ecclesiastical Record* that had set the legislation in motion. Tierney, however, was not reassured. "I have been reading a list of books that have been prohibited in Canada," he said in the Dáil, "and I certainly cannot say that that list is by any means a credit to the Canadian Government."[81] It was, in some ways, a response to Devane, who had admired the Canadian censorship.

Meanwhile, Professor Ernest Alton, an independent TD who represented Trinity College, raised the concern of Irish censorship degrading into a form of cultural isolationism that would effectively cut the country off from the best in contemporary and foreign thought.[82] Hugh Law, who had served on the Joint Select Parliamentary Committee that examined British theatre censorship in 1909 when he was an MP for the Irish Parliamentary Party and now represented Donegal as a Cumann na nGaedheal TD, was likewise sceptical. While he agreed with the censorship of indecent newspapers, he argued that the censorship of books should have been avoided, claiming that the Irish people were a newspaper-reading public, not a book-reading public.[83] William Thrift agreed with Law in insisting on the threat of newspapers as particularly pernicious and in pleading for more discernment when it came to books.[84] For his part, Bryan Cooper, who had been critical of the film censorship, noted that by institutionalising censorship the government would only create an illegal trade in books. "The more stringent you make the penalties," he warned, "the greater the incentive to the literary bootlegger. It will be easier to put a thick volume of Voltaire in your pocket than to produce a dozen bottles of whiskey, and yet in New York bottles of whiskey appear as if by magic."[85] Despite such pleas for caution, the momentum in both society and government at this time was such that they were all but ignored. What is perhaps less recognised is that these critics tended not to be against censorship, but merely the potential form of it being enacted. When the bill was being drafted in the committee stage, Tierney, for example, opposed a motion made by one of his colleagues that would have made all Censorship Board meetings open to the public.[86] Despite this, the IVA attacked Tierney, Law, Thrift, and Alton as attempting to amend the legislation in the debates to aid "the circulation of pernicious literature in this country."[87] As we will see, this demonising of moderates would be a common strategy employed by censorship campaigners.

Meanwhile, other groups continued to work back channels by contacting politicians privately. The CTSI, for one, sent a letter to all deputies denouncing Tierney and Law for proposing to delete the section of the bill prohibiting birth control "propaganda" and for seeking to allow individuals to import prohibited books if they were for personal use.[88] A month later, the CTSI changed tack and wrote to Tierney personally. They claimed that, like him, they sought to strengthen the legislation, but that they disagreed with his way of doing so. To this end, they proposed that Law meet with a deputation of the CTSI to discuss potential amendments.[89] At the same time, Tierney had come under pressure from others, including E. J. Gwynn, the provost of Trinity College Dublin, to push for amendments that would render the legislation more liberal.[90] The Irish Women Citizens' and Local Government Association also lobbied for laxer legislation, informing Tierney that one of their committees was "not convinced" with the claims made in the CEL's report on the circulation of immoral literature, as they had found that it was lower than the levels described.[91] While it is possible that some Irish writers worked behind the scenes, there is no evidence that they agitated for freedom of expression, either individually or collectively, in these more surreptitious ways despite the fact that some TDs and senators, like Hugh Law and Oliver St. John Gogarty, were authors themselves, and many Irish writers, like Yeats and Lady Gregory, had cordial relationships with politicians from across the political spectrum.

Public Actions and Debate

With the Oireachtas engaged in lengthy debates over the fate of the bill, it became increasingly evident that something had to be done to curb the sort of grassroots censorship that took place in Delvin and the turbulence that occurred in the Carnegie Trust. For instance, at the Kilkenny Carnegie Library committee meeting on 19 December 1923, Father Ambrose Coleman, the author of the *Irish Ecclesiastical Record* article that sought to guide library committees on how to assert Irish Catholic values, suggested that the works of Bernard Shaw be withdrawn from circulation. The committee, whose members included priests, politicians, and a librarian, unanimously agreed with Coleman's proposal.[92] Local reaction was not entirely positive, with a *Kilkenny People*'s reporter having at first thought it was a joke. The reporter then wondered whether the committee had actually read Shaw's works and lamented the idea of not being able to read "probably the most brilliant writer for the stage using the English language as a medium of expression" and "the most widely read dramatic author now living."[93] That he was a Protestant, a socialist, and a contrarian had evidently marked Shaw as an author whose work and ideas should not be allowed to infect impressionable citizens.

While the library in Kilkenny merely refused to allow Shaw's works to be borrowed, the public library in Galway was rumoured to have attained a Delvin-esque level in burning his books in October 1928. At the library committee's meeting at the end of the month, Gilbert Lynch, a former Labour TD, demanded to know if the rumours were true. Father O'Dea denied that Shaw's works had been burned but admitted that they had been placed on reserve and were only available for consultation if a person obtained the permission of the committee. However, O'Dea confessed that the archbishop of Tuam, who had been named censor when the library committee took over the buildings and books from the Carnegie Trust in 1924, had burned several books. Lynch was furious that public property had been destroyed and demanded a full list of the burned books. O'Dea was reluctant to comply, suggesting, in an erroneous nod to Catholic doctrine, that the archbishop was infallible.[94] As might be expected, the book burning and committee meeting received coverage in the national press.[95] At the next sitting of the Dáil, William Thrift asked General Richard Mulcahy, the minister for government and public health, to confirm the facts of the case and whether he intended to take any measures to prevent the destruction of similar property in Ireland. Following intense questioning from several TDs who considered the issue important in light of the censorship bill that they were currently discussing, Mulcahy told them that as minister he could only oversee how the library committees spent the tax money they received and ensure that it was not used for any purposes beyond normal expenses. To this, Seán Lemass archly asked: "Such as making bonfires?"[96]

In the meantime, public debate continued in both the Catholic and the secular press. The *Irish Rosary* noted how the bill demanded the consent of at least four members of the Censorship Board to ban a publication.[97] This raised the fear that the Censorship Board could be rendered ineffective by two Protestant members if they were at odds with three

Catholic members. Because of the relatively loose morals that the Catholic press associated with Protestantism, it was only a matter of time before such an occasion, or crisis as they viewed it, occurred. Given that, in the main, censorship was being legislated to protect a largely Catholic Irish nation from the evils of a largely Protestant English press, the conflation here of Protestantism and foreignness is not wholly surprising, especially coming from a sectarian source. *The Standard*, meanwhile, although in a somewhat more subdued manner, praised the bill and the tenor of the Dáil debates.[98]

For their part, AE and the *Irish Statesman* did yeoman's work in presenting liberal critiques of the legislation throughout the late summer and early autumn of 1928.[99] He began his campaign in August and September, which allowed him to attempt to define the terms of the debate before the Dáil returned in October from its summer recess. From the beginning, AE insisted that people could not "be made moral by Act of Parliament. Real virtue exists only when the soul, having vision both of good and evil, exercising free will, chooses what is good. We believe the man who is constrained to be moral and sober by another is no better in the eyes of Heaven than the man who, in practice, is neither moral nor sober."[100] By making the case for free will and the freedom to exercise it, he effectively cast Ireland as an anti-Garden of Eden, one that would not allow citizens the ability to test the mettle of their virtue when confronted with the forbidden fruit. In this sense, the proposed bill would be contrary to God's ways. Arguing the classic liberal position, AE believed that all literature should be allowed to circulate and that through proper competition in the marketplace between good and bad literature, good would inevitably prevail. The onus was rather on the state to provide better education and ensure that good literature was made available. Looking to the United States and Britain, he noted that the only effect of banning *Ulysses* was that doing so advertised the book and caused people who were otherwise ignorant of literature to read it. This was the inevitable fate that awaited books banned in Ireland: popularity by infamy. He feared that it would only result in the country making itself ridiculous in the eyes of the world.

The proposed legislation also set off a flurry of letters to the editor in the *Irish Times*, the sole paper that sided with the *Irish Statesman*. This began at the outset of September with one correspondent suggesting that even watering down the bill would not be beneficial because "there could be no guarantee that, in the course of time, changes would not be made by other parties oppressive to many who are accustomed to use their own free will and discretion as to what they read."[101] Therefore, the bill should be rejected wholesale. Others disagreed, with another correspondent pointing out that all freedoms, including freedom of speech, have limits.[102] For the most part, contributors vacillated between anti-censorship and pro-censorship viewpoints, making the letters-to-the-editor section of the *Irish Times* a proper agora in which all sides could argue their points freely.[103] Yet the paper, showing its own bias, also printed a lengthy commentary that explained Milton's *Areopagitica* and condemned censorship.[104]

A few weeks later, Yeats published an article in the *Irish Statesman* entitled "The Censorship and St. Thomas Aquinas." Taking a religious line similar to AE's, Yeats argued that the bill's definition of *indecent* as that which was "calculated to excite sexual passion" was "ridiculous to a man of letters" and "must be sacrilegious to a Thomist."[105] Yeats found it baffling that the Catholic lawyers who designed the bill could have made such a blunder because the philosophy of St. Thomas was the official philosophy of the Catholic Church. The Church in its artistic renderings of the Virgin Mary had often favoured more sumptuous, maternal figures, not the cold, sexless women of Puritanism. As Thomist Cardinal Mercier once declared, "*Anima est in toto corpore*," meaning "the soul is in the whole body." Unfortunately, Irish politicians and the greater society had ignored this belief, and their Catholicism was at this time infused with a Victorian bourgeois prudery. Yeats thus proposed that they should be forced to study "Titian's *Sacred and Profane Love* and ask themselves if there is no one it could not incite to 'sexual passion.'"[106] He admitted that immoral painting and literature existed and that they were bad art. But it was nonsense to attempt to compel aesthetic judgment with a hard-set definition. Instead, the decision should be left to educated men of letters and art who knew what should be excluded. The heart of his argument was therefore that censorship should be guided by a cabal of artists.

Yeats published another criticism of the censorship legislation, but this time abroad in *The Spectator* on 29 September.[107] While the *Irish Rosary* used Douglas's article, published in England, to provoke a moral panic and censorship legislation in Ireland, it appears as though this was Yeats's attempt to embarrass Ireland abroad and thus force officials to reconsider the issue. In this way, the international dialectic works in the opposite direction by seeking to make censorship less restrictive. Yeats's chief argument was that the TDs who had designed the bill did not believe in the principles it espoused and the mechanisms it sought to put in place. Its definition of *indecency* and the vague phrase "subversive of public morality" would permit the minister for justice "to exclude *The Origin of Species*, Karl Marx's *Capital*, the novels of Flaubert, Balzac, Proust, all of which have been objected to somewhere on moral ground, half the Greek and Roman Classics, Anatole France and everybody else on the Roman index and all great love poetry."[108] Although the government claimed that it did not intend for this to happen, Yeats argued that "in legislation intention is nothing, and the letter of the law everything, and no Government has the right, whether to flatter fanatics or in mere vagueness of mind to forge an instrument of tyranny and say that it will never be used."[109] "I know from plays rejected by the Abbey," he continued, "that the idealist political movement has, after achieving its purpose, collapsed and left the popular mind to its own lawless vulgarity."[110] He ended on a fatalistic note, foreseeing the continued exodus of Irish artists into exile should the state maintain its war against freedom of the intellect by passing the legislation.[111]

In retrospect, one of AE's masterstrokes was to recruit Sean O'Faolain to write an article on censorship, in many ways offering a genealogy of the Irish liberal intellectual and the counter-cultural press, with O'Faolain's *The Bell* later assuming from AE's the *Irish Statesman* the mantle of Ireland's chief socio-political antagonist and literary promoter.[112] Studying towards his MA at Harvard on a Commonwealth Scholarship, O'Faolain was well-placed to offer a comparative perspective as Boston was notorious at the time for a puritanical censorship that was orchestrated by the Catholic Church.[113] The tension in censorship policy, he noted, lies in the compromise between "the ideal of the individual and the need of the masses for ordered community living."[114] He also questioned how any one person, acting as censor, could possibly determine "what did or did not accord with the aims of their people" and claim to be one of the "true interpreters of the civilisation of their century."[115] The effect of the censorship in Boston was that the city was routinely mocked and publishers were rumoured to attempt to have their titles banned there so that they could use the infamy to advance sales elsewhere. Somewhat presciently, O'Faolain suggested that this was the fate in store for Ireland.

Despite such interventions, AE recognised that, in the days ahead of the bill being tabled, some form of literary censorship was inevitable. He therefore turned his attention to concentrating on the form that it would take. In particular, he lamented that the definition of *indecency* was "extraordinary" for its condemnation of any form of natural passion between people. "There should be clear guidance given to the censors," he insisted, "that they are not entitled to range over the whole field of thought, or to pronounce that the doctrine of evolution, and what it implies, is detrimental to public morality, or that socialism or communism or syndicalism or any other isms, however we mislike them, are too evil to be considered by people living in the Free State, and books advocating such social philosophies must not be permitted to be read."[116] He was particularly critical of such religious organisations as the CTSI and the IVA that had withdrawn and burned books, fearing that they would be empowered with the office of a censor. Most troublesome, however, was the fact that decisions would be made in camera and that authors and publishers would not be able to defend themselves before a tribunal, thereby denying them their basic legal rights. In the coming weeks, the *Irish Statesman* maintained a regular focus on the Dáil debates, reporting and commenting on the proceedings. In many ways, the articles became appeals to TDs to make the bill more liberal, AE desiring that the works targeted by the censorship be explicitly pornographic in nature and not be loosely defined as contrary to public morality.[117]

The biggest coup in his campaign was securing an article from Shaw, which AE trumpeted in the issue that preceded its publication, evidently seeking to garner more publicity. "It is quite possible once the measure becomes law that Mr. Shaw's opportunities of addressing Free State audiences will be severely limited," he boomed, noting that "the action of the Galway Public Libraries Committee has proved to a world that is still chuckling over the revelation that the West is very much awake to the necessity of safeguarding the national mind against Shavian contamination. And few things are surer than that the strongest kind of pressure will be used to compel the rest of the country to follow Galway's lead in this matter." Yet AE suggested that while Shaw's books had been taken out of circulation, Shaw, ever the showman and magnet for controversy, would lament "that he has been denied a bonfire."[118]

Shaw opened his polemic by arguing against the belief that people love nothing more than political liberty:

> As a matter of fact there is nothing they dread more. Under the feeble and apologetic tyranny of Dublin Castle we Irish were forced to endure a considerable degree of compulsory freedom. The moment we got rid of that tyranny we rushed to enslave ourselves. ... The latest demonstration of Irish abjectness is the supplanting of constitutional law by the establishment of a Censorship extending in general terms to all human actions, but specifically aimed at any attempt to cultivate the vital passion of the Irish people or to instruct it in any function which is concerned with that passion. It is, in short, aimed at the extermination of the Irish people as such to save them from their terror of life and of one another.[119]

Like Yeats, he saw in the legislation an ironic turn away from Thomist Catholic philosophy and envisioned the destruction of the more attractive images of saints throughout Ireland, the Irish mistakenly conflating "loveliness with debauchery" rather than "loveliness with blessedness."[120] Given such a mentality, even the priest who referred to fertility or homosexuality should be defrocked and cast into hell for eternity. Because of this rejection of knowledge in favour of ignorance, clandestine instruction would flourish, and "everything that is evil in it will be protected and nourished, and everything that is honest and enlightening in it will be discredited and suppressed."[121] Shaw was particularly critical of Ireland's refusal to allow birth-control literature into the country, noting that this would harm, not help, its people. As a result, while the world was interested in Ireland's cause for independence in the nineteenth century, in the twentieth not a soul could care less. The fault, he argued, lay with Irish politicians and "a handful of morbid Catholics, mad with heresyphobia, unnaturally combining with a handful of Calvinists mad with sexphobia."[122] To shake off the chains and to restore greatness to Ireland, the only solution was to force themselves to "face new ideas," prove "all things," and defend all that is good.[123] Upon reading the essay, T. S. Eliot immediately registered his "pleasure" to find himself "in almost complete agreement with anyone so eminent as Shaw."[124]

Yet Shaw's article was not so welcome in other quarters. "Never was there a damper political squib," commented one writer in *The Standard*. Shaw "seemed to think that he was launching a thunderbolt. The thunderbolt is much more akin to a boomerang, for it reveals once more the writer's congenital defects." These defects included a concern for ecclesiastical art that was "only a humorous pretence; he is really anxious lest the contraception propaganda, which is a preliminary to that mechanistic Utopia which he has recently expounded [in *The Intelligent Woman's Guide to Socialism and Capitalism*], should be interfered with."[125] Like Sean O'Casey, Shaw was at this time an easy target in the Catholic press owing to his Protestant, Anglo-Irish background, his avowed left-wing politics, and his work in an artistic profession.

From this point, Shaw and Yeats were to remain publicly silent on the issue of censorship until 1932, when they founded the Irish Academy of Letters, more on which will be said in the next chapter. In the meantime, the Catholic press continued to fight against the bill's critics.[126] Concurrent events in England would also inform the direction of the legislation. Indeed, what occurred in England attests once again that international contexts must be considered to better understand how Irish writers were affected by and resisted censorship as well as how pro-censorship campaigners and politicians similarly turned abroad for inspiration while seeking to stem foreign influences on national culture.

Literature in the Dock

On the surface, the lesbian English author Radclyffe Hall has very little to do with Ireland. Yet the difficulties that she ran into with her novel *The Well of Loneliness* provided important context for Ireland's censorship legislation. Hall's prior novel, *Adam's Breed*, sold twenty-seven thousand copies in its first six months and won both the Femina Vie Heureuse Prize for best English novel and the James Tait Black Memorial Prize for fiction.[127] Despite this success, she had difficulty finding a publisher for *The Well of Loneliness* as editors were wary of taking on a book that dealt explicitly with lesbianism. Jonathan Cape, however, was more amendable, respecting Hall's sales figures and appreciating her innovative work.[128] To frame reception of *The Well of Loneliness*, the press hired the celebrated sexologist Havelock Ellis to write a foreword. Advance publicity in newspapers carried excerpts to drum up sales: "Apart from its fine qualities as a novel by a writer of accomplished art," Ellis wrote, "it possesses a notable psychological and sociological significance."[129] In this way, it was branded as a publishing event, being the first novel that openly and compassionately dealt with lesbian love.

Some critics were sympathetic, seeing the novel as illustrating "the pitiful loneliness of sexual perversity" and believing that, despite its structural and artistic flaws, it was "sincere, courageous, high-minded, and often beautifully expressed."[130] However, not all reviews were so receptive. Unsurprisingly, James Douglas, the Northern Irishman much reviled by modern writers and much beloved by conservatives and the Irish Catholic press, came out against the book. In the 19 August 1928 edition of the *Sunday Express*, he famously wrote: "I would rather give a healthy boy or a healthy girl a phial of prussic acid than this novel. Poison kills the body, but moral poison kills the soul."[131] He was utterly unflinching in his condemnation of homosexuality and its effects on public health and the nation's youth, stating "that sexual inversion and perversion are horrors which exist among us today. They flaunt themselves in public places with increasing effrontery and more insolently provocative bravado. ... The consequence is that this pestilence is devastating the younger generation. It is wrecking their lives. It is defiling their souls."[132] Douglas further noted that the "adroitness and cleverness" of the narrative "intensifies its moral danger. It is a seductive and insidious piece of special pleading designed to display perverted decadence as a martyrdom inflicted upon these outcasts by a cruel society."[133]

What critics have missed in Douglas's invective is that he drew a direct link between the prosecution of Hall's book in England and the censorship legislation being debated in Ireland.[134] Indeed, Douglas suggested that it "may be that the establishment of a similar Censorship Board will be found necessary in this country," although he noted that England's law was "sufficient if it be properly administered" and hoped that Joynson-Hicks would duly prosecute *The Well of Loneliness*.[135] Given Douglas's standing in religious quarters, such polemics in the English press would have encouraged many Irish legislators and emboldened pro-censorship groups to proceed in their attempts to control literature.

In response to the controversy, Cape sent copies of Hall's book to Joynson-Hicks and the director of public prosecutions. He claimed that if the authorities were able to show him "that the best interests of the public will be served by withdrawing the book from circulation," he would do so.[136] In submitting the novel to the authorities, he wished to avoid the sort of prosecution that Vizetelly had incurred. Two days later, Joynson-Hicks asked him to cease publication of the novel, to which Cape agreed.

Hall lamented Cape's decision, noting that the novel did not incite depravity, but rather was "calculated to encourage mutual understanding between normal persons and the inverted, which can only be beneficial to both and to society at large."[137] Like Shaw, she regarded herself as a pioneer who had become a persecuted martyr. Meanwhile, public opinion was decidedly divided. While Lord Beaverbrook's conservative newspapers, including the *Sunday Express*, attacked the book and promoted censorship, the *Daily Herald* promoted anti-Joynson-Hicks sentiment. The home secretary's extrajudicial intervention, which skirted due process and functioned as a "backdoor censorship," was denounced by journalists as well as many of Joynson-Hicks's constituents and erstwhile supporters. Some writers, including E. M. Forster and Virginia Woolf, protested that Hall's novel was "restrained and perfectly decent, and the treatment of its theme" was "unexceptionable."[138] In the weeks that followed, other authors publicly denounced Joyson-Hicks's censorship. Bernard Shaw was blunt: "If this sort of thing is to happen and no protest be made against it, no books will be published at all in England." He had read the novel "carefully" and insisted that "it ought not to have been withdrawn" as it "speaks of certain things that people ought to know about."[139] Given his past struggles, Shaw's preference was for Cape to hold his ground and force the authorities into a highly publicised trial. Yet many of the authors that Hall's lawyers approached "made it clear that they were not going to risk their reputations by showing sympathy with an unpopular cause."[140] In this case, they viewed the cause as lesbianism and not freedom of expression.

Faced with what appeared to be an impossible situation in England, Hall published her book in Paris with Pegasus Press. As shipments landed at Dover, they were seized by British authorities. In response, Pegasus retained counsel to demand the release of the books.[141] Meanwhile, people complained that when returning to Britain from abroad, they had had their personal copies of the novel confiscated despite the fact that no legal decision had been rendered.[142] Joynson-Hicks defended the action by noting that he had "to deal with immoral and disgusting books" and averring that there "must be some limit to the freedom of what a man may write or speak in this great country of ours."[143]

Two days later, debate began in the Dáil on the Censorship of Publications Bill. With Hall's book and its treatment by authorities being covered in the pages of the British press, they informed Ireland's own censorship debates. The *Irish Rosary* complimented James Douglas's attacks while within a matter of weeks Shaw made public statements on both Hall's situation and the Irish legislation. Moreover, Irish newspapers reported on Hall's case for their own readers. From Cork to Belfast, the Irish read that Cape had ceased publication of the novel in bending to the wishes of the Home Office.[144] There was also front-page coverage of the seizure of the imported copies from Paris.[145] *The Well of Loneliness* was even reviewed in Ireland, although quite negatively, with *The Independent* lamenting in terms redolent of James Douglas that the book "discloses sins that up to this have been hid from novel readers and sins which had better been left in their obscene obscurity."[146] Attesting to the book's renowned contentiousness, J. J. Byrne, a Cumann na nGaedheal TD representing Dublin North, suggested during the Dáil censorship debates that the legislation should allow for the banning of such books as D. H. Lawrence's *Lady Chatterley's Lover*, Flaubert's *Salammbô*, and Hall's *The Well of Loneliness*.[147] The case was therefore important not only for providing people of all opinions with an example of a wrongful or a just censorship, but also for influencing politicians on the shape that Irish censorship should take.

Just as those first Dáil debates on the Irish Censorship of Publications Bill ended, rumours spread that the Home Office was going to take action against the sale and distribution of the novel.[148] By the end of October, a summons was issued against Jonathan Cape and Pegasus Press, and a trial was set for 9 November to determine whether the 247 seized copies of *The Well of Loneliness* should be destroyed.[149] Hall joined Cape and Pegasus's London representative in the Bow Street Police Court, where the prosecutors and defence attorneys both admitted that the book was skilfully written, and even the presiding magistrate agreed with the defence that it "contained matter for great public good."[150] However, when Desmond MacCarthy, one of the day's foremost literary critics, was called by the defence to give his views on the novel, the magistrate refused to admit opinion as evidence, thereby excluding the testimony of the many authors, booksellers, educationists, and librarians that the defence had intended to call as witnesses. For their part, the prosecution limited itself to contending that the book's theme of "the physical and sexual relations between Lesbian women" was obscene.[151] A week later, the magistrate rendered his verdict: the book was an obscene libel, and it must be destroyed. Whether or not it was well written was irrelevant: "The more palatable the poison," he argued in terms reminiscent of Douglas, "the more insidious."[152] When Jonathan Cape and Pegasus Press launched an appeal, they were unsuccessful, with the presiding judge declaring that he considered the book "disgusting," "obscene," "dangerous," and "corrupting."[153] As with the initial reception of the book, the trial and the appeal were widely reported in Irish newspapers.[154]

As British authorities ended one controversy with the burning of *The Well of Loneliness*, another emerged that would likewise hang over the Irish censorship debates. On 20 February 1929, the very day that the Dáil resumed deliberating the censorship legislation, Scotland Yard seized several hundred copies of Norah C. James's *Sleeveless Errand*.[155] James's novel tells of the final forty-eight hours in the life of a young woman, who, having been deserted by her lover, is determined to commit suicide. Before she does, she meets a young man who is distraught over his wife's infidelity. Together, they roam the underworld of London, drinking in bars across the city before killing themselves. James addressed the media, claiming that her novel was "in no way immoral" and suggesting that the only possible justification for "the seizure is the frank language the book contains." She argued that the English were "hypocritical," for as "long as you say what you mean you are condemned, but if you only hint at it you are considered clever, and it passes the censor."[156] The novel's publisher, Eric Partridge, who was issued a summons to appear before the magistrate in Bow Street Police Court, was "dumbfounded," knowing "no earthly reason why it should not be published."[157] As with Radclyffe Hall's trials, the case was followed closely in the Irish press.[158]

The seizure of James's novel was raised in Parliament later that week. Harry Day, a Labour MP and the former manager of the magician Harry Houdini, asked Joynson-Hicks exactly how many books had been confiscated over the course of the first two months of 1929. Admitting that six had been "intercepted," Joynson-Hicks then deflected by noting that he had also seized "photographs and all kinds of matter of a very unpleasant character." Yet he said that he did not "in any sense exercise a literary censorship," narrowly defining the term as a process by which "every book should be read by the body of censors." When he was notified of *Sleeveless Errand*, he merely informed the director of public prosecutions, who then applied for and obtained a warrant. Members of Parliament questioned whether this was the best way of handling "clearly obscene publications." One believed that the censorship should be "formally appointed" rather than implemented through "this indirect means," while another rejected Joynson-Hicks's sophistry, insisting that he was, in fact, a censor.[159]

On 4 March, James and Partridge appeared in court. The prosecutor presented *Sleeveless Errand* as "told in a form of conversations by persons entirely devoid of decency and morality, who ... tolerated promiscuity." Furthermore, he added, "Blasphemy is freely indulged in by practically all the characters, and filthy language and indecent situations appear to be the keynote." In response, the defence attorney claimed that the book's objective was "to hold up to horror the mode of life, language and habits of a certain section" of society. He emphasized the fluid nature of morality, and that what was written in the book was true of a different generation than what the authors of the 1857 Obscene Publications Act had in mind.[160] The old debates on realism were resuscitated once again, pitting on one side the view that the purpose and effects of such literature were to debase, corrupt, and deprave people, against, on the other side, the view that such works merely held the mirror up to nature. The issue boiled down to two fundamental aspects. The first was whether obscenity was found in the literature that represented society or in the society that was reflected in the literature. The second was whether the duty of literature was to uplift and idealise or to reveal society's ills and possibly provoke reform. In the end, the magistrate ordered the destruction of the 517 seized copies.[161]

As it happens, one of the presses that had rejected James's book was Jonathan Cape. James first approached Cape with her book as she had been their publicist since 1926. Edward Garnett, the banned writer of *The Breaking Point* and veteran of the 1907–9 campaign, was at this time Cape's main editor, and he had written a "glowing report" recommending that Cape publish *Sleeveless Errand*. However, Cape demurred, suggesting that other authors might become jealous if their publicist's book became a success, suspicious that she was promoting her own work over theirs.[162] Always helpful to talented writers, Garnett suggested that James contact Partridge at Scholartis Press, while telling Partridge that *Sleeveless Errand* was "very well written" as "a real diagnosis of the War generation's neurotics." "The author's technique," he noted, "is admirable."[163]

In Paris, Jack Kahane had caught wind of its fortunes and Garnett's admiration. A friend of Sylvia Beach, Kahane saw that there was a market for novels that had been banned in England and knew that by living in France he would be protected from the reach of English law. Following the trials of Hall and James, Kahane sent a notice that appeared in London papers announcing that he was prepared to publish any book with literary merit that had been banned in England. Over the course of his career, he would have a major impact on the world of letters, publishing Henry Miller's *Tropic of Cancer* and Lawrence Durrell's *The Black Book*, scandalous classics by the Marquis de Sade and John Cleland, and several Irish books, including James Joyce's *Pomes Penyeach* and *Haveth Childers Everywhere* and Frank Harris's *My Life and Loves*.[164] It was a trade that was carried on by his son Maurice Girodias, who published Vladimir Nabokov's *Lolita* and William S. Burrough's *Naked Lunch*; like his father, Girodias also published daring books by Irish authors, notably Samuel Beckett's novel *Watt* and his Molloy trilogy, and J. P. Donleavy's *The Ginger Man*.[165] Over the years, many of these titles would be banned in Ireland.

By the end of March, Kahane had secured a deal to publish *Sleeveless Errand*.[166] To drum up business, he paid Garnett to write an introduction. Running just a little over two pages, Garnett's preface summarised the trial and suppression of the novel, taking issue with Joynson-Hicks for being "zealous in his mission to clear out the literary Augean stable."[167] It lacked the vigour and weight of Shaw's prefaces or even the preface to *The Breaking Point*, but Garnett's support as one of London's leading editors was important for a first-time novelist whom the law had effectively labelled as obscene.

If the novel was a cautionary tale for its readers, then perhaps its afterlife – the seizure, the trial, and the publicity they garnered, coupled with its publication and success abroad – could have served as a cautionary tale for its censors. For English publishers, it warned them once again that they had to tread carefully when handling challenging subjects and frank writing; for censors, it served as a notice that their efforts to suppress a book could contribute to its celebrity. Scholars of British modernism have argued that these cases, taken together, represented the attempts of authorities to control the sexual liberation of women that was unleashed by wartime conditions and how literature sought to represent such issues.[168] For Irish politicians, the English cases suggested that their own legislation was a step in the right, more prudent direction as it protected the minister for justice by creating an independent Censorship Board as opposed to leaving him open to charges, as happened to Joynson-Hicks, of acting as a one-man censorship. These English obscenity cases thus form part of the larger context of Irish censorship legislation. Indeed, they reflect the international dialectic of censorship in demonstrating how censorship controversies in one polity can inform legislation and controversy in another and at times even incorporate some of the same people.

Irish Legislation and Its Reception

When the Dáil resumed its debates on the censorship bill, TDs were particularly anxious about how the term *indecent* would be interpreted. There was also much discussion of the nature of complaints, how they could be lodged, and who could lodge them.[169] Of particular concern were the questions of whether books had to be read in their entirety, something that would repeatedly be an issue in the succeeding decades, and whether birth-control literature needed to be explicitly included or if it was covered by *obscenity* and *indecency*.[170] The latter provided fodder for discussing what exactly was meant by "principles contrary to public morality" and how this phrase could or even should be defined. Meanwhile, some cautious deputies worried that the legislation would enable busybodies, fanatics, and cranks to decide what others should and could not read in the privacy of their own homes.[171]

Fitzgerald-Kenney introduced the bill in the Seanad on 10 April.[172] It was fitting that Sir John Keane, who for many years would be a major opponent of institutional censorship, provided the opening speech.[173] His introduction set the tenor for what was to follow and highlighted the deficiencies in the level of the Dáil debates: "It has been said by some people of consequence that so popular is this measure in the country, and so influential are the forces behind it, that anybody who has the temerity to oppose it in principle will no longer be acceptable in public life."[174] His main concern was that in the past the state had been preoccupied with hygiene in the physical world, including the cleanliness of food, farms, and cities. He thus suggested that they should proceed with caution because censorship involved a move towards the state's control of hygiene of the mind. While he emphasized that "indecency" is a concept that is relative to cultural and historical contexts, he admitted that modern literature posed a distinct problem. But this was a rhetorical strategy. As an obsession with the sexual is imbricated in modern literature, Keane claimed, the only truly effective means of prohibiting publications was to burn all books wholesale, otherwise *some* questionable literature would inevitably invade and infect the body politic.

The bill's focus on the sexual was further flawed as it allowed for what Keane memorably called "the camouflage of sex." In effect, the expression of the sexual could be claimed as the cause of a book's banning while the more problematic issues might be other aspects of the book that the censor would not be obliged to discuss. Indeed, the insidious nature of the camouflage of sex is that it would lead to these other issues being removed from public discussion.[175]

However, the majority of senators were in favour of the bill, including Oliver St. John Gogarty, who later had two of his own novels, *Going Native* (1940) and *Mr Petunia* (1946), banned under the very legislation that he supported. In the later stages of the debate, Gogarty suddenly expressed some reservation, arguing against banning the classics and in favour of the need to consider "the value of a work from a humanitarian or artistic standpoint where the higher expression of a nation's will and energy is represented in art."[176] Despite such interventions, the Censorship of Publications Act became law on 16 July 1929.

As might be expected, the Catholic press followed the debates in the Oireachtas with considerable interest. The *Irish Rosary* reported its frustration at the length of time that the legislation took to pass, arguing that when faced with any other national crisis, the government would normally act swiftly and decisively.[177] *The Standard*, meanwhile, relished the intricacies of the political process, provided significant detail on the amendments, and explained how these would impact the mechanisms of censorship.[178] However, it remained critical of the disparaging remarks levelled by several politicians against such organisations as the CTSI and the IVA.[179] Although they were disappointed that the law did not make the censorship more restrictive, the paper warned that to "resist it would be fatal for any party."[180]

For its part, the *Irish Statesman* was resigned even before the Dáil resumed debating the bill. Despite its pugnacious articles in the autumn, in February it told its readers that while the proposed legislation was "disagreeable ... to people born in and accustomed to intellectual freedom," it was "a pale thing beside the general censorships set up by the new European autocracies." AE hoped for the best, suggesting that Ireland would be "one of the last homes of freedom" as long as "our moral fanatics do not deprive us of it by trying to prevent us reading literary masterpieces."[181] As the legislation was debated, the paper complimented politicians on improvements made to the bill, such as obliging censors to consider the literary, scientific, or historical importance of a book and granting them the power to contact the author and publisher. This latter aspect was important in the case of an Irish press because the loss of the Irish market would be far more costly to them than a foreign press, and in the long run it could potentially ruin Irish literature and the Irish book trade.[182] Taking stock of the process, the *Irish Statesman* was, on the whole, at peace with the outcome, although it took exception to what it considered the government's bungling. "In an evil moment," they opined, "Ministers permitted themselves to be influenced by the din of a strident minority who had convinced themselves this was a golden opportunity not only to suppress pornographic stuff, but to enforce prohibitions on any and every kind of book that ran contrary to their prejudices or soared above their limited intelligence," concluding that they had done so because they had calculated that "it would be simpler to give the fanatics what they asked on the very cynical ground that the mass of the Irish people did not care two straws one way or the other."[183]

In the end, the *Irish Statesman*, its contributors, and other writers were conspicuous in their rather impotent fight: while they waged an admirable polemical battle in the autumn once the legislation was introduced, they had not done much of anything with regard to participating in the process or inundating TDs with letters in the same way as pro-censorship groups had done. As a result, they limited themselves to sniping from the sidelines while others concretely influenced the final legislation. Their articles might have had some impact, but their fight was neither exhaustive nor strategically sophisticated, with their ineffectiveness encapsulated by their relief that the legislation was "much better than at one time seemed possible." Indeed, they were encouraged that politicians had found "a middle way" and hoped that something would be done "to keep in check for the future the zealots whose antics have made us a laughing-stock to the outside world."[184]

While the *Irish Statesman* had a rosy take on the legislation, the Censorship of Publications Act did not assuage concerns over problematic terminology. Despite the extensive debates, it borrowed from British law, with *indecent* vaguely "construed as including suggestive of, or inciting to sexual immorality or unnatural vice or likely in any other similar way to corrupt or deprave."[185] At least, it could be argued, reference to the equally obscure term *public morality* was expurgated from earlier drafts of the legislation, which could have led to broader interpretations. Yet the Censorship Board was to be composed of "fit and proper" people, with no definition of those characteristics provided.[186] A book could only be referred to the Censorship Board if it was "indecent or obscene or advocates the unnatural prevention of conception or the procurement of abortion or miscarriage or the use of any method, treatment or appliance for the purpose of such prevention or such procurement."[187] However, the Censorship Board had to simultaneously consider the publication's "literary, artistic, scientific or historical merit" and its general tenor; the language in which it was produced; the extent of the circulation such a book might have; and the class of reader that might be reasonably expected to read it.[188] For a book to be banned, not more than one member could dissent from the report and at least three members had to assent to it.[189] The same conditions applied to periodicals, but they were banned for three months, whereas books were banned indefinitely.[190] The minister for justice was the sole party that could revoke a prohibition order, and they could do this only after consultation with the Censorship Board.[191] Those prosecuted for knowingly trading and circulating banned publications could be fined from fifty to five hundred pounds and imprisoned from three to six months with the possibility of hard labour.[192] Reflecting the influence of concurrent British debates, the act placed limitations on the reporting of judicial proceedings that discussed indecent matter, including medical details that were "calculated to injure public morals" and stories that entailed divorce and conjugal rights.[193] The 1929 act therefore repealed and replaced the Obscene Publications Act of 1857 that had been adopted from British law under the first two acts of the Oireachtas. As such, Ireland became a more independent country in terms of how the state enforced norms and mores in the cultural sphere. Yet over the following decades, many Irish writers would echo Shaw in suggesting that as a direct result of this national independence, they and their fellow citizens had lost considerable freedoms.

The institution of censorship in Ireland thus created an entirely different regime for writers to navigate. Whereas under British law they could mount a defence and an appeal, and decisions were guided by jurisprudence, the Censorship of Publications Act empowered a small number of their fellow citizens, who were not necessarily versed in the nuances of the law, with the authority to ban their books. Moreover, the censors did not have to justify their decisions. In many respects, literature would be criminalised, and yet writers, unlike people accused of the most heinous of crimes, had been stripped of the right to a fair trial. Although the government would publish lists of banned books to inform booksellers and librarians, this publicity that the banned books would receive was severely limited compared to the wide coverage that censorship trials had afforded writers and books in Britain. In this respect, the censorship could more effectively silence immoral and obscene writing. Like British censorship, Irish censorship was post-publication, but because most publishers and printers of books resided in Britain, they could not be prosecuted in Ireland. As a result, Irish censorship had to focus on the books themselves and ensure that they did not circulate in the country. The other major difference between the two polities was Ireland's creation of the Censorship of Publications Board. As we have seen with Joynson-Hicks and his handling of *The Well of Loneliness* and *Sleeveless Errand*, the censorship in Britain was directly overseen by the home secretary, which caused members of the public and Parliament to question his judgment. Because people had to submit complaints directly to the Censorship Board, Ireland's minister for justice was prudently insulated from the process and thus could remain above the fray in controversial rulings to act as an appellate judge.

This point raises once again the international dialectic of censorship. In the immediate post-independence period, Ireland claimed and sought to carve out for itself a distinct culture. This was dependent upon the passage of legislation that would ensure that Irish values, however vaguely or narrowly they were interpreted, were encoded in law, were protected from external forces, and were nurtured to assist with the nation-building process.[194] Censorship would be at the fore of such efforts, effectively dictating what was permissive in Irish society and thus determining in many ways the formation of present and future generations. Yet the Irish legislation was not crafted in a vacuum. As this chapter has shown, Irish politicians and social reformers were influenced by censorship regimes in other countries, including Britain, Canada, the United States, France, Australia, New Zealand, and South Africa. While the new Irish law was therefore essential for founding a singular national institution, it was undergirded by international contexts and the legal structures and jurisprudence of elsewhere. Indeed, while it effectively created a distinctive rupture with the tradition of British censorship law by creating an in camera institution of five censors, it also sought to insulate the Irish minister for justice, unlike his British counterpart, from charges of acting as a censor. Paradoxically, though, it revealed common concerns, as the Irish legislation incorporated the spirit of Britain's Judicial Proceedings Act and maintained the British legal definitions of *indecent* and *obscene*.

The British cases against Radclyffe Hall's and Norah C. James's novels are of further importance to the international dialectic of censorship as they created the impetus for presses to be founded on the continent to circumvent the censorship of daring and risqué literature. Existing beyond the jurisdiction of English courts, these presses, including Jack Kahane's Obelisk Press, his son Maurice Girodias's Olympia Press, and, even earlier, Sylvia Beach's Shakespeare and Company, published the works of such notable Irish authors as James Joyce, J. P. Donleavy, and Samuel Beckett, all of whom would eventually be banned in Ireland and whose books would not have been issued by presses in the Anglophone world for fear of prosecution, pecuniary loss, and penal sentences. These international networks were thus a direct result of censorship, and they in turn would impact the literature of Ireland, Britain, and the United States.[195]

One of the most provocative aspects of the censorship debates in Ireland was the focus on Irish writers and their potential to subvert the nationalist revolution via their challenges to idealism. While there were elements of this expressed in the cases of Joyce, MacNamara, and Robinson, the fear of Irish writers became much more explicit in the post-independence period. Just as Moore and Shaw had been attacked for their realism, which was considered a perverse reaction against idealism by those who supported censorship in Britain, so O'Casey was charged with sullying the memory of the Easter Rising of 1916 and the Irish hero-martyrs by not approaching the conflict with due devotion and reverence in *The Plough and the Stars*. Four days after Kevin O'Higgins attended the premiere of the play, of which he did not approve, and the day after republicans caused a ruckus in the Abbey Theatre, O'Higgins announced the formation of the Committee on Evil Literature, yet scholars have not previously drawn a link between these events. That O'Higgins had also met with R. S. Devane, one of the most prominent members of the IVA and a leading pro-censorship polemicist, to conspire to create a welcoming reception for censorship legislation, attests to the blend of nationalism and Catholicism that informed the legislation. Because Irish writers could claim their place within the Irish nation, there was a need to target those like O'Casey for undermining Irish culture, norms, and mores not only through indecency or obscenity, but also through their representation of the nation in their art. Post-independence anxieties thus informed the legislation, which sought to create a cohesive and coherent body of citizens that were distinctly Irish and could work towards building and establishing the new country.

The international dialectic of censorship is further evident in the way that both pro- and anti-censorship campaigners used the press. The *Irish Rosary* looked to James Douglas's article, published in an English paper, to give their demands for censorship greater currency and to demonstrate that censorship was not limited to Ireland, but was also being called for by those elsewhere who feared the modern tide of obscene and immoral publications. Similarly, Yeats wrote articles against the Irish censorship in both Irish and English papers, each having its own target audience. In the former, he attempted to persuade readers that the principles guiding the impending legislation were counter to Catholic Thomist philosophy, which embraces sensual art; in the latter, he sought to ridicule the Irish bill and thus embarrass the government abroad in the hope that doing so might impel moderate amendments. In this sense, the international dialectic is a true dialectic in how the ebb and flow moves between Ireland and elsewhere, in how thought within the nation's borders can be influenced from beyond its borders, and in how both pro- and anti-censorship crusaders can use the national and international press to their advantage.

This chapter demonstrates that, during the 1920s, writers in Britain and Ireland failed to organise as effectively as they had in the past. While many were sympathetic to their causes, no group of writers meaningfully coalesced to support either Hall or James. Rather, the opposite happened, with some openly stating that they would not help what they considered to be a lost cause, defend a work that they esteemed to lack sufficient aesthetic quality, or be associated with a taboo subject. Several writers thereby suffered from a combination of resignation, snobbery, and fear that prevented them from defending the larger cause of freedom of expression. Meanwhile, in Ireland writers organised polemically, with AE and the *Irish Statesman* advancing the liberal case. However, despite the significant interventions by such veterans of censorship struggles as Shaw and Yeats, Irish writers did not organise socially or politically. Except for Padraig de Burca in his representation of the Catholic Writers' Guild, no Irish writer stood before or submitted a written statement to the CEL. The situation recalls the 1892 hearings into the censorship of plays in Britain when only William Archer criticised the institution, unlike the 1909 hearings in which several writers testified and submitted evidence. Likewise, while writers in Britain worked to meet with politicians and affect the direction of censorship legislation throughout the 1907–9 campaign, some twenty years later Irish writers did not do so either before the bill was drafted or as it was debated in the Oireachtas. The few Irish writers who were elected officials, including Hugh Law and Oliver St. John Gogarty, offered some criticism from within the halls of power, but they were in the decided minority. Incredibly, Yeats resigned his Seanad seat as the bill was being discussed in the Oireachtas. Irish writers would now have to live with the consequences of not vigorously acting in concert. However, as we will see, they would quickly come to understand that they had to organise with considerably more savvy and fortitude.

Chapter Five

A Made-in-Ireland Resistance: The Rise and Fall of the Irish Academy of Letters

Despite the debates and concerns engendered by the legislation, the first years of institutional censorship in Ireland were relatively calm, with the government, writers, and society cautiously waiting to see how it would function. One exception, however, was the *Catholic Mind*, which bemoaned literary decadence and effectively demanded that the censorship protect Ireland from immoral writers.[1] They further complained that realist literature was only concerned with the physical part of life, which was "the least important" because "it is in the spiritual plane that the essence of life lies."[2] People should strive for better, they suggested, by reading the sort of religious literature provided by the CTSI.[3] Reflecting the international dialectic, there was some anxiety that the censorship would not be up and running soon enough to prevent offensive foreign papers from invading and infecting Ireland.[4]

In the meantime, the CTSI was preparing itself for the battle ahead by selecting five hundred individuals "of steady judgment" to systematically examine books and periodicals and submit offensive material to the Censorship Board.[5] In many ways, this usurped the function of the IVA, with the CTSI now adopting the dual approach of producing Catholic literature and organising people to thwart the circulation of immoral literature. This was partially in response to a confrontation that the CTSI's executive secretary, Frank O'Reilly, had with the government. On 8 October 1929, before James Fitzgerald-Kenney, the minister for justice, had the opportunity to nominate people to the Censorship Board, O'Reilly submitted a copy of Warwick Deeping's *Roper's Row*.[6] O'Reilly was concerned with a page on which he believed the book's hero made a plea for birth control. Fitzgerald-Kenney, however, concluded that "he could not undertake to refer it to the Censorship of Publications Board merely because on one page out of 400 there are a certain number of rhetorical questions recording doubts on the question of contraception running through the mind of the hero." While the book perhaps "treads on delicate ground," it "could scarcely be called indecent or obscene, and the rhetorical questions" that were the focus of O'Reilly's concern "could not be construed as an advocacy of contraception within the meaning of the Act" when read "in the light of the rest of the chapter."[7] This was a remarkable admission of how unprepared the government was. Instead of waiting for the Censorship Board to meet and allowing it to determine the book's fate, the minister himself read the chapter and came to his own decision. This was not to happen again; in the future, the Censorship Board was the front line. Also of importance is that the minister refused to ban a book because he considered the objectionable passage in light of the general tenor of the book. This followed the letter of the law, but it was a precedent that would be unknown to the future Censorship Board and thus did little to affect their decisions.

O'Reilly was not placated by the response and sent an ill-advised letter that could have done permanent damage to the CTSI's reputation with both the Department of Justice and the Censorship Board. Attempting to go over the minister's head, he wrote to William T. Cosgrave, the president of the executive council, to lodge anew his complaint of the book and what he viewed to be Fitzgerald-Kenney's shocking lack of moral direction. More disturbing still, O'Reilly threatened the government: "I do not intend to let the matter rest where it stands," he wrote. "I shall publish the correspondence with comments, unless you may be able to induce a change of heart and a change of attitude in the Department concerned."[8]

When Cosgrave inquired with Fitzgerald-Kenney as to the rationale behind his decision, the latter responded that "this book is a good illustration of the difference between a positive and a negative censorship."[9] The matter appears to have been dropped thereafter. An internal memorandum suggests that civil servants were not in favour of any action, for O'Reilly had attempted "to make the President a Court of Appeal from the Minister for Justice in the matter of the Censorship of Publications Act" and this sort of precedent "should be discouraged."[10] The episode seems to have spurred O'Reilly and the CTSI to organise their campaign of over five hundred readers in the hope that such methods would translate into better results.

While religious groups thus became further galvanised with the passage of legislation, writers remained slow to respond. When the latter would finally organise by founding the Irish Academy of Letters (IAL) in 1932, the censorship was a well-established institution. This delay would prove to be fatal to writers' objective of ensuring that the censorship would not be so zealous as to target books that were literary alongside those of more dubious quality. However, by becoming the first anti-censorship group in Ireland to have significant social capital and political connections, they were able to lobby for precedent-setting decisions on the part of the minister for justice. Indeed, their perceived importance came from drawing their members not only from within Ireland but also beyond its shores to include Irish authors living abroad and a number of notable British and American writers of Irish heritage. This strategy of incorporating literary lions from around the world gave the IAL international bona fides to demonstrate that Irish censorship would not only impact those living in the country, but also hinder the universal values of freedom of expression and access to literature. Yet the IAL's international appeal, despite signalling the nation in its name, would generate a hostile dialectical reaction in Catholic nationalist circles that would cast the IAL as an enemy of and a threat to the purity of the Irish people. Caught between these two poles once the censorship was up and running, the government would be forced to determine the future course of the institution.

The First Years of the Censorship Board

Although the act was passed in the summer of 1929, the Censorship of Publications Board was only formed in early 1930. As it got to work, a campaign was launched against it not by Irish writers or religious organisations, but rather from abroad by the German-American author George Sylvester Viereck. Viereck was disappointed with the banning of his book *My First Two Thousand Years*, particularly because, as he told Cosgrave, he had fought in verse and prose for the Irish nation in the years leading up to independence. "You yourself," he reminded him, "told me that some of my war poems were smuggled into Ireland and printed by the men who fought for Irish freedom."[11] Cosgrave attempted to intercede on Viereck's behalf but was assured by the minister for justice that the Censorship Board had acted according to the law and arrived at its decision in a professional manner.[12] He thus informed Viereck of his regret, but also noted that the "Board is composed of respected distinguished citizens of different faiths, possessing a wide knowledge of conditions in the Irish Free State, and alive to anything which might be calculated to offend susceptibilities here."[13] Viereck said that he sympathised with the nation's right to determine its own standards, then impishly concluded: "I just see from newspaper dispatches that Ireland is riding on the wave of depression and that her exports are higher than ever."[14] Shaw's prophecy that censorship would cause those who had once supported Ireland to turn away from the country came to pass even more quickly than he had imagined.

By the time that it issued its first annual report on 8 May 1931, the Censorship Board had examined eighty-seven books, of which it had banned seventy-eight.[15] Several of the banned books were on contraception, eugenics, and sexology, such as Bertrand Russell's *Marriage and Morals*, Havelock Ellis's *Studies in the Psychology of Sex*, Marie Stopes's *Married Love* and *Early Days of Birth Control*, and Margaret Sanger's *The New Motherhood* and *What Every Mother Should Know*. Serious literature was targeted with the banning of Aldous Huxley's *Point Counter Point*, which had the distinction of being the first book interdicted under the legislation, Radclyffe Hall's *The Well of Loneliness*, W. Somerset Maugham's *Cakes and Ale*, William Faulkner's *Soldiers' Pay*, and Thomas Wolfe's *Look Homeward, Angel*.[16] Of the twenty-six periodicals examined, eighteen were banned. The Censorship Board expressed frustration with local newspapers for publishing the titles of prohibited books, a practice, they lamented, that was tantamount to advertising censored materials, although the intent was, in part, to inform librarians, booksellers, and citizens. Noting that the "demand for censorship was general and persistent," the board was also disappointed that, except for the CTSI, there had been only "little assistance."[17] In particular, the reading public and library committees were encouraged to become more engaged. The Censorship Board thus sought to make people aware that the censorship's success rested entirely upon their vigilance and participation.

The complaint forms available in the government files attest that the CTSI was the chief source for submissions. In the first year of operations, twenty-seven formal complaints were made by Frank O'Reilly on behalf of the CTSI and only three by other citizens.[18] Over the next two years, forty-three formal complaints were lodged by O'Reilly and six by others. The public was therefore not reading books with a critical eye towards discovering and submitting obscene and indecent material. The difference between the figures for the CTSI and other members of society can perhaps be partially attributed to people believing that the CTSI was doing a sufficient job. Moreover, others might not have had the means or knowledge of how to lodge a complaint. This latter point is especially relevant in terms of people from the lower classes, who would generally not have had enough leisure time, education, or access to read some of the literature, would not have complained because it was entertainment that targeted them, and would not have been able to supply the Censorship Board with copies of the offending publication as the cost of doing so would have been prohibitive. Furthermore, it is possible that many people did not share the CTSI's resolve to censor their neighbours' reading habits. There also remains the likelihood that the difference in the number of complaints made by the CTSI and the public is perhaps reflective of a general ignorance of how censorship worked and demonstrates the assumption that the onus for the functioning of the institution was perceived to be entirely on the state.

Given these circumstances, it is worth considering how complainants were reading books and what they considered censorable. Unfortunately, most complaint forms do not appear to have survived. Curiously, despite being one of the most notorious novels of the time, Joyce's *Ulysses* does not seem to have ever been submitted, meaning that, as the censored book registry attests, it was never banned in Ireland. Even for many existent complaints, there are neither pages marked nor comments made. This leaves us with an imperfect understanding of many overall trends and tendencies and completely in the dark about what the rationale was for submitting certain books. As a result, there is no way of knowing how exactly these people were reading such banned Irish works as Liam O'Flaherty's *The House of Gold* and *The Puritan*, Frank Harris's biography of Bernard Shaw, Austin Clarke's *The Bright Temptation*, George Moore's *A Story-Teller's Holiday*, Samuel Beckett's *More Pricks than Kicks*, and Sean O'Casey's *Windfalls*.

A further difficulty lies in determining whether the Censorship Board concurred with a reader's specific complaint in banning a book. In all cases where a book was banned, the decision simply notes the number of members who agreed to ban the work and either that it was "in its general tendency indecent" or that it advocated "the unnatural prevention of conception," both of which are generic phrases pulled from the legislation. Although the latter is self-explanatory, decisions did not detail what exactly the indecent aspects were, thereby leaving it to the literary scholar to guess based on their own reading of the book or, in cases where pages were marked, finding a copy of the submitted edition and determining what on those pages might have been considered indecent. In some instances, even the qualitative comments are not helpful, with O'Reilly complaining that Sherwood Anderson's *Horses and Men* was "deliberately indecent"; that Lionel Britton's *Hunger and Love* was "altogether a depraving book"; and that Arthur Mortimer's *The Wall* was "very morbid and unhealthy, and quite unfit for reading."[19] Such remarks were commonly echoed in other complaints. Yet some were considerably clearer with regard to how exactly the book was indecent. Marjorie Worthington's *Come, My Coach!*, for example, was said to be "unhealthy and immoral generally" for featuring a Catholic priest "with strange ideas, living apart from the Church," and who was "a co-respondent" in a case "involving a married woman."[20] While John Cowper Powys published *Weymouth Sands* in the United States, in Britain he issued it in a redacted version under the title *Jobber Skald*, but even this edition was considered too risqué for Ireland as it was "based on sexual suggestion"; the CTSI flagged several incidents for the Censorship Board, which duly banned the book.[21]

In some cases, the Censorship Board was tested in its interpretation of books under the terms of the legislation. While Joseph Warren Beach's *Glass Mountain* was submitted because of one "blasphemous allusion to 'God the Father,'" it is uncertain if the Censorship Board prohibited it because of blasphemy, which in itself would not have warranted a banning, or if it was because of some other aspect.[22] The English translation of Max Brod's *Reubeni, Prince of the Jews* was similarly complained of by the CTSI on religious grounds because, although it was historical, it referred "to the duplicity and other defects of the Popes and Papal Government that are better forgotten. Some of it may be true, most of it exaggerated and disrespectful, and none of it edifying reading for Catholic youth."[23] Here we see once again the fight between idealists and realists, with the CTSI insisting that even historical facts should be prohibited when they do not accord with national and religious ideals. The Censorship Board banned the book, but because no reason was given other than that it was "in its general tendency indecent," there is no way to determine if they were similarly idealistic readers or if they had other concerns. Rather dubiously, O'Reilly complained of English suffragette author and actress Cicely Hamilton's *Modern Russia* because she agreed with "Russian modern doctrines and future works by her should be watched carefully."[24] The Censorship Board did not officially consider her left-wing politics problematic, instead banning the book because it advocated birth control. However, it would be worth keeping in mind Sir John Keane's warning that books whose politics were considered antithetical to those of the censors could be potentially banned under "the camouflage of sex."

This "camouflage of sex" is evident in the complaints of several books that combined sexual indecency with religious and political unorthodoxy. In many instances, these were banned. Ralph Bates's *The Olive Field*, which details conditions in Spain before the civil war, was said to be "full of blasphemy of a particularly odious kind," "reeking with communist doctrines," and "indecent in very many places."[25] Similarly, the CTSI complained of Walter Duranty's *One Life, One Kopek*, which focuses on the ante- and post-revolutionary periods in Russia. While it noted that Duranty was "regarded as an expert on Russian affairs," it lamented the book's "indecency, immorality, blasphemy, and general communistic outlook."[26] Meanwhile, F. Tennyson Jesse's *Act of God* was submitted because it was "definitely anti-Christian, blasphemous in places, as well as indecent in others. It is calculated to have a very unsettling effect on the weak reader."[27]

Some cases attest that the Censorship Board acted responsibly in rejecting what it considered to be unsubstantiated complaints. In one instance, it disagreed that Thomas W. Broadhurst's *Blow the Man Down* should be banned because it depicted "a prostitute introduced into the life of the sailors with appropriate language + incidents."[28] Despite his public standing as the secretary of the CTSI, O'Reilly had a number of his complaints rejected, including those for Bruce Graeme's *The Penance of Brother Alaric*, George Limnelius's *Tell No Tales*, Charlotte M. Brame's *A Mad Love*, E. W. Savi's *The Beauty Market* and *The Power of Love*, F. E. Baily's *Pleasure Pets*, and Thomas Bell's *Equestrian Portrait*.[29] In the case of the latter, O'Reilly said that it was a "very nicely written book, so nice that the reader is inclined to accept the sacrament of Matrimony as unnecessary" based on its treatment of "illicit love as part of everyday life."[30] The Censorship Board either did not share the opinion that this interpretation was enough to warrant banning the book or felt that it was an erroneous or exaggerated reading. Likewise, the Censorship Board disagreed that Perry Colson's *Please Take Me Next Time* should be proscribed, despite the complainant lamenting that "the whole trend" of it was "wrong," particularly the passages detailing the "extenuation of homosexuality."[31]

In one instance, someone – whether a crank, an absurdist, or a philosopher – submitted the Censorship of Publications Act itself. They emphasized words in the article stating that the Censorship Board should ban "any *indecent* medical, surgical or *physiological details* the publication of which would be calculated to injure public morals." "What the _____ are these?" they asked, censoring themselves. "Is not the human body the Temple of God?" Indeed, they pointed out, St. Paul asserts this in the sixteenth verse of the third chapter of his Epistle to the Corinthians. Therefore, the complainant considered "that to make imputations against His handiwork is Anti-God and Anti-Religious."[32]

One of the few Irish books for which a complaint survives is Sean O'Faolain's *Midsummer Night Madness*, a collection of short stories that takes the Anglo-Irish War of 1919–21 as its subject. O'Reilly lodged the complaint, but he did not comment on the book or individual stories, instead pointing to passages on twenty-five pages that mostly refer to descriptions of a sexual nature.[33] Two years later, O'Faolain wrote to the Department of Justice asking for permission to import copies of the banned book before Christmas.[34] They not only allowed him to do so, but also, incredibly, said that he could distribute them to friends.[35] Such an allowance was a general practice of sorts, with the librarian of Trinity College Dublin repeatedly being granted permission to import banned novels and works on birth control and sex. However, the minister for justice emphasized that this was contingent on the librarian acting as a censor himself by placing them "in a special press" and only issuing them to *certain* readers upon request.[36] Such permission was not a foregone conclusion as others were routinely denied if the Department of Justice did not consider their appeal reasonable. For example, when one citizen asked to import a copy of Sinclair Lewis's banned novel *Elmer Gantry* because he collected Lewis's works, he was refused permission as he was adjudged not to have provided an exceptional reason.[37] Despite such care in attending to their duties, the Censorship Board would get swept up in some controversies stemming from their decisions.

Sean O'Faolain's *Midsummer Night Madness* and the Return of Edward Garnett

When *Midsummer Night Madness* was banned on 19 April 1932, O'Faolain had only recently returned to Ireland after living abroad for six years: three in Boston while studying towards his MA at Harvard and three in the greater London area teaching English. During his time in England, he established a close relationship with Edward Garnett, the influential editor at Jonathan Cape. For O'Faolain, Garnett was a sympathetic and critical reader who was formative in his development as a writer. Excited by O'Faolain's talent, Garnett composed a laudatory preface for *Midsummer Night Madness*, with which O'Faolain was "as pleased as punch."[38]

It was a considerably more engaged and bracingly polemical preface than the one that Garnett had written for *Sleeveless Errand.* In many ways, it was similar to George Moore's preface for Vizetelly's translation of *Piping Hot!* At the time that Moore was writing, Zola and Vizetelly had yet to run afoul of English officials, and the Frenchman was largely unread in the country. Moore thus took the occasion to introduce Zola as a great writer and chronicler of the age, make the case that his work was a much-needed social intervention, and argue that he would be a litmus test for freedom of expression in England. Similarly, at the time that Garnett wrote his preface for O'Faolain's novel, O'Faolain had yet to publish a book. Yet as with Moore, Garnett's own experiences with censors stirred him to incitement.

Garnett opened by stating that O'Faolain's *Midsummer Night Madness* was "one of the best" books to have come out of Ireland. The fault for the paucity of good Irish writing, he charged, did not lie with Irish writers, but rather the Irish people, who were "the most backward nation in Europe" and the "least aware of critical standards."[39] Garnett identified himself as an Anglo-Irishman who had always taken an interest in Irish literature.[40] However, he lamented that on too many occasions when he had read a manuscript of Irish prose or poetry, the author "had no individual insight, or no fresh observation of life," but rather drew from the romances and legends of yore. This "literary conservatism" was too "parochial" for a modern literature.[41] Every recent Irish writer of note, he claimed, citing Moore, Wilde, Shaw, Joyce, and O'Flaherty, "had to emigrate to find a welcome outside his own land." Ireland, he said, was dominated by peasants who lacked interest in "any intellectual subject whatever," making it a place "where many questions, social, literary and religious can never be discussed with the same freedom of thought as in any other civilized country." Furthermore, he alleged that the censorship had led to a "sterile, apathetic, rigid atmosphere" that threatened literature in Ireland.[42]

Garnett suggested that by accepting *Midsummer Night Madness*, the Irish could "rebut" charges that they were ignorant and intolerant and would show that they could "recognize a fine piece of literature frankly Irish in both atmosphere and character and an author essentially Irish in spirit."[43] He held up Daniel Corkery's recent polemical study, *Synge and Anglo-Irish Literature*, in which Corkery denounced most modern Irish writing in English as being foreign. By spouting such rot, Corkery did little more than perpetuate conservatism and ignorance.[44] In contrast, Garnett praised O'Faolain's book for incarnating "the Irish sensitiveness to place and emotional mood, in a style free and flowing, punctuated by passages of that brutal frankness which is the case of the younger generation."[45]

Garnett's preface seemed to impel a reaction from censors and zealots. None of the twenty-five pages that the CTSI indicated on the complaint form refer to Garnett's introduction, but the tone and substance of his preface would have keyed people into prurient readings of a work that presented a direct challenge to literary and social norms. The Censorship Board duly banned *Midsummer Night Madness*, making Garnett's preface a self-fulfilling prophecy. Liam O'Flaherty, who had already had two of his novels banned in Ireland, congratulated Garnett on his "great" preface.[46] For his part, Garnett admitted to Wren Howard, Cape's business partner, that he had written it "in the hope of raising a shindig over the book."[47]

Irish critics differed from the Censorship Board and tended to agree with Garnett in their estimation of O'Faolain's book. Reviewing it in the *Irish Independent*, the dramatist T. C. Murray suggested that it was "hardly a wise impulse" that moved O'Faolain to accept Garnett's preface, which he considered "distempered." Murray countered by defending the censorship, insisting that "while no one wishes to curb the freedom of the artist, here in Ireland freedom and licence have not yet become interchangeable terms." Yet he admired O'Faolain's work, remarking that the stories were representative of "genius in the making, if not of genius itself. Seldom has such prose come out of Ireland in the last decade. Its ease of strength is astounding, and one often pauses in the progress of a tale, held by its magic." While he regretted what he perceived to be the marring of the stories "by the writer's too naturalistic tendencies," Murray looked forward to O'Faolain "as an outstanding figure in that school of writers whose strength derives fundamentally from their power of quickening the English language into new life by investing it with qualities essentially Gaelic in their origin."[48]

The reviews in the *Irish Times* and the *Times Literary Supplement* likewise noted Garnett's preface, although they considered it rather well-founded.[49] In the latter, Austin Clarke praised O'Faolain for showing "human nature distorted by political, religious and racial passions" and depicting "objectively a mental world of distorted values, a world in which a cowardly murder may pass as patriotism while a sexual sin is regarded with sanctimonious horror. He deepens that sense of fantastic unreality which must always puzzle the thoughtful in a time of mob passions."[50] Meanwhile, Frank O'Connor gave a mixed review in the *Dublin Magazine*, but he lauded O'Faolain for his craft as a storyteller and the "rich texture" of his prose.[51]

It could be that the CTSI's attention to the book was drawn by Murray as it submitted its complaint the week after his review appeared. This would have given the reader enough time to purchase a copy and to mark up the potentially indecent and obscene passages. Without mentioning "The Small Lady," the complaint form draws particular attention to that story, in which the eponymous character is kidnapped by an IRA column for having informed to the authorities and caused the death of several of their comrades. During her imprisonment at a monastery, the sensuous woman seduces one of the young IRA fighters. Shortly thereafter, she is executed; meanwhile, a priest absolves the youth of his sin. At fifty-nine pages in length, "The Small Lady" represents 23.5 per cent of the text. However, thirteen of the book's twenty-five marked pages, or 52 per cent of the purportedly indecent and obscene material, are found in the story. If we account for the fact that the listing of objectionable pages on the complaint form indicates that the final two stories of the collection were not marked and were potentially left unread, the length of "The Small Lady" would account for 31.6 per cent of the read text.[52] These figures reveal that the story was disproportionately objectionable when compared to the others in the book. While such number crunching is helpful to demonstrate how *quantitatively* objectionable the story appeared to the complainant, it cannot shed light on how *qualitatively* objectionable the material was; that is, while it might have had a higher percentage of objectionable passages than the other stories, these passages might have been thought less offensive than those that were marked elsewhere. But the centrality of the story – it is the fourth of seven – and the fact that it is the longest and most panoramic in the collection, speaks to its importance in understanding the others and the author's intent. That it alone was singled out and praised in all the aforementioned reviews further indicates how contemporary opinion believed it was the most significant and compelling of the book.[53]

Despite the overwhelming critical praise that *Midsummer Night Madness* received and its almost instant banning, authors did not unite around it as a cause célèbre. There are some possible reasons for this failure to organise. Most evidently, O'Faolain had been out of the country for the better part of six years and had only just settled in Dublin, where, having grown up in Cork, he lacked deep ties to the local literary scene. Moreover, despite his book's literary bona fides, it was sexually provocative and thus perhaps not enough of a borderline case upon which to base a protest. At the same time, Irish writers appeared to be waiting to see how the censorship worked once it had some time to operate. It was only later in 1932, more than two years after the Censorship Board was formed, that writers would finally coalesce, although it would take the old guard to mobilise the younger generation. When they did finally begin to lobby the government, it would be over a book written by an Irishman, but one who was living abroad, was already well-established, and whose banned book was not a realist tale set in Ireland, but a fantastical fable set in Africa.

The Irish Academy of Letters

In a delayed reaction to the institutionalisation of Irish censorship, Bernard Shaw and W. B. Yeats founded the Irish Academy of Letters in September 1932.[54] As Ireland's two Nobel laureates and veterans of censorship campaigns, Shaw and Yeats were well-suited to lead the charge. The Academy was to constitute a body through which writers could wage organised resistance, leading it to become known as the "Academy of Immorality" in more conservative sections of society that viewed its membership as "sufficient to blast it forever in the eyes of all decent Catholics and non-Catholics" alike.[55] After some correspondence on the subject, Shaw donated fifty pounds for secretarial expenses to begin the venture.[56] Although he fully supported the project, Shaw declined Yeats's offer to sit as the Academy's first president, citing his residence in London as making it too difficult to undertake the task effectively. Instead, he suggested that AE would be a more adequate president owing to his Dublin address and his having "the requisite Jehovesque beard and aspect."[57]

The two men composed a plan for an organisation consisting of "twenty-five members who had written creatively 'with Ireland as the subject matter,' plus, as associates, ten Irishmen whose work was distinguished but who did not fall within the definition."[58] The invitation that they sent to prospective members emphasized the importance and purpose of the Academy. Just as AE had expressed his concerns that the legislation would negatively affect the Irish book trade and the development of Irish literature, Shaw and Yeats argued that censorship could lead to confining "an Irish author to the British and American market, and thereby make it impossible for him to live by distinctive Irish literature." Although the Academy members could only be counted by dozens, they believed that "in Ireland there is still a deep respect for intellectual and poetic quality." By wielding their influence "collectively and unanimously," it was hoped that they could ensure that censors would hinder neither the writing process nor their livelihoods.[59]

Invitations were sent to and accepted by AE, Elizabeth Bowen, Ernest Boyd, Shan Bullock, Austin Clarke, Padraic Colum, John Eglinton, St. John Ervine, Oliver St. John Gogarty, Stephen Gwynn, F. R. Higgins, Joseph M. Hone, T. E. Lawrence, Shane Leslie, Alice Milligan, Frank O'Connor, Sean O'Faolain, Liam O'Flaherty, Eugene O'Neill, Seumas O'Sullivan, Forrest Reid, Lennox Robinson, Edith Somerville, Walter Starkie, James Stephens, L. A. G. Strong, and Helen Waddell. Meanwhile, Douglas Hyde, T. C. Murray, James Joyce, Lord Dunsany, and Sean O'Casey refused. Hyde felt that as he had devoted his life to Gaelic culture, "it would be unfitting to join an academy whose writers are all Anglo Irish."[60] Murray initially declined membership because he accepted the principles of and need for censorship.[61] However, he relented and joined after much petitioning by AE.[62] Knowing that Joyce would need some prodding, Yeats sent him a private letter alongside the invitation: "Of course the first name that seemed essential both to Shaw and myself was your own, indeed you might say of yourself as

Dante said 'If I stay who goes, if I go who stays?' Which means that if you go out of our list it is an empty sack indeed. ... The Academy will be a vigorous body capable of defending our interests, negotiating with Government, and I hope preventing the worst forms of censorship."[63] Joyce was thankful for Yeats's kind words and hoped that the IAL would be successful in its endeavours, but he politely declined their offer.[64] Yeats publicly lamented the "disappointment" of Joyce's refusal, reasoning that he had not joined "simply because he is an anti-Academician."[65] While that might be so, after his deal with Maunsel fell through Joyce had asked Yeats for help to publish *Dubliners*, telling him that he would be doing a service to the literature of their country. It would seem that he was in no hurry to help the younger generation of Irish writers by lending his name to the fight against censorship. Just as he had shifted his strategy from polemics to aesthetic engagement with censorship in the 1910s, in his exile, Joyce had withdrawn from the social and political world of Irish literature. For his part, Lord Dunsany considered the classification of members and associates to be divisive and counter to the Academy's mandate to act uniformly, although the fact that he was invited as an associate might have led to his principled stand.[66] When he was elected a second time two years later as a full member, Dunsany graciously accepted.[67]

O'Casey was considerably more antagonistic. Still angry with Yeats for having rejected his play *The Silver Tassie* for the Abbey Theatre in 1928, O'Casey was perhaps bound to rebuff the invitation, even though he held a lifelong admiration of Shaw.[68] Relishing the occasion, O'Casey sent a copy of his refusal to the *Irish Times*, which happily published it. He opined, taking an implicit swipe at Yeats, that "the censorship of dull authority embattled in this Irish Academy of Letters will be much more dangerous to the Irish authors of the future than the *Domine dirige nos* [Lord, guide us] censorship exercised by the State and the Church." Moreover, he claimed that "The statement that there is still in Ireland 'a deep respect for intellectual and poetical quality' is a little above the truth."[69] In one fell swoop, he managed to revenge himself upon Yeats and insult pretty much all his audience. The letter provoked AE to admit that the Academy would be better off without such an unpredictable and abrasive member.[70] Christopher Murray has suggested that it created a further sense of solidarity among Academy members.[71] While it likely generated some internal cohesion, the letter might also have damaged the Academy's public image. If such were the case, then O'Casey's assessment of the place of the intellect and poetry in Ireland would become a self-fulfilling prophecy when the mandate and political influence of this new organisation were tested the following year in its unsuccessful attempt to overturn the banning of Shaw's *The Adventures of the Black Girl in Her Search for God*.

Shaw's book has as its protagonist the unnamed Black girl, who, having learned about God and organised religion from white missionaries in the jungles of Africa, begins to raise questions that her instructors cannot answer without revealing their own ignorance. When she asks where God might be found and is told by a missionary that He said, "Seek and ye shall find me," she sets off on her adventures.[72] In her travels, she meets the God of the Old Testament, the God of Noah, the God of Job, the preacher Ecclesiastes, Micah, a Roman soldier, Jesus, Saint Peter, a wandering Jew, scientists, an artist, and Mohammed, all of whom offer her unsatisfactory views of life, religion, and God. Finally, she stumbles upon Voltaire cultivating his garden. She is swayed by his wisdom, joins him in his work, and takes a redheaded Irishman (an unmistakable Shaw) for her husband. Satisfied with manual labour and later in her role as mother to her "charmingly coffee-coloured children," she recognises the impudence that she once had in setting out to search for God.[73] As Voltaire argues, God would probably not be interested in her, and she would not be able to stand before Him in all of His power and glory. The story therefore systematically attacks several major religions. Just as problematic as this blasphemy were the many wood-carved images of the Black girl and her antagonists, the former, although in silhouette, depicted as naked throughout.

Constable, Shaw's long-time London-based publisher, released the book on 5 December 1932. Five additional printings were needed to meet the demand of the Christmas rush. A total of fifty-seven thousand copies were sold in the first month. Nine more printings followed between 1933 and 1936, representing another forty-eight thousand. In the United States, a further forty-seven thousand copies were printed and sold.[74] The book was a solid success.

Meanwhile, a rather harmless scuffle emerged in County Wexford that predicted the larger debates to follow and echoed the sort of unofficial censorship to which Brinsley MacNamara's father had been subjected. At a meeting of the County Wexford Bee-Keepers' Association, one member proposed that Shaw, who had joined the association four years earlier, should have his membership revoked because of his book's blasphemy.[75] To make his case, he read two passages from the book: one mentioned that Jesus had been persuaded by Peter that he was the Messiah; the other stated that there was not one Christian among the Apostles and that Judas was the only one who showed any common sense.[76] "A man who makes observations of that kind," he said, "directs his sarcastic ridicule at the very foundations of Christianity, and should not be associated, even remotely, with our Association."[77] Other members, however, feared that if this precedent were made, they would be compelled to sign a paper stating that they were not atheists.[78] At its subsequent meeting, the beekeepers voted unanimously against hearing the proposal any further.[79] The chairperson defended Shaw and regretted that the case had garnered the association much negative publicity.[80] Therefore, instead of taking a pious stance on a well-known heretical, socialist, and feminist writer, the association responded with tolerance and much support. In this case, social pressures appear to have dissuaded conservatism and promoted liberalism.

More traditional sources of literary reception were likewise liberal in their approbation of Shaw's novella.[81] However, one person lamented that while Shaw had come under attack, John Farleigh, the book's illustrator, had got off unscathed for his "insolent" drawings: "It is a pity the critics were not up to the other side of their job, when they could have harassed the artist as well as the author so that they might enjoy a well deserved burning together."[82] Although the Irish government would burn neither Shaw nor Farleigh, on 1 May 1933, *The Adventures of the Black Girl in Her Search for God* was made the subject of a prohibition order. Yet given the fact that fifty-seven thousand copies had been sold following the book's first month of publication alone, much of the damage had already been done. The government's goal was therefore to contain it by having the book withdrawn from libraries and preventing its further purchase and circulation.

Three weeks following the announcement of the book's banning, the IAL began its campaign to have the prohibition order revoked. On 22 May, in his capacity as the Academy's secretary, AE wrote to Patrick J. Ruttledge, the minister for justice. After "a close reading" of Shaw's book, the Academy was determined to "contest the legality of the ban" because "there is nothing whatever indecent or obscene in it, nor does it directly or by suggestion advocate the unnatural prevention of conception or the procurement of abortion." AE thus asked Ruttledge, as "the sole court to which an appeal can be carried," to receive a deputation of Academy members.[83] The next day, the Department of Justice asked Brian MacMahon, the secretary to the Censorship Board, for his opinion on the matter. MacMahon responded: "To my mind the illustrations are the only justification under the Act. The Board seemed to consider the general tendency of the book to be bad. They also considered that the pictures were such as would not be allowed, for example, to pass through the post."[84]

The Department of Justice, likely not wishing to give the Academy ammunition and perhaps in acknowledgment of their potential political and social clout, told them that the minister would regretfully be unable to receive the deputation. It tempered this rejection by raising the possibility of repeal as "the Minister may after consultation with the Censorship of Publications Board revoke any prohibition order." Fortunately for the IAL, the minister intended "to re-consider the case."[85] The next day, Ruttledge personally invited AE to discuss matters. AE acknowledged the department's effort on the Academy's behalf and thanked Ruttledge, informing him that a deputation of Academy members comprised of himself, Yeats, Frank O'Connor, and F. R. Higgins would attend the meeting.[86]

Before this, however, Shaw encouraged Yeats to direct everyone's attention to John Farleigh's illustrations. "The revered censors are not nudists," he wrote, "and probably regard a nude negress as the last extremity of obscenity."[87] Such comments have led R. F. Foster to conclude that "GBS handed WBY an unexploded grenade, and then bombarded him with tongue-in-cheek instructions about how to handle it."[88] Yet Shaw's suggestion to raise the issue of the illustrations constituted a shrewd strategy. He added in another letter to Yeats that "as the word obscene can hardly apply to my text, I wish some member of the Dáil would ask Mr Ruttledge whether, if I issue a special edition for Ireland with the negress depicted in long skirts, the ban will be withdrawn."[89] However, this course of action was never undertaken.

After receiving the IAL delegation, the Department of Justice informed the Censorship Board of the meeting and reminded them that the minister could revoke the prohibition order. To help the minister arrive at a decision, they were asked to provide him with their "full and detailed views" concerning the book. They duly sent Ruttledge their rationale:

> In our opinion this book is a blasphemous composition, deliberately offensive to the cherished sentiments of the vast majority of the people, irrespective of religious opinion. On the grounds of this offensiveness it has been excluded from certain public libraries in Great Britain, but under the statutes governing our proceedings, we are not allowed to determine our decisions by considerations of this character.
>
> However, quite apart from such considerations, the Board was unanimously of the opinion that the book was objectionable in its references to sex, indecent in its general tendency, and liable to corrupt in sexual matters. In coming to this considered opinion the Board was largely influenced by the book's attitude of contemptuous disregard of the usually accepted standards of morality, in conjunction with the coarseness and vulgarity of its illustrations.[90]

In return, the Department of Justice told them that "It is difficult to find in the book substantial justification for the statement that it 'was objectionable in its references to sex, indecent in its general tendency, and liable to corrupt in sexual matters.'"[91] Thus, the minister was seriously considering a revocation order. In effect, the Censorship Board's judgment was found to be questionable, which gave credence to the Academy's suspicion that the book had been unjustifiably banned. At the same time, the minister was warned by a civil servant that it "may be dangerous to over-rule the Censorship Board" as they were "doing good work" and they did "not appear to be unreasonable."[92] Ruttledge was further cautioned against action as he had already issued a prohibition order and revoking it would make him appear indecisive and incompetent. In this way, the Department of Justice began to reel in the minister from making any rash decisions and to effectively make the case against not just repeal of Shaw's book, but the mechanism of appeal itself.

Needing more guidance, Ruttledge contacted the attorney general. The latter, having read the book, responded: "I approached the question as to whether the ban on the book should be withdrawn as if I were a Judge in the Court of Criminal Appeal deciding whether the verdict of 'guilty' by a jury should be set aside." Although he found "ample evidence to support" the charge of blasphemy, he believed that there was a lack of evidence to support the claim that the book was in its general tendency indecent. The board, he noted, determined the book to be coarse and vulgar because of the illustrations featuring the naked body of the Black girl. "Apart from this," he summarised, "they rely upon the contemptuous disregard of the usually accepted standards of morality to support their finding that the book is in its general tendency indecent." He agreed that its free circulation could cause problems, "no doubt" outraging "clergymen of all denominations." Its "attraction or danger," he argued, "lies in that attacks upon the Christian and other religions are lightly dressed in Shavian garb." In the end, he feared that revoking the prohibition order would stimulate a greater demand for the book than if it had been simply left alone from the outset, and therefore "it would be a serious matter for the Minister to interfere with the ruling of the Censorship Board."[93] As they admitted to Ruttledge, the Censorship Board was not empowered to ban works based upon blasphemy. One question that arises, however, is whether blasphemy is a form of indecency. This was never debated, but there might have been some room for this interpretation of the guidance that books could be banned for their likelihood "to corrupt or deprave." The attorney general allowed that the minister simply had to refer to the illustrations of the Black girl. But while the illustrations might be judged *legally* indecent, he hesitated in a manner that suggests he did not consider them as such in his own aesthetic evaluation.

Having weighed the attorney general's opinion, the minister for justice suggested that the IAL should be informed that he would not revoke the ban. "In any event," he said, "revocation might have awkward consequences; the Board might resign as a protest."[94] This reveals that some consideration was given to ignore the attorney general's advice. In the end, the minister was not as concerned with the legal basis for his action as he was with the political repercussions. In this case, there appears to have been some calculation between the costs of either the potential mutiny of the Censorship Board or a prolonged and perhaps public campaign waged by the Irish Academy of Letters.

Anxious to know the minister's decision after almost two months had passed, the IAL requested an update.[95] When none was forthcoming, they wrote to him again.[96] On 1 August, they received a blunt response that Ruttledge had "decided not to revoke the Prohibition Order."[97] Not surprisingly, the IAL was dissatisfied. F. R. Higgins, who had recently replaced AE as secretary, wrote asking for an explanation as to why the book was banned.[98] The department said that "it is not the practice to supply information concerning reasons for Prohibition Orders."[99] Therefore, "the Minister regrets that he can add nothing" else.[100] The government would comment no further.

Yeats, though, already knew of the book's fate by 30 July. In a letter to Shaw, he described running into an inebriated Ruttledge at the Abbey Theatre during an intermission. Ruttledge told Yeats: "I have been trying to get round that book but I cant [*sic*] get round it. Nothing to be done. If I take the ban off it, what happens? All the censors resign."[101] He likely signed the prohibition order as he had all others: without giving much thought to the book and having full confidence in the Censorship Board's decision. Like the attorney general, had he been a member of the board he might not have moved to ban the book. Yet despite this potential difference in opinion, it does not appear that he ever raised any questions regarding other decisions or hesitated to sign future prohibition orders, instead ensuring that institutional censorship ran smoothly and caused him few troubles.

Before Yeats told him of his run-in with Ruttledge, Shaw had predicted that the government would remain unmoved. In a letter to his Polish translator, Shaw lamented the extreme nature of censorship in Ireland. His exasperation is noteworthy as the practice had yet to reach the heights of the early 1950s, when, as we shall see, an average of almost three books per day were banned. As the Irish censorship "bans many books and authors unchallenged in Poland," he wrote, "I do not expect it to give way to a Freethinker of Irish Protestant birth."[102] When he was informed of the government's decision, he told Yeats: "You can't prosecute a Government: the King can do no wrong." He suggested that continuing their fight would only result in "a triumph for the enemy," and thus felt that it was a hopeless cause: "When the *force majeure* is on the other side it is the greatest of mistakes to attempt any sort of compulsion. Articles and Miltonic essays may be hurled at the Government if the editors and publishers can be induced to print them: that is all." However, "I shall not protest: if the Churchmen think my book subversive they are quite right from their point of view."[103] After so many censorship battles that had largely left matters unchanged, Shaw was decidedly pessimistic. Unfortunately, the matter was dropped and no further action was taken by the Academy.

By this time, the Catholic press had caught wind of the Academy's efforts and started a counter-campaign by further attacking the novella. The *Catholic Mind* focused on the blasphemous aspects of Shaw's book, which they considered indecent.[104] For its part, the *Catholic Bulletin* mocked the efforts of writers to lobby the government, while making the unfounded nationalist claims that Shaw and Yeats were working "with the help of anti-Irish press magnates in England" and that the Academy was an "alien pest." It also made ad hominem attacks on the IAL's members in referring to their "Souper connections and Charter School upbringing, appearances in public courts for obscene publications, divorce publicity, and cognate blazonries," with special rancour reserved for Shaw and Yeats as the leaders of this "parade of putridity."[105] Published in August and September, the articles were unnecessary: by this time, the government and the Academy were reconciled to the book's banning and the reality of Irish censorship. The Catholic papers must have soon realised this as they made no further mention of the case, smugly triumphant in their silence.

In the end, the banning of *The Adventures of the Black Girl in Her Search for God* represented a definite failure on the part of the IAL and a sound defeat of freedom of expression. If the Academy was unable to defend Shaw's book, then lesser-known Irish writers and those who wrote more risqué material stood little chance of avoiding censorship or having bans repealed. Although the censorship files in the National Archives are incomplete, the fact that they contain no other mention of the Academy suggests that it did not continue to lobby the government. At its Annual General Meeting on 20 November 1936, Frank O'Connor and Sean O'Faolain openly declared that the Academy was moribund and had not followed its mandate to publicly protest the banning of books.[106] Yet this direct challenge by its younger members provoked no renewed sense of collective purpose. Indeed, O'Faolain came to consider that the Academy had become little more than a literary social club, holding an occasional banquet and bestowing awards on its members' work.[107] Writing to Yeats at the outset of 1934, Shaw had likewise complained that the "prizegiving [*sic*] business has no sense in it." If they were to recognise literary achievement, then "the prize should be for the worst English novel. That would at least amuse the public. Donkey races are always popular."[108] It was vintage Shaw, deploying devastating humour to criticise the Academy for straying from its foundational aim of combating censorship; instead of pushing for reform, the Academy was reduced to celebrating its own members. The IAL's archives in the National Library of Ireland support these assertions: they extensively detail awards but make no mention of challenging bans in the wake of Shaw's book. As a result of this change in its *raison d'être*, from the Academy pressuring the government to rewarding literary achievement, institutional censorship did not encounter any significant challenge or critique for the next few years. Thus, while the banning of Shaw's book was originally seized upon as the occasion to affect legislative change, it instead revealed the Academy's impotence, marking its celebratory launch as the beginning of a quick trip into political irrelevance.

Despite this ineffectiveness, the Academy was important for establishing the organisational resistance of writers in Ireland. While it no longer fought against censorship, the IAL gave direction to the next generation of Irish writers. Having been active in the IRA, O'Connor, O'Faolain, and O'Flaherty did not need to be told the importance of sacrificing themselves to a cause. Rather, the IAL under the leadership of Shaw, Yeats, and AE, all veterans of censorship battles in Britain and Ireland, showed them how to canalise their politics through an organisation that actively engaged with the democratic process, thereby creating a template for them and the organisations that they would later cofound and helm. No longer would Irish writers abstain en masse from the political process as they had during the CEL's hearings in 1926 and the Oireachtas debates in 1928 and 1929. At the same time, the work of the IAL was not accompanied by the polemics of those earlier periods. The absence of writers in the public sphere while they worked backdoor channels meant that politicians did not have larger social pressures to bear and could make decisions without much scrutiny.

The banning of Shaw's book and the interventions of the IAL attest to the wisdom of Irish legislators, having learned from the criticisms that Joynson-Hicks faced in the British trials of Hall and James, in establishing a censorship board. In this sense, the international dialectic worked in favour of the government as the minister for justice was able to say that the case was out of his hands and that the Censorship Board was autonomous, despite his having the power to overturn their decisions. Yet, as George Sylvester Viereck attested, the censorship also had a negative effect in terms of how Ireland was perceived by writers from elsewhere who were otherwise supportive of Irish independence. Thus, while the government was shielded from criticism via the separation between itself and the Censorship Board, the actions of the board could still reflect negatively on both the government and the country.

For Irish writers, as Garnett suggested, censorship would only accelerate their exodus and exile. It would, in effect, alienate them from their home country and force them to find acceptance abroad. This international dialectic was reinforced in the claims of Shaw and Yeats that Irish censorship would effectively kill a native Irish literature by forcing Irish writers to turn to markets in Britain and America and hinder the flourishing of a native Irish book trade. With their Nobel prizes, Yeats and Shaw were globally recognised as literary lions, and they used their social capital to found the IAL to lobby for freedom of expression. They also recruited Irish writers of international repute, although they unfortunately failed to draft the exiled Joyce and O'Casey. In fact, O'Casey's public and caustic rejection might have damaged the IAL's reputation and thus their social and political capital. Yet they did succeed in attracting Lord Dunsany, T. E. Lawrence, Eugene O'Neill, and L. A. G. Strong, major writers of Irish heritage who were born in Britain and America, thereby representing for its time a broad definition of what it means to be an Irish writer. However, as the Catholic, nationalist press was quick to suggest, the IAL was an alien group of writers: alien in their adherence to non-Irish values, alien in their places of abode, alien in their backgrounds, and alien in supposedly being financed by foreign sources. Such hostility, coupled with government inertia, would lead to the failure of the IAL to get the banning of Shaw's book overturned and set a moderate precedent in the workings of Irish censorship. In the coming years, Irish writers would conduct themselves as the generation before them did during the 1907–9 campaign in Britain: they would marry the two strategies of politically directed social organisation and polemical intervention.

Chapter Six

International Networking: Establishing Irish PEN

In the initial decades after its founding in 1921, the celebrated organisation PEN International adapted when confronted with existential threats. Now well-known as being dedicated to defending freedom of expression and assisting exiled and imprisoned writers, its origins were considerably more modest as it was established as a society to promote collegiality among its members and literature to the greater world. The story of how it grew into its more militant incarnation as it reacted to the turbulent politics of the twentieth century is fascinating. And the role that Irish PEN played in that movement, at times aligned, at times seemingly at odds, is equally absorbing.

As the prior chapters have shown, Irish writers understood themselves to be part of an international community and considered this an essential element in their struggles with censorship. In many ways, joining PEN was part of a persistent push towards the international, as evidenced in George Moore's and Bernard Shaw's experiences in England, the use of the British press by Irish writers as legislation was being debated in the Dáil, and the composition of the membership of the Irish Academy of Letters (IAL). Yet this push went against the grain of the nationalist culture of exceptionalism and insularity that dominated Irish social discourse and politics in the post-independence period. Somewhat paradoxically, the inward-looking impulses of the people and politicians and the internationalist tendency of writers were both part of larger trends, with nationalist governments and isolationism more frequently becoming the order of the day in polities across the Western world. As the early history of Irish PEN reveals, in keeping with their colleagues in other countries, Irish writers increasingly insisted on humanist values, emphasizing the correlation between universal rights and internationalism and between restricted freedoms and nationalism.

Despite changing contexts, this turn to PEN maintains a continuity with what we have seen thus far. Indeed, the history of Irish PEN and its interweaving with the international organisation shows how many of the older generation, among them John Galsworthy, Bernard Shaw, and Hugh Law, continued to affect and influence the strategies of Irish writers. Yet a younger generation of Irish writers, led by Sean O'Faolain, would now take up the reins in the fight for freedom of expression, aligning themselves much more concertedly with a well-organised and energetic international body of their peers. Inspired by their forebearers, they founded Irish PEN in the hope that belonging to a wider body of artists would help them to challenge censorship in Ireland by enabling them to work more concertedly and radically than writers had in the past.

The Founding of Two PENs

While the IAL attracted a constellation of literary stars through the pull of the country's two Nobel laureates, PEN International had significantly humbler origins. Its founder, Catherine Amy Dawson Scott, was a little-known Cornish author whose power resided in her keen energy, sociability, and organisational skills. The idea for PEN can be traced to its precursor, the To-Morrow Club, which Dawson Scott formed in 1917 to provide a literary hub that would be supportive of young writers. At weekly dinners, these youth mingled with more established authors that she invited, including Shaw, Galsworthy, Lord Dunsany, Siegfried Sassoon, and T. S. Eliot. Thrilled with the success of her work, she soon envisioned creating an organisation whose frontiers would know no bounds.[1]

In the wake of World War I, there was an increasingly positive view of international co-operation. Ventures undertaken in this spirit were seen as ways of forming and nurturing relations between countries to stave off such catastrophic conflicts. The best-known result of this movement, the League of Nations, was created in 1920 under the terms of the Treaty of Versailles.[2] In many respects, PEN was founded to do in the cultural sphere what the League was founded to do in the political sphere. In the summer of 1921, Dawson Scott came up with the idea of PEN and its acronym, which stood for Poets, Essayists, and Novelists. Motivated in large part by her horror at the suffering and hatred that had consumed so many people during the war, she founded PEN as a humanitarian group that would promote tolerance and friendliness between writers from different nations.[3] Over the years, it would have to balance the tensions between national differences and a united vision of humanity, but, at the outset, it was optimistic about the future.

Recognising that she lacked the gravitas of a more accomplished writer to attract people to the cause, Dawson Scott leaned a good deal on Galsworthy, who was elected the first president of PEN and remained in the position for eleven years. Marjorie Watts – Dawson Scott's daughter and biographer, as well as a pivotal administrative force in the group's early years – recalls that her mother and Galsworthy were united in their commitment to internationalism.[4] In accepting Dawson Scott's offer to help found PEN, Galsworthy told her that "Anything which promotes the internationality of art is good."[5] In many ways, it was to incarnate the Enlightenment ideal of a Republic of Letters.[6]

Some forty people were asked to attend PEN's first dinner meeting on 5 October 1921. Dawson Scott's invitation made it appear less grandiose than her designs, noting that a "dinner club" would enable writers to meet.[7] Perhaps inevitably, the gap between its reality of hosting soirées and its lofty internationalist objectives drew some commentary. Shaw originally balked at the idea, claiming that "literary men should never associate with one another ... because their minds inbreed and produce abortions." However, he relented, joining "on the International basis, not the prandial one."[8] A few years later, he claimed that PEN was a social Ponzi scheme "formed to gratify" Dawson Scott's "craze" for "literary society. No other reason for its existence has ever been alleged or discovered; but it has resulted in innumerable dinners, luncheons and receptions for literary guests taking place all over Europe. ... I joined because John Galsworthy said I must. He, presumably, joined because Mrs Dawson Scott said he must. That is how the Club is recruited. I avoid it as I would the plague."[9]

Work began almost immediately to expand the base of its membership across London and the greater world. Oddly, while Shaw and Lennox Robinson were offered membership, W. B. Yeats and AE were invited to join as honorary members because they were considered Irishmen. Other international members were likewise made honorary members in January 1922, among them Knut Hamsun, Maurice Maeterlinck, Anatole France, and Georg Brandes. These men were also asked to found national centres in their respective countries – Norway, Belgium, France, and Denmark – as were Thomas Hardy (England), Edith Wharton (USA), Gabriele D'Annunzio (Italy), Maxim Gorky (Russia), Gerhart Hauptmann (Germany), and Stephen Leacock (Canada).[10] In February 1922, France created the first centre outside of London; Spain, Belgium, Norway, Sweden, Romania,

Bulgaria, Czechoslovakia, Denmark, Italy, and the United States were likewise established by the end of 1923. The number of clubs grew to nineteen in 1924, and by then over three hundred members belonged to the London Centre alone.[11] Attesting to the power of PEN to have some effect on the wider world, their 1926 International Congress was held in Berlin, the first such event to come to the German capital in the post-war period. Hermon Ould, the first full-time secretary of PEN, recalled that "the moral effect" of the Berlin Congress "was enormous," as it showed good will towards German authors and helped to combat the isolationism into which the country had fallen under the harsh terms of the Treaty of Versailles.[12]

Despite such interventions, PEN steadfastly claimed in these years that it was above and beyond politics. A great deal of this had to do with Galsworthy's vision of the organisation. In 1922, he drafted a charter of five principles that provided the ethos for PEN's early functioning: one, it stood for literature in the artistic sense, not journalism or propaganda, and sought to diffuse such art; two, it stood for amicable relations between writers of a country and between writers of different countries; three, it demanded that its writers not advocate for war; four, it supported humane conduct; and five, it rejected using such words as *nationalist*, *internationalist*, *democratic*, *aristocratic*, *imperialistic*, "or any other words with definite political significance" as "PEN has nothing whatever to do with State or Party politics."[13] The contradictions are glaring: PEN was founded on international principles and sought to include writers from all nations, and yet it claimed that it was apolitical, or "supra-political."[14] However, it has evidently been guided by a liberal and humanitarian ethos, both of which are political in nature. Stranger still, in discussing his outlook for PEN, Galsworthy was pessimistic about the ability of writers to exert influence and provoke change, claiming that "Writers have no great, at least no direct influence on world affairs. Such influences as they exert are vague, and, as it were subterranean."[15] The comment is even odder considering Galsworthy's own engagement in the 1907–9 censorship campaign. Moreover, when his play *Justice* was staged in London's West End in 1910, it was so affecting that Winston Churchill, the home secretary at the time, attended several performances and enlisted Galsworthy to help draft legislation to reform the penal system.[16] In that case, he most definitely impacted political and judicial affairs and the treatment of prisoners.

Galsworthy's desire to remain apolitical was tested in PEN's early years in relation to discussions of censorship. The subject first reared its head at the 1927 Congress in Brussels. This was a watershed gathering remembered more today for having produced PEN's first official charter, the three principles of which remain largely unchanged:

1. Literature, national though it may be in origin, knows no frontiers and should remain common currency between nations in spite of political and international upheavals.
2. In all circumstances, and particularly in time of war, works of art, the patrimony of humanity at large, should be left untouched by national or political passion.
3. Members of P.E.N. will at all times use what influence they have in favour of good understanding and mutual respect between nations.[17]

The only major amendment to the charter in the years since has been the addition of a fourth principle stating that PEN supports the unhampered transmission of thought and freedom of expression, a decidedly liberal position.

At the time, Galsworthy succeeded in dismissing the issue of censorship by arguing that it would become political. He believed that discussion of censorship at congresses should "be avoided like Satan himself."[18] Unwilling to risk his popularity and apolitical status, he even refused to support Radclyffe Hall and her novel *The Well of Loneliness*.[19] Ignoring Galsworthy's wishes at the Vienna Congress in 1929, the same year that Ireland passed the Censorship of Publications Act, PEN members made a formal announcement on the subject. Although they sympathised with measures taken by the League of Nations and governments to protect children from immoral books, PEN believed that "authors ought to have the chance to give free expression to their thoughts and that the free circulation of artistic works ought not to be hindered." As a result, PEN expressed "its regret that latterly the authorities in different countries have confused great classical works and the sincere work of modern authors with the productions of an objectionable industry."[20] Galsworthy's desire to steer clear of such politics made him a lightning rod for criticism, especially during the 1932 Budapest Congress, where he was charged with hypocrisy for refusing to become involved on behalf of writers and members of PEN who had been incarcerated as political prisoners.[21] Despite such caution, PEN thrived under Galsworthy's tenure, and the foundations for international collaboration between writers were solidly laid.

While PEN clubs were quickly founded in much of Europe, Ireland was slow off the mark. Watts wrote to inform Lady Gregory that they saw her as the ideal president of a Dublin Centre, but the project seems to have come to naught.[22] A proposal was launched again in November 1928 when Hermon Ould contacted Hugh Law, who, as we have seen, sat as a member of the Joint Select Parliamentary Committee in 1909 and had recently spoken in the Dáil against the Censorship of Publications Bill. In the summer of 1929, AE and Law drew up a shortlist of potential founder-members.[23] International PEN was "delighted" at the news.[24] But fearing more Irish ineptitude, Ould wrote to them again. "Yesterday the Iceland P.E.N. was formally established," he taunted. "Ireland ought not to lag behind Iceland!"[25] The strategy of touching the writers' sense of national pride worked, with the Irishmen immediately responding that the forthcoming formation of an Irish Centre could be formally announced.[26]

By December, the Irish PEN Centre was established by a handful of writers, with Law, Walter Starkie, Lennox Robinson, Michael Tierney, C. P. Curran, George O'Brien, Winifred Mary Letts, and Edmund Curtis on the executive committee, Yeats as president, and Lady Gregory and AE as vice-presidents.[27] The timing is important as it was only a matter of months since the Censorship of Publications Bill had passed into law and International PEN had taken a formal stance against literary censorship at the Vienna Congress. By the first General Meeting at the Peacock Theatre in the spring of 1930, they had increased membership to twenty-seven.[28] Within a year it grew to thirty-six members, including Daniel Corkery, F. R. Higgins, Edith Somerville, T. C. Murray, Peadar O'Donnell, P. S. O'Hegarty, Rutherford Mayne, and Maurice Walsh.[29]

Despite the impressive list of authors, the organisation quickly went to pot. One contributing factor might have been that, as Law noted, many prominent Irish writers lived in London, and with the exception of Stephen Gwynn, none had opted for membership in Irish PEN.[30] In the meantime, the IAL appears to have consumed writers' political attention and activities. As for its ability to work with its international confederates, Irish PEN seems to have been oblivious to PEN's meetings and the merits of transnational solidarity. Indeed, Ould repeatedly asked Law to propose representatives to attend the annual congress.[31] He also had to prod Law to see if he could perhaps find a London-based Irishman to be a delegate for the International Council meeting.[32]

To get some idea of how quickly Irish PEN slipped into utter shambles, one need look no further than the preparations for the 1931 International Congress at The Hague. Towards the end of 1930, Ould informed Law that five nations, including Ireland, were invited to speak "on the condition of literature today in their own countries, with special reference to the dissemination of foreign books."[33] However, Irish PEN did not send a delegate. At a time when Ireland had joined the global club of writers and was given the opportunity to introduce itself, and when it was immediately confronted by institutional censorship that was established, in part, to prevent the circulation of foreign literature and ideas, its writers failed to seize the occasion to discuss how books written by other peoples were – and were not – disseminated on the island.

The only time that Irish PEN appears to have taken an active political stand in these early years was to rebuff international collaboration because of national politics. In the early 1930s, PEN had begun to agitate on behalf of its members who had been incarcerated for expressing ideas counter to state ideologies. This was a particularly contentious issue in Ireland. During the Anglo-Irish War, Irish rebels were imprisoned by colonial British forces, and during the Civil War, anti-Treatyites were imprisoned by the Irish Free State. Although Ireland was no longer officially at war, the IRA remained active, and some of its members were currently incarcerated for fighting against government forces that they believed prevented the establishment of an Irish Republic that would unite the entire island. Hugh Law hoped that Ould and International PEN would not find the Irish "heartless," but understand that given the "particular circumstances affecting this country at the moment," their participation in the campaign would likely be "a possible source of domestic controversy," and thus they felt that it was wiser to refrain.[34] And refrain they did, to the point that the Dublin Centre ceased to exist in all but name.

Given that he complained that the IAL had become a spent political force, it should come as little surprise that Sean O'Faolain revived the twice-abandoned Irish PEN. As it happens, O'Faolain had been in contact with Ould for over two years before he took up the reins. In March 1932, Ould sent promotional material to O'Faolain, who was then residing in England, hoping that he would join.[35] Knowing that O'Faolain was preparing to return to live in Ireland, Ould emphasized that PEN was "very anxious that the Irish Centre should, as far as possible, get into the hands of fairly young people."[36] O'Faolain suggested that the timing was not propitious for him. He further warned Ould of local conditions that stood in the way of the success of Irish PEN: Dublin was small "and liable to break into cliques," and it was not "a wealthy lazy city like London," being a place where people worked and had little time or money for salons. Under such circumstances, he suggested a partnership formed by an older president who could adeptly navigate local politics and attract people alongside an energetic young secretary to undertake the grunt work.[37] Ould, however, continued to groom O'Faolain, inviting him to PEN activities while he remained in England.[38]

By 1934, Ould and Dawson Scott had become upset over the fortunes of Irish PEN. C. P. Curran, who was supposedly the secretary, no longer responded to their correspondence. For his part, AE suggested that now that O'Faolain was settled in Ireland he would be "an ideal person" to resuscitate it.[39] Yet, being a young writer and the main breadwinner of his family, O'Faolain was reticent to do so.[40] A few months later, Ould tried O'Faolain again.[41] Prompted into service, O'Faolain asked for information regarding the qualifications for membership and sounded Ould out on his "opinion as to the attitude of any nationalistically minded centre towards the 'English' control" of PEN, which he noted was "a point of possible import" for Irish writers.[42] Ould reassured him that there was no English control and that "every centre is entirely autonomous."[43]

O'Faolain attended the International Congress in Edinburgh that spring as Ireland's sole delegate and returned convinced of PEN's mission. He wrote to Ould in October to announce that, with him as the new secretary, the Dublin Centre was up and running with a younger and more politically engaged cohort. Their objectives, O'Faolain said, were "To bring together XXXXXXXXXX all Irish writers with a view to creating the atmosphere and conditions most favourable to the development of lit. in Ireland, and to promote the friendly co-operation of all writers with similar objects in their own countries in the interests of international understanding and goodwill." He admitted that the crossed-out words read "in friendly co-operation," and that "their deletion is an interesting comment on our difficulties."[44] Despite such headaches, within a couple of months they had brought membership up to thirty-five. Of the invigorated centre, O'Faolain noted: "We are keen to make it alive to the need for defence of Liberty of expression, a hot question in this island."[45] A year later, membership had more than doubled to seventy-two.[46]

O'Faolain's arrival at PEN was fortuitously timed. His view of the organisation as a tool that could be used for political engagement aligned well with PEN International's new president, H. G. Wells, who had assumed the position following Galsworthy's death in 1933. Wells was a committed internationalist, having written an important pamphlet to promote the League of Nations in 1919 and devoted a good part of his life to spreading the gospel of international socialism.[47] His fearlessness in confronting opposition and maintaining principled stances made the international congresses during his presidency contested affairs. Such leadership was needed for an organisation that valued the international dimensions of literature and freedom of expression while much of Europe convulsed under the totalitarian threats of nationalist governments in Southern, Central, and Eastern Europe.

Wells's first International Congress occurred in the scenic Croatian (then Yugoslav) city of Dubrovnik at the end of May 1933. Hitler had seized control in Germany that January, and his National Socialist Party won the March election, which was marred by brutal Brownshirt tactics. Soon thereafter, he was given dictatorial powers. On 10 May, there were massive book burnings across Germany, with the largest such event taking place in Berlin's Opernplatz, where forty thousand people gathered to hear Joseph Goebbels and watch the destruction of over twenty-five thousand "un-German" volumes. The infringements on freedoms in Germany became a grave concern for PEN. At the London Centre's April dinner, Henry Nevinson, known for his crusading journalism and progressive politics, called members' attention to "the treatment of writers and other intellectuals in Germany" and asked what PEN proposed to do.[48] Telegrams were then dispatched to PEN centres around the world to gauge members' opinions.

In the meantime, it was suggested to wait for the International Congress so that the matter could be aired in a public forum that would hopefully lead to consensus. PEN vowed to act decisively by asking the German delegates to explain why such distinguished writers as Heinrich and Thomas Mann, Stefan Zweig, and Erich Maria Remarque were not admitted as members and why Alfred Kerr had been asked to resign as their centre's president.[49] For most, the rationale for the exclusion of these figures was obvious: the Mann brothers were vehemently opposed to the Nazis, Remarque was considered an anti-war writer and Goebbels had recently banned his classic *All Quiet on the Western Front* for being unpatriotic, and Zweig and Kerr were Jews. In interviews leading up to his departure from England, Ould told one journalist "that the abuses and crimes in Germany" would be discussed and that he would "be the very first to vote for the expulsion of the Hitlerites from the 'literary community.'"[50] In its pre-congress coverage, *The New York Times* referred to the "Nazi-controlled German P.E.N. Club," whose delegates would "defy world criticism of the Nazi attitude toward liberal authors."[51] The battle was to live up to its hype and set PEN on a decidedly more politicised course from which it has rarely veered.

Wells set the tone on the congress's opening day with his presidential address. He began by noting that PEN was founded on the idea of international co-operation, but that this value was existentially threatened. There was now a tension between those who were open towards constructing a world community and those who sought a return to discipline and insularity. They were at a crossroads, and delegates had to decide along which path they were to lead PEN.[52] The next day Henry Seidel Canby, a Yale University professor, noted that "There are again abroad in the world aspects of chauvinism which debase the spirit" of humankind and cause people to persecute others and rob them of their freedom. He thus called upon members "to take definite steps to prevent the individual centers ... from being used as weapons of propaganda in the defence of persecution inflicted in the name of chauvinism, racial prejudice, and political ill will."[53] Benjamin Crémieux, an active member of International PEN who later fought in the French Resistance and died in the Buchenwald concentration camp, believed that the Canby Resolution did not go far enough, while the Fascist apologist Filippo Marinetti, who has been referred to as "PEN's arch tormentor in the 1930s," applauded its moderation.[54] Seen as a compromise that still reflected PEN's values, it passed unanimously and was to form the basis for any action against all PEN centres that did not adhere to the three articles of the organisation's charter. In a raucous session that afternoon, the German delegates, led by the self-proclaimed Nazi writer Edgar von Schmidt-Pauli, protested Ould questioning their relationship with Hitler's regime and left the congress. At the London meeting of the International Executive Committee on 8 November 1933, the actions of German PEN were judged to be antithetical to PEN's values, and von Schmidt-Pauli, recognising the discrepancy, withdrew the Berlin Centre from the association. To fill this "unfortunate gap," exiled German writers were welcomed to form a new German PEN.[55]

When O'Faolain resuscitated Irish PEN, this was the newly energised association to which they belonged. And O'Faolain became quickly aware of PEN's liberalism when he attended the next congress in Edinburgh in June 1934. In the lead up to the event, PEN International maintained its anti-censorship stance in founding what it called the "German Library of the Burned Books." It contacted well-known authors, scientists, artists, and intellectuals from around the world to contribute works. The resulting library was inaugurated in Paris on 10 May 1934 to mark the one-year anniversary of the burning of books by Nazi leaders and their supporters.[56] Meanwhile, the first order of business in Edinburgh was a resolution moved by the British novelist Ernest Raymond: "That the P.E.N. stands for liberty of expression throughout the world and views with apprehension the continual attempts to encroach upon that liberty in the name of social security and international strategy. It affirms its belief that the necessary advance of the world towards a more highly organised political and economic order renders a free criticism of administrations and institutions imperative from all points of view."[57] Raymond was most concerned with new British legislation that was being proposed to allow authorities to search one's library or desk should they suspect one of supporting communism, socialism, or pacifism. The British scaremongers, he charged, were no better than the Nazis. He was warmly applauded by the delegates as he then turned his focus on them: writers had a great responsibility to critique, to push for social progress, and thus they would always be among the first to be attacked, "the angry bosses being quite ruthless because we are generally much more clever than they are and much more intelligent, and wielding a much more potent instrument, those selected, carefully chosen, and written words, because in aim at least we move the spirit of man."[58] A number of others then stood to voice their opinions, all in favour of freedom of speech. Despite an attempt by Marinetti to water down the resolution so that freedom of expression only applied to "real writers, but not to the pamphleteers," Raymond's resolution was carried unamended.[59]

With O'Faolain in the audience, the expulsion of German PEN in hindsight, and further challenges ahead, Wells charted the political course for PEN in his presidential speech. He said that they should, if possible, avoid politics. However, he asked, "what if Politics and Politicians and Police and Soldiers and so forth lift themselves up and presume to lay hands on literature and science? What if they attack books? What if they attack that free movement of the human mind which we call Science? What then? Can the P.E.N. Club still remain serene and say it has nothing to do with Politics?" His response was emphatic: "When Politics reaches up and assaults Literature and the liberty of human thought and expression, we have to take notice of Politics. If not, what will the P.E.N. Club become? A tourist agency – an organisation for introducing respectable writers to useful scenery – a special branch of the hotel industry." PEN's mission was thus clear: it could have "no justification for associating itself as a society with any party or school of thought. If and when National Socialism or Fascism invades the liberties of thought and literature, the P.E.N. must fight National Socialism or Fascism. But it must confine its fight to that issue." He also noted that freedom of expression was not only infringed upon by Fascist countries. Even in Britain, the Lord Chamberlain still determined what could be said in the theatre.[60] PEN, Wells said, had to wrestle with these situations.

Closer to home, a reborn Irish PEN had to grapple with such existential questions and determine how to organise considering that writers, and freedoms of expression more broadly, had been targeted by censorship legislation. The congress was a formative experience for

O'Faolain, illustrating how PEN was supposed to work and suggesting what the objectives had to be for the new centre in Dublin. In this way, the international context was essential for understanding how Irish writers would position themselves in relation to censorship and freedom of expression.

The Early Years of Irish PEN

From 1934 to 1937, Irish PEN under O'Faolain's leadership reflected the direction of PEN International under Wells and his successor, the French author Jules Romains. Both bodies came to vigorously defend freedom of expression and in so doing fought censorship head-on. The first rule of the reformed Irish Centre stated that the organisation's *raison d'être* was "to bring together all Irish writers of standing with a view to creating the atmosphere and conditions most favourable to the free development of literature in Ireland; and to make contact with all writers with similar objectives in their own countries in the interest of international understanding and goodwill."[61] The phrase "free development of literature in Ireland" was an indirect statement that Irish PEN was against censorship and would fight for the free circulation of literature, and this adherence to defending freedom of expression was aligned with their internationalist perspective. O'Faolain asserted that PEN's function is defined "by some such statement as our Rule One. After that all centres will interpret their ideas according to the circumstances of the time and place."[62] Like many delegates from other countries, O'Faolain was happy to align the national with the international, but he felt that the day-to-day running of any centre could only be undertaken with a degree of sovereignty to act according to local conditions.

However, it took Irish PEN some time to act. At a dinner on 30 October 1935, Lord Longford expressed hope that the Dublin Centre "would make itself a literary and intellectual force in the country."[63] Two weeks later, they held a public debate on the motion that the Censorship Board had exceeded its powers, the event attracting extensive newspaper coverage. The speakers included O'Faolain, Stephen Gwynn, Monk Gibbon, and A. E. Malone. O'Faolain opened by lamenting that the board had banned so many books – an average of more than one hundred per year. "It was clear," he emphasized, "that all the banned books were not in truth and in fact in their general tendency indecent or obscene," and that those with real artistic and literary value had been interdicted. One participant responded that restraint had always been used in societies and that living in them would be otherwise impossible, insisting that "no person who accepted the Catholic point of view would place the claims of Art before those of morality, truth and goodness." Most of those present wavered between these views. Confronted with this equivocation, O'Faolain withdrew the motion.[64] While Galsworthy had warned PEN to avoid the subject of censorship like the devil, Hermon Ould rather encouraged such measures as the staged public debate. "I am delighted to see that your Centre has been expressing itself on the subject of the censorship," he told Malone. "[T]his is good P.E.N. work."[65]

By this time, censorship had become a focus of PEN International. At the Barcelona Congress in 1935, the English and American Centres proposed a joint motion "that freedom of expression and publication is an inalienable right of all creative workers; that any censorship of literature hinders authors in their work, and is treason to the right of conscience, and should be resisted by all authors." Moreover, "the first duty of all governments to the author is to see that he is not hampered in that pursuit."[66] Recognising that in some countries authors were not in a position to put such principles into practice, they called on PEN International to make "demands as may be necessary whenever the occasion arises."[67] The resolution passed unanimously and would have considerable impact on how Irish writers confronted censorship.

Indeed, Irish PEN continued to reflect the more general movement of the international organisation towards defending freedom of expression. At a meeting on 12 May 1936, the executive committee of Irish PEN voted on a motion that was critical of the government's suppression of the IRA's newspaper, *An Phoblacht*. The protest was made irrespective of the members' different views on the opinions expressed in the paper, and rather focused on the matter of the government "perpetuating an evil tradition of tyrannical suppression." However, after some debate, no agreement was reached because, although all members accepted the principle of the motion, some felt that the paper "continued a tradition that had, in the past, displayed an ambiguous attitude towards 'the right to free speech.'"[68] They thus decided to adopt a policy on "the Censorship Question" at the Annual General Meeting (AGM) that autumn.

Censorship again became a hot-button issue following the banning of O'Faolain's novel *Bird Alone*, for which the Censorship Board issued a prohibition order on 29 August 1936. When Frank O'Connor returned from a trip to Italy some three weeks later, he wrote a letter of protest to the *Irish Times*. Registering his own shock at the banning, he was astonished that citizens had not been outraged "against a step which is obviously not intended to protect the Irish people against evil literature, but to destroy the character and prospects of Irish writers in their own country." There was not, he claimed, an indecent line in the entire book. "I admit," he wrote, "that by adopting the profession of literature O'Faolain has put himself outside the pale of decent society, and shown himself unworthy of our great Gaelic heritage of intolerance and illiteracy; but does not the law go too far in denying him the rights accorded to a murderer?" It would be a step up from the current state of affairs in Ireland, he argued, should writers be raised to criminal status by at least having the possibility of being publicly tried before their peers. Even in Fascist Italy, he had been able to purchase many books that were banned in Ireland and others that were openly critical of Mussolini's dictatorship.[69] O'Connor's letter sparked a brief campaign of protest by figures such as Lynn Doyle, who referred to the Censorship Board as a "secret tribunal," and A. E. Malone, at the time the organising secretary of Irish PEN, who claimed that the censorship amounted to little more than "legalised slander."[70]

Not being one to hold his tongue and always enamoured with the possibility of being at the centre of a melee, O'Faolain wrote "The Dangers of Censorship," an essay that appeared in the November issue of *Ireland To-Day*, the country's leading progressive periodical of the time.[71] Addressing the recent banning of *Bird Alone*, Francis Hackett's *The Green Lion*, and Austin Clarke's *The Singing-Men at Cashel*, he argued that "while it is undoubtedly an indignity to be publicly proclaimed as a pornographer, we could bear with that, confident of our own integrity as artists, and indifferent, as artists, to a form of insult which is rapidly becoming quite meaningless by indiscriminate use, if we did not believe that the chief results of the Censorship are to debase the public conscience, to bring the law into disrepute, and to limit, not the growth of the author, but the growth of the nation."[72] Reflecting broader concerns about what was happening on the continent, he highlighted the tyranny of an unchecked censorship, one that functioned without a proper mechanism of appeal and that in effect rendered citizens unable to form proper consciences, thereby depriving them of free will and the ability to cultivate virtue. He feared that the result of censorship and the mentality that informed it was that Ireland would become infused with national isolationism. In so doing, it would cut itself off from global currents of thought and thereby kill the potential for a dynamic and progressive society. Like the founders of PEN, he saw literature as providing the foundation for a critical-thinking liberal humanism. And like Shaw before him, he believed that for civilisation to make any positive progress, a politics of tolerance needed to be articulated and defended.

At the AGM that same month, O'Faolain addressed the membership of Irish PEN on the subject of censorship, concluding with some frustration: "The very things which we exist to counter tend to defeat us even before we can get into grips with them – the apathy of modern Irish intellectual life, the popular policy of repression with regard to the promulgation of unpopular ideas, the monopoly of politics over every other interest in the public mind. If the club as a whole has not a forward policy, unanimously agreed on, or perpetually considered – which is best of all – it is left, and the committee is left, at the mercy of the effect of these things I have mentioned."[73] As though to underscore his disappointment and sense of failure, the attendance at the AGM was too small to hold a quorum, so the meeting was delayed to December. On this later occasion, there was no mention of censorship.

Unbeknownst to O'Faolain, the Censorship Board discussed the banning of *Bird Alone* at their meeting on 20 November 1936. The minister for justice had requested their observations on an appeal made by several professors from University College Cork and University College Dublin asking for the book's prohibition order to be revoked. The professors had read O'Faolain's novel and believed that "a wrong has been done the author." While they admitted that it concerns the "delicate subject" of premarital pregnancy, "it does so with fitting reserve" and "nowhere does it descend to the level of pornography." Moreover, because of the ban, the public was "deprived of a book of high literary value." As they understood the impossibility of the board's ability to act with infallibly "correct judgment in the case of every one of the huge number of books which come up for consideration," they sought to resolve the issue discretely rather than undertaking a "public press campaign which might embarrass the Board or the Minister." However, they stressed that the mistaken decision should be rectified.[74]

The minister had informed the board that "in no circumstances could he recommend the revocation of the prohibition order in force against 'Bird Alone,'" which begs the question: Why not? Under the terms of the legislation, he was the only means of appeal, but he was likely following the precedent of the case of Shaw's *The Adventures of the Black Girl in Her Search for God*. This allowed the board to not reconsider the issue, and instead emphatically entrench their position. In response, they noted that saying that the book was focused on "a delicate subject" was a euphemism, in effect betraying its unmentionable and therefore censorable nature. They cited the publisher's blurb that said that the book deals with "the conflict between the Church and a young man who rebels blindly against two of its most powerful elements – insistence on spiritual humility and <u>the control of sex</u>."[75] Their interpretation was considerably more condemnatory: "Translated into language more frank and direct, the author presents a 'hero' who advocates and preaches Free Love. This hero ... proclaims a gospel of lust, and forces on the heroine acceptance of fornication as a way of life, in spite of her conviction that their libertinage is 'mortal sin.'" They used the publisher's own words to build their case, underlining what they felt to be particularly damning passages: "Where so much more is involved than the merely physical consequences of love, the novel of sex is renewed, and in 'Bird Alone' gains a quality of significance lost since the days of 'Jude the Obscure.'" They considered the allusion to Thomas Hardy's scandalous final novel, which, they noted, was "derisively" referred to as *Jude the Obscene*, to be "eminently appropriate." While they viewed Hardy's book and Joyce's *A Portrait of the Artist as a Young Man* as the models for O'Faolain's novel, the "grossness" of these predecessors was redeemed "in some measure" by their "literary power," which they found "notably lacking" in *Bird Alone*. The board was particularly critical of the novel's characters: "A hero who revolts against clean living, alias 'control of sex'; a saintly heroine whose orgasm of passion is recorded with Naturalism's art (an unmarried expectant mother whose physical appearance in her last hour the author forces vividly on the reader's eye); the immoral hero's immoral aunt, a London prostitute; her protégé, the hero's grandfather, the 'old lecher'; a circus star who has been paramour successively of the old lecher and of his son – an unsavoury troupe." They thus chastised the protesters for not reading the novel "with a lively consciousness of a censor's responsibility to the adolescent and the inflammable."[76]

What is most revealing is not the expected attacks on immorality and the depiction of unconventional sexuality, nor the arguments that it is the paternal duty of the censor to protect children and arrest the reader's desire. As we have seen already, these are all typical points made in favour of censorship across historical periods, social contexts, and geopolitical borders. Rather, the most candid revelation is that the board considered that *Bird Alone* "must be classed with the many others of foreign authorship already banned as tending to deprave morals."[77] Despite the fact that it is entirely set in Ireland and written by an Irish author currently resident in Ireland and inspired by an Irish novel written by another Irish author, *Bird Alone* is classed as belonging to those works "of foreign authorship." There is thus a mentality central to the Censorship Board's decision-making that classified immoral authors – regardless of their material or their provenance – as non-Irish, meaning that the Irish are necessarily wholesome and moral, and thus only books reflective of this morality should be permitted to circulate in the country. Moreover, their claim that they are in some ways more sophisticated and sensitive readers than the university professors sets them considerably above the general public, in effect emphasizing their credentials as arbiters of taste and their roles as citizen-builders. Here, then, the members of the Censorship Board attested to the direct links between censorship and citizenship and thus demonstrated aspects of the international dialectic. Indeed, they both effectively labelled banned Irish writers as foreign and revealed that they considered themselves and censorship as being at the forefront of national identity formation.

It is curious that a group of professors from two of Ireland's leading universities had banded together and mounted a protest, but then did not follow up on their efforts in a more sustained manner or work in conjunction with O'Faolain or a writers' organisation such as PEN. Instead, the subject of literary censorship all but disappeared from the pages of the press for the remainder of the pre-war period. The only tangible result of the scandal and the inability to repeal the ban or effect any change was that Irish PEN suffered a small but significant wave of resignations: O'Faolain abruptly quit as corresponding secretary and later left PEN for good in 1938, and Francis Hackett, the newly elected vice-president of Irish PEN, fled Ireland and took up residence in his wife's native Denmark.[78] In this way, Hackett's trajectory follows that of James Joyce and Sean O'Casey, writers who left the country in part because of the censorship and intolerance to which they were subjected. In Hackett's case, his wife, Signe Toksvig, also had two of her novels banned in Ireland, which only served to further alienate them from the country.

Like Hackett's experience, the early history of Irish PEN exemplifies facets of the international dialectic of censorship. Most evidently, joining PEN International provided Irish writers contact with and support from an important organisation of their colleagues from other countries. Such a tactic could have allowed them to draw upon wider networks and helped them to bring about negative international attention to the censorship with which they – and indeed their foreign colleagues – were threatened. Thus, Irish PEN afforded the potential for an international body to combat national censorship. Although Irish writers failed to coalesce at first, and in fact failed quite miserably – and repeatedly – compared to their colleagues in many other countries, they were eventually galvanised by O'Faolain and a younger generation, perhaps in part because of their youthful energy, perhaps in part because they had yet to make names for themselves internationally and thus were more dependent upon the Irish market. Yet they also displayed a savvy for understanding the dynamic of the international dialectic, with O'Faolain acknowledging that while PEN sought to have common values and objectives among its members, it allowed national centres to respond independently to local conditions.

While asserting a degree of national sovereignty, O'Faolain understood, as his essay on the dangers of censorship attests, that a zealous censorship could cause the country to descend into isolationism. Safeguarding freedom of expression was therefore a means of maintaining Ireland's connection with global currents of thought and art. Isolationism was a very real threat, especially with the country currently engaged in a years-long tariff war with Britain and world powers increasingly receding from international institutions and electing nationalist governments. This, of course, was borne out by events when, most disturbingly, not only religious and nationalist groups, but also the Censorship Board, an institution of the Irish Free State no less, began to consider banned and risqué Irish writers as foreign, as internal others who had to be controlled and have their writing blocked from circulation for fear that it would hinder idealist attempts to construct a coherent and somewhat homogenous body of national citizens. As we will see, for the next few years, Irish PEN remained active, but, without O'Faolain at the helm, it lacked a commitment to defending freedom of expression and to fighting institutional censorship. Instead, following the wider zeitgeist, the centre recoiled from the international body to which it belonged.

Chapter Seven

Insularity and Reform: Irish PEN in the War Years

As the history of Irish PEN attests, there were times when the Dublin Centre remained sequestered from global currents and world events, in many ways reflecting the isolationism and protectionism that marked the initial decades of post-independence Ireland. This would come to a head during World War II, when Ireland declared itself neutral and stringently enforced that neutrality with strong censorship powers over the press. At the same time, the period would end with what appeared to be a major success for Irish PEN in agitating for reform of the literary censorship through a more systematic method to appeal bans. As we will see, this outcome would align with certain theories promulgated within PEN International that emphasized the links between internationalism and greater protections for freedom of expression.

Before the war, Irish PEN continued to increase its internationalist bona fides. In 1938, in the wake of the departures of such high-ranking politically engaged members as Sean O'Faolain and Francis Hackett, Irish PEN looked to Northern Ireland, where it created a Belfast Centre to complement the activities of Dublin, with the latter being the administrative headquarters. It was hoped that the Belfast Centre would stem "the never-ending emigration of genius that is at once the regret and the pride of Ireland," not only to Great Britain and elsewhere, but across the border to Dublin.[1] Within two years, the membership of Irish PEN had significantly increased, with one hundred writers affiliated with the Dublin Centre and another thirty with the Belfast Centre.[2]

In the lead up to World War II, Irish PEN demonstrated their devotion to internationalism at the Annual Dinner of the Belfast Centre on 22 April 1939. The meeting brought together not only members of the two Irish centres, but also a significant contingent from Scotland. Speeches were made to "appeal for sympathy with those less fortunate writers of other lands who are now without homes, or friends, or countries of their own," with the plight of an increasing number of refugee writers drawing much concern.[3] The overall tenor was one of affirmation of their mission, testifying to the goodwill between writers from different countries. Irish PEN maintained this outlook throughout the war years, with both centres continuing to host members from the other at meetings and dinners.

Such ventures emphasized the importance of international collaboration, and they ensured that Irish writers north and south of the border were both physically and morally supported in continuing their activities. To signify the harmony of Irish PEN, in 1940 the two centres adopted a common letterhead, "a small outward and visible sign of the inward and spiritual grace of goodwill."[4] Ould considered this a noteworthy event, and wished "to God that the common sense which seems to determine our actions would percolate to the governments."[5] He was particularly sensitive to this as he undertook the yeoman's task of helping to settle writers fleeing the conflict. At the time, several national centres in exile had taken up residence in London, where the headquarters of PEN International was situated. In the face of the totalitarianism that had convulsed the continent, there was a general concern that the war was undoing much of the solidarity and collaboration that PEN had established. Moreover, many feared that the political repression in some countries would spell the end of freedom of expression and vibrant literature, and result in the exile, imprisonment, and execution of PEN members.

The difficulty for Irish PEN at this time was that when Ireland declared its neutrality in the war, it caused the national body to withdraw from engagement with the international organisation.[6] Fearing that they would retreat into an isolationist *coquille*, Ould was "loth to think that Irish members will not be as eagerly P.E.N. as ever." It was, he noted, "our job to try and keep up cultural relations as much as we can."[7] Irish PEN might have made a stand against the imposition of repressive measures abroad and shown concern for the plight of their colleagues in other lands, but under the terms of wartime policy in Ireland, they could offer very little support. The Emergency Powers Act, which was passed immediately following the outbreak of the conflict, sought to keep Ireland neutral by presenting the country as a model of impartiality while suppressing anything that might prove to be divisive to national unity. It thereby restricted prejudicial information that it feared might potentially affect the security and preservation of the state. In practice, the state could seize any materials that were deemed to threaten its neutrality and could censor all publications. The result was that it created in Ireland a much more tightly controlled press than what existed in other neutral countries, including Switzerland, Sweden, and Portugal.[8] Given this context, Irish PEN could not offer any message of solidarity through the national press. Had they sent one to the London Centre for broadcast, it could have been intercepted and seized by Irish authorities, and thereafter placed PEN under scrutiny and potentially ruined its ability to work on local issues. This explains, in part, why Ould wrote in March 1940 wondering why "the Dublin Centre has been so silent since the war broke out."[9]

Comparatively, the Belfast Centre bristled with energy. Ould and May Morton, Belfast's enthusiastic secretary, regularly wrote about how the war was impacting their daily lives and to offer support when the other had endured German bombing raids. At one point, Ould admitted his "considerable uneasiness about Eire. It is a subject that one hardly dare discuss, and certainly not with an Irishman."[10] Morton offered her opinion from north of the border: "My own honest conviction is that she is genuinely neutral. ... In the clash of mighty empires, small nations can only continue to exist by the justice (or mercy) of the great ones."[11] The silence of the Dublin Centre could therefore be chalked up to several factors: the effects of the wartime censorship, the absence of international congresses with the advent of war, a decline in the number of visits from foreign writers, and a less politically charged executive. Taken together, these factors would cause the Dublin Centre to be far less inclined to agitate in favour of freedom of expression.[12]

A Neutral PEN in a Neutral Ireland

When Irish PEN finally broke its silence, it did so for rather selfish reasons that also indicated that the Dublin Centre had adopted, in some measure, the government's politics of neutrality. In the spring of 1941, they proposed that the first post-war congress of PEN International should be in Dublin as Ireland might be "the only country in Europe which will have escaped" destruction.[13] Ould welcomed the offer, but noted that as Stockholm, India, and London had been slated to host congresses before the war, they would have priority. He also took the occasion to inform Irish PEN of the rather prohibitive costs of hosting one of these "lavish" affairs, as those in Poland and Holland had each cost about £5000.[14] A month later, PEN International announced that they would hold the congress in London that September, the first such meeting since Prague in 1938. While there was general excitement in PEN that their activities would continue despite the unpropitious conditions, the Dublin Centre protested. Contending that PEN should avoid hosting a congress "in a belligerent country," they argued that one that was neutral, such as Ireland, would be a much more suitable place for "making the delegates welcome in every possible way."[15]

The international executive did not see any problem with a belligerent hosting the congress. As it was, London had been selected several years earlier, and now they were simply proceeding according to plan. In addition, Ould noted that there was already a large international presence of PEN members living in London: "We are in the happy position of being able to muster official delegates from many of the countries overrun by the Nazis" and thus "insure an unusually comprehensive congress." Moreover, he emphasized the current context and what both PEN and London's relative freedom meant to the continent: "So far as France is concerned there does not exist at present a French Centre. You do not need me to tell you that one of the first actions of the Gestapo wherever it spreads is to suppress the P.E.N. Many Free French members will be present at the Congress."[16] Had Irish PEN read regular PEN reports, they would have been aware of the London Centre's concerns and efforts. In the April 1940 issue of *P.E.N. News*, for example, it was noted that "The number of foreign writers in this country is increasing and many of them were members of P.E.N. Centres which flourished until the various forms of dictator aggression decided that they were a menace to a Totalitarian State."[17]

Irish PEN's idea was quixotic at best. Most notably, they do not appear to have considered the impossibility of their own proposition: as they were based in a country that had stringent censorship to ensure that it remained neutral, there would have been considerable tension regarding the press coverage of an organisation that increasingly favoured an Allied victory over the Axis and was openly critical of continental totalitarianisms. The chances are that the government would not have been open to such an organisation holding its international congress on Irish soil, making it unlikely that members would have been issued visas to enter the country.

Despite the reluctance of many of Irish PEN's members to participate in the London Congress, which ran from 11 to 13 September 1941, Peadar O'Donnell, who was the current vice-president of the Dublin Centre, Denis Ireland, and May Morton attended as the official Irish delegates. Other Irish authors of note – Bernard Shaw and L. A. G. Strong among them – showed their support by participating in sessions. In addition to writers, there were representatives from eighteen governments.[18] English PEN issued a press release on holding the congress in the current situation, noting that "the value of the P.E.N. has increased a hundred-fold." Because in times of war officials considered that literature could easily and "even usefully" be marginalised, with writers valued only when they could be employed as propagandists, they warned members that "they have special powers to serve – or to corrupt – civilisation" and proclaimed the "duty of writers" was "to hinder in every way the growth of hatred and contempt for the enemy nation." By fighting against totalitarianism, they were supporting freedom of expression, and "no one has a closer interest in guarding this freedom than writers." Their responsibility was to "keep open as many channels as possible for the movement of ideas" and to repeatedly denounce "any word, any act, any treaty, which debased the dignity and freedom of common men."[19] PEN thus stressed the perceived links between freedom of expression and internationalism, suggesting that a more cosmopolitan and international perspective ipso facto translates into less censorship and a greater exchange of ideas and literature, which would place the global organisation and Irish PEN at odds with one another at several key moments during World War II.

Indeed, schisms continued to appear between PEN International and the Dublin Centre. Many of these were related to the tensions between PEN International defending freedoms at all costs, while Irish PEN defended the country's neutrality. This led to Irish PEN becoming censorious of PEN International following the publication of a seemingly harmless report in *P.E.N. News*. In a tribute to the recently deceased Henry Nevinson, Benjamin Farrington, a Professor of Classics at University College Swansea, noted that as an Irishman he appreciated Nevinson's support of the Irish during the Anglo-Irish War of 1919–21 and the difficult times in which civil liberties were under attack in Northern Ireland. He also registered his regret that Ireland should remain neutral during the war.[20] At a meeting on 20 February 1942, the Dublin Centre passed a resolution that Farrington's comments were "outside the province of P.E.N.," with Austin Clarke writing to protest that Farrington's remarks were "politically controversial."[21]

For someone who was normally so humane and patient with centres across the globe, Ould responded in a most direct and dismissive way. He told Clarke that the memorial meeting for Nevinson had been jointly held by the London Centre and the National Council for Civil Liberties and that representatives of movements with which Nevinson had been involved were invited to speak to his legacy, before impishly concluding that he hoped that the Dublin Centre did "not wish to suggest that we should have <u>suppressed</u> Professor Farrington's remarks?"[22] Ould further inflamed matters by implying that Irish PEN was making a mountain out of a molehill.[23] For his part, Clarke was adamant in explaining the difficult situation in which Irish PEN found itself: "I do not think you realise the real issue. It is an offence here to publish or circularise propaganda against our strict neutrality. Your Committee, therefore, can hardly claim to have the right to circularise matter of such a kind in this country. The banning of P.E.N. News here would injure the Club in public opinion and might wreck it."[24] After further exchanges, Ould became mightily annoyed and puzzled by the Dublin Centre's persistence, wondering whether their "committee feels that it is our duty to suppress all reports of sentiment with which we don't agree."[25]

The exchange is notable for a number of reasons. Being an international organisation devoted to liberal humanist values, PEN saw fit to defend the right for people to speak their own minds, which was particularly important in the current context. At the same time, the tensions that flared up between the international organisation and one of its national centres were inevitable. Throughout its history, such strains have always existed between local concerns and the wider objectives of the organisation, with PEN usually showing some flexibility and understanding, save for in circumstances, such as with the German PEN in 1933, that cannot be reconciled to its charter. In the end, PEN had to insist on its principles and could not waver each time a centre protested. It was, rather, for the centre to be the organ of PEN's values and to disseminate them among their fellow citizens as best as they could. Because PEN had grown increasingly political in the 1930s and become a devoted agitator for freedom of expression in response to the war, it could not in this situation bend to Irish PEN's demands. To some extent, the Dublin Centre could be accused of toadying to Irish politics out of fear that were it to conflict with the law, it would look bad in public opinion, but some members felt that the reputation of Irish PEN should be safeguarded. Indeed, being found guilty of breaching the country's neutrality laws could have led to a very real existential threat for Irish PEN, and its members were simply ensuring its survival. However, it remains the case that in protesting against the publication of Farrington's comments in *P.E.N. News*, Irish PEN proposed that PEN International should be more censorious in its reporting.

A Call to Action

The exchange between Ould and Clarke was symptomatic of Irish PEN's impotence and lack of desire to effect change during the early war years. Yet it also coincided with the advent of a more progressive movement within Irish PEN that would push the Dublin Centre to defend freedoms more aggressively than it had since O'Faolain stepped down as secretary. At the AGM on 15 November 1941, Hanna

Sheehy-Skeffington proposed that a new group be formed to "take some definite action in the matter of the present Censorship of books in Eire."[26] At the next committee meeting, there was some discussion about holding a public debate on censorship. One member stated that authors had not taken advantage of the right to appeal bans to the minister for justice, and thus an author should contest a board ruling. This was followed by a representative of the Irish Society for Intellectual Freedom (ISIF), an organisation recently cofounded by Frank O'Connor, Hanna Sheehy-Skeffington, Lennox Robinson, and Dorothy Macardle, inviting "P.E.N. to send delegates to a proposed meeting of representatives of literary and other societies to formulate an authoritative demand for the removal of the censorship of books." However, the committee decided "that no action be taken in the matter for the present."[27]

A few months later, the executive determined that the censorship of publications was "entirely unsuitable" as it was currently administered. They then received a deputation from the ISIF headed by Sheehy-Skeffington. She had evidently broached the idea of censorship at the AGM to prepare the ground for her group to pressure Irish PEN into acting. The idea appears to have been that if Irish PEN was going to be lax in defending freedom of expression, others would provoke them. After the deputation presented their case, the executive of Irish PEN agreed to hold a symposium on the censorship of books – but not to include, they emphasized, the censorship of publications under the terms of the Emergency Powers Act.[28]

At Jury's Hotel on 30 May 1942, Austin Clarke, the president of Irish PEN, chaired a well-attended debate on "The Censorship of Books in Ireland." Notably absent were those most closely related to the workings of institutional censorship despite invitations for them to attend, including Gerald Boland (the minister for justice) and several members of the Censorship Board. All speakers agreed that the administration of the censorship of publications "shows a lack of common sense, fairness and conscientiousness. The works of famous writers, scholars and scientists are regularly placed on the banned list, and the majority of present-day Irish writers cannot be read in their own country." In response, those present proposed that a Council of Action, to be drawn from various literary and learned societies, should be established to inquire into how the censorship operated and "to deal with cases of injustice and misinterpretation of the Act."[29]

Soon thereafter, the executive of Irish PEN invited other organisations to join the Council of Action, including the IAL and the ISIF; Trinity College; the National University of Ireland; the Booksellers' Association; the National Association of Journalists; the Dublin Literary Society;

the Women's Writers' Club; the Librarians' Association; the Institute of Journalists; the Writers', Artists', Actors' and Musicians' Association (WAAMA); the Book Fair Committee; the Royal Irish Academy; and the Women's Social and Political Union.[30] By September, they had received positive responses from only a few, attesting to the general apathy or hopelessness with which many people regarded the latest crusade.[31] Despite the lack of enthusiasm, Irish PEN dutifully forged ahead with the formation of the council.

Later that autumn, the Council of Action's subcommittee on censorship reported to the executive that David Sears, the vice-president of Irish PEN, had a discussion on the subject with a member of the Department of Justice, who suggested that he broach the matter with Sir John Keane, a senator who, as we have seen, had long fought against censorship. They advised that Irish PEN should ask Keane to delay his proposed motion for censorship reform to give the Council of Action the chance to convene.[32] The council then wrote to the Censorship Board proposing that they should accept a deputation to hear the council's recommendations. Believing that the board was as anxious as they were "to obviate the possibility of error" in their decisions, they were confident that their proposals would be duly considered. Not surprisingly, the Censorship Board firmly rejected the offer, and the Council of Action was informed that they should instead direct any concerns that they had to the minister for justice.[33]

In the meantime, O'Faolain took a more public route of protest. In a letter to the *Irish Times*, he argued that the banning of several recent titles, among them Eric Cross's *The Tailor and Ansty* and Halliday Sutherland's *Laws of Life*, was "an embarrassment to the Government and a humiliation to the people."[34] Others, including the ISIF, seconded him and criticised censorship as it was currently being practised.[35] The groundswell raised by O'Faolain caused parliamentarians to discuss the matter and forced S. A. Roche, the secretary of the Department of Justice, to publicly explain and defend how the institution worked.[36]

Stirred by the Council of Action behind closed doors and Sean O'Faolain's public sortie, Sir John Keane's campaign for censorship reform began when he introduced a motion to the Seanad on 18 November 1942. While the parliamentary debates that followed have been detailed by many scholars, there has yet to be any recognition that much of the support for Keane, and indeed the origins of the reform movement, was rooted in the work that Irish PEN and the ISIF had undertaken for over a year.[37] As he had been in contact with Irish PEN, it is logical that Keane's motion embodied the spirit of the resolution that had been passed at the open debate on 30 May that the Censorship

Board had "ceased to retain public confidence, and that steps should be taken by the Minister to reconstitute the board."[38] To illustrate his argument, Keane focused on three books, each one having been, in his estimation, egregiously banned, two of which had been noted by O'Faolain: Eric Cross's *The Tailor and Ansty*, Kate O'Brien's *The Land of Spices*, and Halliday Sutherland's *Laws of Life*. The inclusion of O'Brien's *The Land of Spices* was also likely the result of Irish PEN's backdoor politicking: the executive noted in the preparations leading to the open meeting that they would only confirm the date "on our learning from Kate O'Brien as to when she can attend."[39] O'Brien had been the focus of Irish PEN in their censorship struggles because they believed that the rationale that underpinned the banning of her novel was spurious at best. However, despite having two of her books banned and being invited to attend the debate, O'Brien remained silent on the subject of censorship and aloof from social organisations that sought to defend her freedom of expression.

The Tailor and Ansty, which Keane described as a book about the pastoral lives and racy fireside banter of an elderly couple from County Cork, is a quasi-anthropological account of the disappearing folkways of the Irish people as much as it is a portrait of a *seanchaí*, a traditional Irish storyteller. Keane argued that its banning had "aroused more indignation ... on the part of those who are interested in the domestic literature and genius of our people than on the part of those interested in that of the wider world."[40] To make his case, Keane read a lengthy excerpt. However, the passage that he read is not included in the parliamentary records, and in its stead is the phrase "*Here the Senator quoted from the book.*"[41] This expunging of the debates was undertaken at the behest of William Magennis, a senator who, as well as having been a champion of the original censorship legislation when it passed through the Oireachtas, was chair of the Censorship Board and a leading member of the Catholic Truth Society of Ireland. Magennis argued against the recording of passages from a banned book, which included "some of the vilest obscenity," because the official reports could be bought for only a few pence. In this sense, the government would make portions of a banned text cheaply available to the public.[42] His worries proved to be well-founded: the *Irish Times* later reported that Keane's criticisms of the Censorship Board were so popular that it was impossible to obtain a copy of the debates and that the state's Stationary Office was forced to ask inquirers to place orders with advance payment.[43] Magennis also tried to intervene by asking Keane to refrain from quoting the book, which Keane claimed was a further example of the work of the "literary Gestapo."[44] In the end, he defended the book as being Rabelaisian, not indecent, and denied that it was written with the intention to deprave or corrupt or to excite others to sexual passion or unnatural vice.[45]

While the banning of *The Tailor and Ansty* was ridiculed as essentially censoring aspects of Irish life, Keane was particularly furious over the censorship of *The Land of Spices*, which he called "a most astounding case."[46] The book is about a "noble character" who, in turn, becomes a nun when she discovers her father's homosexuality, is made the Reverend Mother of an Irish convent, and is named Mother General of the international order to which she belongs. For a single phrase, which discretely alludes to the homosexuality of the nun's father when he is discovered in "the embrace of love" with another man, the entire book was banned.[47] So much, it was suggested, for considering either the literary merit or the general tenor of O'Brien's novel.[48]

Similarly, although the state's position on birth control mirrored the Catholic Church's social teachings, Halliday Sutherland's *Laws of Life*, whose subject is reproductive health, was banned.[49] Indeed, Sutherland's book had been given *permissu superiorum* by the Archbishop of Westminster and was published by the English Catholic press Sheed and Ward. The focus of the debate was the book's discussion of the rhythm method, which, it was argued, was the only aspect that could have possibly drawn the censor's wrath – despite the fact that the rhythm method had long been taught by the Catholic Church.

Keane's main contention was that the censors inadequately attended to their duties, banning almost 1,600 books in the thirteen years since censorship was institutionalised. The problem with this, he claimed, was that no unpaid volunteer who held down a job and had a social life could responsibly read an average of three books a week and pass judgment on them, not to mention the others that were considered and not banned.[50] A further problem was the composition of the Censorship Board, the members of which Keane believed to be "detached from the stream of life and the outlook of youth."[51] Their standards, he claimed, were governed by a Victorian prudery that was at odds with the changing morality of the nation. The biggest loss, he claimed, would be to the literary heritage of Ireland. Not only had scores of the world's masters been banned, causing the Irish to lose touch with global artistic movements, but many leading Irish writers had likewise been targeted. The result was that the current generation was constrained through the censorship of their works and that future generations were robbed of their culture because these books would not be available to them. Had such a system been in place fifty years earlier, Keane argued, Ireland would not have had the "inspirational works" of the "great" George Moore and would have been the poorer for it.[52] The reputation of the country was therefore threatened by a censorship that acted too stringently. The residual effects included a potential paucity of internationally known Irish writers in succeeding generations. On these points, Keane's argument aligned with those of PEN on the importance of literature as the heritage for all of humankind and that its reach was international, not merely local in scope.

There was some support for Keane's motion and his comments. His staunchest ally was Professor Joseph Johnston, a senator representing Trinity College.[53] Johnston suggested that Keane's views might be representative of more people than had been heard in society, the implication being that they would have been heard more frequently if there had not been a culture of informal censorship that punished those who deviated from norms through shunning and other social pressures. Similarly, Desmond FitzGerald, the former Cumann na nGaedheal minister for external affairs and minister for defence, argued against the nationalist view of Irish exceptionalism, stating that censorship was necessary precisely because the Irish were as morally lax as others. If they were more virtuous than other peoples, there would be no need for censorship. The problem, as he saw it, was that the state had inadequately educated the populace. By promoting literacy, the state had given the people the tools to read, but it had not educated them *how* to read effectively and to be discriminating in their tastes. The people were therefore infantilised on two fronts: first, by being undereducated, and second, by being subjected to a censorship that was based upon what children should be allowed to read. Furthermore, he charged that those who argued that Irish writers should be censored for how they represent the nation were ignorant of the Censorship of Publications Act, as such provisions were not included. This was a direct response to senators who claimed that some Irish writers belittled their country merely to be championed in England. Such comments, FitzGerald argued, revealed an inferiority complex more than they said anything about the books.[54] Moreover, they attested to the nationalist anxieties over representation that were evident in the riot provoked by Sean O'Casey's *The Plough and the Stars*.

Unsurprisingly, William Magennis came down hardest against the motion.[55] He opened with an ad hominem attack, portraying Keane as a member of the Anglo-Irish Ascendancy and noting his service during World War I, thereby suggesting that Keane was loyal to England, not Ireland. He then argued that *The Tailor and Ansty* was sex-obsessed and a mere attempt to smear the Irish peasant to foreign readers, and drew people's attention to the fact that *The Land of Spices* was banned because of its allusion to the act of sodomy, which, Magennis reminded his colleagues, was illegal. However, he offered no such indictment of novels that portrayed murder or theft, and the phrase in O'Brien's book is vague enough that it could refer to anything from copulation to a hug. As for Sutherland's book, Magennis provided an exacting description of the differences between *imprimatur* and *permissu superiorum*, detailing how the book was cleared by the Archbishop of Westminster's censor *after* the first edition had been in print and only applied to the revised second edition. The banning of the book was therefore in keeping with the Church censor. Yet he made no attempt to differentiate between the responsibilities of the Church and the state or to recognise the censorship as a secular institution despite the arguments that he had made earlier to dissuade the Seanad that there was a conspiracy between the Censorship Board and the Catholic hierarchy.

Magennis's main preoccupation as a censor was what he called "Lecher-ature." To demonstrate how exacting the Censorship Board was in its decision-making, he held up Liam O'Flaherty's *Famine* as an example of a book that was "very strong meat," yet passed for untold reasons. Despite this, he noted that the more liberal elements in Irish society had chosen to focus on the borderline cases that had been banned, citing Frank O'Connor and Sean O'Faolain as the ringleaders of this cohort. Moreover, he remained unapologetic for writers who, like the oft-banned Norah Hoult, had been forced into exile; the responsibility was placed upon her for having written "horrible and revolting" material for English publishers.[56] He reasoned that it was not the fault of the police or the magistrate if the arrested criminal broke the law.

In the debates that followed, there was a remarkably large number of senators who felt that the Censorship Board might have been acting within the letter of the law, but not within its spirit. Robert Rowlette, who represented Trinity College, reasoned that the problem with censorship was that it was antithetical to the pre-independence struggles of the nation. Echoing Shaw's remarks from over a decade earlier, he said that as opposed to moving towards greater freedom, the Irish people had created shackles with which to control their independent impulses. There was therefore a drive towards collective freedom but a shunning of individual freedom. Rowlette would not support Keane's motion, however, because he was more radical, believing that the Censorship Board should be completely eradicated. In this sense, his views aligned with PEN's belief that the transmission of thought and culture should not be hindered in any way. Other senators agreed that the Censorship Board had made many questionable decisions and should have ignored much of what they had banned as they had only caused controversy and taken away from the otherwise good work that they had undertaken by interdicting truly offensive works. Summarising the debates, O'Faolain referred to the senators who spoke in favour of the Censorship Board as "deplorable" because "they were not fitted by nature or education to intervene on such a subject at all."[57]

In his final address, Keane openly admitted that more than 90 per cent of the country would not have read the books that had been discussed. Like Shaw, he argued that morality was not immutable, and that it was necessary to reflect a changing society with a reformed institution. In tabling the motion, he had intended to promote a discussion on the subject.[58] He argued that Britain's 1857 Act was better than Ireland's 1929 Act because it allowed for an open process in which individuals could defend and appeal their cases before the courts. Instead, Ireland had opted for the infantilisation of its citizenry by creating a society in which adults were denied certain books because they *might* cause harm to young and unformed minds.

In the end, the motion was defeated by a count of thirty-four to two. However, these numbers are deceptive. As the debate demonstrated, there was a growing faction that was dissatisfied with the censorship; the problem was that the motion failed to offer a suitable alternative. At the next meeting of the Censorship Board, Magennis's colleagues congratulated him "on his brilliant defence of Censorship ... and the work of the Board, when refuting the allegations made against them in the Senate. ... They expressed their lively appreciation of their good fortune in having such an able champion in the Senate when so badly needed there, and extended to the Chairman their most sincere thanks for this magnificent effort which resulted in such a striking and memorable vindication of the Board and the whole principle of Censorship."[59]

O'Faolain, though, remained optimistic, imploring the Council of Action "to keep on pressing the matter home."[60] The board, he noted, was elderly, and with continued pressure, more liberal-minded members might be appointed to align with society's evolving views. Writers, he concluded, have always been able to "extract the fundamental thing from the mass of superficial arguments" by the likes of Magennis "because they have always kept the fundamental rights of the individual Irishman in the forefront of their minds and have persistently fought for it in the face of every obloquy."[61] Importantly for them, change was in the air.

At first, Irish PEN did not pay heed to O'Faolain's advice to press on and instead faded from public view. By the summer of 1943, its future appeared particularly dreary as it started to lose its more politically engaged members.[62] It would not begin to take shape again until Seumas O'Sullivan and Kathleen O'Brennan kickstarted it the following year, hoping to recapture "the best element" of "those who had fallen away." Among these was O'Donnell, who caused "the most controversial debate" with a public lecture on "Have We Irish Writers Failed the People?" in which he insisted that writers should be prepared to use their pens "to arouse the public to a consciousness" of the censorship "and the cause of Justice."[63] He succeeded in riling the organisation, which was no small feat considering its recent lethargy. Coinciding with the renewed energy at Irish PEN, Keane proposed amending the legislation in a Senate debate on 19 April 1944, but he withdrew his motion two months later. While this might appear to have been a further sign of an impotent resistance, Keane had backed down because he learned that the government intended to legislate on the matter to provide more adequately for the principle of appeal.[64]

Despite this renewed energy, Irish PEN lagged behind the activities of PEN International, especially in defending and promoting freedom of expression. From 22 to 26 August 1944, the London Centre held a conference to commemorate the tercentenary of John Milton's *Areopagitica*. Aside from L. A. G. Strong, who chaired a session, no other Irish writer appears to have attended.[65] With broad support and enthusiasm over the anniversary of the anti-censorship tract, the event drew considerable attention. However, PEN squandered the occasion to make a firm commitment to the principle of freedom of expression in confusingly giving the conference the theme "The Place of Spiritual and Economic Values in the Future of Mankind." While some participants signalled their desire to speak on the censorship that Milton denounced, Ould insisted that people should keep to the conference's theme.[66] The result was that only three of the thirty-one participants addressed Milton's pamphlet directly. Reviewing the proceedings when they were published the next year under the misleading title *Freedom of Expression: A Symposium*, George Orwell lamented the sidelining of Milton's polemics, claiming that the essays are rather "remarkable for the way in which they *don't* deal with their alleged subject matter." The result was that instead of commemorating "Milton's great plea for liberty, you get this vague bumbling in which the liberty that is supposedly being defended is never clearly defined." Orwell concluded that it was "a depressing book."[67] Between Irish PEN's abstention and the participants' failure to address censorship, freedom of expression seemed to be forgotten as a *raison d'être* of the organisation.

The Bell Steps In

In refusing the occasion to participate in a symposium that purportedly celebrated a canonical anti-censorship pamphlet, Irish PEN missed a golden opportunity to speak against censorship not only in Ireland, but also in the wider world. Moreover, critiquing literary censorship in Ireland would not have caused Irish PEN to run afoul of the wartime censorship that ensured the country's neutrality. It should therefore come as no surprise that it was not Irish PEN who took up Milton's challenge in Ireland, but rather Sean O'Faolain at *The Bell*. With Peadar O'Donnell, O'Faolain cofounded the monthly periodical in 1940. His regular editorials set the tone for the magazine's liberal humanism, which was in line with PEN International and in contrast to the dominant nationalist, Catholic ethos. For O'Faolain, censorship was a symptom of the latter's narrow-mindedness, so it was a topic to which he often returned in his desire to make Ireland more progressive. From his involvements in and resignations from the IAL and Irish PEN in the 1930s to his founding and editing of a journal in the 1940s, there was a career trajectory in which he moved from working within writers' organisations to effect change by galvanising his colleagues and lobbying politicians directly to using a periodical to form public opinion.

This engagement is evident in both the title and argument of O'Faolain's essay "The Mart of Ideas," in which he registered his sadness that "the average man in this country does not care a rap about the Literary Censorship."[68] Ireland, he claimed, had become divided between the people and the intellectuals. The problem was that censorship had prevented the common person from accessing new ideas and, he lamented, from thinking at all. As a result, an intellectual like O'Faolain was lobbying "a brainless morale, a moronic mass" that was impervious to any "intelligent appeal whatever."[69] Putting forth his argument to *The Bell*'s readership, O'Faolain implicitly separated them, too, from the people, implying that they had the independence of thought that was required to promote if not affect change. Yet this "live intelligentsia" was thwarted by the censorship that had intervened in the marketplace of the public sphere, blocking the circulation of ideas and, as John Milton, John Stuart Mill, and Bernard Shaw had argued long before, thereby preventing society's ability to strive for truth and progress. The Irish censorship, O'Faolain concluded, was thus "a wholly negative and destructive piece of machinery" because it prepared "the way for the handing over of all power to the caucus and the mob."[70]

In late 1944, half a year after Keane had withdrawn his proposal to amend the censorship laws, O'Faolain and his colleagues at *The Bell* instigated a public debate to provoke action. It began with an essay by Monk Gibbon, a well-known poet and writer. Even the title of Gibbon's article was chosen to generate as much controversy as possible. As Gibbon later noted, it was originally called "Is there a case for Censorship?" then was changed to "Censorship" before the editors settled on "In Defence of Censorship."[71] Appearing in January 1945, the essay was preceded by an editorial foreword that begged for controversy: "THE BELL has more than once severely criticised the present Literary Censorship. It is only fair to print an article which warmly defends the principle if not the practice of Censorship. We do not however wish Mr. Gibbon's article to be a final curtain on the subject and we invite readers to submit comments."[72]

As the title of his essay implies, Gibbon maintained that while the practice of censorship in Ireland was abhorrent, in some cases he supported it. He noted: "Let the present Board of Censors by all means be anathema, let it even be conceded that a reasonable censorship is almost a contradiction in terms. Let us then debate whether censorship, in any circumstances, is, or can be, justifiable."[73] The lack of informed aesthetic judgment on the part of the censors was perhaps the most significant factor in generating hostility towards the institution. Indeed, banning more than a hundred books per year from the likes of Proust, Hemingway, and Shaw did little to cast the censors in a good light. But Gibbon was not interested in judging censorship as a practice through the lens of a dysfunctional institution. For him, the institution needed a serious overhaul, and there was thus little in the subject that could be debated. This specific institutional focus missed the more interesting question of when exactly censorship might be encouraged by those who would otherwise be opposed to it. To get readers to divorce the localised practice from the principle, Gibbon refrained from referring much to Ireland.

Instead, he began by making public health and paternalistic defences of censorship. Drawing an analogy between nourishment for the mind and nourishment for the body, he argued that if governments could pass food adulteration acts to protect our corporeal health, then they should be able to pass censorship laws to protect our moral health. After all, physical disintegration was no more harmful to a country than moral and social disintegration. He noted that although one book alone might not be responsible for corrupting the people, "the influence of a book is pervasive, by stages, so that though the unintelligent may never read it they may still be corrupted by it when it reaches them at fifth hand. ... The process is invisible, via journalism, via conversation, via the passing sneer, via a gradual change of mental values, handed down strata by strata."[74] Writers who refused to acknowledge their influence were either insincere or had failed in their objectives. Of Ireland's censorship, Gibbon believed that the people had been spared more than they had lost. In the meantime, England and America would keep the good books alive for future generations to read.[75]

Gibbon allowed that there was some merit in what he termed "the toxin and anti-toxin argument," which is an extension of the public health defence.[76] According to this model, as a healthy body has a natural power of resistance, it should be regularly subjected to germs so that it can maintain its ability to survive and does not become overly susceptible to infections. People should therefore be properly educated and cultivate a taste for good things to maintain their moral and social health. In so doing, they could withstand the baleful effects of bad literature. This theory, he argued, works well when people come into contact with germs or diseases in small doses, but when the organism, no matter how robust, is constantly battered, it eventually succumbs. This was what confronted modern society: a veritable tsunami of bad literature that had to be defended against by censorship.

For Gibbon, nineteenth-century French naturalism was to blame for the increased need for censorship, but he considered the ultimate villain of modern literature to be the Swedish playwright August Strindberg, whom he accused "of neurotic raving, of Satanic glee."[77] Whereas a writer such as Guy de Maupassant simply depicted society, Strindberg was a propagandist, attempting to prove that the bad man was really the good man and preaching "The New Morality," which suspiciously resembled "The Old Immorality." He thus concluded that censorship of such propagandists was needed because their points of view were axiomatic and not debatable.

To ensure greater publicity, O'Faolain recruited four eminent figures to respond in the next issue: Bernard Shaw, Sean O'Casey, T. C. Kingsmill Moore (a sitting senator representing Trinity College), and James Hogan (a professor of history at University College Cork). Perhaps in a sign that Shaw had declined in his dotage, he simply reformulated what he had written better elsewhere, most significantly in the prefaces to *Mrs Warren's Profession* and *The Shewing-up of Blanco Posnet*. He did not appear to have even read Gibbon's essay, and his entire focus was on the censorship of plays in Britain, with nary a remark on Ireland. However, given his celebrity, his response would have attracted more people.

It was therefore left for O'Casey to dirty his hands. "Mr. Gibbon's defence of Censorship is," he charged, "a comic medley of fright, fear, superstition, faint piety, greek fire, and a cool desire to keep on the lee side of the counts, knights, and esquires of the Holy Roman Empire."[78] Responding to Gibbon's remark that every community protects its youth through what they eat, O'Casey pointed out the terrible undernourishment of more than 80 per cent of all Dublin children whose fathers had steady employment. Food, he noted, was far more of a necessity than literature, and it was a grave indictment of the state when we worry more about censorship than we do about keeping our youth well fed. He also took exception to Gibbon's conservative world-view that change necessarily equates deterioration. Indeed, he argued, the socialist revolution would steer society in a progressive direction and rid it of much evil. Censorship was merely another tool by which that change was stymied. Irish censorship specifically was a "pompous, ignorant, impudent, and silly practice" that stunted society's growth and made "Ireland a laughing-stock among the intelligent of all lands."[79]

O'Casey rebuffed the notion that there was a dire need for censorship in contemporary society. Reflecting the spirit of Titus 1:15 that "Unto the pure, all things are pure; but unto those who are defiled and unbelieving, nothing is pure," he suggested that those who complained of sexual obsession in modern literature in fact revealed what obsessed them. "No distinguished author would, nor could, make the water-closet, and its spare parts, a main, or semi-main, theme in a novel, play, or poem," he claimed. "Such a thing would be impossible in the first place; and, in the second place, were it possible, such a work would knock the author off his claim to be distinguished."[80] As we have seen before, the sex obsession of censorship is considered to betray the sex obsession of society and the censor. This, he offered, was further evidence that censorship cannot prevent physiological urges.

O'Casey further defended Strindberg, whom he referred to as "one of the greatest playwrights of his time and ours."[81] While he allowed Gibbon the right to banish Strindberg from his own life, O'Casey insisted that Gibbon had no right to banish Strindberg for others. Just as Gibbon considered the work of Anatole France, Jean-Jacques Rousseau, Voltaire, and Guy de Maupassant as tolerable, O'Casey warned that someone else might find these authors dangerous and wish to ban his access to them. Not everyone's tastes run the same, he noted, so we are better off letting people have the choice of what they will and will not read. In the end, O'Casey adopted the classics argument in suggesting that Gibbon would not find any worse in modern literature than he could in older revered works: rape and murder, after all, abound in Shakespeare and the Bible.

The essays by T. C. Kingsmill Moore and James Hogan were considerably shorter and more conciliatory. Moore, who had been Gibbon's teacher, contended that while censorship might in some ways be beneficial, he was against it in practice. Overall, his outlook was liberal. More specifically, he held that the cardinal right of every man was to develop and hold his own opinions; otherwise, sound views could not be formed. Like O'Casey, he therefore objected to Gibbon's beliefs and to being bound to them.[82] Hogan similarly conceded that there was no clear-cut solution to the issue of censorship. The challenge, he agreed, was to stake out the limitations. For him, no censorship should impinge upon pure thought in the realm of such disciplines as mathematics and philosophy. Reflecting the international dialectic, he argued that literature was "the debatable no-man's-land. The fact that it can be infested by aliens and outsiders whose interests may be politically impure or merely commercial leaves it open to disinfection by Censorship."[83] Yet Hogan believed that censorship of literature should be kept to a minimum because political opinion was the real menace to society, the unstated targets of his views being communism and socialism. This, coupled with his allusions to "aliens and outsiders," rather situates him at the conservative end of the spectrum, which attests to *The Bell*'s adherence to its liberal ethos in publishing views that were antithetical to its editors and its belief that an unhindered marketplace of ideas would allow people to strive towards truth.

Gibbon's response followed in the next issue.[84] While he praised Shaw's "studied moderation," which might have had a great deal to do with Shaw's avoidance of directly confronting Gibbon's article, he took exception to most of O'Casey's remarks.[85] He rebutted O'Casey's comment that writers merely take their cues from the world around them, arguing that they derive their material and perspective "from some inner and highly personal psychic conflict" that colours their political and religious outlooks.[86] Gibbon admitted that he had negatively generalised about works of art in the same way that he had blamed others for negatively generalising about religion and that O'Casey and Moore were right to point out that others might attempt to banish his favourite writers from him in the same way as he would do to others. As for Hogan, his desire to censor political opinion frightened Gibbon.

However, he was not able to concede that censorship should not exist. Turning to gossip, he reported that even AE burned Frank Harris's sexually charged memoirs. Moreover, "There is a tale floating round," he added, "that Shaw burnt *Ulysses*."[87] He therefore portrayed writers who were famous for their struggles against censorship as not being against the principle and in fact engaging in the practice themselves. In so doing, he sought to demonstrate that everyone had morals to defend and thus everyone was a potential censor. However, his appeal to unsubstantiated rumour leaves much to be desired, even if it tantalises the imagination to envision AE and Shaw ripping pages from their compatriots' books and tossing them into a fire.

While it would have attracted readers, the debate must have disappointed the editors. It ran its course rather quickly and did not have any of the punch of similar discussions that had taken place in the letters to the editor columns of the national press and between various periodicals. The public's rather tepid response – a meagre four letters – mixed with the authors' discussion of the global issue of censorship as opposed to the localised practice of the Censorship Board, perhaps reflected, as O'Faolain had previously feared, the acceptance of institutional censorship as a part of Irish life. Yet the debate was important for keeping the issue of censorship and the need for reform in the public sphere.

A New Censorship Bill

Later that year, on 10 October 1945, some months after World War II had ended and the wartime censorship had been repealed, Gerald Boland, the minister for justice, introduced a new Censorship of Publications Bill.[88] The legislation was "to effect changes in the machinery of censorship which experience of the working of the 1929 Act has shown to be desirable."[89] Irish PEN had not simply forgotten about the issue, although there is a chance that it had been provoked into action by *The Bell*, with many of its members overlapping as contributors to O'Faolain's periodical. At the AGM on 27 October 1945, David Sears 'spoke on the work of the Council of Action in connection with the Censorship Bill and the interviews of the Council with the Minister for Justice'.[90] When Irish PEN led the Council of Action to impel Ireland towards some measure of reform, it was therefore done behind the scenes. This suggests that they opted for a discreet tack, one that was likely based on the lessons learned in the past: with no public debate, no grand statements, and no essay-writing campaign to publicly embarrass the Censorship Board or the minister, they appear to have been met with less resistance and indeed to have been given some input into the legislation. Yet it is revelatory that they felt that they should not maintain pressure on the government while the bill was debated in the Dáil. This likely stems from one of two factors: either they were assured by Boland that the government had the numbers to pass the legislation, or they did not wish to poison its chances by drawing negative and undue attention.

The most significant change the new legislation brought to the censorship of publications was the creation of an appeal board. It was hoped that this new body, as one senator wryly noted, would make an unworkable and laughable system more workable and less laughable.[91] The legislation was enacted on 13 February 1946. Chief among the changes was that now any five members of the Oireachtas could lodge an appeal collectively, as could the author or publisher of a given work.[92] Moreover, potentially obscene books – not to be confused with books already banned and thus determined obscene – were permitted to enter the country without the threat of seizure by customs officials if they were for personal use.[93] Importantly, the Censorship Board's first consideration was to be "the literary, artistic, scientific or historic merit or importance, and the general tenor of the book," meaning that it could not be banned for a word or an act without bearing in mind the entirety of the work.[94]

Irish PEN had been at the vanguard of those who had been working towards censorship reform, and they had contributed in no small measure to the spirit of the amended act. They would even boast to PEN International later that year that they had been "foremost in the demand for the removal of censorship, which has become almost ludicrous with the banning of books."[95] Compared to the IAL, their sustained efforts alongside politicians and other groups paid dividends. However, this was only the case once the war had ended. As this chapter demonstrates, Irish PEN adhered to the government's laws in ensuring that freedom of expression was tempered during the conflict, to the point of suggesting to PEN International that they censor themselves in their communications. In this sense, their actions emphasize the international dialectic, bearing out PEN International's claims of a link between greater internationalism and increased freedom of expression and thus a corresponding link between insularism and censorship. While they did affect change in a way that created a clearer mechanism to appeal the censorship of literature, they did so only after the war, when the country and borders across the globe reopened. Yet this was a considerable success, effectively increasing the rights of readers, publishers, and writers alike.

Chapter Eight

Equivocal Values: Irish PEN in the Age of Appeal

While the preceding chapter attests to a link between greater internationalism and less censorship, or at least some commitment to appeal in matters of freedom of expression, Irish PEN would, over the course of the next decade, reveal themselves to be more international, and yet less devoted to defending such freedom. Indeed, following passage of the new legislation, Irish PEN became complacent, perhaps because they believed that the censorship would now be more restrained. However, despite holding out the possibility of righting the gross abuses of the Censorship Board or keeping them in check, the Appeal Board refused to revoke certain prohibition orders, and they were not met with requests at the same rate that the Censorship Board banned books. This led to an air of inevitability about bans not being repealed. Moreover, as the Appeal Board would hold their meetings in camera and publishers and writers could not testify before them, the appearance of reform had been created while in reality things remained pretty much unchanged.

This came to light shortly after Frank O'Connor's English translation of the eighteenth-century Irish-language poet Brian Merriman's *The Midnight Court* was banned on 30 April 1946, just two months after the new legislation was enacted. Most incredibly, the case involved the banning of a work that had originally been written in Irish and was published in Dublin, with no such publications having run afoul of censors in the past. It might thus seem that, as with the experience of Zola in England, translations of daring works into the dominant vernacular would be banned while those in a less accessible language were allowed to circulate. However, other English-language translations of the poem, including the most recent one in 1926 by Percy Arland Ussher, were not prohibited.[1] Importantly, though, O'Connor's novel *Dutch Interior*, a voracious attack on provincial

Ireland, was proscribed some six years earlier, and a banned author translating a poem renowned for its ribaldry was almost certain to be scrutinised.

As with George Moore and Edward Garnett, O'Connor had written a preface for the book to frame its reception, but in doing so he might have unwittingly made the case against himself. Rather than referring to Merriman's Rabelaisian style and Swiftian satire, O'Connor presented him as "supremely a realist" who had an "intellectual independence." He also claimed that the poem was "innocuous," although the press had provocatively subtitled it *A Rhythmical Bacchanalia*.[2] Indeed, the young woman who stands before the fairy court to plead her case for finding a husband argues in favour of free love, and at one point, as O'Connor himself put it, "bursts into a furious attack on clerical celibacy." In the end, he admitted that the poem is "an attack on marriage" and that Merriman said such things that "even Yeats himself might have thought twice of writing" some two centuries later.[3] Evidently, the Censorship Board agreed.[4]

In response, Maurice Fridberg, the book's publisher, launched an appeal on 25 June.[5] To this end, the Appeal Board sat for the first time on 9 July. While later records of the Appeal Board's meetings would be as slight as they are for the Censorship Board, they indicated here their individual thoughts on the case, which were perhaps meant to provide some rationale for the precedent that they were about to make and thus serve to guide them in future decisions. Fitzroy Pyle, a professor of English at Trinity College, believed that the book would not "be in the least injurious to the morals of even young people," and "that it was unfair to the translator and the publisher that this particular edition should remain under a ban, while the original and several other translations were not prohibited." Furthermore, he stressed "the literary merit" of Merriman's poem and O'Connor's translation. H. B. O'Hanlon, a Dublin solicitor, thought that the circulation of such a book of poetry would be "negligible."[6] However, the other two members were convinced that O'Connor's translation was obscene. Richard Hayes, a former Cumann na nGaedheal TD and the sitting film censor, argued that "it was as bad as the worst of the recognized 'classics' of pornography." James Hogan, who had participated in the censorship debates on stage with PEN a decade earlier and in the pages of *The Bell* more recently, considered that the book was "indecent beyond dispute" and, having studied the original and seven translations, concluded that "O'Connor had departed from the original text, with resultant increase in the indecency of the poem and a case of what must seem deliberate blasphemy."[7] In the end, only Pyle was in favour of revoking the prohibition order, with Hayes, O'Hanlon, and Hogan against it. Consequently, the appeal was dismissed.

Fridberg and his solicitors were "taken aback" by the decision, wanting to know if the Appeal Board "paid attention to the argument" and "who voted for what and why."[8] Recognising that no response would be forthcoming, Frank O'Connor protested in the *Irish Times*, noting that the Appeal Board had supposedly been established to rectify the Censorship Board's poor decisions, not to grant them licence. In fact, he had not approved of launching the appeal, claiming that he would not consider any of their opinions on literature worthwhile as they were no more than "a group of amiable busy-bodies."[9] However, Fridberg believed that the banning lacked any grounds because neither the original poem nor other translations had been banned. As such, O'Connor concluded, the implication was "that I had deliberately introduced material which was not to be found in any other edition, and this material was sufficiently indecent to justify the banning of the whole work." The process, he charged, was a farce in which "the proceedings of one secret tribunal were approved by another secret tribunal."[10]

Unsurprisingly, Myles na gCopaleen, a nom de plume for the writer better known as Flann O'Brien, ridiculed the situation, noting that "O'Connor confuses law with justice," and suggested that he stop "whingeing." Instead, he should adapt the poem for the theatre, over which the censorship had no control, and produce it "for all who hold that literary censorship is a paternalistic impertinence."[11] This would, he argued, have the added advantage of compensating O'Connor for the financial loss that the banning had cost him. O'Connor's intervention, coupled with na gCopaleen's article, caused a deluge of letters to the editor over the course of more than a month, thereby reopening a discussion that many people thought had been put to bed by the recent legislation.[12]

Incredibly, O'Connor drew the censors into debating with him in the press. Hogan wrote that O'Connor believed that no one, "unless he is a minor poet, or at least of Mr. O'Connor's *literati*, can possibly rise to the level of one of Mr. O'Connor's masterpieces," and that he was "a sublime victim to a wretched clique of obscurantists." Yet, having compared Merriman's original poem with O'Connor's and other translations, and charging O'Connor with introducing blasphemy into the poem, Hogan contended that "Merriman is the victim of his translator."[13] In the end, while he was against the censorship as it functioned in Ireland, Hogan claimed that no Irish judge would allow O'Connor's book to pass. Moreover, the Censorship Board published a response in the *Irish Times* alongside of Hogan's letter to correct what they viewed as O'Connor's misunderstanding of how the censorship functioned. They insisted that they never concluded that he had added something immoral to the original poem because this was not their remit; rather, they judged the book on its own merits. In a similar vein, O'Connor had alleged that they lacked sufficient Irish to determine where he had departed from the original, but this was moot, as they were only supposed to judge the work before them.[14] The effects of these letters were potentially devastating to O'Connor's public case, essentially casting him as arrogant, dismissive of others, and ignorant of the workings of the institution he criticised.

However, O'Connor leapt to the challenge. In considering the responses from those involved in the censorship, he noted that Hogan admitted to having compared his version with the original and other translations to determine that he had introduced blasphemous material, while the Censorship Board said that such considerations were not within their remit.[15] He argued that under the terms of the legislation, which obliged "literary, artistic, scientific or historic merit" to be taken into account, the competence of his translation should in fact be placed at the centre of the decision-making process.[16]

In the weeks that followed, Hogan and O'Connor traded jibes, with Maurice Fridberg, Sir John Keane, Peter Kavanagh, and Percy Arland Ussher joining the fray.[17] When the Appeal Board met while the controversy raged, they discussed how the case was playing out in the pages of the *Irish Times*. Pyle, Hayes, and O'Hanlon confided that they would never have banned several of the titles that the Censorship Board had, while Hogan remained silent on the matter.[18] Pyle proposed that he compose a letter to the *Irish Times*. Admirably, he did not reveal his own judgment in the case to distance himself from his colleagues. Instead, he defended the integrity of the Appeal Board, saying that despite the fact that the book was so short, they had discussed it for an hour and a half.[19]

The controversy ended thereafter. While it had raised a din in the public sphere, there was a familiar deafening silence from Irish PEN. Although they had recently been at the fore of advancing censorship reform, they failed here to intervene by questioning the direction of the newly transformed institution, thereby suggesting that they had become complacent following the passage of the legislation. This lack of vigilance heralded ill for Irish PEN's role as a defender of freedom of expression in the era of appeal. Indeed, as this chapter will demonstrate, not only would Irish PEN fail to defend freedom of expression in Ireland in the coming years, but they would also appear to sell their souls, accepting government subsidies in a tacit exchange for not addressing the issue of censorship.

Writers Censoring Writers

Just before the controversy over the banning of *The Midnight Court* erupted, PEN International held its first post-war congress in Stockholm. With the defeat of fascism and the apparent victory of democracy and liberal human rights in much of Europe, the congress gave PEN members the occasion to take stock. Henri Membré reported on French PEN, noting that after the liberation of Paris in 1944, there was no documentary trace of the centre left behind as everything had been burnt. To accompany this material loss, several members had been killed in fighting or the death camps. Louis Piérard noted that Belgium had likewise suffered. During the war, he said, "the Gestapo visited the president or secretary of the different sections of the Pen Club and tried to find papers on the Pen Club, with their brutality." PEN, he proclaimed, "shall always be the refuge of freedom"; however, he reminded delegates, "If we are to be worthy of the great memory of those who have died and been murdered for the cause of free thought, if the international Pen Club must be worthy of these great names, of these great dead, the Pen Club must become a real force."[20] For his part, the American poet Henry Goddard Leach emphasized that PEN should be based on "tolerance: the right freely to publish and proclaim opinions to which we object."[21] Understanding that it had been targeted by totalitarian regimes because it represented freedom of thought and expression, PEN recognised that these freedoms were essential to its existence. In the new world order, as several delegates passionately argued, PEN had to assert and defend these freedoms vigorously.

While such measures created solidarity and a sense of direction, the congress also became a site of division and vengeance, with a significant faction turning on those who had worked with the Axis powers. This began when the Dutch delegation proposed that a list of collaborators be drawn up and shared between the national centres to make it impossible for them to obtain work. Hermon Ould, however, warned that the resolution was "in the highest degree dangerous," believing that PEN should not "take up the position of inquisitors."[22] One French delegate argued that in 1933 PEN International had revoked the membership of German PEN and that the Germans had gone on to slaughter millions in the concentration camps. Those who profited by collaborating with the killing machine, he said, should not be able to reap any riches.

The debate was acrimonious. For some it became a matter of live and let live; at times, it veered into a contest between absolute liberty of expression, in which anyone was welcome to do or say anything without any consequences, and liberty of expression and freedoms only for those who ensured them for others. The British philosopher and science fiction writer Olaf Stapledon offered the most sensitive response. He noted that the resistance to blacklists was strongest in American and English delegates, reasoning that this divide with their continental European colleagues likely stemmed from the very different experiences they had of the war, with the United States and England having remained free from totalitarian rule. While he believed that blacklists were risky, "the right course is always dangerous." He recognised that "There are certain kinds of liberties which we do refuse to allow. For instance sticking pins in babies! This applies equally to freedom of speech. If it consists in doing something not merely opposed to some established government but to humane public opinion then it must not be allowed."[23] In effect, while PEN stood for freedom of expression, it must stand against what would come to be defined as hate speech and thus denounce those who trafficked in it, thereby evoking the essence of John Stuart Mill's harm principle.

The vote on the resolution was overwhelmingly in favour of drafting and sharing blacklists of collaborators, with sixteen national centres in favour, six against, and three abstentions.[24] As Stapledon suggested, it was mainly the countries most touched by the war who voted in favour. Similarly, those who voted against or abstained from voting, including Ireland, were either neutral or not invaded, and thus they were not directly affected by collaborators. Ould might have recalled his claim from some five years earlier that one of the first actions of the Gestapo in any occupied territory was to suppress PEN, which, as testified by several continental delegates, turned out to be true.

Ireland's vote against the measure might be considered an extension of the country's wartime policy of neutrality. In its coverage of the congress, the *Irish Times* favourably reported that the Irish delegation was unanimously supportive of Ould in repudiating the creation of a blacklist. The paper feared that in passing the resolution, PEN had simply created "a pillory within a pillory." It concluded that as the Irish censorship of publications "had received many buffets in the course of its smug and illiberal existence," it was "good that Irishmen at an international gathering should help to indicate that their people do not endorse wholeheartedly a measure which is as ineptly managed as it is ill-conceived."[25]

The Belfast Centre was likewise against the blacklist. May Morton asserted that "you can't deny anyone the freedom you claim yourself" and that evil could not "be fought by evil – nor 'Nazi' methods be put an end to by either vetoes or atomic bombs. (But I must remind myself that the bitterness shown by some people might be shown by me if I had suffered as they did.)"[26] At their October AGM, the Belfast

Centre unanimously approved of their congress delegates having voted against the resolution.[27] By the beginning of 1947, they received blacklists from the French and Dutch centres, although they did not compile one of their own. They further prepared themselves by determining that should a resolution be moved to abolish the blacklist, their delegates would strongly support it.[28]

Ould understood why the Stockholm Congress was not as literary as he had hoped it would be. It had rather allowed the organisation to assemble, take stock, blow off steam, and begin to consider its future direction. He confided that he found members to be "bent on three things": "(i) to have a good time, (ii) to make as many international contacts as possible and (iii) to air their grievances."[29] All of this was reasonable given the isolation and suffering that so many had experienced during the war, and he trusted that the world would soon settle down to some semblance of normalcy. For Irish PEN, the congress was important for allowing them to burnish their anti-censorship credentials on the international stage. Coming out of the insularity of the war years, Irish PEN was eager to become an active member of the larger community once again, and they did so with a commitment to freedom of expression that they had let slide. Indeed, in refusing to provide a collaborator blacklist or to circulate names, the Irish adhered to a more absolute concept of freedom of expression.

Two years later, PEN International made its greatest post-war commitment to freedom of expression by adding a fourth article to its charter at the congress in Copenhagen. Its wording remains unchanged to this day:

> PEN stands for the principle of unhampered transmission of thought within each nation and between all nations, and members pledge themselves to oppose any form of suppression of freedom of expression in the country and community to which they belong, as well as throughout the world wherever this is possible. PEN declares for a free press and opposes arbitrary censorship in time of peace. It believes that the necessary advance of the world towards a more highly organised political and economic order renders a free criticism of government, administrations and institutions imperative. And since freedom implies voluntary restraint, members pledge themselves to oppose such evils of a free press as mendacious publication, deliberate falsehood and distortion of facts for political and personal ends.[30]

PEN International thus took a principled stance in favour of freedom of expression. Yet in terms of censorship, it appears rather ambivalent:

only censorship that is deemed "arbitrary" is opposed, leaving the question open as to what one should make of a targeted censorship, such as one directed at sexuality. Censorship is also considered undesirable in times of peace, which implies that it is tolerable in times of war. Rather problematically, the notion of freedom as being determined by "voluntary restraint" suggests that artists who fail to use restraint – which could extend from those who intentionally lie to those found guilty of obscenity, indecency, blasphemy, or promoting birth control – are at fault for bringing censorship upon themselves. It is a conflicted statement, but one that, as a collaborative document written by people living in scores of different countries and holding a range of ideological views, was bound to reflect the contradictions inherent in any large group.[31]

The revised charter and energised membership should be considered part of the new internationalism that arose out of another world war. Replacing the League of Nations, the United Nations was at the fore in recognising human rights, which was particularly important in the wake of genocidal mass murder and the totalitarian destruction of freedoms. Like PEN International, the UN was concerned with how to ensure that the worst excesses and crimes against humanity would not be repeated. To do so, the UN's Commission on Human Rights (UNCHR) was charged with drafting a charter. The document, titled the Universal Declaration of Human Rights (UDHR), was accepted on 10 December 1948, with an overwhelming majority voting in favour and only eight countries abstaining.[32]

Most important for PEN, Articles 18 and 19 declare that freedom of thought and freedom of expression are essential rights.[33] These articles, together with Article 20, which states that everyone has the right to assemble and associate peacefully and should not be compelled to belong to an association, are grounded in theories of liberal tolerance. From their experience of the war, the drafters believed that these articles were "universally the first ones dictators will seek to deny and destroy."[34] This belief was borne out in the experience of several European PEN centres, which saw their offices overrun, their files picked through and destroyed, and their members persecuted, tortured, and killed. The United Nations Educational, Scientific, and Cultural Organization (UNESCO) asked PEN to make its members aware of the UDHR. PEN in turn passed the information on to its membership, noting that "for the first time in history," the principles of freedom and the dignity of all people had been proclaimed "with world-wide scope."[35] As Ireland would join the UN in 1955, the UDHR would have an impact upon questions of freedom of expression in the country. In this sense, its censorship would soon be antithetical to its international obligations. For its part, Irish PEN was now put on notice that the international community was moving towards more aggressively defending freedom of expression and combating censorship. However, in the coming years, despite Irish censorship entering its most draconian phase, Irish PEN would not staunchly defend or promote such freedom.

Towards an Irish Congress

Despite such declarations from the international community, Ireland remained committed to the censorship of publications. As we have seen with Frank O'Connor's translation of *The Midnight Court*, for many opponents of censorship, the creation of the Appeal Board had a negative impact by not functioning as a braking mechanism that caused the Censorship Board to consider books more thoroughly. Instead, the Censorship Board essentially adopted a modus operandi of ban 'em all and ask questions later. As Table 8.1 shows, there was an increasing number of books examined, with over four times more submitted in 1954 than in 1946. The ratio of banned books to those examined also increased in this period, from 40.7% in 1946 to 85.0% in 1954. Therefore, either the quality of the books was worse or the standards of the Censorship Board were more puritanical – or some combination thereof. Throughout this period, Irish PEN was obliged to abide by the parent organisation's new charter. It would have been logical, then, to have undertaken whatever it could to promote freedom of expression and to combat state-sanctioned censorship. However, as we will see, this was not the case, even though a golden opportunity presented itself in the early 1950s.

Table 8.1: Figures for the Censorship Board, 1946–54.[36]

Year	Number of Books Examined	Number of Books Banned	Percentage of Books Banned
1946	285	116	40.7
1947	317	164	51.2
1948	329	181	55.0
1949	304	166	54.6
1950	671	410	61.1
1951	717	539	75.2
1952	838	640	76.4
1953	1023	766	74.9
1954	1217	1034	85.0

In February 1948, Irish PEN began to make serious inquiries about hosting an international congress.[37] The first step was to approach the government to determine what level of support they would have: there would be high costs involved in receiving delegates, and securing visas for them would take time and political will. As opposed to broaching the idea of hosting a congress right away, they instead pivoted to garnering government support by meeting with the minister for external affairs to obtain a travel grant for a delegation to attend the congress in Copenhagen.[38] From this moment on, Irish PEN became beholden to government largesse, which would raise doubts about their independence from the state. Yet the expense of attending congresses in far-off places was such that it was well beyond the means of most writers. If the state was serious about supporting the arts and not merely censoring them, then it had to do so with more than words. The issue would always be whether the grants meant that there was a quid pro quo.

By 1950, PEN International was very much in favour of Dublin hosting a future congress and floated 1952 as a possibility.[39] The Belfast Centre also got on board, promising their support in a joint venture. Irish PEN then began to endear themselves to the government, hosting a garden party with special guest Seán MacBride, the minister for external affairs.[40] Later that autumn, following a productive meeting with the secretary of the Committee for Cultural Relations, who assured them of MacBride's support, they began to organise.[41] By the end of March 1951, the minister recommended their submitted proposal.[42] However, a national election was soon announced, and when confronted by uncertain political support following Fianna Fáil's defeat of the Fine Gael-led coalition, PEN International recognised that Ireland would not be able to host the 1952 congress, which was then awarded to French PEN in Nice.[43]

Encouraged by Ould in the immediate aftermath, the Irish tried again for 1953.[44] With a new government in place, Irish PEN had some difficulty accessing the relevant minister and securing a definitive response to their application for funding, so they turned elsewhere. They began by contacting whiskey companies Jameson and Powers, believing that the distillers would fund them with a mind to piercing foreign markets; there would, after all, be receptions at which thirsty delegates would need to be refreshed.[45] Guinness, which had been contacted in the same vein as the distillers, promised £50, and a variety of other businesses committed themselves for a combined £160.[46] By the end of the winter, the Department of External Affairs announced that it would sanction a grant of up to £500, while the Arts Council pledged another £500; this meant, though, that Irish PEN remained short of the estimated £1500 that they needed to host the congress.[47] To this end, they continued to work their connections. Erskine Childers, the minister for posts and telegraphs, contacted several of his colleagues on Irish PEN's behalf. They also sent a representative to meet with Frank Aiken, the new minister for external affairs. In the end, their politicking paid off: Aiken agreed to maintain the funding promised, plus guarantee a further £500 against potential losses.[48] With the financials now in place and with the blessing of the international organisation, Irish PEN could forge ahead with planning the congress.

At no time in the lead-up to the congress did Irish PEN raise the possibility of making censorship an issue. The theme that they chose for the event, "the literature of peoples whose language restricts wide recognition," was a worthy topic at any time, and it was eminently suitable for a country still at pains to revive the Irish language three decades after independence. Yet it appears to have been chosen in part for how far it was from the subject of state suppression. Indeed, Irish PEN actively sought to avoid anything that would cause them to displease their political paymasters. This became evident when the executive discussed whether the issue of censorship should be brought before the congress. Ultimately, it found "that the proposal of any resolution by us would be unsuitable in the circumstances but that if the subject were raised by other Centres we should affirm our adherence to P.E.N. principles of free expression."[49] The circumstances were directly tied to the government's role not only in helping to finance the event, but also in hosting it. Censorship would therefore be an "unsuitable" issue to raise as it would place officials in an awkward situation. Instead of using the occasion to incite change, Irish PEN thus took the view that freedom of expression would be discussed only if other people raised it. The event itself came first.

Held 8–13 June 1953, the Dublin Congress was by most standards a glitzy affair and a rousing success. Seventy delegates from thirty-five centres in twenty-seven countries and over four hundred and fifty participants attended.[50] The festivities opened with a reception held by the minister for education in St. Patrick's Hall, Dublin Castle. The next day, sessions were held at Trinity College, and a luncheon was given by Fógra Fáilte, the Irish Tourist Publicity Board. Then the provost of Trinity hosted a sherry party, and the evening ended with a special performance at the Abbey Theatre of J. M. Synge's *The Playboy of the Western World* and W. B. Yeats's *The Dreaming of the Bones*. The day of 10 June saw one lunch hosted by the president and faculty of St. Patrick's College, Maynooth, and another sponsored by Guinness; these were followed by a mannequin parade of Irish fashions at the upscale Brown Thomas store on Grafton Street and a reception by Seán T. O'Kelly, the president of Ireland, at his official residence in Phoenix Park. On 11 June, the government of Northern Ireland provided a special train to whisk participants to Belfast, where they enjoyed lunch at the city hall, a reception at Queen's University, a bus tour of the city, and a state dinner in the King's Hall before being taken back to Dublin. The following day, there was a bus tour of County Wicklow featuring a visit to the ancient ruins of Glendalough and a buffet meal at Laragh House Hotel in Annamoe. The congress concluded on 13 June with a reception by the president of University College Dublin at Newman House, the congress ball at the swanky Gresham Hotel, which featured a display of Irish dancing, and a farewell speech by the Lord Mayor of Dublin. For those who needed to decompress, participants were offered a post-conference excursion to Killarney for a tour of its famous lakes.[51] Reflecting the perception of superficiality, most newspaper accounts focused on the presence of the actor Peter Ustinov and such literary luminaries as Ignazio Silone and Bertolt Brecht more than the substance of the congress.[52]

Only Myles na gCopaleen would take a contrary view in an article published on the final day, as though timed to have participants leave with a bad taste in their mouths. Arriving late one day "owing to obstruction of my bus by a hunger march staged by a section of our country's 80,000 people who cannot get work and who don't emigrate because they can't find the fare," he had the occasion to reflect on matters: "Why must plain people live in poverty when these 'literary' folk ... can be flown from the ends of the earth to Dublin to talk damn nonsense in twelve languages when they are not guzzling free drink? ... The speakers at the P.E.N. conference I found fascinating inasmuch as they seemed to me ... replicas of our own branch of ineffectual sherry drinkers. ... I honestly begin to suspect that this P.E.N. is an international Fianna Fáil party, in reality simply a junket." He concluded: "Why should Ireland be chosen as the rendezvous of an international society dedicated to the literary arts, since sundry illiterate and pietistical gangs have outlawed the circulation here of nearly all worthy books by native as well as foreign authors? Why honour a country where political clodhoppers trample on people who own minds?"[53] In many ways, he raised the concern that Wells had articulated in his presidential address at the Edinburgh Congress nineteen years earlier: should PEN neglect its responsibilities and duties, it would merely become "an organisation for introducing respectable writers to useful scenery – a special branch of the hotel industry."[54]

There was, in all fairness, some consequential work undertaken at the congress. This included passing a resolution to increase the amount that centres paid to help with the running of the organisation and issuing a press release calling on publishers in large countries to undertake the translation of works written in little known languages; also, a telegram was sent to Juan Perón, the president of Argentina, deploring the arrest of renowned editor Victoria Ocampo for her opposition to his regime.[55] The congress further issued a public message condemning the suppression of Catalan and Basque languages, literature, and culture by the Franco government and deploring that all writers in Spain had been "deprived of freedom of thought, expression and criticism" by being forced "to submit their artistic creations to political censorship." They thus "would welcome the return of Spain to Western principles of mutual respect and tolerance, so that writers could freely and peacefully devote themselves to their creative work."[56] It is rather glaring that PEN did not take the occasion to release a similar message regarding censorship in Ireland that criticised the way Irish writers were in some instances being deprived of freedom of expression. Moreover, this was at the height of the McCarthyist witch hunts of communists in the United States, so the notion of "Western principles of mutual respect and tolerance" was rather debatable.

The French delegates, however, were not so blind to the hypocrisies. They were the first to spoil Irish PEN's party by placing censorship on the agenda of the 8 June meeting of the executive committee of PEN International, which was held just before the congress officially got underway. Drawing attention to the fact that Article IV of the PEN Charter requires members to combat suppression of freedom of expression and limitations on the free circulation of ideas, they emphasized that it was "especially important" to issue a resolution that condemned censorship.[57] After some discussion among the executive, it was decided that such a resolution needed to be sent to the committee stage. By the time that it made its way to the general membership, it had been somewhat defanged: ironically, mention of censorship had been suppressed and instead the resolution more generally praised freedom. In its final form it read: "The Congress solemnly recalls to its members that the defence of the freedom of the mind depends on the free circulation of ideas, on their being freely questioned and discussed, and reminds all members of P.E.N. Centres that they are failing to respect their oath if they tolerate in silence restrictions of any kind on the freedom of thought and expression in the countries they inhabit."[58]

As it happens, Donal Giltinan, a member of Irish PEN's executive, had caught wind of the resolution a month before the congress opened.

That spring, Irish PEN had been debating whether they should broach the subject of censorship at the congress. When Austin Clarke was asked to preside at a literary session, he said that he would only do so if he could chair one "devoted to a discussion of our Literary Censorship" and that he must be allowed to "make a speech about it." Clarke was evidently miffed at having his books banned: *The Bright Temptation* and *The Singing-Men at Cashel* had been banned in 1932 and 1936, and his most recent novel, *The Sun Dances at Easter*, was banned on 3 October 1952. However, Giltinan impressed upon Clarke that it was gauche of him to impose a condition on being extended an honour. Clarke backed down, convinced that some foreign centre would raise the issue. Upon being notified of the French resolution, Giltinan was again concerned. He confided to David Carver, who, following Ould's death in 1951, had become secretary of PEN International, that if anyone were to suggest that Irish PEN supported censorship or did not defend freedom of expression, "he will go back to France a wiser man." Yet he said that he was relieved "because if we hadn't been brought up by somebody, we should have had to engineer some opportunity for discussing our Censorship, without appearing to wash our own unclean linen before the world." Hoping that the motion did not directly implicate Ireland, he was resigned to the issue being raised. Giltinan concluded that he could "foresee all kinds of nastiness ahead" but hoped that the resolution would be introduced *after* the presidential reception and the day in Belfast, thereby avoiding a potential political stink.[59]

As Giltinan suggested, the resolution was conveniently relegated to the final day. Several PEN members voiced their support for the watered-down French resolution. Lord Killanin, the congress delegate for Irish PEN and future president of the International Olympic Committee, declared that Ireland did not have a theatre censorship but did have a book censorship, whereas England had a theatre censorship but did not have a book censorship. In one fell swoop, he broached the issue and dampened its impact, depicting Ireland to be just as liberal – or conservative – as England, the seat of PEN International. He further diluted the issue in stating that the censorship of pornographic literature was "a good thing" and then attempted to postpone debate by suggesting that "censorship should be discussed in detail at a future Congress."[60] The matter was then closed with a unanimous vote in favour of this resolution. Thus, the issue had been raised, Irish PEN was self-satisfied that it had stood up for freedom of expression, and the Irish government had been spared embarrassment.

Aftermath

At a meeting later that month, Irish PEN's executive celebrated the event's "outstanding success."[61] Giltinan informed Carver that the members of Irish PEN "are all as happy as a dog with two tails"; moreover, "The President is pleased, the Government is pleased – indeed, we haven't heard a word of cynicism, which is most unusual in these parts." Now they could turn their "attention to the report on our Literary Censorship for next year's Congress."[62] The subject was therefore to be addressed by Irish PEN, but only after PEN International and the world press had left the country's shores and the spotlight of the national media was turned elsewhere. It could be argued that by hosting such a successful event that refused to be adversarial to the government, Irish PEN would have more political capital to effect change. Yet while they continued to petition successive governments for subsidies and financial support, they did not take up the issue of censorship again.

Meanwhile, reflecting on the Dublin Congress, the German writer Egon Larsen publicly claimed that "Irish colleagues were very anxious that writers from all over the world should find out how much official 'thought control' exists in a country tacitly accepted as part of what we are used to calling the Free World." Many delegates believed that Irish writers had invited PEN to Dublin "in despair about their own impotence in the face of a thought-controlling bureaucracy" and "expected us to rouse the indignation of the cultural world against Eire's censorship." Given a list of banned writers and books, the invitees were bemused to see that the president and his wife shook hands with many distinguished people whose works they were not supposed to read. Larsen acknowledged that PEN was put in a difficult situation of potentially protesting "against this infringement of the freedom of the printed word in a country which had invited us as its guests," and thus they had delayed such discussion until the 1954 congress in Amsterdam.[63]

In response, Giltinan admitted that the Irish chafed under a censorship that "perpetuates as many stupidities as most other institutions of the kind," but he emphasized that it was founded as a result of the democratic process and that the Irish could rid themselves of it immediately should they so decide. It was rather the role of Irish PEN to make the people conscious of it as a restriction, but they did not host the congress to air "our 'despair' and 'impotence' before our guests." Noting that works critical of the censorship circulated freely and that banned writers from abroad were allowed to enter the country, he considered that Ireland was not the "thought-controlling bureaucracy" that Larsen and others had depicted it to be.[64] It was a fair defence of Irish PEN's actions and inactions at the congress and a good reminder that as bad as the censorship of publications was, it had not directly obstructed public debate of the subject. But Irish PEN was also bizarrely apologetic of the censorship of literature and naive in the context of 1953 when the institution was becoming increasingly draconian in its ferreting out of indecency and obscenity in contemporary literature. Even if one were to accept Giltinan's defence, the fact remains that they were worried about the subject being broached well before the congress.

In the lead-up to the 1954 congress in Amsterdam, Irish PEN's executive discussed the topics that were likely to be raised, including censorship.[65] They had some indication of this as South African PEN had passed two significant resolutions. The first emphasized the importance of "safeguarding the freedom of the universities" from political meddling. The second condemned "any attempt to set up a department or organisation for the banning of books, or for the restriction of their distribution or importation."[66] South African writers had reason to fear such policies as that same year the newly elected Nationalist government launched a commission of inquiry into "Undesirable Publications."[67] Given this context, South African PEN's resolutions only make the silence of Irish PEN, when confronted with their own censorship, all the more evident.

Like the Dublin Congress, the Amsterdam Congress treated participants to a whirlwind of tourist hot spots and luxurious events, including, among others, a trip to see the Van Gogh collection at the Kröller-Müller Museum; lavish dinners and receptions at The Hague and Leyden hosted by those cities' mayors; a canal trip in Amsterdam; and a tour of the sand dunes of the North Sea. However, unlike the Dublin Congress, there was objectively more focus on reinforcing PEN's adherence to freedom of expression and other more political matters. Indeed, in his welcoming remarks, Victor E. van Vriesland, the president of Dutch PEN, reminded participants that the PEN Charter speaks of freedom of thought and expression.[68]

The South African resolutions were quickly carried with a unanimous vote.[69] While during the congress Irish PEN remained relatively mute on the subject of censorship, the German PEN centres – West and East Germany – co-proposed two further resolutions: the first demanding the free circulation of all types of literature while deploring books that served to inflame national hatred, racial discrimination, and militarism; and the second declaring that "every obstacle placed in the way of humanist literature is an attack upon humanity."[70] Thus, even a PEN centre living under a totalitarian regime, as was the case in East Germany, raised its voice for freedom of expression, while the members of Irish PEN, living in relative safety, refused to criticise either the Censorship Board or the Irish government. In fact, members of Irish PEN, such as Donal Giltinan and Lord Killanin, publicly defended the censorship and deflected the focus of the argument while attacking those who dared to criticise.

From this moment on, Irish PEN washed its hands of the matter of censorship. Its members were not involved in battling censorship in their own country in any significant way, whether publicly or more surreptitiously through backdoor channels. In the early 1950s, the period in which the Censorship Board worked at its frenzied heights of banning almost three books per day, Irish PEN completely recused itself from its responsibility to fight for freedom of expression, despite the mandate to do so as stipulated in the PEN Charter.

However, it would be unjust to suggest that Irish PEN had completely failed. As their history demonstrates, they wielded a fine fight at times, including protesting bans and working hard to reform institutional censorship. That the creation of the Appeal Board in 1946 led the Censorship Board to abuse its power – because it could simply ban most books brought before it and allow others to challenge its ruling if they thought it was worthwhile – should not diminish Irish PEN's role in helping to bring about the amending legislation. Most people believed that the appeal mechanism would ensure that questionable decisions to ban works could be overturned without implicating the minister for justice and would thereby diminish the potential for political interference or indifference. Yet as the next chapter will reveal, political intervention became necessary when the Censorship Board continued to ban with increasing zeal. What should be taken from this history is that Irish PEN proved themselves to be more capable of affecting institutional change than had the IAL. In working back channels, they showed that the earlier generation of writers had erred in only making their cases against the 1929 legislation in the press. In reality, they should have participated in the process from the beginning and focused their energies on actively organising and working with politicians to determine the functioning of censorship and how it would impact freedom of expression in Ireland.

Irish PEN did play an active role in periodically maintaining censorship in the public eye, but much of this depended upon who was on its executive. In many ways, they lagged significantly behind their counterparts, in Britain and elsewhere, who organised and agitated much more consistently, vigorously, and openly. When O'Faolain steered Irish PEN, he continued in the tradition that he had inherited from Yeats and Shaw at the IAL and from Edward Garnett as his pugnacious booster. Importantly, all three of these men were veterans of the 1907–9 anti-censorship campaign in Britain. Yet when others who lacked O'Faolain's character and talents led the centre, it became more temperate, although, interestingly, more politically astute in working directly with politicians behind the scenes. However, contrary to what we saw in the preceding chapter – where less internationalism translated into greater censorship, and, correspondingly, greater internationalism appeared to translate into greater commitment to freedom of expression – in this chapter, Irish PEN rejoined the international community in the post-war years, but doing so did not correspond with an increased defence and promotion of freedom of expression and a more combative stance against censorship. It is thus impossible to make definitive causal links between insularity and censorship, and between internationalism and freedom of expression, although we might, like PEN International, consider them aligned as a general rule of thumb. Meanwhile, just as O'Faolain left the IAL to run Irish PEN once he became frustrated with the lack of vigour and political action in the former, so he left Irish PEN and soon founded *The Bell*, from the pages of which he led the polemical charge against isolation, conservatism, and censorship in Ireland during the war. As we shall see in the next chapter, a couple of years after he resigned as editor of *The Bell*, he cofounded the Irish Association for Civil Liberty to further fight for freedom of expression and other basic human rights. This would lead to one of the last great battles that Irish writers would collectively wage against censorship.

Chapter Nine

Aligning with Other Intellectuals: The Irish Association for Civil Liberty and Conservative Ireland's Last Great Censorship Moral Panic

When Irish PEN failed to live up to its stated objectives, the Irish Association for Civil Liberty (IACL) would come to take its place as the great defender of freedom of expression in the post-war period. Its first president was Sean O'Faolain, who founded the organisation in 1948 alongside Owen Sheehy-Skeffington, Edgar Deale, Roger McHugh, and Christopher Gore-Grimes. Sheehy-Skeffington was the son of Hanna Sheehy-Skeffington, who was the founder of the Irish Women's Franchise League and, as we have already seen, the one who led the charge against *The Plough and the Stars* before becoming a member of Irish PEN and a co-founder, alongside her son, of the Irish Society for Intellectual Freedom. For his part, Skeff, as he was affectionately known, was a lecturer in French at Trinity College and a senator from 1954 to 1961 and again from 1965 until his death in 1970. Edgar Deale was a founder of the Music Association of Ireland and a governor of the Royal Irish Academy of Music. Roger McHugh was an independent senator from 1954 to 1957 and in 1966 was named professor of Anglo-Irish literature and drama at University College Dublin. And Christopher Gore-Grimes was a respected solicitor.

Such collaboration continued the gradual widening of the circles of solidarity that Irish writers had forged since the institutionalisation of censorship in Ireland. With the Irish Academy of Letters, writers were considerably narrower in their campaigns as the Academy only included a select group of notable authors. Irish PEN brought Irish writers of all stripes into an established international network that comprised not only authors but also editors, publishers, and many others involved in the community of letters. With the IACL, Irish writers would work with others who were not involved in the publishing industry but were intellectuals from the professional classes who valued civil liberties. This would be important as their battles were to be far more confrontational and public than anything that the IAL or Irish PEN had previously encountered.

The date of the IACL's founding is noteworthy as it was the same year that the UN adopted the Universal Declaration of Human Rights. While Articles 18 and 19 directly declare that freedom of thought and freedom of expression are essential rights, the UDHR promotes and seeks to protect other civil liberties that are imbricated in these freedoms. Signatory countries pledge to protect such fundamental rights as "life, liberty and security of person," equality before the law, protection against discrimination, a healthy standard of living, and access to free education. Freedom of thought and freedom of expression both stem from these other rights and undergird them. This was certainly the view of Sheehy-Skeffington, who saw these freedoms as vital to furthering a just and equitable society. As his cousin Conor Cruise O'Brien, himself a diplomat, politician, and leading public intellectual, later recalled: "Owen's whole career was motivated by love of the poor and helpless, and a commitment to freedom of expression, without which human beings cannot, in communication with one another, seek the truth."[1] In this way, the IACL was very much a part of the broader zeitgeist.

It also had a significant precursor in the American Civil Liberties Union (ACLU). Founded in 1920, the ACLU has always been a staunch defender of freedom of expression. It made its name in 1925 when it represented John Scopes, a teacher in Tennessee who was accused of violating a state law that forbid teaching the theory of evolution in schools. In 1929, the ACLU drafted its charter, which affirmed its "Opposition to the censorship of books, plays, radio, talking movies."[2] In one of its earliest and most famous victories, Morris Ernst, a lawyer and high-ranking member of the ACLU, successfully defended Joyce's novel and his right to freedom of expression in the 1933 case *United States v. One Book Called Ulysses*. While the ACLU claims that it is non-partisan, which is true in that it has defended minorities seeking basic human rights as well as neo-Nazis wanting to march in public, the organisation is decidedly liberal in its dogged insistence on the absolute right to freedom of speech.

Unlike the ACLU, the history of the IACL has not been documented.[3] There are several reasons for this, including the impact that the ACLU has had on American and indeed world culture and its enormous membership, which in 2025 stood at over 4 million.[4] Compared to similar organisations, the IACL has left little archival trace of its activities. Despite its role in fighting against censorship in Ireland, much of the IACL's work is only known through newspaper reports, government dossiers in the National Archives of Ireland, and, provocatively, files in the Dublin Diocesan Archives. Furthermore, it has been overshadowed by the newer Irish Council for Civil Liberties (ICCL), which was cofounded in 1976 by Mary Robinson, who went on to become Ireland's president from 1990 to 1997 and later the United Nations High Commissioner for Human Rights from 1997 to 2002. Yet just as the ACLU was an important precursor for the IACL, the IACL helped paved the way for the ICCL and other likeminded groups.

Mirroring Irish PEN in its earliest incarnation, the IACL worked towards the liberalisation of Irish society and greater respect for freedom of expression. Evidently, some of this was due to the crossover in personnel, O'Faolain playing a key role in both organisations during their most combative periods and Sheehy-Skeffington providing considerable impetus to action. With Ireland joining the United Nations in 1955, the IACL would attempt to have Ireland live up to the spirit of Articles 18 and 19 of the UDHR and recognise the importance of a more open society to the well-being of its citizens. They would be fortunate in that Irish norms and mores were slowly moving in a more liberal direction and would result in the country adopting a greater internationalist ethos. For those in power, the outcome of this internationalist turn would be that censorship could not continue to function in the draconian manner that we saw adopted after the creation of an appeal board. As this chapter will show, with the combination of the efforts of the IACL, new government policy, and a changing Ireland, the increased internationalism would realign with greater respect for freedom of expression.

Taking On the Censorship

At the outset of 1950, the IACL found itself embroiled in an important public skirmish over freedom of expression. The episode has its roots in the Censorship Board banning Britain's *Report of the Royal Commission on Population* and the Appeal Board revoking the prohibition order. It was then kicked off by an article in the *Irish Times* by Felim O Briain, a priest and professor of philosophy at University College Galway, who denounced the repeal, believing that the report advocated the unnatural prevention of conception. He declared that "One of the fields of freedom in which Socialists agreed with Liberals was a free morality – the ethics of free love."[5] This liberal morality – or "the liberal ethic," as the issue came to be known – would, O Briain warned, inevitably lead to birth control, abortion, and divorce. While praising the work of the Censorship Board, he chastised the Appeal Board for making the report available and touted the Catholic Church as the one "obstinate opponent" of the liberal ethic in Ireland.

O Briain's article brought an immediate and combative riposte from Sheehy-Skeffington, who condemned O Briain's "fantastically sweeping generalisations" of liberals and socialists. Similarly, he said, "Burning heretics at the stake was once considered useful and justifiable by many of the Catholic clergy, but it would be uncharitable to say that this was what they all stand for to-day."[6] While Sheehy-Skeffington was willing to allow for a diversity of opinions in priests, he lamented that Ireland lacked prominent liberal Catholic thinkers. O Briain defended himself, which brought a further response from Sheehy-Skeffington, and the debate raged in the *Irish Times* between them and several other contributors over the course of more than seven weeks. In addition to the place of liberalism in Irish society, people were divided over whether and on what grounds the report should have been banned, and the role of the Catholic Church and Catholic morality in the state. So impassioned and engaging was the debate that the *Irish Times* quickly issued the correspondence as a book titled *The Liberal Ethic*.[7]

The final word on the matter fell to O'Faolain in an article that he published in *The Bell*. Upon having read *The Liberal Ethic*, he reflected on the controversy's pedigree in nineteenth-century liberalism and expressed his disbelief that such an episode had occurred in 1950: "Surely this is a reprint from *The Irish Times* of 1850? That year would have been about right. Some twenty years out of date is permissible in Dublin: but one hundred and twenty! Had we been even as half-alive then as we now are we should have started to discuss Liberalism not later than the Reform Bill of 1832."[8] He reminded readers that it was the liberals, not the conservatives, who brought in Catholic Emancipation. O'Faolain proffered John Henry Newman as a model for Catholics, arguing that he rose to become a cardinal because in his youth he had the intellectual and emotional courage to become a radical, breaking from the Church of England, converting to Catholicism, and spearheading the Oxford Movement.[9] The problem, he said, was that Irish Catholics tended to be anti-liberal, and "anti-Liberals cut a fine show when they are against something," but, unlike liberals, they not only offer nothing for curing such social diseases as slum housing and racism, but also tend to perpetuate them.[10]

As O'Faolain's essay suggests, *The Bell*, alongside the *Irish Times*, was the major tribune through which writers made their case for a more liberal and tolerant Ireland. The *Irish Times* afforded them immediate interventions in public debates to far more readers, but *The Bell* allowed for longer pieces in which they could reflect more calmly, take stock, and possibly point to new courses of action. In doing so, they were bound to make enemies. O'Faolain's "The Liberal Ethic" was but one of many articles that lamented the power and the tyranny of the Catholic Church in Ireland, seeing it as a conservative force that stemmed the tide of liberalism and positive progress. When John McQuaid, the archbishop of Dublin, dictated in his Lenten regulations of 1944 that no Catholic should attend the traditionally Protestant Trinity College Dublin and that if they did so they would be unworthy of receiving the sacraments, O'Faolain denounced the decree as totalitarian in demanding the absolute, unbending adherence of parishioners.[11] In 1951, when McQuaid, fearing that the Church would lose control over women's reproduction, squashed the Mother and Child Scheme (an attempt to bring a limited measure of universal healthcare to Ireland), O'Faolain was likewise vocal in his criticism.[12] Repeatedly, O'Faolain claimed that the Church and its political adherents engaged in "the throwing of yet another stone on the cairn erected, stone by stone ... on the grave of an adult, informed, intellectual, Catholic conscience. Such a conscience can only live where full liberty of discussion is permitted to the laity, whose fundamental Loyalty to their Church and Faith must otherwise be as useless as the Loyalty of an ignorant, untrained and unarmed army of mercenaries, unfitted to defend the Truth."[13] Such statements by O'Faolain and his confederates brought them and any periodical or organisation to which they belonged under the close watch of the Catholic hierarchy.

In the wake of these polemical battles, the IACL took on the censorship in a way that was in keeping with both O'Faolain's and Sheehy-Skeffington's more confrontational agitations through Irish PEN and the Council of Action. The strategy was provoked by the Censorship Board's exponentially increasing number of bans and, as we saw in the prior chapter, the inability of Irish PEN to provide a meaningful defence of freedom of expression. In March 1956, the IACL launched a campaign against the censorship's banning of books of literary merit, asking people to sign a petition to the taoiseach stating that they sought "a review of the work of the Censorship of Publications Board."[14] The date is noteworthy: Ireland had joined the United Nations the year before, and the country could therefore be expected to live up to the terms of the Universal Declaration of Human Rights, including the protection of freedom of expression.

The origins of the IACL's campaign can be traced to a public talk on censorship that O'Faolain gave to a meeting of Trinity College's Philosophical Society on 23 February 1956. Taking a moderate position, he suggested that the institution of censorship did not need to be altered; rather, they should change "the attitude of the mind of the censors themselves" as he felt that they understood the terms *indecency* and *obscenity* too broadly. Claiming that "Fostering ignorance by protecting alleged innocence could be one of the greatest instruments for the corruption of youth ever introduced," O'Faolain argued that young people were not equipped for going out into the wider world. The students were favourable to his views, further proposing that every ban should be immediately appealed to ensure that there was proper oversight; they also pointed out that the boards were composed of men only, while women should be equally represented.[15] Such interventions attested to the more radical views of the educated youth and suggested that a broader generational shift in public morality might soon occur.

The next night, Father Joseph Deery, the sitting chair of the Censorship Board, addressed members of the Dublin Institute of Catholic Sociology. Deery insisted that while "Ireland was a Catholic country," he did not seek to force his views on others; however, he had to protect the public from harm, questioning what right readers had "to fill their imaginations with foul thoughts and to make themselves familiar with the lowest forms of vice." Admitting that people were free, he said that freedom should not be rendered so extreme as to become licence. Moreover, "It was the view of the Catholic Church that a work of great literary merit could do more harm than one of sheer pornography." Censorship was, he argued, far less harsh in Ireland than it was in Britain, where it could lead to people being fined and imprisoned. As for those who suggested that the censors' banning of the sexual merely revealed their own prurience, he said that this was illogical. One might just as easily say, "'To the healthy, all things are healthy. Stuff him up with strychnine!'" Following the speech, Peadar Ward, the editor of *The Standard*, registered his disapproval of O'Faolain's lecture the night before, denouncing what he viewed as his moral relativism and noting that it was appropriately espoused at a Protestant university.[16]

Conveniently for the IACL, another censorship controversy soon erupted. *The Observer*, a London Sunday newspaper, was unavailable in Ireland on 1 April because it was held by customs authorities, purportedly for an article that was part of a series on "family planning." One member of the IACL was "amazed" with the situation, believing that the "withdrawal of such a paper, which has such distinction and tradition, will ... make our censorship machinery, which has made this country ridiculous in the eyes of the literary world, even more so now."[17] This was considered by one journalist as yet another move by those "who wish to keep us in hair-shirts and sackcloth."[18] In their reading of the Censorship Act, the editors of the *Irish Times* declared that such a seizure by customs was unlawful as they could only confiscate books, not periodicals. They thus surmised, wrongly, that the officials had not acted of their own accord and that the Censorship Board had demanded it.[19] "This point is of importance as an indication of the lengths to which our country's obscurantists will go in their attempt to stamp out the last vestiges of nonconformity," they charged, arguing that it was unlikely that an article could "create a wave of sentiment in favour of birth control." They concluded that the "banning of the *Observer* merely brings the Censorship Board into deeper contempt – and with it, unfortunately, our country."[20] For its part, the Irish Retail Newsagents', Booksellers' and Stationers' Association endorsed the paper's seizure.[21]

Seeing an opportunity to defend freedom of expression, Sheehy-Skeffington informed the chair of the Seanad that he intended to raise the issue of the seizure, especially as he had had his request to import past and future copies of *The Observer* denied by the minister for justice.[22] However, the Sunday edition was available in Ireland the next week.[23] In the end, the episode raised questions with regard to the legality of the seizure and the minister's refusal to allow Sheehy-Skeffington to import a periodical that had not been banned. It appears that there was some extra-legal censorship in Ireland, and without the pressure of the *Irish Times* and Sheehy-Skeffington, *The Observer* would have remained effectively, although unofficially, banned.

On 21 April, the IACL used the momentum generated by their campaign and the *Observer* episode to hold a meeting at Dublin's Mansion House. The event was billed as a discussion on the theory and practice of censorship. Admission was free, with the list of speakers including O'Faolain; Owen Sheehy-Skeffington; the playwright Denis Johnston; Professor James D. Smyth, a former member of the Censorship Board; Thomas Finlay, a Fine Gael TD; and Father Roland Burke-Savage, the censor of the Dublin Archdiocese.[24] Such an array of speakers from distinctly different backgrounds and perspectives was evidently meant to generate healthy debate on the subject and to attract the widest attention possible.

O'Faolain opened the meeting by emphasizing that both he and the IACL accepted the principle of censorship, but that they were against it as it was practised in Ireland. As we have seen, while doing so might reflect one's honest opinion, it is also an important polemical gesture: arguing in favour of censorship reform, not abolition, makes one appear more moderate and one's demands potentially more palatable. For his part, Finlay claimed that the state should use censorship as a defensive and not an offensive weapon. Censorship was necessary, he claimed, to protect the literate masses who had no formal education as their reading habits were in advance of their critical functioning. Smyth referred to his three-month stint on the Censorship Board in 1949 as necessarily coming to an end because of the way the other members interpreted and administered the Censorship Act. He noted that he had abstained from voting on at least two occasions because he had not read the novels in their entirety and spoke of the pressures placed upon the Censorship Board to read only the marked passages because of the volume of books it received. This was an important public admission that would be echoed in the testimonies of other Censorship Board members in the coming year, although its significance appears to have been lost at the time. Johnston was more of a contrarian who argued the libertarian perspective, his main point being that he was absolutely against censorship; he also claimed that the "conspiracy of silence" in Ireland caused people to avoid important issues and was thus a worse form of censorship than that practised by the state. Not surprisingly, Father Burke-Savage defended censorship, although his support was conditional to it working "properly," which he claimed was the case with the current Censorship Board.[25]

Sheehy-Skeffington then stood to refute the arguments in support of censorship. Against the notion that the state must ban certain publications to protect the people's mental health, he argued that if such were the case, then the state should likewise ban everything that endangered physical health, such as cars, surgical instruments, and even canals and rivers. He wondered how one could justify virtue being state imposed, decrying the belief that people can make others virtuous by force: "I wonder how the Almighty, when he placed the Tree of Knowledge in the Garden of Eden, did not have a committee of five sitting round Him." He added that "the power to resist temptation is a necessary part of virtue and it might even be part of the Eternal Plan which tolerates evil – evil could not exist if a Divine Creator did not tolerate it."[26] He thereby employed a provocative hybrid of the typical anti-censorship arguments. Public health is raised, but instead of censorship impeding delivery of a cure, it is mocked for its inability to protect people from actual harm. And instead of censorship being regarded as a pious measure, legislating against free will to protect virtue is seen as antithetical to providence. Tolerance, then, is posited as a divine trait. However, although He granted them free will, God did not exactly tolerate Adam and Eve's dissidence. Yet the essential matter was that evil was not routed from the world as its presence was necessary to test people's virtue.

O'Faolain ended the evening by denouncing the prevailing culture of informal censorship, which he referred to as "a sort of psychosis."

Instead of the present structure of institutional censorship, he appealed for a return to the procedures of British law in which an offending writer was brought before a judge and jury and had the right to face their accuser and defend themselves and their work. In camera censorship and a lack of due process was antithetical to democracy. Like Bernard Shaw in response to the British censorship of plays and Frank O'Connor when *Bird Alone* was banned, he objected "strongly that the right given to an embezzler, a murderer or a prostitute should be denied to Irish writers." Moreover, "It is not good" if "writers are not integrated into the life of the country. ... That means that there is something radically wrong with a country."[27]

The IACL maintained its campaign in the months that followed. On 6 July, Edgar Deale, the IACL's secretary, sent Taoiseach John A. Costello the more than eight hundred signatures of those who supported the organisation's petition. These people, Deale stressed, comprised "a cross-section of our society," not just writers.[28] In addition to repeating the request to initiate an investigation into the workings of the censorship, the IACL submitted a list of reputable authors and classic books that had been censored. It also included a memorandum consisting of five main points. First, the IACL insisted that "the serious reading public" resented the banning of works of literary merit, but that these people remained silent because of the hostility that conservative sections of Irish society would otherwise direct at them. This was, in effect, a social censorship protecting the literary censorship. Second, the practice was inoperable given the number of submitted works that the members of the Censorship Board were expected to read in their entirety. Third, while the public knew of such moral and social tensions as were presented in the list of banned books, the prohibition of these works suggested that the Censorship Board was out of touch with the realities of Irish life. Fourth, though censorship might protect and preserve the innocence of youth while they remained in Ireland, because large numbers of young people were forced by economics to emigrate, the censorship led to a dangerous ignorance when they were exposed to the realities of the greater world. And fifth, the censorship had brought international disrepute to Ireland, making it appear to be intolerant of the freedoms of thought and expression.[29]

The next month, Deale sent Costello legislative improvements drafted by the Legal Subcommittee of the IACL.[30] Among these was the proposition that when the Censorship Board decided to ban a book, the author and publisher should be notified and have ten days to lodge an appeal. If such an appeal were lodged, the prohibition order would not be published until the appeal was determined, thereby allowing the author and publisher to defend themselves. Furthermore, members of the Censorship Board should not be allowed to serve more than one five-year term, and the terms of each member should end in different years, thereby diminishing opportunities for a cabal to form. Finally, demanding that only one copy of a book be submitted to the Censorship Board but six copies to launch an appeal made the latter economically inequitable and thereby prejudicial, and so this requirement should be reformed.[31]

On 3 September, the minister for justice told the taoiseach that while some of the proposals were dismissed as subversive attempts to undermine the censorship, others were thought to be good though merely minor suggestions that did not warrant the time and effort of altering the Censorship Act.[32] The Department of the Taoiseach drafted a letter to the IACL, but Costello deferred his response indefinitely.[33] The IACL, likely figuring that Costello's silence was his response, did not contact him again. And they would have been right: the negative tone of the unsent letter suggests that their expectations for change would not be met. However, by this time the IACL had turned to a different tactic to deal with the censorship, which had been controlled for years by the Knights of St. Columbanus.

Catholic Control of Censorship

As far as censorship is concerned, a marriage was consummated between the state and the Knights around the time of the passage of the 1946 Censorship Act. When William Magennis died earlier that year, John J. Pigott, a professor at St. Patrick's College in Drumcondra, was named to replace him on the Censorship Board. Father Joseph Deery, who had only joined the board in February 1945, was appointed chair. Although people would come and go over the following years, the three other main members were District Judge T. G. O'Sullivan, Christopher J. O'Reilly, and Dermot J. O'Flynn.[34] With these five men, the Censorship Board fell under the control of a cabal of the Knights of St. Columbanus, a conservative Catholic group with direct ties to the hierarchy.[35] The organisation's biographer, Evelyn Bolster, notes that the Knights had always been an influential part of the Oireachtas, with their numbers and ideology affecting a great deal of legislation, including the Censorship of Publications Act.[36] Among the politicians on the roll call of the organisation were several figures who were significant in the first decades of the censorship, including Seán T. O'Kelly, Gerald Boland, William Magennis, and Michael Tierney.[37] While the Knights' role in censorship has been widely acknowledged, it has yet to be documented.[38]

On 22 November 1945, a directive was issued from Ely House, the Knights' headquarters just off of St. Stephen's Green, notifying members that it was their "clear-cut duty" to inform the supreme executive of any obscene or indecent publications.[39] Many lodges throughout the country dutifully set about forming Evil Literature Committees.[40] The Waterford Council feared that it would have to foot the expense of purchasing books for submission, but it was reassured by a member of the Censorship Board that it only needed to complete the complaint form and the board would obtain its own copy and check the passages in question. This was undertaken because the Censorship Board was sensitive to the fact that the Waterford Council was "submitting so many books at a fairly heavy cost."[41] In this instance, the board was flexible in the interpretation of its regulations when it meant that the institution would smoothly run along conservative lines.

A more direct link between the activities of the Knights and the Censorship Board became evident in 1949. On 15 September, T. A. Buckley, a member of the Cork Council, notified Eugene Kavanagh, the supreme secretary, of an article in *The Bookseller*.[42] In one recent issue, a publisher was quoted as saying that the appeal mechanism was easily accessed and that upon protest a revocation was almost assured. Kavanagh's response was blunt: "The Supreme Knight is taking a keen interest in this Censorship business. By the way, the Board consists of four members of the Order and one other – all Catholic."[43] The same day, Kavanagh sent to Professor B. F. Shields the article and a copy of his letter to Buckley.[44] At this time, Shields was one of the members of the Censorship Board who was also a Knight. He confirmed that publishers had had an easy time appealing bans: of the fifteen applications for revocation, thirteen had succeeded.[45] From the increased numbers of publications submitted in the following years, we might infer that there was a concerted effort to submit a barrage of potentially obscene and indecent books to make up for the few that were successfully appealed. In other words, if the appeal mechanism was going to function liberally, conservative groups would swamp the Censorship Board. That the Supreme Knight from 1951 to 1957, Christopher J. O'Reilly, was a member of the Censorship Board during these same six years further attests to a direct connection between the two groups and how they viewed their duties.

Buckley was involved in a similar case at the outset of 1951 when he informed Kavanagh that Nevil Shute's *A Town Like Alice*, a recent bestseller, was rumoured to have had its prohibition order revoked when store owners complained to the authorities that they had been stuck with hundreds of copies in stock.[46] Kavanagh then suggested to Pigott that booksellers were contravening the law. Pigott in turn asked Brian

MacMahon for some explanation. By this time working as the secretary to both the Censorship Board and the Appeal Board, MacMahon called the report a "ridiculous fabrication," noting that under both the 1929 and 1946 acts, booksellers were not able to lodge appeals and that alerting authorities to stocks of banned books would have resulted in prosecution, not openness to their lobbying.[47] When other concerns warranted examination, Kavanagh sent his queries directly to MacMahon, who then provided sympathetic, detailed responses.[48] However, the Knights remained anxious, leading them to closely watch the Appeal Board. The suspicion with which the Knights held the Appeal Board was again apparent when the magazine *Lilliput*, which had already been banned on two prior occasions, was complained of for a third time in October 1951.[49] This led to their frustration that the legislation did not make the prohibition of periodicals permanent.[50]

Further concern about combating the more liberal elements in Irish society was raised when a member of the Knights' Tyrone Council alerted Ely House that *The Bell*, after a two-year hiatus, was to be issued again under the editorship of Peadar O'Donnell. "We have a suspicion that this magazine may not be up to the requirements of the Catholic Church," wrote one member, "and we would appreciate your views on same."[51] Kavanagh responded: "If and when this magazine is published we shall keep a strict watch on its outlook."[52] Liberals were thus suspected as potential fifth columnists, and, as such, their activities were closely monitored.[53]

By 1954, the Knights, like the CTSI two decades earlier, had established a well-organised secretive network functioning across the country to support the censorship. In April, one of the Dublin councils submitted a list of eight proposals that would control books and periodicals more effectively.[54] These included amendments to the existing legislation to license bookshops and libraries; to allow the Censorship Board to examine publications on its own initiative; to oblige all wholesalers and distributors to have in their possession a current register of prohibited publications, with penalties applied to offending parties; to decentralise the Censorship Board to attract the interest of people in other parts of the country and facilitate submissions; and to tighten regulations for the importation of publications. It was also proposed that members should garner more support by asking others to assist them with ferreting out evil literature and pressuring those who undermined the censorship through the sale and distribution of immoral publications to change their ways. This was yet another example of how social censorship worked alongside of official, institutional censorship.

The IACL was therefore waging its war on censorship against the weight of social and political orthodoxy. However, an opportunity to liberalise the institution soon presented itself. The beginning of the IACL's campaign coincided with the departure from the Censorship Board of T. G. O'Sullivan in March and Father Deery in June. In November, Christopher Gore-Grimes gave a lecture to the Criterion Club in Dublin, saying that he hoped that at least one of the two vacant positions on the Censorship Board would go to a religious minority as only Catholics had been members for the past ten years. Protestant representation, he noted, was in keeping with the Censorship Board's traditional composition.[55] The IACL's campaign paid off when, instead of staunch, conservative Catholics, two more liberal men were appointed on 5 December: R. R. Figgis and Andrew F. Comyn. Figgis was a Protestant Dublin businessman, had been a contributor to *The Bell*, and had served on the board of the Arts Council of Ireland, of which O'Faolain was the director from 1956 to 1959. Comyn, a Catholic lawyer from Cork, had a lower public profile. Because only two dissenting voices were needed to overturn the decision of three members to ban a publication, the new appointments created a seismic shift in the way that the Censorship Board came to operate.

Indeed, the Censorship Board quickly divided into two factions – one composed of Pigott, O'Reilly, and O'Flynn, the old guard of conservative Knights of St. Columbanus, and the other of Comyn and Figgis – who came to loggerheads over the interpretation of how their duties were defined and how they viewed indecency and obscenity. The major sticking point was that Comyn and Figgis wished to read books in their entirety and to take literary merit into account, whereas the other three believed that a questionable passage was reason enough to ban a book. A memorandum written for Archbishop McQuaid mentions that a directive was issued to make Catholic Action societies sensitive to the efforts of the IACL to impede the work of the Censorship Board.[56] Given its details, it was most likely written by one of the three Knights on the Censorship Board. Its author believed that, from the outset, the purpose of the IACL's campaign had been to fill the vacancies on the Censorship Board with its nominees, and that Comyn and Figgis "are there, to block (or veto) a majority decision. The number of prohibition-orders are nothing to what they were formerly."[57] This outcome was blamed on the IACL's "campaign of vilification" against the Censorship Board. Moreover, Comyn and Figgis "seem to consider that their main duty is, not to protect the public from indecent literature, but to protect the authors and publishers of such from censorship."[58] The new appointees based their decisions on the principle that artistic merit should override moral matters, as permitted under Section 6.2 of the 1946 Censorship Act. It was therefore lamented by Church insiders that "the presence of these two gentlemen on the Board at the same time, (or any two of the same kidney, for that matter) would mean a slow and painful (but not too slow) death for censorship."[59]

By May 1957, the more conservative bloc of the Censorship Board could no longer sit in the same room with Comyn and Figgis. As chair, Pigott refused to hold further meetings until things could somehow be resolved to align their views or the minister for justice intervened. Meanwhile, because from June to December of the year before there were not enough members to have a quorum, the number of untreated submissions grew. Understandably, conservative, pro-censorship sections of Irish society were infuriated at what they considered a year of wasted opportunity and the failure of the institution to properly function.[60] In this environment, censorship, which had always had its critics for being either too harsh or not harsh enough, was rendered a farce. The authority of Oscar Traynor, the minister for justice, would have been entirely eroded had this continued. In this sense, the barrier that the Irish legislation had created to protect the government from censorship blowback was crumbling. By September, Traynor had had enough and called Pigott into his office.

In his account of the meeting with Traynor, which he submitted to McQuaid, Pigott claimed that the Censorship Board had not been called to order in four months because of the intransigence of Comyn and Figgis. These two men were accused of sharing the views of the IACL by considering works in their entirety as opposed to focusing on marked passages, as had been the practice of the Censorship Board since Pigott became a member. Comyn and Figgis, he emphasized, therefore regularly voted against the other three members. "If the authors happened to be persons of the standing of, say, Steinbeck or Huxley," claimed Pigott, "their names were sufficient to give them a free passage, however filthy the matter. It must be said, however, that in the case of books openly deriding chastity the two recalcitrant members voted with us and banned them."[61] Here, *recalcitrance* is defined as a refusal to allow censorship to function smoothly by debating matters for too long, as opposed to a refusal to discuss other aspects of a publication than those found in a purportedly indecent or obscene passage. He revealed that the difficulty arose mostly over "Freudian inspired novels where the obscenity was presented under the cloak of some social, political or military cause."[62] The origins of indecency and obscenity were therefore of central concern: were they the product of a writer or were they the product of a society that the writer merely depicted? The more liberal members clearly held the latter, naturalist, reformist viewpoint, whereas the conservative members held the former and condemned writers for having the temerity to even speak of such things. At issue was whether this debate would be allowed to take place in Ireland so that questions could be raised as to how society was structured and whether individuals would continue to be victimised, castigated, punished, and rejected by their society for differing from the dominant morality.

Another point of debate was the question of omnibus volumes. The refusal of Comyn and Figgis to ban such a volume that included already banned material by John Steinbeck and Ernest Hemingway became the moment of truth for the Censorship Board. Pigott appealed to the attorney general, who informed the Censorship Board that it had to ban the book because "a publication which incorporates a prohibited book, clearly identifiable as such, is ipso facto itself a prohibited book."[63] Pigott then met with Traynor in June to share some passages from books that Comyn and Figgis had refused to ban; apparently, Traynor was not impressed with their decisions. Pigott then asked the minister to force the resignation of the other two men, but Traynor stated that he could not do so under the terms of the law.[64]

As no meetings were called over the summer, Traynor summoned Pigott at the beginning of September. After discussing the deadlock, Traynor asked Pigott for his resignation. When Pigott reminded Traynor that he could not do so, Traynor suggested that he might be forced to dissolve and recompose the Censorship Board.[65]

By this time, the government was under pressure to make such changes. Some of this came from the IACL, but the attitude of the Fianna Fáil government that took office in March was completely different to that of the coalition government that had preceded it. The government elected in 1957 would, in the coming year, usher in the First Programme for Economic Expansion, which guided Ireland's aggressive effort to attract foreign capital and business for the first time since independence. For a new generation, the opening of the country's borders would have to be aligned with a broader, more tolerant cultural mentality, thereby making an archconservative Censorship Board an anathema. In this sense, the new administration was aligned with PEN International's belief that greater internationalism both necessitated and was driven by greater freedom of expression.

Soon after his meeting with Traynor, Pigott submitted his resignation.[66] In the weeks afterwards, O'Reilly and O'Flynn followed suit. In the stead of these three men, Judge J. C. Conroy, F. T. O'Reilly, and Emma Bodkin were appointed on 28 October.[67] This was significant: the members of the Knights of St. Columbanus had effectively relinquished the organisation's control of the Censorship Board. However, the appointment of Emma Bodkin was perhaps the most unnoticed and yet most radical aspect of the recomposition: for the first time in the institution's nearly three decades, a woman was included. The ramifications of this were of both real and symbolic importance. Not only was a woman treated as an equal to men in her ability to determine a book's potential indecency and obscenity, but also she was not considered to need protection by men from the potentially harmful effects of being exposed to such literature. In this regard, the government went beyond what even the IACL had proposed.

The change in personnel with the appointments of Figgis and Comyn was simply in keeping with the way that the institution had been run, with people being replaced once they stepped down. It was left to the minister for justice to decide whom he should appoint in their stead. Although the actions of the IACL would have provided an impetus for the selection of these two men, there was also a creep towards a more liberal society. A part of this would have been instigated by the residual disgust elicited in some corners over the fallout of the Mother and Child Scheme. A clearer division between Church and state was needed to placate a growing number of people in Irish society who saw their civil rights being infringed upon by the Catholic hierarchy. Furthermore, because of the massive number of banned books, most glaringly in the first half of the 1950s, the legitimacy of the institution was quickly eroding. Indeed, it was impossible for members of the Censorship Board to say that they had thoughtfully considered so many books while working full time in other employment. But, as their private comments revealed, this was not their concern as they believed that any vulgarity should condemn a book regardless of its literary merit. The changes that occurred in the composition of the Censorship Board were therefore the result of factors both internal (the resignation and death of members) and external (the appointment of new members and louder calls for a more liberal institution).

A Moral Panic for the Ages

With the arrival of the new members of the Censorship Board in October 1957, stirrings of trouble quickly took the form of a tidal wave that became Ireland's last great censorship moral panic. Hints of what was to come can be traced to the beginning of November, when one of the provincial councils of the Knights of St. Columbanus contacted Ely House to inquire into the reason behind the resignations of the three Knights from the Censorship Board.[68] Some felt that the men had betrayed the membership. More importantly, the communication demonstrates once again that the Knights' control of the Censorship Board was an open secret that the more conservative sections of Irish society counted on to further shape national culture. Ely House's response was that the members resigned to call into question the legitimacy of the current Censorship Board, hoping that doing so would force the minister to dissolve it and reconstitute a new one along the lines of the old.[69] As this did not occur, another strategy was needed. By this time, Dermot O'Flynn had already contacted "various societies and bodies in an effort to create a certain amount of public opinion."[70] A directive was then sent to councils across the country to ensure that their members were being vigilant in their respective communities by continuing to ferret out evil publications in libraries and bookshops.[71]

At the beginning of December, Archbishop McQuaid emerged from the shadows to begin a new campaign against evil literature. Speaking to a conference of the leaders of the Catholic youth organisations of Dublin, which catered to more than twenty thousand children, he noted the increasing number of "foul books" on sale in the city. In response, the attendees unanimously passed a resolution urging the authorities to take immediate action.[72] The next day, Pigott issued a press release in the form of an interview with the *Irish Independent* in which he referred to the IACL as "the traditional enemies of censorship."[73] Between the timing of the interview – one day after McQuaid announced a renewed influx of evil literature in Ireland – and Pigott's constant communication with McQuaid throughout the controversy, it appears that the archbishop had convinced Pigott to take his story public to garner momentum for the battle ahead.

The success of the campaign's launch is evident in the reaction that it evoked from politicians. Phelim Calleary, a Fianna Fáil TD, broached the subject in the Dáil on the same day that Pigott gave his statement, asking Traynor, his own minister for justice, about the Censorship Board. In particular, he wanted to know how many publications had been banned since 1954. Traynor, who was barraged with more questions about the effectiveness of the Censorship Board as it was currently composed, announced that the figures for the number of publications banned in 1954, 1955, 1956, and 1957 were, respectively, 1045, 537, 323, and 75. When pressed on the decreasing efficiency, he responded that the machinery had remained unchanged and that the numbers dropped starkly because there were very few Censorship Board meetings held during the previous two years. He reminded his colleagues that at times there were not enough members to have a quorum and at others the chair refused to hold meetings. The current Censorship Board had

Traynor's full confidence and, he believed, needed time to demonstrate its competence.[74]

Meanwhile, O'Faolain issued a counterattack by rejecting Pigott's claim that the IACL was an enemy of censorship, noting how the organisation had always stated its acceptance of some form of control, especially with the growth of the pornography industry. However, it had long been critical of how the censorship was structured and functioned in Ireland, with O'Faolain citing the prohibition of books by twelve Nobel laureates and scores of authors of world repute as evidence of the institution's shortcomings. He then praised the minister for justice for upholding and defending the Censorship Act by demanding that censors genuinely consider works for their literary merit.[75]

Over the next month, a series of letters to the editor in Irish newspapers further inflamed matters.[76] Owen Sheehy-Skeffington questioned the professionalism of Pigott and the work of the Censorship Board when he was a member, noting the impossible task of reading in their entirety all of the books that had been submitted during that period.[77] Edgar Deale corrected Pigott's claim that the IACL now controlled the Censorship Board as none of the five censors were members.[78] Pigott responded by charging that Sheehy-Skeffington belonged "to the liberal school of thought – that school which would substitute the authority of man for that of God and asserts that every individual is free to do whatever he wishes, provided it is not obviously against the common good."[79] Sheehy-Skeffington readily accepted the label of liberal and claimed that Pigott must secretly deplore "the Creator's behaviour in making the forbidden fruit so freely and dangerously accessible in the Garden of Eden, contenting Himself with bestowing a liberal free will on Adam and Eve and actually enjoining and expecting them to be virtuous by free choice."[80] He then facetiously pointed out that Pigott had banned every book the board's secretary had passed him for consideration: "In such circumstances," he archly added, "I am surprised that he never absentmindedly banned the board's minute book instead of signing it."[81] Sheehy-Skeffington sought to assure Pigott "that liberalism no more necessarily leads to the sexual orgies of his fevered imagination than the acceptance of Catholicism necessarily leads to burning women alive as a public spectacle for the greater glory of God."[82] The "anti-liberal totalitarians of Church and State," he concluded, did more to foster evil than to fight it.[83]

While this exchange took place, the government was swamped by sections of the public that sided with McQuaid. Letters poured into the taoiseach's office from the Catholic youth groups that were present for the archbishop's lecture.[84] The minister for justice responded by noting that the Gardaí were as informed as ever in their duties to be on the lookout for indecent and obscene publications and that there was no evidence that evil literature was being sold in Ireland. Each group was asked to provide hard evidence if it had it. In the end, they were told that now that the Censorship Board was operable again, the potential for the circulation of questionable literature was diminished.[85]

Aware that its response would do little to dissuade these groups, the government held a meeting to discuss the matter. Éamon de Valera, taoiseach once again, suggested that a public statement should be issued and that the Gardaí should visit bookshops suspected of selling immoral publications and prosecute offenders. Traynor, though, was against the idea, stating that the Gardaí had enough work at present and that if the public was concerned by such literature, people only had to submit complaints to the Censorship Board.[86]

Meanwhile, the Knights of St. Columbanus continued its campaign. Councils from across the country successfully lobbied a number of booksellers not to sell questionable publications and vowed to remain vigilant in their inspection of shops.[87] The Knights also enlisted the help of D. J. Bridgeman, who was the secretary of the Irish Retail Newsagents', Booksellers' and Stationers' Association (IRNBSA) and had spoken on the organisation's behalf over thirty years earlier when he appeared before the Committee on Evil Literature. Bridgeman assured the Knights that he was working "in his own quiet way" to support their cause.[88] Soon thereafter, the IRNBSA issued a public statement that its members were against evil publications and would continue to help combat the menace.[89] At the end of February, Ely House issued another directive encouraging local councils to remain active and to send any questionable publications to the Censorship Board.[90]

By this time, other groups had begun to get involved. On 16 January, Dublin City Council, concerned with the harmful effects of the purportedly increasing amount of undesirable literature being imported into the country, asked the government to take the necessary measures to rectify the situation.[91] Two weeks later, William MacNeely and James Fergus, respectively the bishops of Raphoe and Achonry, contacted de Valera on behalf of their peers. During a meeting of the Standing Committee of the Hierarchy held earlier that month, the prelates had concluded that while the existing legislation was adequate, the regulations to enforce it were not being energetically applied by the present Censorship Board. To remedy this situation, the bishops suggested several possible amendments to the legislation, among them increasing the membership of the Censorship Board to twenty people and, to cope with the number of submissions, having several committees of three decide the fate of books.[92] Given that the proposals resembled those from other groups who in the past had sought to change the institution to no avail, there was little chance that the government would be amenable to such reform. Despite this, de Valera told them that he was carefully considering their suggestions.[93]

Meanwhile, the Catholic hierarchy issued a press release. Contrary to all reports, they noted that an increase in evil publications in Ireland was "confirmed by the strongest evidence."[94] Furthermore, they made an unfounded link between literature and the growth of juvenile delinquency and reminded parents to be vigilant in warning their children about the dangers of evil books to their spiritual welfare.[95] In his Lenten pastoral published under the title *Evil Reading Matter is not Literature*, the archbishop of Cork "warned that it was grievously sinful to write, and it might lead to grievous sin to read, any book or paper that was in any way indecent."[96] The Lenten pastoral of the bishop of Killaloe similarly cautioned his flock, singling out travelling vendors of the Bible and books that purported to deal with spiritual matters because they might be subversive if they had yet to receive the imprimatur of the Church.[97] Other bishops indirectly attacked evil literature by addressing the rise of immorality and materialism and the need for Catholics to reject temptation.[98] Meanwhile, the government was trying to remain out of the spotlight and to determine the best way in which to proceed.

There was some consideration of the Censorship Board's members at this time, suggesting that the government sought to protect itself from charges of being weak. To counter this wavering, Traynor told de Valera that there was no increased threat; rather, it was a conspiracy created and supported by the Catholic organisations that were whipped into a frenzy by McQuaid. The archbishop, Traynor believed, was acting petty, feeling slighted at not being consulted on the recent appointments. Traynor counselled that unless the campaign was met with full force, the government would suffer serious damage. Because the initial criticism of the Censorship Board was directed at Comyn and Figgis, who were appointed by the former Fine Gael coalition government, Traynor told de Valera to show Costello this implicit attack of his decision-making. By doing so, de Valera could enlist the opposition to counter the power of the Catholic hierarchy. He noted that it was important to rally "the responsible members of the various parties in the Dáil to the support of the institutions of the State so that the Hierarchy may be led to see at the outset that this Government and those which preceded it were carrying out their duties faithfully in accordance with the powers conferred on them."[99] Traynor assured de Valera that he "took particular pains to select persons to whom the Church authorities could not possibly take exception."[100] It is therefore understandable that some people felt that the crisis was yet "another Coalition mess left behind for Fianna Fáil to clear up."[101]

Taking Traynor's advice, de Valera held a private meeting with Costello, who affirmed his confidence in the Censorship Board and implied that he would support the government and not resort to political opportunism by criticising its decisions in the matter.[102] De Valera also informed Bishop Fergus that there was no evidence to prove that the number of evil publications in Ireland had increased. However, had they done so, it was because of the difficulties concerning the membership and functioning of the Censorship Board for the past two years. The Catholic hierarchy would not have been able to dispute this claim, and in fact de Valera's point placed some of the responsibility for the problem on those whom the Church had supported. Furthermore, the Censorship Board was working "harmoniously" and conscientiously since its reconstitution in October 1957. In the end, the onus for making indecent and obscene literature disappear was placed on the hierarchy and its followers, for if they would lodge complaints, the Censorship Board would consider them.[103]

Unfortunately for Traynor, Joseph Blowick, a deputy representing Clann na Talmhúain, the farmers' party, remained beyond the inter-party agreement. During question period on 1 May, Blowick asked for the number of books and periodicals awaiting consideration and the number submitted and dealt with by the Censorship Board in the past year. Traynor responded that as of 1 October 1957, 525 books and 8 periodicals had been submitted but had yet to be dealt with by the Censorship Board. As of 1 April 1958, these stood at 695 books and 43 periodicals. During that same period, 412 new books and 82 periodicals were submitted; meanwhile, the Censorship Board had considered 242 books and 47 periodicals.[104] Although they were working admirably, examining 40 books and 8 periodicals per month, they had not been able to keep up with the rate at which publications were submitted. When Blowick asked Traynor if, considering these figures, he believed that the Censorship Board was up to the task, Traynor reiterated his confidence in it, noting that sometimes delays could not be avoided owing to logistics, but that this was not the fault of the censors themselves.[105] Blowick then proposed amending legislation to combat the increased circulation of evil literature; Traynor, however, noted that the machinery was sufficient, that the Censorship Board was capable as it was currently composed, and that any complaints about specific cases should be submitted for consideration.[106] While Blowick's actions might be thought to be the product of an independent spirit, his questions were actually a part of the Knights' final attempts to discredit the Censorship Board. Indeed, earlier that spring, M. L. Burke, the Knights' supreme secretary, sent Blowick the comments and questions that he had agreed to ask in the Dáil. Blowick, it turns out, was a member in good standing of the Knights' Claremorris Council.[107]

The efforts by Blowick were merely the fizzling out of the last great moral panic waged by conservative Catholic Ireland against evil literature. Once they received de Valera's letter, McQuaid and his colleagues no longer pursued the matter. After that, few Catholic organisations and lay groups contacted de Valera, thereby suggesting that they were reconciled to the government's position. Traynor's strategy of staying on message and forging solidarity between the two major parties had won the day. Being politically savvy people, the Catholic hierarchy would have understood this and decided to wait and see what the results of the new Censorship Board would be. In the meantime, McQuaid was occupied by another censorship controversy: his refusal to bless the 1958 An Tóstal theatre festival. The festival's decision to stage Sean O'Casey's *The Drums of Father Ned* and a dramatic adaptation of James Joyce's *Ulysses* led to McQuaid's public refusal and the event's ultimate collapse.[108] Perhaps the hierarchy was flexing its muscles because it realised that it had indefinitely lost control of the Censorship Board and felt the need to have its power publicly acknowledged. For the bishops, the censorship was thereafter resistant to their whims.

Towards the 1960s

While the censorship had shown itself to be somewhat malleable with the changes that took place in the board's composition in 1956 and 1957, it demonstrated stability in weathering the attacks launched at it during the winter of 1957–8. This stability was the result of several factors. First, as Table 9.1 reveals, the new Censorship Board was not exactly liberal: in its first five years, from 1958 to 1962, it banned an average of 395 books per year.

These numbers were closer to how the Censorship Board of the late 1940s performed, with the caveat that the percentage of examined books that were banned in the first three years shrank significantly from the earlier part of the 1950s. The larger numbers examined in 1958 and 1959 were the result of the backlog that had occurred from the Censorship Board's inactivity over much of 1956 and 1957. The number of books banned per year was still significantly higher than it had been in the first sixteen years of censorship, when just over a hundred books were annually banned, but this was also the result of more complaints being

Table 9.1 Figures for the Censorship Board, 1958–62[109]

Year	Number of Books Examined	Number of Books Banned	Percentage of Books Banned
1958	911	487	53.5%
1959	797	402	50.4%
1960	518	291	56.2%
1961	631	408	64.5%
1962	539	389	72.2%

submitted. It is important to note that the books banned in the post-1957 era were largely of the pulp fiction variety and that the Censorship Board no longer banned the established classics. The newly composed Censorship Board was therefore not much different to those that had come before it in terms of its willingness to ban books, only now it appeared to take artistic merit into account and thereby banned fewer literary works. There was thus a high degree of institutional stability despite a slightly more liberal outlook on the part of the censors, meaning that the government's confidence in the new Censorship Board not to undermine the institution was well placed.

However, the numbers of books submitted remained similar to what they were in the early 1950s when the Knights first began their campaign against evil literature, thereby indicating that they and like-minded individuals were still active in this later period. More disturbing for those who believed that the Censorship Board would now be governed by a more liberal ethos, the ratio of books banned to those examined started to increase significantly in 1960. While established classics were now safe, contemporary works were not so lucky. In the new decade, the Censorship Board was tested by the changing times in which the nascent civil rights and feminist movements began to exert themselves with some force. As we will see in the next chapter, this conflict between the old and new guards was represented in the banning of a young crop of Irish writers, led by the likes of John McGahern, Edna O'Brien, and John Broderick. Confronted by this turn of events, Irish writers and liberals recognised that *plus ça change, plus c'est la même chose*. In the end, the answer for how to reverse this trend would be found in not just personnel changes, but continuing societal shifts and structural institutional reform.

The history of the IACL's battles with censorship attests to how effective sustained pressure can be when writers work alongside a broader collective of individuals. Furthermore, as we have seen in the cases of

George Moore, Bernard Shaw, the IAL, and Irish PEN, reform is dependent not only upon the obstinacy of the writers and their strategies of resistance, but also a confluence of social forces that impel institutional transformation. As beacons of stability, institutions remain relatively impervious to change when they are buffeted by critics but have overwhelming public and political support. In the wake of the failed Mother and Child Scheme, there was more taste for a separation of church and state, and with the advent of the government's neoliberal First Programme for Economic Expansion, there was a desire to open the country's borders to outside business. The international dialectic is therefore evident in both the IACL's reflection of a global move towards greater internationalism and the Irish government's concomitant opening of the country for business and liberalising of its Censorship Board. In this respect, Ireland's more liberal censorship and greater internationalism reflected PEN's belief in the correlation between internationalism and freedom of expression. Yet after the supposedly internal liberal change of personnel, censorship continued to attempt to hold back progressive forces. To maintain its relevance in a more progressive era, the censorship would need to be subjected to meaningful reform. As the next chapter will reveal, a new generation of writers and intellectuals would be at the fore in demanding this change.

Chapter Ten

Towards the Liberalisation of Censorship: John McGahern, Edna O'Brien, and the Censorship Reform Society

At the same moment the Irish government radically altered the direction of the Censorship Board by appointing two liberal – or at least less conservative – members, the British government sought to reform its censorship laws to fall in line with changing values. This was part of a long process that had begun in 1954 when the Society of Authors approached the government on the matter.[1] On 21 November 1956, the Conservative MP Antony Lambton introduced a bill that proposed to amend the Obscene Publications Act of 1857, noting that authors and publishers found it too difficult to determine in advance what might be prosecuted, and thus they tended towards self-censorship.[2] Even then, at times they had to deal with printers refusing to handle their work. This led to what was considered a "liberal lull" in which respectable publishers shied away from some serious literature and pornographic publishers were emboldened to ramp up operations. Furthermore, because interpretation of the law was based on the Hicklin test, which Lambton described as hanging "like a London fog above every case of obscenity," artistic merit was not considered, thereby posing a "threat to genuine literature." To counter this, they needed legislation to define "artistic literature." Congratulating the government on such progressive reform, the Labour MP Kenneth Robinson cited Judge Learned Hand's decision in the 1934 American appeal trial over the banning of Joyce's *Ulysses* that "the proper test of whether a book is obscene is in its dominant effect." To determine this, one had to consider the work's reputation and critical reception, which the existing law in Britain did not allow magistrates to do.[3] After much discussion, a select committee was struck. Their report led to a new bill being tabled on 18 November 1958.[4]

After much debate, the Obscene Publications Act became law on 29 July 1959. The legislation still maintained that obscenity was defined by its tendency to "deprave and corrupt." However, it allowed that if a work was proven to be "in the interests of science, literature, art or learning," then those responsible for its publication and circulation could "not be convicted of an offence." To ascertain whether a book met this threshold, the law "declared that the opinion of experts" could be admitted.[5] In Ireland, artistic and scientific merit were supposed to impact whether a book should be banned, but, as we have seen, unlike a judge overseeing a censorship trial in Britain, many censorship boards did not abide by jurisprudence, with personal morality determining their decisions.

The new legislation's allowance for literary merit was tested the next year when Penguin published two hundred thousand copies of D. H. Lawrence's *Lady Chatterley's Lover*. The public prosecutor launched legal action before the book hit stores, with the trial beginning on 20 October 1960. Representing Penguin was the law firm Rubinstein, Nash & Company, who were the defence attorneys for the trial of Radclyffe Hall's *The Well of Loneliness*. Now permitted to call on witnesses to testify to the book's literary value, the defence invited more than thirty people to give evidence, including the authors Rebecca West, E. M. Forster, and Cecil Day-Lewis, the critics Raymond Williams and Noel Annan, the politician and author of *Obscenity and the Law* Norman St. John-Stevas, and the publishers Sir Stanley Unwin and Sir Allen Lane, the latter being the founder of Penguin. The testimonies depicted Lawrence as a giant of world literature and *Lady Chatterley's Lover* as a work of considerable art with a moral purpose. On 2 November, the jury concluded that Penguin was not guilty of publishing an obscene article.[6] This was a massive victory for writers and freedom of expression more generally: there was now a legal precedent as well as a law that distinguished between literature and pornography. Given that many Irish authors published with English presses, this inevitably affected the course of Irish literature. Unlike Joyce, Beckett, and Donleavy in the previous decades, they would no longer have to deal with presses on the continent to publish daring and risqué works.

Following the decision, Northern Ireland's Parliament debated whether they should permit Lawrence's book to circulate in the six counties as the Obscene Publications Act did not apply there. Indeed, the country's censorship law was determined by local legislation, which raised the spectre of them having their own trial.[7] However, the Northern Irish minister of home affairs said that if *Lady Chatterley's Lover* were published in England, it would be difficult to prohibit it in Northern Ireland.[8] A few weeks later, the attorney general of Northern

Ireland warned that while he found the book to be "a work of literature," adults should not leave it lying around where "young people" might read it.[9]

When Penguin released the book in the week after the trial, the *Irish Times*'s London correspondent described the scenes to obtain copies as "a rush roughly proportionate to that experienced by the big department stores during the January sales." Retailers quickly sold out, with one shop owner claiming that he had sold 2,500 copies in three hours.[10] As *Lady Chatterley's Lover* was banned in Ireland on 21 March 1932 and the prohibition order was still in effect, Irish readers could not avail themselves of copies unless they smuggled them in or applied for a special permit to have them imported. Yet the London verdict, which was widely reported by Irish papers, would resonate in Ireland in the succeeding decade.

As noted in the last chapter, while the current Censorship Board was more liberal than its predecessors, it was not liberal compared to what was occurring in England and the United States. In a globalising world, with the tide of modernisation and liberalisation sweeping across Western polities, Ireland increasingly came under both external and internal pressure to open the country to outside influences and be more tolerant, if not accepting, of different attitudes. Such openness was evident in its entry into the United Nations in 1955, adoption of the First Programme of Economic Expansion in 1958, and application for membership in the European Economic Community.[11] Religious mores also began to change with the reforms ushered in by the Second Vatican Council of 1962–5, better known as Vatican II. Organised by Pope John XXIII, Vatican II reassessed the Church's role in a rapidly modernising world to ensure its relevance. As part of its reforms, it allowed for the use of vernacular languages in the saying of Mass and reading of the Scripture, which facilitated adherents' understanding of what was being said.[12] Ireland was also not immune to the many movements that would impact the course of world history in the 1960s, including the civil rights movement, which became particularly relevant with the eruption of the Troubles in Northern Ireland in the latter part of the decade, and the rise of second-wave feminism, which would challenge the patriarchy of Irish society and the Catholic Church. These shifts towards a less obscurantist, more open and democratic worldview would cause further conflict in cultural, social, political, religious, and legal spheres. In Ireland, as elsewhere, censorship remained a bulwark against the waves of liberal forces.

While men of the old guard like Archbishop McQuaid remained convinced that censorship was necessary to stem the tides of change and refused to adopt the reforms proposed by Vatican II, there had been recent signs that religious views of censorship were changing. This shift was in part propelled by the emergence of a younger generation of clergy that was more in tune with the times. One of the foremost members of this clergy was Father Peter Connolly, a Jesuit priest and professor of English at Maynooth. In 1957, Connolly authored an essay entitled "Censorship and Moral Classification of Films" in *The Furrow*, a journal founded in 1950 that bills itself as a voice for "the contemporary Church." Connolly admitted that a Catholic society like Ireland "cannot subscribe to the liberalist rejection of all censorship and to absolute freedom of speculation and discussion."[13] However, he agreed with the relativistic position that "what is a proximate occasion of sin for one person or group may not be so for another."[14] Furthermore, recognising that cinematic, like literary, analysis needed sophisticated knowledge of the medium, he argued that experts should be consulted before bans were issued. In this sense, Connolly was in keeping with politicians in the United Kingdom. Most importantly, he prepared the ground in this essay for another article that would influence the political fortunes of censorship legislation in Ireland.

Simply titled "Censorship," Father Connolly's second essay on the subject appeared in the July 1959 issue of *Christus Rex*, a journal founded in 1947 to guide Irish priests in their social work. Examining how the censorship of literature functioned, Connolly called for a more liberal institution. Outlining what he deemed to be a "reasonable" censorship, he said there should be an attempt "to balance the claims of the common good against the claims of individual freedom" and "the rival claims of various groups in the community." The state, he argued, did not have an unlimited right to coerce: "Therefore, in whatever way it protects public morality civil law should define as narrowly as possible the limits placed on individual freedom."[15] He thus rejected censorship that was too rigid and that did not allow for moral latitude. Yet Connolly also insisted that individuals must limit their rights at times for the sake of the greater common good. In this sense, freedom of expression could not become absolute license. Like anti-censorship crusaders, Connolly recognised the value of people having their virtue tested. As he reasoned, "it is surely one of the marks of maturity not to ignore or deny or be continually at the mercy of [highly excitable] states but to control them by comprehension, to distance and handle them by science, wit, humour, imagination, compassion or contemplation." Similarly, those who regarded thoughts of or taking pleasure in sex as immoral were guilty of falling into "a Manichean-Puritan confusion," as the Church only forbid "the arousal of *extra*-marital venereal pleasure."[16] He further warned pro-censorship advocates that in any society, the meaning of "words like 'indecent' and 'obscene' constantly develop with changing fashions and taste."[17]

Just as importantly, Connolly scrupulously differentiated literature and pornography. He posited that "a genuine literary work provides more [of] a stylistic or imaginative paraphrase of obscenity than the thing itself for it is incorporated with comedy or satire, poetic verve or tragedy." Meanwhile, "pornography connotes mediocrity, commercialism and certain narrative features such as the 'stark' banal four-letter word and a traditional vocabulary for direct action on the patient so that nothing interferes with simple sexual stimulation."[18] Connolly was thus sensitive not so much to subject matter, but to the way in which that subject matter was treated. To make his case, he defended Kate O'Brien's *The Land of Spices*, arguing that its ban for a single reference to homosexuality penalised not only the author, but also "the average reasonable adult."[19] In this respect, his essay became a policy paper of sorts for the new iteration of the Censorship Board, making the case for a more balanced censorship that would avoid banning literature and instead focus on preventing the circulation of pornography. The problem was that a new generation of Irish writers was about to enter the scene. With their frank treatment of taboo subjects having some affiliation with Lawrence's aesthetics, their works would test the ability of the Censorship Board, the government, and Irish society to respond to literature that challenged traditional morality in a world that increasingly embraced liberal values.

As the above discussion illustrates, Ireland in the late 1950s and 1960s was set to continue the course of increasing liberalisation. A part of this was due to the forces of liberalisation that were sweeping across much of the Western world and that would affect the direction of Irish culture as the country increasingly projected itself outwards by joining organisations and implementing policies that were pointedly internationalist. According to the general tendency of the international dialectic, such movement would entail liberal reforms to, if not wholesale abolition of, censorship. This would be in keeping with what was occurring in Britain with the first changes to the Obscene Publications Act in over a century, which resulted in winning meaningful freedom of expression in literature. As this chapter will attest, such changes in Ireland would only come after further personal, political, and social struggles, and would depend upon an alignment of targeted organisational forces with wider acceptance of liberal values in Irish society and politics.

John McGahern: Silence, Exile, and Loss of Employment

Often regarded as one of Ireland's most important prose masters, John McGahern began his career with wide recognition for his talent.[20] In 1962, even before his first novel, *The Barracks*, was published, the Irish Arts Council awarded its opening chapters the AE Memorial Prize.[21] Published by Faber and Faber in London, *The Barracks*, a semi-autobiographical work that follows the life of a young family who live in a police garrison in rural Ireland, was hailed by critics. In the *Irish Press*, the novelist Benedict Kiely praised McGahern's "careful naturalistic prose" that reminded him "of Brinsley MacNamara." His sentences moved, Kiely claimed, "as steadily and unhurriedly as the flow of the river past the barracks in which Elizabeth Regan [*sic*] dies," leaving the impression "of experience sincerely grappled with and of understanding and of truth known intimately."[22] In the *Irish Times*, Bruce Arnold acclaimed "the resilience and supple strength" of McGahern's prose and its "powerful," "haunting," and "poetic" qualities.[23] In the *Irish Independent*, John D. Sheridan likewise lauded McGahern's writing, especially his "vivid and satisfying" descriptions of nature that evoked "the discontent and bewilderment and frustration" of Elizabeth Reegan. While Sheridan considered *The Barracks* "a novel of distinction," he warned potential readers that some of its "accounts of the body" were "crude." Similarly, "the Holy Name occurs frequently ... and there is a fair sprinkling of one of our commonest and ugliest vulgarities." Yet he concluded that although these elements marred the work, McGahern's novel was "marked by sensitive writing and seriousness of purpose."[24] By April, *The Barracks* topped the bestseller list in Dublin, ahead of even Ian Fleming's *On Her Majesty's Secret Service*.[25]

While the novel was not banned, Faber was worried enough that it contacted Christopher Gore-Grimes in his capacity as a solicitor to advise on the book's use of the word *fucking*. Gore-Grimes suggested that, despite the fact that the current Censorship Board was "much more liberal and intelligent than the former" ones, the press might instead use "f – " to avoid the risk of being censored.[26] McGahern, however, believed that the book would not be banned because it had won the AE award and Professor Hogan, who was a member of the Appeal Board, had been on the nomination committee. He thus insisted, as Joyce did in his dealings with Maunsel, that they let it stand and not deform his work; in this, Faber acquiesced.[27] However, it appears that, as with Joyce again, the printer intervened and the word appeared in proofs as "f___"; when McGahern protested, Charles Monteith, a Northern Irish editor who oversaw many of Faber's authors, assured him that it would be restored.[28] Although the book did not run afoul of Ireland's official censors, McGahern's father, fearing local opinion, complained: "If he can write, why can't he write about South America or some of those exotic places. ... They ran Brinsley McNamara's [*sic*] father, you know, out of Delvin." Meanwhile, the priests in Ballinamore, County Leitrim, were reported to have removed *The Barracks* from the town's library as it was "unfit for parochial consumption."[29] While it did not face official censorship, there was thus social and informal censorship of McGahern's first novel.

At the beginning of May 1965, Faber published McGahern's second novel, *The Dark*. Another semi-autobiographical book about a young man who comes of age in rural Ireland, it was marketed as being "impelled forward by ambition and sexuality, guilty and uncontrolled, by a twisted puritanical and passionate religion, and above all by a strange, powerful and very vigorous relationship between a son and a widower father."[30] With such advance publicity, customs officials detained copies of the book. The *Irish Times* lamented the seizure as continuing the sad tradition of the country's poor treatment of its writers. Noting the banning of Joyce, O'Casey, O'Connor, O'Faolain, Brendan Behan, and the "palpable disgrace" of censoring Shaw's novella, they cursed the "shameful and shoddy" censorship of Irish literature and the inevitable fate that awaited McGahern's book.[31]

Meanwhile, *The Dark* received widespread praise. In England, *The Guardian* likened it to Joyce's *A Portrait of the Artist as a Young Man*, although instead of fleeing into silence, exile, and cunning, McGahern's protagonist rather retreats into "acceptance, domicile, [and] sullen responsibility," wreaked by "religious guilt, masturbation, [and] vocational doubt" in an Ireland that is little more than a "prison of prejudice and modified poverty."[32] Terence de Vere White, a novelist himself and the literary editor of the *Irish Times*, regarded McGahern as Joyce's successor and declared that *The Dark* was "most remarkable" and written in "concentrated and evocative" prose. However, he feared that it would be banned as it details "the suppressed sex of the widower, of the priest, but principally of the boy himself. He is an addict to self-abuse, and this, not unnaturally, causes him to wonder and to worry about his future as a priest. Sex is rampant." Yet White was convinced that it was not meant "to titillate or to shock," rather seeing the book as possessing a "wholeness of artistic integrity."[33] Without addressing the legislation or the Censorship Board directly, White argued that the book's literary and artistic merit outweighed any of its potentially obscene or indecent passages.

In the meantime, several Irish readers were not happy that they were deprived of the book themselves. Contrary to the general silence of the public towards bans in the past, many readily voiced their discontent. One person suggested that with the public now aware of the book's seizure, whether or not it was banned it would "be widely read in Ireland," and "a high percentage" of those who read copies smuggled into the country would "do so purely to seek out the allegedly salacious passages."[34] Another citizen lamented that, as Yeats had said during the riot that greeted Sean O'Casey's *The Plough and the Stars*, "we have disgraced ourselves again," as the book's seizure was "a clear indication of the narrow, puritanical, and boorish mentality" of Irish institutions.[35] And a third person referred to it as a "disgusting, prurient and philistine act" that could be remedied by flagellating officials with "a long pole and a whip."[36] The *Munster Express* caught wind of the complaints and similarly charged that the "name of Ireland was once more dragged into the muck by faceless men acting on orders from some hidden authority." Faber and Faber, they noted, was a "highly reputable" press that "does not publish filth." After all, McGahern was a prize-winning author and advance reviews had been entirely favourable, with *The Dark* signalling the arrival of a potential "Golden Age of writing in Ireland."[37]

Brendan Corish, a Labour TD from Wexford and a future tánaiste (the deputy head of the Irish government), asked John Lynch, the Fianna Fáil minister for finance and a future taoiseach, to comment on the seizure of McGahern's novel. Lynch said that it had not been seized but had rather been detained, with copies sent to the Censorship Board for assessment.[38] One TD joked that the title of the book rather reflected "the state of mind of the Customs authorities," warning that "a marriage between John Knox and Mrs. Grundy could not produce healthy offspring."[39] Less than a week later, on 24 May 1965, *The Dark* was banned; on 9 July, an appeal was dismissed. For his part, McGahern was "a little ashamed" that Ireland "was making a fool of itself yet again."[40]

As with *The Barracks*, McGahern and Monteith feared in advance that *The Dark* would be banned in Ireland. Monteith worried about the opening scene in which the narrator's father, who sleeps with him following the death of his wife, uses the boy to excite and masturbate himself. However, he insisted that McGahern should not delete the passage as it was central to the book, suggesting instead that it simply needed "a little toning down – even a little deliberate imprecision."[41] He was also afraid that McGahern's father might sue for libel, but two of McGahern's sisters had read the manuscript, and they felt that their father would not give any trouble, in part because the life described in the book did not align with the family's reality and in part because his father would not dare to risk his own reputation.[42] Despite this confidence, McGahern tempered the incestuous elements of the book, rewriting the scene to do away with "the realistic detail" and instead make it "more rhythmic and imaginatively more vicious."[43] Yet such aesthetic and narrative ambiguity had little impact on the Censorship Board, who were evidently able to decode it.

The banning of *The Dark* was rather ironic as only the year before, based on his success and future promise, McGahern was awarded the Irish Arts Council's £1000 Macaulay Fellowship. The prize allowed him to take a year off from his teaching position at St. John the Baptist school in Clontarf to complete his second novel. To this end, he spent time both in London and on the continent.[44] In the wake of the banning, the press fussed about the fact that during his sabbatical, McGahern had met and married Annikki Laaksi, a well-known Finnish theatre producer, and had honeymooned in Russia.[45] Reflecting the international dialectic, the implication was that the censorship protected the God-fearing nation, as the cosmopolitan McGahern had been cavorting with foreign artists and communists and his work was infused with un-Irish values. As might be expected, the *Irish Times* protested what they considered to be a manifestly unjust banning.[46] Attesting to changing attitudes, the *Irish Independent* agreed that the Censorship Board had acted without justice and common sense, denouncing the ban because they found that it was not prurient and feared "the danger of an official libel on its author."[47] The English papers also chipped in, with Mary Kenny, who later cofounded the Irish Women's Liberation Movement, writing in *The Guardian* that it "is not hypocrisy or despotism which provokes this ban: it is a simple case of arrested intellectual development."[48] This cultural and intellectual stagnation simply buttressed the outdated thinking of the Censorship Board. Despite such public protest, things remained as they were until McGahern's banning had further effects that recalled the treatment of both Brinsley MacNamara and his father.

In February 1966, a little over eight months after *The Dark* was banned, it emerged in the press that McGahern had not resumed teaching duties since his sabbatical had ended in the autumn of 1965. When asked whether he had been dismissed, Father Patrick Carton, the school manager, said that McGahern was simply not "re-appointed."[49] Carton believed that it was not "advisable" to have him return and said that McGahern left a discussion that they had had "perfectly satisfied." For his part, McGahern claimed that just before returning to Dublin, he had received a telegram informing him that he would no longer be employed at the school. He then contacted the Irish National Teachers' Organisation (INTO) regarding the matter, but Father Carton told them that McGahern was "well aware of the valid reason which would render his resumption of duties" impossible.[50] After meeting with Carton in Dublin, McGahern left for London. Meanwhile, the INTO said that it did not represent McGahern as he no longer had a position in the country and therefore had ceased to be a member.[51] It thus denied any responsibility to defend the case. Well before the book was published, McGahern was fatalistic, dreading that were it to be banned, he would probably lose his job.[52] As he confided to one friend, he was "sickened" that he would be disgraced, and the thought that it might not be possible for him to live in Dublin was "the worst."[53] In this sense, censorship had very real affective, social, and economic consequences.

McGahern believed that he was dismissed because he had authored *The Dark*, in effect refuting Carton's claim that he was not reappointed. When he won the fellowship, he had secured a leave of absence, under the terms of which he should have been reintegrated the following year. McGahern admitted that just before his scheduled return in September, he had a motorcycle accident while in Spain that delayed his planned trip to Dublin. He had, however, notified both the Department of Education and Father Carton of his condition. McGahern tried to see Carton in October, but the priest had left on holidays, which delayed their meeting until November. During their discussion, McGahern said that Carton raised the issue of his being wed in a civil ceremony without the consecration of the Church. When McGahern asked Carton whether he could obtain another teaching post if he were to get married by a priest, Carton told him that he could not in the Dublin diocese, but perhaps in a rural school. The priest then admitted that he had been dismissed in part because of *The Dark*, but the way in which he said it led McGahern to believe that it was the main reason. As he left the office, Carton scolded him: "You have gone and ruined your life. ... And you have made my life a misery as well. I can't put my head out the door these days but I'm beset by bowsies of journalists."[54] At the same time, McGahern heard that Archbishop McQuaid had asked the INTO to drop his case in return for supporting their pay negotiations.[55] D. J. Kelleher, the general secretary of the INTO, confided to him: "If it was just the auld book, maybe – maybe – we might have been able to do something for you, but with marrying this foreign woman you have turned yourself into a hopeless case entirely." He also wondered why McGahern would "marry this foreign woman when there are hundreds of thousands of Irish girls going around with their tongues out for a husband."[56] Later reflecting on the episode, McGahern referred to the union as "a paper tiger," for the Church had "all the power."[57]

Most astounding was McGahern's refusal to publicly engage with the scandal and lead a charge against the authorities of both church and state. He had, in effect, been doubly censored, now unable to sell his book or work as a teacher. Yet McGahern offered no treatises on freedom of expression or letters to the editor denouncing his treatment by the INTO and the Church, and he failed to seek legal counsel to challenge both his firing and the INTO's poor representation of his case. Likewise, there was no coalescence of writers around him. Echoing Joyce's exile on the continent and stymied creativity following his long battles with Maunsel, McGahern moved to London and would not publish another novel until *The Leavetaking* in 1974, almost a full decade after *The Dark,* later admitting that he was so affected by the situation that he "didn't manage to write for three or four years."[58] Moreover, like Joyce and MacNamara, McGahern would respond to censorship through his aesthetics rather than polemics, *The Leavetaking* being a semi-autobiographical account of his marriage to a foreign woman and his firing from a Dublin school for not living in accordance with Catholic morality.

In the meantime, Owen Sheehy-Skeffington raised a motion in the Seanad to discuss the failure of the minister for education to ensure that McGahern could resume his teaching post. However, the cathaoirleach (the Speaker) refused to allow the point of order, denying that there was any ministerial responsibility in the matter. Sheehy-Skeffington balked, incredulous that the Oireachtas voted for £14 million for teachers' salaries and yet the minister claimed to have "no power, no responsibility, no capacity" to see that McGahern was "not deprived of his right to make a living." The cathaoirleach abruptly ended the discussion.[59] The *Irish Times* referred to this, with no little irony, as a form of censorship, with the cathaoirleach effectively banning a Seanad inquiry into what had now become known as "the McGahern Affair."[60] Yet the judgment should not have been a surprise as the current cathaoirleach was Liam Ó Buachalla, a longstanding Fianna Fáil senator who, during the censorship debates in the early 1940s, argued passionately against Sir John Keane's appeals for a more liberal censorship.[61]

While the *Irish Times* continued to protest McGahern's treatment, Sheehy-Skeffington wrote an article on the controversy for *Censorship,* a journal published in London by the anti-communist, CIA-sponsored Congress for Cultural Freedom. Sheehy-Skeffington claimed that the worst aspect of McGahern's "victimisation" had been that "the closed circuit clerical machine," which "wielded its absolute power," denied his right to make a living because he had written a banned book.[62] The problem stemmed from the fact that under the Irish system of education, school managers, who were almost always local priests, had total control of personnel with no input from either parents or the government. "The State pays the piper," he quipped, "but the Church calls the tune."[63] When McGahern finally had an audience with Father Carton, the priest was exceptionally frank, complaining: "What entered your head to write that book! Such a terrible schemozzle you caused. I couldn't take you back after that. There would be an uproar if I did."[64] As Carton informed McGahern that he could not be employed in Dublin, Sheehy-Skeffington argued that he could not have made such a statement without having first consulted McQuaid.[65] He concluded that Ireland "has one of the most successful educational systems in the world: its aim is to prevent the children from thinking for themselves. In all too many cases it is eminently successful; and our Censorship Board does all ... to see to it that as few of us as possible ever grow up." Yet he noted an "increasing resistance to such attitudes. Though many a battle still remains to be won, the head-shrinker ... is meeting with tougher skulls in the Ireland of to-day, tougher because they contain minds that claim the right to grow."[66]

Given Sheehy-Skeffington's lead, it should come as no surprise that the Irish Association of Civil Liberty got involved. Edgar Deale, the IACL's secretary, argued in the press that McGahern's civil liberties had been infringed upon by taking away his right to employment. Importantly, he had not been found guilty of professional fault and had received several teaching awards during a relatively short but distinguished career. Deale requested that the minister for education "institute some instrument of appeal to which teachers and public servants who lose their employment (without breach of contract) for reasons unconnected with their efficiency at work could have recourse so that justice would not only be done but would be seen to be done."[67] Unsurprisingly, he drew a blunt rebuke from one priest, who argued that because a teacher not only taught subjects but also had a "moral influence" on future generations, Deale was yet another in a long line of secular liberals who had tried to undermine the national cause.[68]

On the surface, the McGahern affair attested to the continuance of a conservative, Catholic, nationalist censorship that worked hand-in-glove with the Church to maintain a tight control on morality in Ireland. Just as Brinsley MacNamara's father had suffered pecuniary loss as a teacher because his son had written a scandalous book that was burned in the streets of Delvin, so McGahern, half a century later, had his book banned by the state and lost his teaching post. Neither MacNamara nor

McGahern made public comments or statements fighting for the freedom of expression or defending the right to have gainful employment in the absence of professional negligence or abuse. In McGahern's case, resistance instead came from members of the public and the IACL, but without the explicit involvement of writers. Despite the lessons learned from past struggles, Irish writers again reverted to silence, impotence, and stasis. Yet the fact that other citizens had begun to speak more freely and protest the censorship, the collusion of the Church and the state, and the abuse of human rights in the name of protecting morality reveals that new fault lines had formed and that a cultural shift was taking place, however modest it might be.

Edna O'Brien and the Censorship Reform Society: Confrontation and Impelling Change

As Edna O'Brien embarked on her writing career, her mother told her that she "hoped and prayed" that she "was not about to bring ignominy and disgrace" on her family.[69] Nevertheless, O'Brien remains one of the Irish writers most associated with being banned. Indeed, following her death on 27 July 2024, when *The Guardian* asked several contemporary Irish writers to comment on her legacy, Anne Enright, Colm Tóibín, and Eimear McBride all opened their reflections by noting the censorship of her early work.[70] Like McGahern, O'Brien represented a new generation; her unapologetic and honest depiction of the interior lives of Irish women, their sexual relationships, and the social and cultural forces that attempted to circumscribe them was very much in keeping with the zeitgeist of the 1960s and the women's liberation movement. The result was the banning in Ireland of her first five novels: *The Country Girls* on 13 June 1960, *The Lonely Girl* on 4 June 1962, *Girls in Their Married Bliss* on 7 December 1964, *August Is a Wicked Month* on 29 November 1965, and *Casualties of Peace* on 12 December 1966. O'Brien contested the decisions, but her appeals were dismissed. Just for good measure, *Girl with Green Eyes*, a movie for which O'Brien had adapted the screenplay from *The Lonely Girl*, was banned in Ireland upon its release in 1964.[71]

Publicly, O'Brien denied that the bans angered her, and she refused to write articles and essays on the subject.[72] As she prepared to launch *August Is a Wicked Month*, she said that she was "astounded" that her books were banned in Ireland while they were so popular elsewhere. However, she would not omit anything, asserting, as Joyce and McGahern had before her, that "Taking out an offending word or passage is taking part of the totality of something good. You might just as well take a leg or an arm of a piece of sculpture and say then it deserves its place in an art gallery." Literature that troubles souls, she claimed, is "healthy and invigorating" because "it's by abrasion that people's prejudices are aroused." The problem was that some people "don't distinguish between works that are outspoken with a fierce moral undertone and those which have no moral undertone." Before her fourth book was banned, she travelled to Dublin from her home in London on a "crusade" to change the "climate of suppression."[73]

In many respects, O'Brien used her candour and photogenic appeal to broadcast her views further afield.[74] As one journalist noted at the time, she "has always made good newspaper copy. Her news value probably springs from a combination of things – her frank exploration of the adolescent and maturing female; her straightforward responses to interviewers; her refusal to pretend that her writing is not to some extent autobiographical and, not the least important factor, perhaps, that rapt, wool-gathering look of hers that the earlier photographs used to present to us in the world's newspapers and magazines."[75] In this respect, although she refused to write essays and articles, her interviews were as performative as the self-interviews that Shaw conducted for papers and were simply another way of drawing attention to her work and making a public case for freedom of expression. At one point, O'Brien even circulated a rumour that a priest in her native County Clare had bought copies of *The Country Girls* to publicly burn them, but when the *Irish Times* sent a reporter to investigate the matter, they concluded that, like the purported burning of Shaw's books in Galway more than thirty years earlier, it had never happened.[76]

While O'Brien was confronted by a hostile reception from officialdom, she was welcomed by other sections of Irish society. Accompanying her on the dais for an event in Limerick in April 1966, Father Peter Connolly gave a glowing lecture on her novels.[77] It was so popular that the hall was "full to overflowing half an hour before the time the meeting was due to start."[78] Those in attendance included the mayor and several clergy members.[79] One paper reported that "The physical oppression of the atmosphere made it seem for a while as if Ireland, the sow who eats her farrow, was about to turn again on this enigmatic, 33-year-old literary bonham." Yet when a poll was taken asking those present if they had read at least one of O'Brien's books, there was "a forest of raised and waving arms."[80] One man who wondered how it was possible to read banned books was told that he lacked "the right contacts."[81] When another person complained about a passage in *The Country Girls*, O'Brien remarked that it revealed more about "you as a person than me." She noted that people were capable of "great depth and variation of thought, from the almost mythical to the obscene," and that to give only "a fraction of someone's inner thought is to abuse them and diminish them. What makes us love people is their imperfection as much as their perfection." When she was asked why she lived in England, Connolly came to her defence, explaining that she had told him that she felt she could not write as freely in Ireland "because of the narrowness of the atmosphere. ... It was a social not a religious pressure and other writers in other countries ... had experienced it as well."[82] Confronted by censoriousness, she had followed into exile the banned Moore, Shaw, Joyce, O'Casey, Hackett, Hoult, and McGahern.

In his talk, Connolly quoted freely from O'Brien's novels, celebrating "the high spirits of the first two, and their cheerful, natural, rural ribaldry which expressed for him the spirit of the countryside." As for artistry and style, he commended her "spareness" and "the merging of scene and mood, the simple and essentially dramatic technique," while her characters were "something new in Irish fiction," with Kathleen's innocence being "not amoral but premoral." However, he felt that the second two novels lacked the same quality, being uneven and tending to increase the quantity rather than the quality of sexual description. Yet he ended by praising O'Brien's development and tendency to break new ground with each book, concluding that he was "more interested in her work than in any other novels appearing at the moment in Ireland."[83] Coming from a priest and professor of Connolly's stature, this was high praise for O'Brien. Indeed, his esteem for her as Ireland's most exciting novelist was considered by many the most salient point of the evening, and they expected that it might encourage the minister for justice to inject "some greater sanity" into the Censorship Board.[84]

O'Brien was adept at exploiting these methods of engaging people directly and using the new media to her advantage. In November 1966, just as *Casualties of Peace* was being published and only months after the McGahern affair, she appeared on a current events program on Raidió Teilifís Éireann (RTÉ), Ireland's national broadcaster. There was some concern that a banned novelist would be able "to talk on television and to young, impressionable people at that. Suppose some of the teenagers were to ask Miss O'Brien about S-E-X, what mightn't she say to them?"[85] Of course, the young people in the audience did ask O'Brien pointed questions, and her responses were deemed to be "thoroughly sensible, reasonable and wholly unsensational."[86] This was the public persona that she had adopted: the rational and frank voice of women and sex, which went counter to the conservative Catholic morality of Ireland's official culture as promoted by church and state. O'Brien's forthrightness and her use of the new media allowed her to connect more readily with the younger generation and to make a case for a new morality.

Commentators noted how "because she is a colourful personality," she and her writing were "the subject of wide discussion and controversy." More specifically, the journalist Bruce Arnold claimed that O'Brien had a positive effect by shining light on the fact that, because writers did not have the right to a public trial and the banning of their works deprived them of their livelihoods, the censorship was "unconstitutional." He thus hoped that a "Censorship Reform Society" would soon be established, asking his readers if they would continue "to accept the arbitrary judgment which stifles in Ireland this woman's words and her life."[87] The problem was that this was a common refrain echoed down the ages that had failed to provoke significant structural change.

Meanwhile, O'Brien's fifth novel, *Casualties of Peace*, was warmly received by reviewers. In the *Irish Times*, Mary Holland opined: "Let us pray that this novel, at least, of Edna O'Brien's will not be banned in Ireland." The experience that it relates "is one which seems particular to the dark side of Irish Catholicism, the darting, furtive guilt about sex which begins at our first convent kindergarten and maims too many of us for too many years afterwards."[88] Although Augustine Martin, a lecturer of literature at University College Dublin, was less laudatory in the *Irish Press*, he praised O'Brien's breakaway from the semi-autobiographical mode as indicating artistic growth and extolled her prose, which had evolved from the simpler linear style of the earlier novels to a "more metaphorical and densely structured" writing.[89] Both reviewers were enamoured with her style, suggesting that the novel's literary merit would perhaps keep it from being banned despite its challenging subject matter.

However, just a week later, in the days before she appeared on RTÉ, it was discovered that customs officials were holding a consignment of *Casualties of Peace* because they had submitted a copy to the Censorship Board and were awaiting their decision before either releasing or destroying the books. A number of shop owners had not even ordered copies because they feared that the book would be banned and they would be left with the unsellable stock.[90] Given the interdiction of her first four novels, the *Irish Times* called the situation "predictable."[91] Now back in London, O'Brien voiced her dismay, believing that "the air seemed to be clearing after the talks we had in Limerick."[92] Matters got worse by the beginning of December when she returned to Dublin. As she passed through the airport, the five copies of *Casualties of Peace* that she was carrying were confiscated, despite the novel not being banned at the time.[93] Until then, there had never been as much reporting of a novel being potentially banned, and it is possible that, given her media savvy and penchant for spectacle, O'Brien might have hoped for or even provoked the seizure.[94] Of course, her book would soon be banned. Yet as O'Brien suspected, despite the official position, there appeared to be a wider taste for and momentum towards change.

There is considerable irony in customs officials confiscating O'Brien's books as she had come to Ireland to address the inaugural meeting of the Censorship Reform Society (CRS). This was in keeping with her engagements before large live audiences that were duly reported in the pages of the national press. The CRS's event, scheduled at the Gate Theatre on 4 December 1966, had garnered considerable advance publicity, with papers noting that O'Brien and her fellow writers Hugh Leonard, James Plunkett, and Brendan Kennelly would be among the featured speakers. The other invitees included Bruce Arnold, who had defended and promoted the work of both McGahern and O'Brien and initially proposed the formation of the CRS, and the actor, writer, and theatre producer Micheál MacLiammóir.[95] Upon opening, the Gate's four hundred seats were quickly filled, with patrons forced to crowd in the aisles; a hundred more had to be turned away.[96] As one of the speakers, Christopher Gore-Grimes, who had been central in the IACL's activities in the 1950s, charged that the censorship was unjust and doubted, like others, that it was constitutional in depriving artists and publishers of the right to defend their work. Meanwhile, Plunkett argued that the censorship made the case against itself by banning "virtually every Irish writer to achieve eminence in the rest of the world." Leonard contended that the war between the writer and the censor arose from the fact that the former "dealt in truth" while the latter sought to protect "the conventions of a surface morality."[97] In an act of defiance, two actors read from *Casualties of Peace*. O'Brien also noted that she was not afraid to let her sons, aged eleven and thirteen, read *The Lonely Girl* as "there was nothing in it which would harm their future lives."[98]

As might be expected, while the panellists called for reform, many of those present positioned themselves as not being in favour of absolute freedom. Ireland should, they agreed, continue to stem the tide of pornography. In one of the more historically enlightened moments, the theatre director Jim FitzGerald noted that while Sean O'Faolain and Frank O'Connor "had fought a gallant battle against obscurantism" decades earlier, "they did not win."[99] Therefore, the CRS would take up the mantle of these predecessors to usher in a more liberal age. The audience "warmly endorsed" the speakers' views.[100] With those in attendance being broadly drawn from different sectors of society, Irish writers had once again joined forces with people from beyond their profession to advocate and agitate for institutional reform.

When *Casualties of Peace* was banned later that month, O'Brien said that she had reluctantly "come to the conclusion that the banning of books, especially by Irish writers, is as automatic as daylight." For her, being censored was akin to "hanging a label around a person's neck to mark him out as a leper." Having envisaged that the CRS's meeting would impact the Censorship Board's decision, she was baffled that the Irish censors had not been more "aware of their ridiculousness."[101] Jonathan Cape, the publisher of *Casualties of Peace*, claimed to have "expected it to be banned," although they had hoped that "the climate of opinion was changing."[102] The CRS duly condemned the ban, calling it "a clear case of the faulty workings" of the institution, which was "being widely used to censor the works of Irish writers who portray an unflattering or satirical image of Ireland, or who are too honest in their presentation of human faults and failings."[103] O'Brien's book, they insisted, was neither indecent nor obscene, and it had artistic and literary merit. Defiant, they vowed to lobby Brian Lenihan, the minister for justice, to amend the legislation. In a context that was increasingly liberal, writers were organised and well-placed to provoke governmental action.

A New Censorship Act

In the wake of the banning of *Casualties of Peace*, the *Irish Times* contacted several people involved in the decision to ask them what they thought of Edna O'Brien as a writer. Incredibly, some members of the Censorship Board and the Appeal Board candidly responded. Joan Ryan, the sole woman on the Censorship Board, found that *Girls in Their Married Bliss* did not have the same quality as O'Brien's first two novels, but she thought that *August Is a Wicked Month* was "a very sincere book." While she would not allow her teenage daughter to read it, she hoped that children read books that would "give them a broad enough view so that they can read anything" as adults. However, she declined to discuss *Casualties of Peace*. Her colleague Michael Binchy admired O'Brien's work, although he did not approve of everything she wrote. Kevin O'Hanrahan Haugh, a supreme court justice and the chair of the Appeal Board, found O'Brien to be "a most entertaining writer" and her books "amusing and clever."[104]

Meanwhile, the paper solicited others to comment on O'Brien's work. Sean O'Faolain found her first two novels "fresh, delicate, original," but considered *Girls in Their Married Bliss* "rather coarse and unlikeable." One priest went on the record that he enjoyed her books, while Terence de Vere White rated her "a natural writer, although not a heavy-weight," rather "a most nimble light-weight, hard to beat in her own class." The poet Brendan Kennelly thought that O'Brien had "increased in skill" in her more recent work, seeing her tone and vision as indebted to F. Scott Fitzgerald and Albert Camus and her perspective as informed by post-Simone de Beauvoir feminism.[105]

With the recent foundation of the Censorship Reform Society and the controversial banning of yet another of O'Brien's novels, the intent behind the article was clear: to raise doubts about the censorship and to provide ballast to claims that the Censorship Board and the Appeal Board were not properly functioning. Moreover, it appeared that such bans conflicted with the direction in which society was moving and even the opinions of several censors. In this context, the demands of the CRS for censorship reform, the recent controversial banning and treatment of John McGahern and Edna O'Brien, and changing mores and norms in the wider society forced the government to seriously consider amending legislation. Father Connolly had warned politicians of this in his 1959 article, noting that while no law or censorship could keep in step with advanced opinion, it had to at the very least represent majority opinion.[106]

To this end, on 27 April 1967, Lenihan announced that he was ready to introduce "a very short Bill."[107] He would later confess that he had been affected by the McGahern affair, and, after discussing the censorship with Sean O'Faolain, he set about reforming the legislation.[108] Under the proposed law, a book would only be prohibited for up to twenty years, and appeals could be made at any time, instead of being restricted to the first year after a book was banned. As opposed to past debates in which legislation was presented and discussed in terms that suggested the Irish people were wholly in favour of censorship, Lenihan noted that the terms "indecency," "obscenity," and "censorship" had provided "a perennial source of controversy," meaning that any bill would necessarily be criticised. While he felt that the censorship was still supported by "the vast majority" of Irish people, he admitted that the system had its critics and that some of their concerns were justified. In particular, he acknowledged that many prohibited works "have achieved recognition among responsible people here and abroad as being important works of literature," "a good proportion" of which were by Irish authors who were "regarded as being among the finest writers in any language." Lenihan's proposed legislation therefore took into consideration that morality was not immutable but was given to considerable flux over time. "A decision that commanded pretty general approval in the 1930s," he noted, "would not necessarily meet with the same measure of approval now. Standards of what is permissible change. The fantastic and unparalleled social and technological changes that have taken place in the last 40 odd years ... have in my opinion, led to a quite definite change in the general toleration of outspokenness in literary productions."[109] In this sense, he recognised that Irish society was moving in a more liberal direction and that institutional censorship had to follow suit.

Michael O'Higgins, a Fine Gael TD from County Wicklow, applauded the proposed legislation, but suggested that ten years would be a more appropriate period of prohibition as moral, cultural, and literary standards were changing with increasing pace. Similarly, he recommended allowing an appeal to be lodged on behalf of a book not only once but perhaps every five years. To ensure that literary merit was properly considered, he proposed that at least one member of both the Censorship Board and the Appeal Board should be a writer, literary journalist, or publisher. Citing Father Connolly's 1959 article in *Christus Rex*, O'Higgins noted that the state should not be duplicating Church doctrine and that there had to be some balance between the common good and individual freedom. Seán Dunne, a Labour TD from Dublin, commended Lenihan for having the courage to propose reform instead of letting matters stagnate in "an area of political activity and of legislation in which one could easily revel in holier-than-thou exercises." Like his colleagues, Dunne sought a middle ground, lamenting that Irish people could not enjoy Shaw, O'Faolain, and O'Connor, while they were "read in every part of the known world" and had introduced many people to Ireland through their writing. To this end, he was in favour of the legislation, but he, too, supported a shorter time limit for bans. He also queried what Ireland's position would be if it were to join the European Economic Community, which Lenihan admitted was a "big question." There was thus some concern as to whether Ireland's censorship would conflict with its continued international turn. However, Lenihan did note that the number of books being banned was "substantially on the decrease," with 442 censored in 1963, 353 in 1964, 288 in 1965, and 158 in 1966.[110]

Two weeks later, Lenihan proposed to reduce the term of a ban from twenty to twelve years. While this drew praise from many members, others saw it as "pandering to so-called liberal thought." Yet O'Higgins insisted that while it was understandable that someone might regret the state of contemporary culture and prefer that things were as they had been twenty years ago, it was the duty of the Oireachtas to legislate for the current world. This then set off an acrimonious argument between TDs over who was liberal and who was "holier-than-thou."[111]

What is clear, however, is that most politicians were more susceptible to liberal rather than conservative opinion. While the CRS had influenced the proposed amendment and the tenor of the debates, the Catholic Church was all but ignored.[112] McQuaid, though, still had a network of spies who reported back to him. One informant worried that the CRS posed "an imminent and formidable danger" and informed him that the Vigilance Committee recommended "a comprehensive theological, legal, and literary enquiry into the present system of civil censorship, to provide the information necessary to meet the attack." Being "aware of the need for secrecy," they suggested approaching individuals in a "discreet" manner.[113] McQuaid was also notified that the CRS was contacting priests to become members, but that clergy had been warned by colleagues that they risked having their names exploited in the cause of liberalism.[114] The archbishop's sole suggestion was to wait until the spring of 1967, when he proposed that an essay defending censorship be published in *Studies*.[115] There would be no moral panic organised, nor would there be a concerted sortie of bishops condemning evil literature and anti-censorship crusaders. It appeared that McQuaid and Catholic Ireland recognised that censorship was going to be rendered more liberal and that there was very little that they could do about it in the new climate. In some respects, this mirrors the belated polemical responses by Irish writers and their lack of social organisation in the 1920s when confronted with the creation of institutional censorship. In both cases, Irish writers in the 1920s and the Catholic hierarchy in the 1960s appear to have accepted that any effort that they made to further their cases would hopelessly go against the grain. Another public defeat for the Catholic hierarchy would only serve to damage their authority.

When he introduced the amended bill in the Seanad on 7 June 1967, Lenihan stated that the key proposal was to limit the life of prohibition orders to twelve years, which he considered "a reasonable way" to address the "valid criticism of our system of censorship that many books stand banned for all time which are accepted as being important literary works." As he noted, if people felt that a book was still objectionable, it could then, according to the Censorship Board's discretion, be banned anew.[116] While some colleagues might think that his proposed changes did not go far enough, he said that they were identical to those that were advocated by no other critic than Sean O'Faolain, who had recently made a number of suggestions along these lines on radio and in public lectures to support the demands of the CRS. In the end, Lenihan argued, the bill represented "what might be called a middle course between a liberal view and a very conservative view."[117]

The first to address the matter was Garret FitzGerald, a Fine Gael senator and a future taoiseach. FitzGerald believed that "there is no part of our legislation which has done such damage to this country and brought it into such discredit as our censorship." While he, like everyone who spoke on the matter, recognised the need to censor pornography, he denounced the censorship of works of literature. Furthermore, he argued that "the State ought not to intrude into the private moral lives of individuals, unless public morality is threatened," and that it should allow for "the maximum freedom for adult individuals with reasonable protection for the young and immature." Therefore, "the onus of establishing the need for, desirability of or workability of a particular system of censorship or control of immoral literature lies on those who advocate the system of control. It must be shown that what is done is the minimum necessary and that interference with the freedom of the individual is minimised." This was, in fact, the classic liberal position as proposed over a century earlier by John Stuart Mill. FitzGerald welcomed reform as he believed that the censorship had infringed too much upon individual freedom by placing an inordinate value on common morality. However, he felt that the proposed amendment was too minor and questioned the relevance of the institution and whether it was the best way of tackling the problem. Rather than take credit for these ideas, FitzGerald said he had been inspired by Father Connolly's 1959 article in *Christus Rex*, which effectively protected him from charges of moral laxness. He also suggested that Lenihan should reduce the time limit on bans to ten years and argued that writers should have the right to be heard in their defence and that people should be able to import a banned book on their person for their personal use.[118] FitzGerald's stance was unsurprising for many people as he was a prominent member of Tuairim, an organisation of Catholic intellectuals that, from its founding in 1954 to its heyday in the 1960s, was influential in persuading governmental institutions to adopt more liberal policies. Indeed, Tuairim organised a few public talks by Father Connolly on censorship to instigate substantial reform, including the Limerick meeting that featured both him and Edna O'Brien.[119]

FitzGerald was supported by John McQuillan, a National Progressive Democrat from Roscommon, who welcomed amending the legislation and praised Lenihan for undertaking a thankless job. Yet McQuillan viewed the bill as "a limited, timid, tattering attempt ... to remedy the green mould of the green curtain imposed here practically since 1929." Registering his amazement "at the brass neck of the socalled [*sic*] leaders of our society who talk about behind the blue curtain, the Iron Curtain and all the other sorts of curtain which exist elsewhere," he emphasized their hypocrisy in erecting one "to keep our people out of touch with world literature through the application of this reprehensible censorship." Reflecting the international dialectic, he denounced nationalist attempts since independence to protect Irish people from "outside ideas." In the end, he argued, "Great harm has been done to our community through the mentality that has been brought here as a result of censorship." However, he believed that the proposed amendment was merely cosmetic, brought on by the fact that, under the former taoiseach Seán Lemass, the government, "when they found out that they were not European in their outlook, decided that some step would have to be taken just in case there was the slightest possibility we would be allowed into the European Community." Indeed, he lamented that the Irish lagged well behind European thought, and he argued that "blame must be laid fairly and squarely on the shoulders of those who have been advising over the years on what the moral commitments are and how our censorship laws should react."[120]

Sheehy-Skeffington likewise congratulated Lenihan for taking a step in a more liberal direction. The result of the censorship, he said, was the infantilisation of the people, for while others grew up, the Irish, mollycoddled and sheltered as they were, simply got taller. He insisted that "you cannot legislate to make people virtuous," that virtue had to be tested, and that free will must be allowed free rein, for without temptation, virtue was merely the absence of vice. In the end, he was an extreme liberal, asserting that "I am against all censorship by the State."[121] Yet recognising that he was the only abolitionist, he tried to reduce the time limit on bans to seven years. When Lenihan refused, Sheehy-Skeffington suggested ten and asked for a vote. Ten years was, in fact, what the CRS had proposed to Lenihan, indicating that the CRS and the IACL were likeminded and that Sheehy-Skeffington might have first proposed seven to make his request for ten appear to be more moderate.[122] It turns out that Lenihan was similarly prudent, believing that fifteen years "might suffice" but proposing twenty when he introduced the legislation to "play safe"; indeed, he was "fortified by the views of the speakers for the Opposition" and more than happy to lessen it.[123] In the end, the Seanad preferred a twelve-year limit to a ten-year limit by a vote of twenty-six to ten. The relative closeness of the vote and the small margin between the two time limits attest to how the culture and politicians had changed.[124]

Over the four days of thoughtful debates, senators, with the exception of Sheehy-Skeffington, agreed that while the Censorship Board had been reasonable in its more recent incarnations by avoiding the zealotry of the initial decades, pornography still had to be stymied.

Many also believed that Ireland had to take its place in an increasingly globalised world and could no longer withdraw into an isolationist coquille. One of the more interesting moments occurred when Gerald Boland recalled introducing the amending legislation in 1946 as minister for justice. He claimed that he was "always against censorship" because it was "humbug to try to enforce it" and was glad that the Irish were now "looking for a change." Having read those past debates in preparation for discussing the proposed amendment, Dónall Ó Conalláin, an independent senator representing the National University of Ireland, considered that their predecessors in the Oireachtas had, with almost the sole exception of Sir John Keane, acted in a "spirit of inquisition" and "could be incorporated in a work of science fiction by somebody like George Orwell." Moreover, he claimed that the Irish had too often "unjustifiably charged writers with indecency and obscenity when, in fact, they were merely attempting to mirror society as they found it and were being true to themselves and to the discipline of their craft." The Irish had now matured, he argued, and thus had come to accept "that there is no area of life that is unfit to be explored by the writer provided he illuminates it with the light of artistic truth." Perhaps they had realised "that the writer is necessarily anti-establishment or at least he cannot afford to be pro-establishment if his work is to be of any significance either as art or as social comment. He is committed to the truth as he sees it even if he treads on the toes of people who may imagine themselves to be above criticism."[125] Such views suggested that Moore's naturalism and the works of his Irish successors would soon find a more receptive audience in Ireland than they had in the past.

The bill became law on 11 July 1967. As the twelve-year time limit was now official, the thousands of books that had been banned prior to 1955 were free to circulate.[126] Throughout the debates, politicians showed that they were aware that the vast majority of banned works had been cheap pulp fiction and were now long out of print. Meanwhile, the works of literary merit remained available. This was a victory for more liberal-minded critics, especially when combined with Lenihan's promises to appoint only people with some knowledge of and respect for literature to both the Censorship Board and the Appeal Board to ensure as much as possible that pornography, and not works of artistic merit, was targeted. There had been a considerable change in Ireland's regard for literature in the decade since the last great campaign waged by Archbishop McQuaid and Catholic organisations against evil literature. Censorship was therefore a litmus test for how liberal the country had become – or desired to become.

As the bill was discussed in the Oireachtas, several TDs attested to the necessity of the legislation. There was an increasing belief in Ireland, shared by H. G. Wells and PEN International over thirty years prior, that as a country skewed more towards the international, there would necessarily be a commitment to greater freedom of expression and thus less censorship. Moreover, just as the trials of Hall's and James's novels provided context for the Irish crafting their censorship legislation to protect the government from responsibility for decisions to ban publications, so the British trial of *Lady Chatterley's Lover* in 1960 provided the context for the Irish government to liberalise the institution of censorship by amending the law.[127] Thus, the international dialectic can work to render censorship more conservative or more liberal, depending upon the situation. This is borne out in one exchange wherein Erskine Childers, the minister for transport, contacted Lenihan, the minister for justice, to suggest that customs should not have the power to confiscate questionable and even banned publications because "from the standpoint of the tourist industry," such seizures were "undesirable."[128] Not only would the tourist industry be affected, but, officials feared, so would Ireland in its application to join the European Economic Community as censorship would potentially cause its policies to appear unaligned with the federation's more liberal objectives.

The government was aware, as several politicians attested, that the current institution was not responding to society's changing norms and mores. As they admitted, the failures of the censorship arose in no small part from the fact that censors had grown "to regard themselves as a moral Authority rather than a Body appointed to enforce the provisions of an Act of the Oireachtas." Moreover, they were sensitive to the reality that "Irish Writers in particular" had "been harshly treated."[129] In this sense, Irish writers were no longer posited as internal enemies who infected the body politic with cosmopolitan ideas and values and threatened the fabric of the national culture, but rather were sources of pride who had brought positive attention to Ireland from across the world. Changes thus had to follow to maintain the institution's legitimacy and to better reflect current norms and mores. The government therefore came to recognise that morality was not an eternal or immutable ideal; morality was, rather, something that moved with the times, and censorship had to reflect that reality.

Coda

Edna O'Brien's *Casualties of Peace* was the last book by an Irish author to be banned under the Censorship of Publications Act of 1946. The only Irish writer to have new works banned under the 1967 act was Lee Dunne, a working-class Dubliner who had five novels proscribed: *Paddy Maguire Is Dead* on 1 November 1972, *Midnight Cabbie* on 18 December 1974, *The Cabbie Who Came In from the Cold* on 18 June 1975, *Maggie's Story* on 3 November 1976, and *The Cabfather* on 15 December 1976. With the prohibition orders on Dunne's novels lapsing once the twelve-year time limit had passed, no books by Irish authors have been prohibited in Ireland since 1 January 1989.

The 1967 Oireachtas debates demonstrated that Ireland had become more liberal and cosmopolitan in its outlook. This shift was driven by both internal and external factors. As we have seen, Irish writers played important roles over the years in gradually pulling the country away from the nationalist, isolationist, and obscurantist outlook of the post-independence period, often forging coalitions at home and abroad with people from other professions who similarly believed in the necessity of freedom of expression. Their decades of polemics, political lobbying, and social organisation paid off at times, but never as decidedly as they had in the 1960s. What was needed was not only a series of controversial bans, such as occurred with John McGahern and Edna O'Brien, but also the alignment of these cases with larger injustices and the good fortune of a shift in public opinion large enough to make it politically viable for those holding the reins of power to liberalise the institution.

One of the best cultural artefacts to capture that change in mood is Peter Lennon's documentary *Rocky Road to Dublin*. In early 1966, at the height of the McGahern affair, Lennon, the Irish-born Paris correspondent for *The Guardian*, wrote a series of scathing letters to the editor of the *Irish Times* protesting the impotence of the state, its collusion with the Church to deprive McGahern of his livelihood, and its efforts to ensure the dominance of a conservative Catholic morality in Ireland. As he said at the time, "Public debate of social problems provides some check on a possible abuse of power; public criticism, far from being destructive, stimulates all sides into a healthy reassessment of conflicting points of view. But to have a point of view people must first be informed."[1] Lennon returned to Dublin the next year to document Irish society with acclaimed French cinematographer Raoul Coutard. Asking post-independence Ireland "What do you do with your revolution once you've got it?" *Rocky Road to Dublin* criticises the Church and state for having stymied economic, cultural, social, and intellectual progress, while showing how the younger generation was calling for and had begun to impose some change. Recording the parochialism and dogmatism that underscored the Irish educational system – in which schoolboys, prodded by priests, stood to recite catechism and puppet diatribes against indecent books, plays, and films – Lennon also discussed the banning of McGahern's *The Dark*. While he featured the commentary of such notable liberal critics as Sean O'Faolain and Conor Cruise O'Brien, his main focus was Father Michael Cleary, a renowned priest who had adopted less traditional approaches to dealing with youth, most notably in his frank discussions of sex. When the film was premiered at Cannes, it became part of a revolution as the festival was closed down amid the protests that engulfed France in the student strikes of May 1968. These years – from 1965 to 1968 – were therefore pivotal for how Ireland had begun to shift, however modestly, as a part of the broader cultural and social changes that were sweeping across the Western world.

Indeed, since the outcome of the *Chatterley* trial in 1960, Irish writers have not been impacted by censorship in the United Kingdom, where they have continued to publish their books with the largest presses and to garner prestigious literary awards. On 26 July 1968, almost a year after the Oireachtas liberalised Irish censorship law, Britain abolished the censorship of plays with the passage of the Theatres Act of 1968, thereby ridding itself of the last vestiges of government control of the theatre. The legislation was the fruit of a two-year process that included the work of a joint select parliamentary committee. Yet under the terms of the new law, the theatre was not completely free. Rather, as Shaw had predicted several decades earlier, it was now subject to the criminal courts, wherein the director and producer could be charged with overseeing an obscene performance. However, it also took into consideration whether impressionable audiences "were likely, having regard to all relevant circumstances, to attend" the production.[2] This addendum meant that the *virginibus puerisque* litmus test, which imagined a play's impact upon maidens and youths, would not factor into decisions regarding what adult audiences could or could not see. Also, people could not be convicted of an offence if the performance "was justified as being for the public good on the ground that it was in the interests of drama, opera, ballet or any other art, or of literature or learning." Moreover, like the Obscene Publications Act of 1959, expert opinion could be admitted in any proceedings.[3]

The roughly ninety years of censorship struggles encountered by Irish writers that are covered by this book allow for an overall impression of movement from a more repressive, conservative world to one that is more permissive and liberal. Yet while we might speak of a larger trajectory that is inclined towards increases in freedom of expression, history and society tend to move in swings of the pendulum, however subtle and uneven they may be. In its multifarious forms, both official and unofficial, censorship remains a threat to writers' freedom of expression and ability to make a livelihood by their pens, as well as the rights of readers and audiences to access literature, theatre, and ideas. When societies assess their morality, new concepts and philosophical outlooks, competing notions of what is and is not permissible, the rights of individuals, and their pursuit of the collective good, there will always be tension between freedom of expression and censorship. The outcome, as we have seen, is not only determined by how writers respond to the times, but also how far and in which direction the pendulum swings.

This image of the pendulum brings us back to the tensions between the local and the wider world in the international dialectic of censorship. As the introduction argues, the international has been imbricated in censorship from its very origins. In ancient Rome, the duty of the censor was doubly to assess the fitness of a person's morals and to determine their citizenship status. If one did not live up to the mark, they were administratively cast out of the tribe and not granted the same rights as their neighbours. Modern and contemporary censorship, as this book has shown, maintain this dynamic. From the point of view of censors, the banned writer's work is considered unfit to be circulated, read, watched, listened to, or performed within the boundaries of the polity. In this sense, the writer is determined to be unfit themselves, possessing a different morality from that of their fellow citizens. The censored writer, as much as their work, is thus labelled as perverse, a pollutant that threatens to infect and harm the body politic. Often, this perversion is understood to be the manifestation of a diseased mind and soul, the result of the writer harbouring cosmopolitan values and having adopted foreign aesthetics. The banned book or play is thus the product of, at best, someone who holds divided loyalties between the nation and a globalised art, or, at worst, a traitor who seeks to transform, if not destroy, the pure, national culture.

When George Moore and Bernard Shaw worked in Britain, it was easy to consider these Irishmen as hostile to the nation. They were not truly British, it could be argued, despite their holding British passports and being able to vote in British elections, so their attraction to the French Zola and the Norwegian Ibsen was merely a way for them to rebel against and deviously subvert British values. Yet when Moore and Shaw, alongside the many Irish writers discussed in the preceding chapters, were later banned in Ireland, there was a much more complex negotiation between the national and the international. Both men were born in Ireland, but they resided for much of their lives in Britain, and they were influenced by continental models, thereby rendering them suspect in the eyes of many censors. This was also the case for James Joyce, Sean O'Casey, Norah Hoult, Kate O'Brien, Samuel Beckett, and Edna O'Brien, who long lived abroad in exile. For others, such as Sean O'Faolain, a Catholic who had fought in the IRA, who spoke Irish, and who returned to live in Ireland for much of the mid-century, the charges of otherness were harder to make stick, so his criticism of nationalism and the Church was cast as the revisionism of a traitor or, slightly more generously, a dupe who supported British colonialism.[4] His censored fiction thus attested to the fact that he did not share the same values as the majority of Irish people and sought to undermine the nation.

Censors thereby engage in the international dialectic by casting people and works from beyond their borders as threats. In this way, censorship becomes a *cordon sanitaire* erected to maintain national purity and cohesion. Simultaneously, censors suspect domestic writers of harbouring cosmopolitan and alien values and often label them as enemies of the people. Indeed, censorship labels – and libels – the banned object and writer as counter and foreign to the local. At the same time, censors look abroad for inspiration from other polities and groups to manage and craft censorship and to control the direction of national culture and society. In Britain, for example, the French trials of Baudelaire and Flaubert were contemporaneous to and provided context for the passage of the Obscene Publications Act of 1857. Similarly, in Ireland, the trials of Radclyffe Hall's *The Well of Loneliness* and Norah C. James's *Sleeveless Errand* informed the Irish government's decision to shield, to some extent, the minister for justice from claims that they were a censor by creating a censorship board. Moreover, when researching censorship in 1926, the government-appointed Committee on Evil Literature looked overseas to regimes in Britain, Canada, the United States, France, Australia, New Zealand, and South Africa. Thus, while the Irish sought to institute a made-in-Ireland censorship that would be shaped by and in turn shape Irish culture and values, the government examined what other countries had established and how their censorships functioned.

Despite these efforts to control culture and morality, censorship in any democratic society must negotiate between national conditions and larger international forces. This was especially the case in the periods following each of the two world wars, when internationalism was increasingly the order of the day. While this outlook did not last long in the 1920s and 1930s, it was a powerful and seemingly unstoppable force in the second half of the twentieth century, when globalisation as we have come to recognise it began to move at an astounding pace, apparent not only in the growth of multinational corporations and free trade agreements, but also in the spread of universal human rights, the establishment of the United Nations, and the federation of countries into what would become the European Union. While there were, as this book shows, times of a "liberal lull," the trajectory of the twentieth century was largely one of a greater shift towards a more liberal opening of borders and culture. Such openness to the global tended to be followed by a concomitant curtailment of censorship. Indeed, in both Britain and Ireland, the 1950s and 1960s saw significant changes to the machinery of censorship that were a direct response to a more liberal populace. In Ireland, this was due, in part, to an increasing unease with a conservative Catholic ethos, a cultural shift that was reflected more generally in the world with the adoption of the reforms proposed under Vatican II. Yet, as chapter 10 reveals, the government was also pragmatic, aware that its efforts to join the European Economic Community might be hindered should the country remain out of step with the more liberal laws on the continent. It also understood that censorship could hurt tourism when unsuspecting visitors had their books confiscated by customs officials. Thus, while there were still those who desired to maintain a relatively strict and puritanical censorship, the wider culture, global trends, economic pressures, and political realties made liberalising the institution a necessity. In this sense, censorship reform responded to a combination of internal and external forces, that is, both the national and the international, which are always in tension with one another.

As for the censoring institutions, they, too, engage in an international dialectic. When countries censor writers from elsewhere despite being their dominant market, then censorship in one polity has the potential to affect the development of other national literatures. This was particularly the case for Irish writers who worked and published in Britain.

With the threat of the Lord Chamberlain's blue pencil and the possibility of having their books prohibited by a judge under the terms of the Obscene Publications Act, there were very real pressures for Irish writers to curb the content and the aesthetics of their work. Furthermore, as Bernard Shaw and Father Peter Connolly asserted over the years, Western democratic states and governments derive their legitimacy from people's adherence to and acceptance of the law and current morality. They, and PEN International, therefore concluded that a more conservative and insular polity would be more censorious and prioritise the collective, while a more liberal and open polity would protect and promote freedom of expression and individual rights. Certainly, this was what occurred in both Britain and Ireland over the course of this study: when Ireland became an independent country and then engaged in a long-lasting tariff war with Britain, and later when it remained neutral during World War II, it erected and maintained its censorship. Similarly, when both Britain and Ireland became more liberal following World War II, prepared the ground for post-war globalisation and neoliberal policies, joined the United Nations, and began to consider applying to the European Economic Community, they liberalised their censorship laws. However, while we might allow, in a general sense, that a more cosmopolitan and tolerant democratic society might be less censorious, whereas a more nationalist, conservative, insular society might be more censorious, it would be wrong to assume that the internationalist perspective of a government and people *always* means that they will be less censorious than an insular government and people. Indeed, in the late nineteenth and early twentieth centuries, when Britain's empire was at its largest, it actively censored plays and publications. Likewise, Ireland's most zealous period of censorship coincided with the post-war period, overlapping with its dismantling of the censorship that ensured the country's neutrality during the war, its formation of an appeal board to allow people to contest questionable rulings, and its entry into the United Nations.

Whatever the reality, many Irish writers over the century covered by this book remained convinced that insularism would lead to stasis and regression and the eventual downfall of the nation. It was in part for this reason that they equated greater internationalism with freedom of expression and, conversely, insularity and nationalism with censorship. Moreover, they sought out colleagues and publishers from other countries to help them to circulate their work and for moral, intellectual, and political support, thereby forming a modern Republic of Letters. This internationalism led them to join such organisations as PEN and to be inspired by other national free speech organisations, including the ACLU in the United States. Indeed, they appealed to freedom of expression as a universal right that knows no boundaries, that should be fiercely protected, and that would, theoretically, lead to social, political, and cultural progress. They thus highlighted a catalogue of international martyrs, including Socrates, Jesus, and Galileo, that attests to how censorship can cause a great deal to be lost not only for the country, but also for all of humankind. Within certain Millian limits, often noting the harm that pornography could cause, they claimed that freedom of expression superseded parochial, local demands. They thus refused to be cast as subversive fifth columnists who sought to pervert and undermine national morality, arguing that they rather wanted to ensure that the country and its culture survived by adopting and adapting new ideas and new ways of seeing the world. In so doing, they found literary inspiration in other countries while in turn rendering Irish writing more widely recognised and achieving a prominent place for it in world literature. As this study illustrates, when examining how Irish writers engaged with censorship in their polemics, their politics, and their social organisation, it is essential to consider how the international dialectic is deeply imbricated in censorship. Irish writers and their censors, in both Ireland and elsewhere, understood the relationship that censorship has to the tensions between the national and the international, and the ways that they responded to one another attests to this dynamic.

Thusly considering Irish writers in both national and international contexts allows us to understand the different forces that impacted them and that they themselves helped to augment or to diminish. This widening of the lens through which we examine Irish writing and the sociology of Irish literature allows the critic and the student alike to have a more sophisticated understanding of how writers function within the nation and the world as well as how they react to both internal and external forces. Censorship and freedom of expression were constant issues for Irish writers to negotiate in their writing as well as in their lives, affecting their aesthetics as much as their ability to publish, make their livelihoods, and live among their fellow citizens. At times, these issues were pushed to the fore; at others, they remained in the background, although they always threatened to assert themselves at any given moment. Some writers were more active in their fight, others more resigned; but all of them were affected. Indeed, Irish writing was inevitably shaped by censorship and the refusal of many authors to succumb to its threat. In the end, any account of modern Irish literature must contend with this legacy.

Appendix

Books Written by Irish Writers That Were Banned in Ireland[1]

In the table that follows, books are listed according to the dates on which they were first banned. In some cases, new editions of banned books were also banned; this is indicated following the title of the book. New editions of banned books are not granted a number in the left column, which only registers unique entries. In a few instances, the new editions carried different titles, which are also noted.

The final column indicates under which of the acts the book was unbanned. In most cases, this was the 1967 act, which, as discussed in chapter 10, revoked the prohibition orders for books after a duration of twelve years from the end of the year in which they were banned. In these cases, if a book was banned in 1954 or earlier, it was unbanned in Ireland as of the passage of the 1967 legislation; for a book that was banned in, say, June of 1960, the book was unbanned as of 1 January 1973.

When in the final column a specific date is indicated under the 1946 act or 1967 act, this refers to the date a book was unbanned by a successful submission to the Appeal Board. In some cases, books were unsuccessful in their appeal; the date of the unsuccessful plea is likewise provided.

In a few instances, the final column also indicates whether a variation order was issued. A variation order was granted following a successful request to the Appeal Board to publish an amended version of the book. Under such terms, parts of the book could be modified or removed to make this specific edition acceptable for circulation. These cases detail whether the order was accepted or denied and the date on which a decision was rendered.

As *Censorship and the Irish Writer* attests, defining what makes a writer Irish has long been a contentious political act. For the most part, I have included writers found in such reference works and databases as

Robert Welch's *The Concise Oxford Companion to Irish Literature* and Bruce Stewart's *Ricorso*. It is, however, too difficult to know how many Irish writers might have published under pseudonyms, especially in cases involving some of the hundreds, if not thousands, of banned works of pulp and pornographic fiction. Moreover, there are scores of books written by people having notably Irish names but whose backgrounds I have been unable to discover. Given these challenges in identifying all of those who are listed in the registers, there is a distinct possibility that many more books written by Irish authors were prohibited over the years.

Table A.1: Books Written by Irish Writers That Were Banned in Ireland

	Book	Author	Date that the Prohibition Order was Issued	Revoking Order
1	*Confessions and Impressions*	Ethel Mannin	14 October 1930	1967 Act
2	*The House of Gold*	Liam O'Flaherty	30 October 1930	1967 Act
3	*Ragged Banners*	Ethel Mannin	11 May 1931	1967 Act
4	*Bernard Shaw*	Frank Harris	21 December 1931	1967 Act
5	*Boy*	James Hanley	21 December 1931	1967 Act
6	*Common-Sense and the Child*	Ethel Mannin	25 January 1932	1967 Act
7	*The Puritan*	Liam O'Flaherty	16 February 1932	1946 Act, 22 August 1947
8	*Midsummer Night Madness*	Sean O'Faolain	19 April 1932	Appeal dismissed 21 January 1951; 1967 Act
9	*The Bright Temptation*	Austin Clarke	16 September 1932	1946 Act, 8 October 1954
10	*Ebb and Flood*	James Hanley	12 October 1932	1967 Act
11	*A Story-Teller's Holiday*	George Moore	17 January 1933	Appeal dismissed 6 July 1951; 1967 Act
12	*The Martyr*	Liam O'Flaherty	27 March 1933	1967 Act
13	*A Hillside Man*	Con O'Leary	1 May 1933	1967 Act
14	*The Rocky Road*	John Brophy	1 May 1933	1967 Act
15	*The Adventures of the Black Girl in Her Search for God*	Bernard Shaw	1 May 1933	1946 Act, 20 January 1948
16	*Shake Hands with the Devil*	Rearden Conner	25 October 1933	1967 Act
17	*Shame the Devil*	Liam O'Flaherty	12 May 1934	1967 Act
18	*More Pricks than Kicks*	Samuel Beckett	20 October 1934	1946 Act, 25 April 1952

(*Continued*)

Table A.1: (Continued)

	Book	Author	Date that the Prohibition Order was Issued	Revoking Order
19	*The World Went Mad*	John Brophy	20 October 1934	1967 Act
20	*Rude Earth*	Rearden Conner	20 October 1934	1967 Act
21	*Windfalls*	Sean O'Casey	3 December 1934	Appeal dismissed 17 June 1947; 1967 Act
22	*As the Fool*	Francis Plunkett	6 April 1935	1967 Act
23	*Stoker Bush*	James Hanley	11 February 1936	1967 Act
24	*The Singing-Men at Cashel*	Austin Clarke	2 May 1936	1946 Act, 24 June 1947
25	*The Green Lion*	Francis Hackett	6 June 1936	1946 Act, 13 April 1951
26	*Bird Alone*	Sean O'Faolain	29 August 1936	1946 Act, 24 June 1947
27	*Pluck the Flower*	John Brophy	22 September 1936	1967 Act
28	*The Ramparts of Virtue*	John Brophy	21 October 1936	1967 Act
29	*Mount Prospect*	Elizabeth Connor	21 October 1936	1967 Act
30	*Mary Lavelle*	Kate O'Brien	24 December 1936	Appeal dismissed 6 July 1951; 1967 Act
31	*A London Story*	George Buchanan	25 March 1937	1967 Act
32	*Eve's Doctor*	Signe Toksvig	25 March 1937	1946 Act, 9 December 1952
33	*Hollywood Cemetery*	Liam O'Flaherty	4 May 1937	1946 Act, 13 April 1951
34	*Coming from the Fair*	Norah Hoult	8 December 1937	1967 Act
35	*Castle Corner*	Joyce Cary	8 March 1938	1967 Act
36	*Rags and Sticks*	Louis Lynch D'Alton	13 May 1938	1967 Act
37	*Lifer*	Jim Phelan	10 June 1938	1967 Act
38	*The Sword of Love*	Rearden Conner	13 October 1938	1967 Act
39	*Chaos*	Shaw Desmond	7 November 1938	1967 Act
40	*Nine Years Is a Long Time*	Norah Hoult	16 January 1939	1967 Act
41	*I Knock at the Door*	Sean O'Casey	10 May 1939	1946 Act, 16 December 1947
42	*Julie*	Francis Stuart	14 July 1939	1967 Act
43	*Gentleman of Stratford*	John Brophy	6 December 1939	1967 Act
44	*Four Women Grow Up*	Norah Hoult	11 April 1940	1967 Act
45	*Julie*	Ethel Mannin	7 May 1940	1967 Act

(*Continued*)

Table A.1: (Continued)

	Book	Author	Date that the Prohibition Order was Issued	Revoking Order
46	*Dutch Interior*	Frank O'Connor	10 July 1940	1946 Act, 26 January 1951
47	*Charley Is My Darling*	Joyce Cary	11 September 1940	1967 Act
48	*Rolling in the Dew*	Ethel Mannin	5 November 1940	1967 Act
49	*Green Glory*	John Brophy	10 December 1940	1967 Act
50	*Green Ladies*	John Brophy	5 April 1941	1967 Act
51	*The Land of Spices*	Kate O'Brien	5 May 1941	1946 Act, 18 February 1949
52	*The Bay*	L. A. G. Strong	8 July 1941	1946 Act, 23 April 1948
53	*Waterfront*	John Brophy	11 September 1941	Variation order dismissed 20 October 1950; 1967 Act
54	*Smilin' on the Vine*	Norah Hoult	8 October 1941	1967 Act
55	*Red Rose*	Ethel Mannin	10 November 1941	1967 Act
56	*The Squire of Shaftesbury Avenue*	Vivian Connell	9 December 1941	1967 Act
57	*Going Native*	Oliver St. John Gogarty	20 January 1942	Appeal dismissed 14 August 1947; 1967 Act
58	*Cactus*	Ethel Mannin	20 January 1942	1967 Act
59	*Herself Surprised*	Joyce Cary	12 February 1942	1967 Act
60	*Sophia*	St. John Ervine	12 February 1942	1967 Act
61	*Life Boat*	Signe Toksvig	12 February 1942	1967 Act
62	*Two Days in Aragon*	M. J. Farrell	25 March 1942	1967 Act
63	*Pictures in the Hallway*	Sean O'Casey	6 May 1942	1946 Act, 16 December 1947
64	*Commonsense and Morality*	Ethel Mannin	8 June 1942	1967 Act
65	*The Tailor and Ansty*	Eric Cross	28 September 1942	1946 Act, 20 January 1948
66	*Augusta Steps Out*	Norah Hoult	28 September 1942	1967 Act
67	*Captain Moonlight*	Ethel Mannin	12 March 1943	1967 Act
68	*The Furys*	James Hanley	7 April 1943	1967 Act
69	*The Blossoming Bough*	Ethel Mannin	15 June 1943	1967 Act
70	*No Directions*	James Hanley	15 June 1943	1967 Act
71	*The Peacock Is a Gentleman*	Vivian Connell	15 June 1943	1967 Act
72	*The Chinese Room*	Vivian Connell	20 December 1943	1967 Act
73	*Alone We Embark*	Maura Laverty	20 December 1943	1946 Act, 9 October 1953

(*Continued*)

Table A.1: (Continued)

	Book	Author	Date that the Prohibition Order was Issued	Revoking Order
74	*Stephen Hero*	James Joyce	6 November 1944	1946 Act, 13 April 1951
75	*There Were No Windows*	Norah Hoult	10 January 1945	1967 Act
76	*... and Blackthorns*	Jim Phelan	27 February 1945	1967 Act
77	*The Horse's Mouth*	Joyce Cary	30 April 1946	1967 Act
78	*The Midnight Court*	Bryan Merriman, translated by Frank O'Connor	30 April 1946	Appeal dismissed 9 July 1946; 1967 Act
79	*Mr Petunia*	Oliver St. John Gogarty	30 July 1946	Appeal dismissed 17 June 1947; 1967 Act
80	*Land*	Liam O'Flaherty	30 July 1946	1967 Act
81	*Selected Stories*	Norah Hoult	30 July 1946	1967 Act
82	*House Under Mars*	Norah Hoult	30 September 1946	1967 Act
83	*The Moonlight*	Joyce Cary	30 September 1946	1967 Act
84	*City of Departures*	John Brophy	10 January 1947	1967 Act
85	*He Had My Heart Scalded*	Ernest Gébler	14 March 1947	1967 Act
86	*Lift Up Your Gates*	Maura Laverty	9 May 1947	1967 Act
87	*Time, Gentlemen! Time!*	Norah Hoult	9 May 1947	1967 Act
88	*The Devil Among the Tailors*	Rearden Conner	10 October 1947	1967 Act
89	*The Common Chord*	Frank O'Connor	12 December 1947	1967 Act
90	*The Story of Adam Verity*	Shaw Desmond	9 January 1948	1967 Act
91	*Frank Harris, His Life and Adventures*	Frank Harris	5 May 1948	1967 Act
92	*Quench the Moon*	Walter Macken	30 June 1948	1967 Act
93	*The Trials of Oscar Wilde*	Edited by H. Montgomery Hyde	15 September 1948	1946 Act, 14 December 1948
94	*The Golden Sleep*	Vivian Connell	6 October 1948	1967 Act
95	*Tarry Flynn*	Patrick Kavanagh	3 November 1948	1946 Act, 14 December 1948
96	*Growing Up*	Olivia Manning	3 November 1948	1967 Act
97	*The Name's Phelan*	Jim Phelan	1 December 1948	1967 Act
98	*My Love to the Gallows*	Rearden Conner	9 March 1949	1946 Act, 17 June 1949
99	*Redemption*	Francis Stuart	16 September 1949	1967 Act
100	*A Fearful Joy*	Joyce Cary	13 January 1950	1967 Act
101	*In a Harbour Green*	Benedict Kiely	13 January 1950	1946 Act, 18 July 1950
102	*I Am Alone*	Walter Macken	10 February 1950	1967 Act

(Continued)

Table A.1: (Continued)

Book	Author	Date that the Prohibition Order was Issued	Revoking Order
103 *Rose Forbes*	George Buchanan	10 March 1950	1967 Act
104 *Hunger of the Heart*	Rearden Conner	9 June 1950	1946 Act, 18 July 1950
105 *The Iron Hoop*	Constantine Fitzgibbon	21 July 1950	1967 Act
106 *The Flowering Cross*	Francis Stuart	10 November 1950	1967 Act
My Life and Loves – New Edition of *Frank Harris, His Life and Adventures*[2]	Frank Harris	10 November 1950	1967 Act
107 *Traveller's Samples*	Frank O'Connor	13 April 1951	1967 Act
108 *The Hounds of Cloneen*	Vivian Connell	8 June 1951	1967 Act
109 *Windfall*	John Brophy	24 July 1951	1967 Act
110 *Vagabond Cavalry*	Jim Phelan	14 December 1951	1967 Act
111 *Good Friday's Daughter*	Francis Stuart	8 February 1952	1967 Act
112 *December Bride*	Sam Hanna Bell	4 April 1952	1967 Act
113 *Turn the Key Softly*	John Brophy	4 April 1952	1967 Act
114 *The Bogman*	Walter Macken	13 June 1952	1967 Act
115 *September in Quinze*	Vivian Connell	25 July 1952	1967 Act
116 *Cousin Emily*	Constantine Fitzgibbon	25 July 1952	1967 Act
117 *A Place to Live*	George Buchanan	25 July 1952	1967 Act
118 *The Sun Dances at Easter*	Austin Clarke	3 October 1952	Appeal dismissed 9 December 1952; 1967 Act
119 *Prisoner of Grace*	Joyce Cary	7 November 1952	1967 Act
120 *The Closed Harbour*	James Hanley	7 November 1952	1946 Act, 30 January 1953
121 *Wreath for a Redhead*	Brian Moore	12 December 1952	1967 Act
122 *A Man of Parts*	Vivian Connell	6 February 1953	1967 Act
123 *The Fields at Evening*	Ethel Mannin	13 March 1953	1967 Act
124 *The Hill of Howth*	L. A. G. Strong	12 June 1953	1967 Act
125 *A Portrait of My City*	Brian Talbot Cleeve	12 June 1953	1967 Act
126 *The Wildes of Merrion Square: The Family of Oscar Wilde*	Patrick Byrne	10 July 1953	1946 Act, 9 October 1953
127 *Lucifer and the Child*	Ethel Mannin	10 July 1953	1967 Act

(*Continued*)

Table A.1: (Continued)

	Book	Author	Date that the Prohibition Order was Issued	Revoking Order
128	*Lover under Another Name*	Ethel Mannin	9 October 1953	1967 Act
129	*The Chariot*	Francis Stuart	9 October 1953	1967 Act
130	*A Different Face*	Olivia Manning	9 October 1953	1967 Act
131	*Irish Moon*	Shaw Desmond	13 November 1953	1967 Act
132	*Birth of a Dark Soul*	Brian Talbot Cleeve	19 February 1954	1967 Act
133	*The Prime of Life*	John Brophy	19 February 1954	1967 Act
134	*Adam and Eve*	Shaw Desmond	19 February 1954	1967 Act
135	*Honey Seems Bitter*	Benedict Kiely	12 March 1954	1967 Act
136	*Journey into Print*	Norah Hoult	14 May 1954	1967 Act
137	*The Night Winds*	Brian Talbot Cleeve	18 June 1954	1967 Act
138	*The Singing Stone*	Rearden Conner	15 October 1954	1967 Act
139	*Watt*	Samuel Beckett	15 October 1954	1967 Act
140	*The Pilgrimage*	Francis Stuart	11 March 1955	1946 Act, 5 August 1955
141	*Not Honour More*	Joyce Cary	10 June 1955	1967 Act
142	*Judith Hearne*	Brian Moore	8 July 1955	Appeal dismissed 7 October 1955; 1967 Act
143	*There Was an Ancient House*	Benedict Kiely	8 July 1955	1946 Act, 14 October 1955
144	*City of Scandals*	John Brophy	13 January 1956	1967 Act
145	*The Doves of Venus*	Olivia Manning	13 January 1956	1967 Act
146	*The Ginger Man*	J. P. Donleavy	13 January 1956	1967 Act
147	*Molloy*	Samuel Beckett	13 January 1956	1967 Act
148	*The Nimble Rabbit*	John Brophy	13 January 1956	1967 Act
149	*Levine*	James Hanley	11 May 1956	1946 Act, 3 August 1956
150	*The Flight from the Enchanter*	Iris Murdoch	8 June 1956	Appeal dismissed 27 July 1956; 1967 Act
151	*The House of Cain*	Rearden Conner	29 January 1957	1967 Act
152	*Soldier of the Queen*	John Brophy	28 March 1957	1967 Act
	The Lonely Passion of Judith Hearne – New Edition	Brian Moore	3 February 1958	1967 Act
	The Chinese Room – New Edition	Vivian Connell	21 July 1958	1967 Act
	Waterfront – New Edition	John Brophy	21 July 1958	1967 Act
	Mary Lavelle – New Edition	Kate O'Brien	1 September 1958	1967 Act
	A Fearful Joy – New Edition	Joyce Cary	20 October 1958	1967 Act

(*Continued*)

Table A.1: (Continued)

	Book	Author	Date that the Prohibition Order was Issued	Revoking Order
153	*Borstal Boy*	Brendan Behan	3 November 1958	Appeal dismissed 16 January 1959; Variation order dismissed 21 April 1961; Variation order granted 17 February 1970; 1967 Act
	Herself Surprised – New Edition	Joyce Cary	3 November 1958	1967 Act
	Ragged Banners – New Edition	Ethel Mannin	17 November 1958	1967 Act
	The Golden Sleep – New Edition	Vivian Connell	1 December 1958	1967 Act
	Confessions and Impressions – New Edition	Ethel Mannin	19 January 1959	1967 Act
	Lifer – New Edition	Jim Phelan	19 January 1959	1967 Act
	Cactus – New Edition	Ethel Mannin	6 April 1959	1967 Act
	Shake Hands with the Devil – New Edition	Rearden Conner	6 April 1959	1967 Act
	The Evil Men Do – New Edition of *Honey Seems Bitter*	Benedict Kiely	29 June 1959	1967 Act
	The Lonely Passion of Miss Judith Hearne – New Edition	Brian Moore	29 June 1959	1967 Act
	The Horse's Mouth – New Edition	Joyce Cary	24 August 1959	1967 Act
	Frank Harris: My Life and Adventures – New Edition	Frank Harris	28 September 1959	1967 Act
154	*The Country Girls*	Edna O'Brien	13 June 1960	1967 Act
155	*The Pilgrimage*	John Broderick	24 March 1961	1967 Act
156	*Kings, Lords, and Commons*	Anthology, translated by Frank O'Connor	3 July 1961	1946 Act, 12 December 1961
	The Naked Rich – New Edition of *September in Quinze*	Vivian Connell	29 January 1962	1967 Act
157	*A Severed Head*	Iris Murdoch	12 February 1962	1967 Act

(*Continued*)

Table A.1: (Continued)

	Book	Author	Date that the Prohibition Order was Issued	Revoking Order
158	*The Lonely Girl*	Edna O'Brien	4 June 1962	Appeal dismissed 3 August 1962; 1967 Act
159	*An Answer from Limbo*	Brian Moore	27 May 1963	Appeal dismissed 3 January 1964; 1967 Act, 2 November 1973
160	*Famous Trials Ninth Series: Roger Casement*	H. Montgomery Hyde	1 June 1964	Appeal dismissed 9 October 1964; 1967 Act
	Girl with Green Eyes – New Edition of *The Lonely Girl*	Edna O'Brien	6 July 1964	1967 Act
161	*A Singular Man*	J. P. Donleavy	2 November 1964	1967 Act
162	*Girls in Their Married Bliss*	Edna O'Brien	7 December 1964	Appeal dismissed 9 April 1965; 1967 Act
163	*The Dark*	John McGahern	24 May 1965	Appeal dismissed 9 July 1965; Variation order granted 11 August 1970; 1967 Act
	The Chameleons – New Edition of *The Pilgrimage*	John Broderick	18 June 1965	1967 Act
164	*August Is a Wicked Month*	Edna O'Brien	29 November 1965	Appeal dismissed 28 January 1966; 1967 Act
165	*The Ferret Fancier*	Anthony C. West[3]	6 June 1966	1967 Act
166	*The Native Moment*	Anthony C. West	6 June 1966	1967 Act
	My Life and Loves, Fifth Volume	Frank Harris	7 November 1966	1967 Act
167	*Casualties of Peace*	Edna O'Brien	12 December 1966	Appeal dismissed 27 January 1967; 1967 Act
	My Life and Loves[4]	Frank Harris	6 January 1969	1967 Act
	The Ginger Man	J. P. Donleavy	14 April 1969	1967 Act
168	*Paddy Maguire Is Dead*	Lee Dunne	1 November 1972	Appeal dismissed 13 April 1973; 1967 Act
169	*Midnight Cabbie*	Lee Dunne	18 December 1974	1967 Act
170	*The Cabbie Who Came In from the Cold*	Lee Dunne	18 June 1975	1967 Act
171	*Maggie's Story*	Lee Dunne	3 November 1976	1967 Act
172	*The Cabfather*	Lee Dunne	15 December 1976	1967 Act

Notes

Introduction

1 Archer to Lady Mary Murray, 1 November 1907, in *William Archer: Life, Work and Friendships*, by Charles Archer (London: George Allen & Unwin, 1931), 321.

2 There are too many studies to note without reproducing a massive bibliography. For the sake of brevity, I have provided some key works here for three of the earliest of modern Irish writers who figure largely in this book to give readers an idea of the many individual author-based studies of censorship that exist. For studies of George Moore and censorship, see Troy J. Bassett, "Circulating Morals: George Moore's Attack on Late-Victorian Literary Censorship," *Pacific Coast Philology* 40, no. 2 (2005): 73–89; Mark Llewellyn and Ann Heilmann, "George Moore and Literary Censorship: The Textual and Sexual History of 'John Norton' and 'Hugh Monfert,'" *English Literature in Transition, 1880–1920* 50, no. 4 (2007): 371–92; Jane Jordan, "'Literature at Nurse': George Moore, Ouida, and Fin-de-siècle Literary Censorship," in *George Moore: Influence and Collaboration*, eds. Ann Heilmann and Mark Llewellyn (Newark: University of Delaware Press, 2014), 69–81; and Katherine Mullin, "'The Sort of Girl I'd Like to See Behind the Bar at the King's Head': Barmaids and Censorship in George Moore," in *George Moore: Influence and Collaboration*, eds. Ann Heilmann and Mark Llewellyn (Newark: University of Delaware Press, 2014), 83–97. For James Joyce and censorship, see Joseph M. Hassett, *The "Ulysses" Trials: Beauty and Truth Meet the Law* (Dublin: The Lilliput Press, 2016); Clare Hutton, *Serial Encounters: "Ulysses" and the "Little Review"* (Oxford: Oxford University Press, 2019); David Weir, "What Did He Know and When Did He Know It: The *Little Review*, Joyce, and *Ulysses*," *James Joyce Quarterly* 37, nos. 3–4 (2000): 389–412; Paul Vanderham, *James Joyce and Censorship: The Trials of "Ulysses"* (New York: New York University Press, 1998); Katherine

Mullin, *James Joyce, Sexuality and Social Purity* (Cambridge: Cambridge University Press, 2003); and Jonathan Goldman, ed., *Joyce and the Law* (Gainesville: University Press of Florida, 2017). For Bernard Shaw and censorship, see Lauren Arrington, "The Censorship of *O'Flaherty V. C.*," *SHAW: The Annual of Bernard Shaw Studies* 28 (2008): 85–106; L. W. Conolly, "*Mrs Warren's Profession* and the Lord Chamberlain," *SHAW: The Annual of Bernard Shaw Studies* 24 (2004): 49–95; Brad Kent, "Censorship," in *George Bernard Shaw in Context*, ed. Brad Kent (Cambridge: Cambridge University Press, 2015), 199–206; Brad Kent, "Bernard Shaw, the British Censorship of Plays, and Modern Celebrity," *English Literature in Transition, 1880–1920* 57, no. 2 (2014): 231–53; Brad Kent, "Censorship and Immorality: Bernard Shaw's *The Devil's Disciple*," *Modern Drama* 54, no. 4 (Winter 2011): 511–33; Brad Kent, "Shaw, *The Bell*, and Censorship in 1945," *SHAW: The Annual of Bernard Shaw Studies* 30 (2010): 161–74; Brad Kent, "The Banning of Bernard Shaw's *The Adventures of the Black Girl in Her Search for God* and the Decline of the Irish Academy of Letters," *Irish University Review* 39, no. 2 (Winter 2008): 271–94; and Bernard F. Dukore, *Bernard Shaw and the Censors: Fights and Failures, Stage and Screen* (London: Palgrave Macmillan, 2020).

3 See, for example, David Bradshaw and Rachel Potter, eds., *Prudes on the Prowl: Fiction and Obscenity in England, 1850 to the Present Day* (Oxford University Press, 2013); Rachel Potter, *Obscene Modernism: Literary Censorship and Experiment, 1900–1940* (Oxford University Press, 2013); Adam Parkes, *Modernism and the Theater of Censorship* (Oxford: Oxford University Press, 1996); Celia Marshik, *British Modernism and Censorship* (Cambridge: Cambridge University Press, 2006).

4 See, for example, Michael Adams, *Censorship: The Irish Experience* (Dublin: Scepter Books, 1968); Senia Pašeta, "Censorship and Its Critics in the Irish Free State, 1922–1932," *Past & Present* 181 (November 2003): 193–218; and Peter Martin, *Censorship in the Two Irelands, 1922–1939* (Dublin: Irish Academic Press, 2006). The Irish historian Donal Ó Drisceoil is the exception to this tendency in respect to his focus on Irish writers; see his essay, "A Dark Chapter: Censorship and the Irish Writer," in *The Oxford History of the Irish Book, Volume V: The Irish Book in English, 1891–2000*, ed. Clare Hutton (Oxford: Oxford University Press, 2011), 285–303. However, like his colleagues, Ó Drisceoil does not concern himself with larger philosophical questions. For a more literary account of Irish censorship, see Eibhear Walshe, "Censorship, Law and Literature," in *Irish Literature in Transition: 1940–1980*, ed. Eve Patten (Cambridge: Cambridge University Press, 2020), 169–84.

5 Marshik, *British Modernism and Censorship*, 3.

6 *Oxford English Dictionary*, s.v. "censorship," accessed 28 October 2024, www.oed.com/dictionary/censorship_n.

7 For examples of works that adopt this more capacious definition of a censor, see Matthew Fellion and Katherine Inglis, *Censored: A Literary History of Subversion and Control* (Montréal: McGill-Queen's University Press, 2017); Bradshaw and Potter, *Prudes on the Prowl*; Potter, *Obscene Modernism*; and Paul Blanshard, *The Irish and Catholic Power* (Boston: Beacon Press, 1953), which features a chapter titled "Censorship, Official and Unofficial," 72–109.

8 Viscount Brentford, *Do We Need a Censor?* (London: Faber and Faber, 1929), 9. Joynson-Hicks was 1st Viscount Brentford.

9 For more on this distinction, see Mogens Lærke, "Introduction," in *The Use of Censorship in the Enlightenment*, ed. Mogens Lærke (Leiden: Brill, 2009), 9.

10 Danilo Kiš, *Homo Poeticus: Essays and Interviews* (New York: Farrar, Straus and Giroux, 1995), 90–1.

11 Kiš, *Homo Poeticus*, 92.

12 Morris Ernst and Alexander Lindey, *The Censor Marches On: Recent Milestones in the Administration of the Obscenity Law in the United States* (New York: Doubleday, 1940), 212.

13 Library studies have been particularly good in teasing out the implications of such distinctions between censorship and selection. The seminal essay in the field is Lester Asheim, "Not Censorship But Selection," *Wilson Library Bulletin* 28 (1953): 63–7; Asheim revisited and revised aspects of his argument three decades later in "Selection and Censorship: A Reappraisal," *Wilson Library Bulletin* 58 (1983): 180–4. For other studies that make this distinction, most of which draw upon Asheim's work, see Michael K. O'Sullivan and Connie J. O'Sullivan, "Selection or Censorship: Libraries and the Intelligent Design Debate," *Library Review* 56, no. 3 (2007): 200–7; Tony Doyle, "Selection versus Censorship in Libraries," *Collection Management* 27, no. 1 (2002): 15–25; and Eli M. Oboler, *Defending Intellectual Freedom: The Library and the Censor* (Westport: Greenwood Press, 1980), 17–20, 63–8. For more on the role of librarians with regard to censorship, see also Francis M. Jones, *Defusing Censorship: The Librarian's Guide to Handling Censorship Conflict* (Phoenix: Oryx Press, 1983).

14 In an era of digital texts, shelf space is a less significant factor.

15 A. E. Astin, *Cato the Censor* (Oxford: Clarendon Press, 1978).

16 *Oxford English Dictionary*, s.v. "obscene," accessed 28 October 2024, www.oed.com/dictionary/obscene_adj.

17 Bernard Causton and G. Gordon Young, *Keeping it Dark: Or, the Censor's Handbook* (London: Mandrake Press, 1930), 74.

18 Alec Craig, *The Banned Books of England and Other Countries: A Study of the Censorship of Literary Obscenity* (London: George Allen & Unwin, 1962), 44.

19 Jonathan Israel, "Introduction," in Spinoza, *Theological-Political Treatise*, ed. Jonathan Israel (Cambridge: Cambridge University Press, 2007), viii–xxxiv;

and Jonathan Israel, "French Royal Censorship and the Battle to Suppress the *Encyclopédie* of Diderot and D'Alembert, 1751–1759," in *The Use of Censorship in the Enlightenment*, ed. Mogens Lærke (Leiden: Brill, 2009), 61–74.

20 D. H. Lawrence, *Pornography and Obscenity* (London: Faber and Faber, 1929), 13.

21 Lawrence, *Pornography and Obscenity*, 15.

22 James Joyce, *A Portrait of the Artist as a Young Man*, ed. Jeri Johnson (Oxford: Oxford University Press, 2008), 172–81.

23 Allison Pease, *Modernism, Mass Culture, and the Aesthetics of Obscenity* (Cambridge: Cambridge University Press, 2000), 34.

24 Pease, *Modernism, Mass Culture, and the Aesthetics of Obscenity*, 36.

25 Harry M. Clor, *Obscenity and Public Morality: Censorship in a Liberal Society* (Chicago: University of Chicago Press, 1969), 217. Clor uses the term "obscenity" for what Lawrence describes as "pornography" and Joyce describes as "improper art."

26 Ernest Renan, "What Is a Nation?" in *Nation and Narration*, trans. Martin Thom, ed. Homi Bhabha (London: Routledge, 1990), 8–22.

27 For a study on how modern liberal societies have their own censorship regimes, see Sue Curry Jansen, *Censorship: The Knot that Binds Power and Knowledge* (Oxford: Oxford University Press, 1991). There are legions of studies on liberal democracies that define their parameters and undergirding philosophies. Examples include William A. Galston, *Anti-Pluralism: The Populist Threat to Democracy* (New Haven: Yale University Press, 2018); John McGowan, *Pragmatist Politics: Making the Case for Liberal Democracy* (Minneapolis: University of Minnesota Press, 2012); Michael J. Perry, *The Political Morality of Liberal Democracy* (Cambridge: Cambridge University Press, 2009); and Bryan T. McGraw, *Faith in Politics: Religion and Liberal Democracy* (Cambridge: Cambridge University Press, 2010).

28 John Stuart Mill, *On Liberty*, in John Stuart Mill, *On Liberty, Utilitarianism and Other Essays*, 2nd ed., eds. Mark Philp and Frederick Rosen (Oxford: Oxford University Press, 2015), 91.

29 The term "conservative democracy" has been applied to Turkey under the leadership of Recep Tayyip Erdoğan. In this context, and in relation to similar societies in much of the Maghreb, it refers to democracy in a theocratic society, which is, as will be seen, pertinent to Catholic Ireland, although in these more recent forms the theocratic societies in question are Islamic. Prior to the rise of the term "conservative democracy," political scientists instead used a range of synonyms to describe similar societies, including "defective democracy" and "illiberal democracy." See, respectively, Wolfgang Merkel, "Embedded and Defective Democracies," *Democratization* 11, no. 5 (2004): 33–58, and Fareed Zakaria's influential

essay "The Rise of Illiberal Democracy," *Foreign Affairs* 76, no. 6 (1997): 22–43. As the title of Zakaria's essay suggests, much of the work on this topic has examined polities that have taken illiberal turns as opposed to being illiberal from the beginning. For a similar perspective, see Nancy Bermeo, "On Democratic Backsliding," *Journal of Democracy* 27, no.1 (January 2016): 5–19.

30 Clive Bell, *On British Freedom* (London: Chatto & Windus, 1923), 1.

31 Bell, *On British Freedom*, 53–71.

32 *Proclamation of the Irish Republic*, National Museum of Ireland, accessed 28 October 2024, www.museum.ie/en-ie/collections-research/collection/resilience/artefact/test-3/fb71e3dc-2e95-4406-bc46-87d8d6b0ae5d.

33 Blanshard, *The Irish and Catholic Power*, 3–4.

34 Blanshard, *The Irish and Catholic Power*, 48.

35 Harold C. Gardiner, *Catholic Viewpoint on Censorship*, 2nd ed. (Garden City: Image Books, 1961), 21. The first edition was published in 1958.

36 Gardiner, *Catholic Viewpoint on Censorship*, 23.

37 Gardiner, *Catholic Viewpoint on Censorship*, 50. Original emphasis.

38 For an account of censorship in this regard, see Brian Fallon, *An Age of Innocence: Irish Culture, 1930–1960* (New York: St. Martin's Press, 1998).

39 J. H. Whyte, *Church and State in Modern Ireland, 1923–1970* (Dublin: Gill & MacMillan, 1980), 365. For other studies of the influence of the Catholic Church on post-independence Irish politics, see Patrick Murray, *Oracles of God: The Roman Catholic Church and Irish Politics, 1922–37* (Dublin: University College Dublin Press, 2000); and Dermot Keogh, *The Vatican, the Bishops, and Irish Politics, 1919–39* (Cambridge: Cambridge, University Press, 1986).

40 Tom Inglis, *Moral Monopoly: The Rise and Fall of the Catholic Church in Modern Ireland* (Dublin: University College Dublin Press, 1998), 77–82.

41 Fearghal McGarry, "Independent Ireland," in *The Princeton History of Modern Ireland*, eds. Richard Bourke and Ian McBride (Princeton: Princeton University Press, 2016), 123.

42 Inglis, *Moral Monopoly*, 68.

43 Andrew F. Comyn, "Censorship in Ireland," *Studies: An Irish Quarterly Review* 58, no. 229 (1969): 42.

44 Tom Inglis, "Religion, Identity, State and Society," in *The Cambridge Companion to Modern Irish Culture*, eds. Joe Cleary and Claire Connolly (Cambridge: Cambridge University Press, 2005), 69.

45 Gary A. Boyd, "Supernational Catholicity: Dublin and the 1932 Eucharistic Congress," *Early Popular Visual Culture* 5, no. 3 (2007): 325. See also Rebecca Troeger, "Voices of the World": National Identity and Musical Space at the 1932 Eucharistic Congress," *Éire-Ireland* 50, nos. 3–4 (2015): 59–73; and

David G. Holmes, "The Eucharistic Congress of 1932 and Irish Identity," *New Hibernia Review* 4, no. 1 (2000): 55–78.

46 Donat O'Donnell, *Maria Cross: Imaginative Patterns in a Group of Modern Catholic Writers* (London: Chatto & Windus, 1954), 111. Donat O'Donnell was O'Brien's nom de plume.

47 Bruce Francis Biever, *Religion, Culture, and Values: A Cross-Cultural Analysis of Motivational Factors in Native Irish and American Irish Catholicism* (New York: Arno Press, 1976), 268–9, 306–7.

48 Anthony Keating, "Censorship: The Cornerstone of Catholic Ireland," *Journal of Church and State* 57, no. 2 (2015): 289.

49 James M. Smith, *Ireland's Magdalen Laundries and the Nation's Architecture of Containment* (Notre Dame: University of Notre Dame Press, 2007).

50 There were many such institutions in Ireland, notably the "mother and baby homes," in which infant mortality was significantly higher than the national average; in many instances, the authorities donated the corpses to science without their mothers' knowledge or buried them in mass, unmarked graves. See Caelainn Hogan's excellent, devastating book *Republic of Shame: Stories from Ireland's Institutions for 'Fallen Women'* (London: Penguin, 2019).

51 For a comprehensive survey of how sexuality was expressed, repressed, marginalised, and criminalised in Ireland over the course of the past hundred or so years, see Diarmaid Ferriter, *Occasions of Sin: Sex and Society in Modern Ireland* (London: Profile Books, 2009). See also Aongus Collins, *A History of Sex and Morals in Ireland* (Cork: Mercier Press, 2001).

52 Finola Kennedy, "The Suppression of the Carrigan Report: A Historical Perspective on Child Abuse," *Studies: An Irish Quarterly Review* 89, no. 356 (2000): 354–63; and James M. Smith, "The Politics of Sexual Knowledge: The Origins of Ireland's Containment Culture and the Carrigan Report (1931)," *Journal of the History of Sexuality* 13, no. 2 (2004): 208–33.

53 John A. Murphy, "Censorship and the Moral Community," in *Communications and Community in Ireland*, ed. Brian Farrell (Dublin: Mercier Press, 1984), 51. In Irish, "Sinn Féin" means "ourselves alone" and is the name of a nationalist political party that has long advocated for an independent, non-partitioned Ireland.

54 Aodh de Blácam, "Poison in the Wells," *Irish Monthly* 65, no. 766 (April 1937): 271.

55 De Blácam, "Poison in the Wells," 272.

56 P. J. Gannon, "Art, Morality and Censorship," *Studies: An Irish Quarterly Review* 31, no. 124 (1942): 415.

57 Julia Carlson, ed., *Banned in Ireland: Censorship and the Irish Writer* (Athens: The University of Georgia Press, 1990), 23, 40.

58 Many canonical historical surveys insist on the importance of literary and other forms of censorship to the maintenance of a conservative, Catholic society in post-independence Ireland. See, for example, J. J. Lee, *Ireland 1912–1985: Politics and Society* (Cambridge: Cambridge University Press, 1989), 159–61; F. S. L. Lyons, *Ireland since the Famine* (Oxford: Clarendon Press 1979), 674–6; and Whyte, *Church and State in Modern Ireland*, 37.
59 Michel Foucault, *Discipline and Punish: The Birth of the Prison*, trans. Alan Sheridan (New York: Vintage, 1995), 27.
60 Gardiner, *Catholic Viewpoint on Censorship*, 10.
61 Dr. Cornelius Lucey, "The Freedom of the Press," *Irish Ecclesiastical Record* 50, no. 840 (1937): 584.
62 Foucault, *Discipline and Punish*, 110.
63 Judith Butler, *Excitable Speech: A Politics of the Performative* (London: Routledge, 1997), 132.
64 For a study of how censorship has extended to all sections of Ireland, including government, business, churches, educational institutions, and professional organisations, see Brendan Ryan, *Keeping Us in the Dark: Censorship and Freedom of Information in Ireland* (Dublin: Gill & Macmillan, 1995). As a sitting senator in 1985, Ryan proposed the first freedom of information legislation in Ireland; it was never passed. Ireland's first Freedom of Information Act was passed into law in 1997. For more on the links between democracy and access to information, see Patrick Smyth and Ellen Hazelkorn, eds., *Let in the Light: Censorship, Secrecy and Democracy* (Dingle: Brandon, 1993).
65 Foucault, *Discipline and Punish*, 111.
66 Plato, *Republic* (Perseus Digital Library, accessed 21 October 2024), www.perseus.tufts.edu/hopper/. 377b.
67 Plato, *Republic*, 378a.
68 Plato, *Republic*, 380c.
69 John Milton, *Areopagitica*, in *The Major Works*, eds. Stephen Orgel and Jonathan Goldberg (Oxford: Oxford University Press, 2008), 239.
70 Milton, *Areopagitica*, 247.
71 Milton, *Areopagitica*, 240.
72 Milton, *Areopagitica*, 259.
73 Milton, *Areopagitica*, 263.
74 Milton, *Areopagitica*, 265.
75 Mill, *On Liberty*, 5.
76 Mill, *On Liberty*, 8.
77 Mill, *On Liberty*, 65.
78 Mill, *On Liberty*, 33.
79 Mill, *On Liberty*, 63–4. Original emphases.
80 Mill, *On Liberty*, 77.

81 Mill, *On Liberty*, 77.
82 Bernard Shaw, preface to *The Shewing-up of Blanco Posnet*, in *The Doctor's Dilemma, Getting Married, and the Shewing-up of Blanco Posnet*, by Bernard Shaw (London: Constable, 1911), 377.
83 Jürgen Habermas, *The Transformation of the Public Sphere: An Inquiry into a Category of Bourgeois Society*, trans. Thomas Burger (London: Polity Press, 1992), 33.
84 Habermas, *The Transformation of the Public Sphere*, 58.
85 W. T. Stead, "Government by Journalism," *Contemporary Review* 49 (January 1886): 654.
86 Frederick Schauer, *Free Speech: A Philosophical Enquiry* (Cambridge: Cambridge University Press, 1982), 15–16.
87 Mill, *On Liberty*, 12–13.
88 Mill, *On Liberty*, 82.
89 See, for example, Stephen L. Newman, "Finding the Harm in Hate Speech: An Argument against Censorship," *Canadian Journal of Political Science* 50, no. 3 (2017): 679–97; Ivan Hare and James Weinstein, eds., *Extreme Speech and Democracy* (Oxford: Oxford University Press, 2009); Saul Levmore and Martha C. Nussbaum, eds., *The Offensive Internet: Speech, Privacy, and Reputation* (Cambridge: Harvard University Press, 2011); Mark M. Carroll, "'All for Keeping His Own Negro Wench': Birch v. Benton (1858) and the Politics of Slander and Free Speech in Antebellum Missouri," *Law and History Review* 29, no. 3 (2011): 835–97; Eric Barendt, "Copyright and Free Speech Theory," in *Copyright and Free Speech: Comparative and International Analyses*, eds. Jonathan Griffiths and Uma Suthersanen (Oxford: Oxford University Press, 2005), 11–34; and Carol Loeb Shloss, "Privacy and the Misuse of Copyright: The Case of *Shloss v. the Estate of James Joyce*," in *Modernism and Copyright*, ed. Paul K. Saint-Amour (Oxford: Oxford University Press, 2011), 243–59.
90 See, for example, Charles Booth's multivolume *Life and Labour of the People in London* (London: Macmillan, 1892–97). The first volume was originally published as *Life and Labour of the People* in 1889 before it was collectively issued with the other works. This was a landmark study in the foundation of British sociology.
91 R. Brimley Johnson, *Moral Poison in Modern Fiction* (London: A. M. Philpot, 1922); and de Blácam, "Poison in the Wells".
92 For a compelling study of how discourses of sexual health, which is a specific form of public health, affected the direction of Irish literature and, in some instances, coincided with censorship, see Lloyd (Meadhbh) Houston, *Irish Modernism and the Politics of Sexual Health* (Oxford: Oxford University Press, 2023).
93 Jonathan Dollimore, *Sex, Literature and Censorship* (Cambridge: Polity Press, 2001), xi. Original emphasis.

94 Morris Ernst and William Seagle, *To the Pure ... : A Study of Obscenity and the Censor* (New York: Viking, 1928), 130; and Samuel Beckett, "Censorship in the Saorstat," in *Banned in Ireland: Censorship and the Irish Writer*, ed. Julia Carlson (Athens: The University of Georgia Press, 1990), 146.
95 Mill, *On Liberty*, 68.
96 Stanley Cohen, *Folk Devils and Moral Panics: The Creation of the Mods and the Rockers*, 3rd ed. (London: Routledge, 2002), vii–viii.
97 Cohen, *Folk Devils and Moral Panics*, xxxv.
98 Cohen, *Folk Devils and Moral Panics*, xliv.
99 Cohen, *Folk Devils and Moral Panics*, 7–8.
100 For the SSV as a precursor of the NVA, see Katherine Mullin, "Poison More Deadly than Prussic Acid: Defining Obscenity after the 1857 Obscene Publications Act (1850–1885)," in *Prudes on the Prowl: Fiction and Obscenity in England, 1850 to the Present Day*, eds. David Bradshaw and Rachel Potter (Oxford University Press, 2013), 11–29.
101 Julia Carlson, "Introduction," in *Banned in Ireland: Censorship and the Irish Writer*, ed. Julia Carlson (Athens: The University of Georgia Press, 1990), 2.
102 Carlson, *Banned in Ireland*, 72.
103 Irish writers also have a long lineage of those who refused to engage with censorship in the polemical, political, and social spheres. Samuel Beckett's celebrated essay attacking censorship, which is cited earlier in the introduction, was only published some fifty years after he wrote it. Like Beckett, the oft-banned Liam O'Flaherty, Kate O'Brien, and Norah Hoult lived abroad for much of their lives, remained silent on the subject of censorship, and failed to organise against it. Despite their importance to Irish literature and their being banned on multiple occasions, the relative inaction of such writers means that they do not appear as major figures in this book.
104 See, for example, Kevin Whelan, "The Green Atlantic: Radical Reciprocities between Ireland and America in the Long Eighteenth Century," in *A New Imperial History: Culture, Identity and Modernity in Britain and the Empire, 1660–1840, ed.* Kathleen Wilson (Cambridge: Cambridge University Press, 2004), 216–38.
105 See, for example, Joe Cleary, *The Irish Expatriate Novel in Late Capitalist Globalization* (Cambridge: Cambridge University Press, 2021); and Joe Cleary, *Modernism, Empire, World Literature* (Cambridge: Cambridge University Press, 2021).
106 See, for example, Pilar Villar-Argáiz, ed., *Literary Visions of Multicultural Ireland: The Immigrant in Contemporary Irish Literature* (Manchester: Manchester University Press, 2013).

1: Setting the Template: George Moore and the Public Face of Resistance

1 Pease, *Modernism, Mass Culture, and the Aesthetics of Obscenity*; and Marshik, *British Modernism and Censorship*.

2 Declan Kiberd, *Inventing Ireland: The Literature of the Modern Nation* (Cambridge: Harvard University Press, 1997); and Nicholas Grene and Chris Morash, eds., *The Oxford Handbook of Modern Irish Theatre* (Oxford: Oxford University Press, 2016).

3 Joan FitzPatrick Dean, *Riot and Great Anger: Stage Censorship in Twentieth-Century Ireland* (Madison: University Wisconsin Press, 2004); Peter Martin, *Censorship in the Two Irelands*; and Adams, *Censorship*.

4 Ernst and Seagle, *To the Pure ... : A Study of Obscenity and the Censor*, 46.

5 George Moore, *A Communication to My Friends* (London: Nonesuch Press, 1933), 8.

6 George Moore, *Letters of George Moore* (Bournemouth: Sydenham, 1942), 63. Le Café de la Nouvelle Athènes, which Moore frequented, was a meeting place for impressionist painters in the Pigalles neighbourhood of Paris.

7 Adrian Frazier, *George Moore, 1852–1933* (New Haven: Yale University Press, 2000), 104.

8 For a study of how the English engaged with French literature in the nineteenth century and the perceived immorality of French writing, see Juliette Atkinson, *French Novels and the Victorians* (Oxford: Oxford University Press, 2017).

9 Elizabeth Ladenson, *Dirt for Dirt's Sake: Books on Trial from Madame Bovary to Lolita* (Ithaca: Cornell University Press, 2007), 22.

10 The original court decision reads: "L'ouvrage déféré au tribunal mérite un blâme sévère, car la mission de la littérature doit être d'orner et de recréer l'esprit en élevant l'intelligence et en épurant les moeurs plus encore que d'imprimer le dégoût de vice en offrant le tableau des désordres qui peuvent exister dans la société." Ladenson, *Dirt for Dirt's Sake*, 25–6.

11 The original reads: "Ce n'est pas pour mes femmes, mes filles ou mes soeurs que ce livre a été écrit; non plus pour les femmes, les filles ou les soeurs de mon voisin. Je laisse cette fonction à ceux qui ont intérêt à confondre les bonnes actions avec le beau langage." Ladenson, *Dirt for Dirt's Sake*, 57.

12 Émile Zola, "Naturalism in the Theatre," in *A Sourcebook on Naturalist Theatre*, trans. Albert Bermel, ed. Christopher Innes (London: Routledge, 2000), 51.

13 George Moore, *A Modern Lover* (New York: Garland Publishing, 1984), 77–8.

14 Guinevere L. Griest, *Mudie's Circulating Library and the Victorian Novel* (Bloomington: Indiana University Press, 1970), 41–2.

15 John A. Sutherland, *Victorian Novelists and Publishers* (Chicago: University of Chicago Press, 1976), 24.
16 Griest, *Mudie's*, 87–101.
17 Pierre Coustillas, introduction to *Literature at Nurse, or Circulating Morals: A Polemic on Victorian Censorship*, by George Moore, ed. Pierre Coustillas (Sussex: The Harvester Press, 1976), 12.
18 Peter Keating, *The Haunted Study: A Social History of the English Novel, 1875–1914* (London: Secker & Warburg, 1989), 24.
19 Pierre Coustillas, introduction, 13.
20 Griest, *Mudie's*, 137–40.
21 Herbert Maxwell, *Life and Times of the Right Honourable William Henry Smith, M.P.*, vol. 1 (Edinburgh: William Blackwood and Sons, 1893), 87.
22 Griest, *Mudie's*, 145.
23 "Mudie's Select Library: Notice," *Saturday Review*, 27 October 1860, 536. The italics, in the original, emphasize the relation between his morality and his business.
24 Nicola Wilson, "Circulating Morals (1900–1915)," in *Prudes on the Prowl: Fiction and Obscenity in England, 1850 to the Present Day*, eds. David Bradshaw and Rachel Potter (Oxford University Press, 2013), 52–3.
25 "Mudie's Library," *Saturday Review*, 3 November 1860, 550.
26 Nicola Wilson, "Circulating Morals," 53–4.
27 Simon Eliot, *Some Patterns and Trends in British Publishing, 1800–1919* (London: Bibliographical Society, 1994), 44–9.
28 Eliot, *Some Patterns and Trends*, 128.
29 Sutherland, *Victorian Novelists and Publishers*, 218–25.
30 Moore, *A Communication to My Friends*, 21.
31 Moore, *A Communication to My Friends*, 33–4.
32 Review of *A Modern Lover*, by George Moore, *Spectator*, 18 August 1883: 1069.
33 Coustillas, introduction, 16.
34 George Moore, *Literature at Nurse, or Circulating Morals* (London: Vizetelly, 1885), 4.
35 Moore, *A Communication to My Friends*, 58–9.
36 Frazier, *George Moore*, 104–5.
37 Matthew Arnold, "Up to Easter," *Nineteenth Century* XXI (May 1887): 638–9. For more on the origins of the New Journalism, see Laurel Brake, "Journalism and Modernism, Continued: The Case of W. T. Stead," in *Transatlantic Print Culture, 1880–1940: Emerging Media, Emerging Modernisms*, eds. Ann Ardis and Patrick Collier (London: Palgrave Macmillan, 2008), 149–66; J. O. Baylen, "The 'New Journalism' in Late Victorian Britain," *Australian Journal of Politics & History* 18, no. 3 (December 1972): 367–85; and Kate Campbell, "W. E. Gladstone, W. T.

Stead, Matthew Arnold and a New Journalism: Cultural Politics in the 1880s," *Victorian Periodicals Review* 36, no. 1 (2003): 20–40.

38 W. T. Stead, "The Future of Journalism," *Contemporary Review* 50 (July 1886), 664.

39 W. T. Stead, "Government by Journalism," *Contemporary Review* 49 (January 1886): 653–74.

40 Stead, "The Future of Journalism," 670.

41 George Moore, "A New Censorship of Literature," *Pall Mall Gazette*, 10 December 1884, 1–2. Reprinted in Coustillas, *Literature at Nurse*, 27–32.

42 Moore, "A New Censorship," 28.

43 Moore, "A New Censorship," 32.

44 Sylvanus, letter to the editor, *Pall Mall Gazette*, 15 December 1884. Reprinted in Coustillas, *Literature at Nurse*, 42–3.

45 Robert Langstaff de Havilland, letter to the editor, *Pall Mall Gazette*, 13 December 1884. Reprinted in Coustillas, *Literature at Nurse*, 37–9.

46 Peter Keating, *The Haunted Study*, 254.

47 George Gissing, letter to the editor, *Pall Mall Gazette*, 15 December 1884. Reprinted in Coustillas, *Literature at Nurse*, 44–5.

48 Ernest Vizetelly, *Émile Zola, Novelist and Reformer: An Account of His Life and Work* (London: John Lane, 1904), 243.

49 Frazier, *George Moore*, 104–5.

50 Moore, *A Communication to My Friends*, 64.

51 Ernst and Seagle, *To the Pure*, 93; Frazier, *George Moore* 115.

52 George Moore, *Avowals* (self-pub., 1919), 105.

53 Moore, *Literature at Nurse*, 16–17.

54 Moore, *Literature at Nurse*, 7–17.

55 Moore, *Literature at Nurse*, 18.

56 Moore, *Literature at Nurse*, 19.

57 Moore, *Literature at Nurse*, 20.

58 Moore, *Literature at Nurse*, 21.

59 For a survey of how Moore deployed prefaces throughout his career, see Kathi R. Griffin, "The Prefaces of George Moore," in *George Moore: Spheres of Influence*, eds. Kathryn Laing and Mary Pierse (Liverpool: Liverpool University Press, 2023), 57–78.

60 George Moore, preface to *Piping Hot!*, ed. Émile Zola (London: Vizetelly & Co., 1887), vi.

61 Moore, preface, x, xviii.

62 Moore, preface, xvii.

63 The book is now more commonly known in English as *The Earth*, the alternate meaning of Zola's title. See, for example, Émile Zola, *The Earth*, trans. and eds. Brian Nelson and Julie Rose (Oxford: Oxford University Press, 2016).

64 Vizetelly, *Émile Zola*, 225.
65 "The Maiden Tribute of Modern Babylon," *Pall Mall Gazette*, 6 July 1885, 1–6.
66 "The New Crusade," *Pall Mall Gazette*, 12 August 1885, 11.
67 "The Hyde Park Demonstration," *Pall Mall Gazette*, 24 August 1885, 11.
68 "Street Literature," *Pall Mall Gazette*, 29 August 1885, 11.
69 Edward J. Bristow, *Vice and Vigilance: Purity Movements in Britain since 1700* (Dublin: Gill and Macmillan, 1977), 112; and William Alexander Coote, *A Romance of Philanthropy* (London: National Vigilance Association, 1916), 19–20.
70 Coote, *A Romance of Philanthropy*, 16–17.
71 Bristow, *Vice and Vigilance*, 202.
72 Vizetelly, *Émile Zola*, 257.
73 Vizetelly, *Émile Zola*, 262.
74 "My Life and Publications," *Pall Mall Gazette*, 24 March 1888, 2.
75 *Hansard*, 8 May 1888, vol. 325, c. 1708.
76 *Hansard*, 8 May 1888, vol. 325, c. 1709.
77 *Hansard*, 8 May 1888, vol. 325, c. 1710.
78 *Hansard*, 8 May 1888, vol. 325, c. 1715–17.
79 *Hansard*, 8 May 1888, vol. 325, c. 1719.
80 Edward de Grazia, *Girls Lean Back Everywhere: The Law of Obscenity and the Assault on Genius* (New York: Random House, 1992), 44.
81 *Hansard*, 11 May 1857, vol. 145, c. 103.
82 *Regina v. Hicklin*, (1868) L.R. 3 Q.B.D. 360.
83 Ernst and Seagle, *To the Pure*, 130.
84 For a good review of the ramifications of the act and the Cockburn ruling in the period before Moore and Vizetelly, see Katherine Mullin, "Poison More Deadly than Prussic Acid: Defining Obscenity after the 1857 Obscene Publications Act (1850–1885)," in *Prudes on the Prowl*, Bradshaw and Potter, 11–29. In 1877, Charles Bradlaugh and Annie Besant were prosecuted for publishing Charles Knowlton's *Fruits of Philosophy*, which advocates birth control. Bradlaugh and Besant were not sentenced, and the publicity of the trial caused sales of the book to soar from a few hundred a year to 120,000. See Norman St. John-Stevas, *Obscenity and the Law* (London: Secker & Warburg, 1956), 70–4.
85 *Daily News*, 11 August 1888, 6.
86 Henry Vizetelly, *Extracts Principally from English Classics: Showing That the Legal Suppression of M. Zola's Novels Would Logically Involve the Bowdlerizing of Some of the Greatest Works in English Literature* (London: Vizetelly, 1888). For Moore's hand in the work, see Joseph Hone, *The Life of George Moore* (1936; repr., Westport: Greenwood, 1973), 151.

87 "Mr. Vizetelly's Defence of M. Zola," *Pall Mall Gazette*, 20 September 1888, 7. Vizetelly also printed it at the outset of *Extracts*.
88 Vizetelly, *Extracts*, 3–4.
89 "A Plea for a Literary Censorship," *St. James's Gazette*, 22 September 1888, 3.
90 George Moore, *Confessions of a Young Man* (London: Swan Sonnenschein, 1888), 237.
91 Moore, *Confessions*, 339.
92 "Vizetelly and Zola's Novels," *Pall Mall Gazette*, 18 September 1888, 10.
93 "No More Translations from Zola," *Pall Mall Gazette*, 31 October 1888, 10.
94 William Alexander Coote, ed., *Pernicious Literature: Debate in the House of Commons, Trial and Conviction for Sale of Zola's Novels, With Opinion of the Press* (London: National Vigilance Association, 1889), 3.
95 Vizetelly, *Émile Zola*, 285.
96 "Stopping a Vile Trade," *Pall Mall Gazette*, 15 February 1889, 5.
97 "Sensational Literature and the National Vigilance Association," *Bookseller*, 4 May 1889, 445.
98 "Holywell Street Panicstricken," *Pall Mall Gazette*, 1 June 1889, 6.
99 Vizetelly, *Émile Zola*, 297–8.
100 "The Vizetelly Prosecution," *Pall Mall Gazette*, 26 June 1889, 7.
101 Moore, *Avowals*, 107. He made this same claim again later; see Moore, *A Communication*, 71–2.
102 Rachel Potter, introduction to *Prudes on the Prowl: Fiction and Obscenity in England, 1850 to the Present Day*, eds. David Bradshaw and Rachel Potter (Oxford University Press, 2013), 1–10.
103 Anthony Cummins, "Émile Zola's Cheap English Dress: The Vizetelly Translations, Late-Victorian Print Culture, and the Crisis of Literary Value," *Review of English Studies* 60, no. 243 (2008): 127–9.
104 Frazier, *George Moore*, 116.

2: Evolving Tactics: Bernard Shaw, Relentless Antagonism, and Organised Resistance

1 Elizabeth Carolyn Miller, *Slow Print: Literary Radicalism and Late Victorian Print Culture* (Stanford, CA: Stanford University Press, 2013), 90.
2 *Star*, 2 November 1888. Reprinted in Bernard Shaw, *Agitations: Letters to the Press, 1875–1950*, eds. Dan H. Laurence and James Rambeau (New York: Frederick Ungar, 1985), 12–13.
3 Matthew J. Kinservik, *Disciplining Satire: The Censorship of Satiric Comedy on the Eighteenth-Century London Stage* (Lewisburg: Bucknell University Press, 2002), 55–94.

4 L. W. Conolly, *The Censorship of English Drama, 1737–1824* (San Marino: Huntington Library, 1976), 13–45.
5 For studies of these trends over time, see Conolly, *The Censorship of English Drama*; John Russell Stephens, *The Censorship of English Drama, 1824–1901* (Cambridge: Cambridge University Press, 2010); and Steve Nicholson, *The Censorship of British Drama, 1900–1968*, 4 vols. (Exeter: University of Exeter Press, 2003–15).
6 Bernard Shaw, *The Diaries, 1885–1897*, ed. Stanley Weintraub, vol. 1 (University Park: Pennsylvania State University Press, 1986), 151–2; *Note-book of the Shelley Society* (London: Reeves and Turner, 1888), 1.
7 *Note-book of the Shelley Society*, 8.
8 Edward Pigott to Lord Lotham, 29 December 1885. Kew LC 1/453.
9 Edward Pigott, Memorandum for Sir Spence, 29 January 1886. Kew LC 1/469.
10 Charles Wilmot to Sir Ponsonby, 14 April 1886. Kew LC 1/469; and Edward Pigott, Memorandum, 18 May 1886. Kew LC 1/469.
11 See *The Theatre* (August 1885); *The Artist* (August 1885); and *Musical Review* (2 January 1886). All reprinted in *Note-book of the Shelley Society*, 13.
12 *Note-book of the Shelley Society*, 11.
13 Shaw, *The Diaries, 1885–1897*, vol. 1, 167.
14 *Note-book of the Shelley Society*, 8, 36.
15 *Note-book of the Shelley Society*, 51. For Pigott's estimate, see his Memorandum, 18 May 1886. Kew LC 1/469.
16 "The Shelley Society," *Daily Telegraph*, 8 May 1886, 3.
17 Bernard Shaw, "Art Corner," *Our Corner* (1 June 1886): 370–3. Reprinted in *Shaw Review* 15, no. 1 (1972): 35.
18 See, for example, his entries on 15 December 1886, 13 April 1887, 14 December 1887, and 15 October 1890, in Shaw, *The Diaries, 1885–1897*, vol. 1, respectively, 221, 259, 323, 659; and 9 March 1892 and 4 August 1892, Bernard Shaw, *The Diaries, 1885–1897*, vol. 2, ed. Stanley Weintraub (University Park: Pennsylvania State University Press, 1986), 803, 841. For a discussion of Shelley's influence on Shaw, see Roland A. Duerksen, "Shelley and Shaw," *PMLA* 78, no. 1 (March 1963): 114–27.
19 There is some debate as to when exactly they met, but their first meeting likely occurred in the British Library in 1883. Michael Holroyd, *Bernard Shaw: The Search for Love*, vol. 2, 1856–1898 (London: Penguin, 1990), 134–5. For a record of their relationship, see Thomas Postlewait, ed., *Bernard Shaw and William Archer* (Toronto: University of Toronto Press, 2017).
20 A. M. Gibbs, *Bernard Shaw: A Life* (Gainesville: University Press of Florida, 2005), 112.
21 Henrik Ibsen, *Ibsen's Prose Dramas*, trans. William Archer (London: Walter Scott, 1890–91).

22 Bernard Shaw, "Fragments of a Fabian Lecture 1890," in *Shaw and Ibsen: Bernard Shaw's The Quintessence of Ibsenism and Related Writings*, ed. J. L. Wisenthal (Toronto: University of Toronto Press, 1979), 87.
23 Joan Templeton is one of the few critics to make the important distinction that Shaw did not argue that Ibsen was a socialist; indeed, she rebuts those who have said the contrary. For her valuable debunking of the falsehood in contemporary accounts and academic studies over the years, see Joan Templeton, *Shaw's Ibsen: A Re-Appraisal* (London: Palgrave Macmillan, 2018), 40–9.
24 In his history of the Théâtre Libre, Antoine refers to himself at the time of its founding as being employed by the gas company and never having played before a real audience. André Antoine, *Le Théâtre Libre* (Paris: Ressources, 1979), 3.
25 "The Theatre Libre Company in London," *Evening Telegraph*, 5 February 1889.
26 J. T. Grein and C. W. Jarvis, "A British Théâtre Libre (A Suggestion)," *Weekly Comedy* (30 November 1889). Cited in Jan McDonald, "Continental Plays Produced by the Independent Theatre Society, 1891–8," *Theatre Research International* 1, no. 1 (1975): 16–17.
27 Neil Blackadder, "Dr. Kastan, the Freie Bühne, and Audience Resistance to Naturalism," *New Theatre Quarterly* 14 (1998): 357–65. For an early account of the European independent theatre movement, see Anna Irene Miller, *The Independent Theatre in Europe: 1887 to the Present* (New York: Benjamin Bloom, 1931).
28 George Moore, *Impressions and Opinions* (London: David Nutt, 1891), 226.
29 Moore, *Impressions and Opinions*, 243.
30 "The Theatres," *Daily News*, 23 February 1891.
31 "Ibsenility," *Era*, 28 February 1891.
32 Santley to the Lord Chamberlain, 7 March 1891. Kew, LC 1/564.
33 Memorandum by Pigott, 14 March 1891. Kew, LC 1/565.
34 "'Ghosts'," *Era*, 21 March 1891, 10.
35 These last two quotes were cited by William Archer in "'Ghosts' and Gibberings," *Pall Mall Gazette*, 8 April 1891.
36 For references to his work on the proofs from May through to July and the delivery of his copy, see Bernard Shaw, *The Diaries*, vol. 2, 721–47.
37 Bernard Shaw, "The Quintessence of Ibsenism," in *Shaw and Ibsen: Bernard Shaw's The Quintessence of Ibsenism and Related Writings*, ed. J. L. Wisenthal (Toronto: University of Toronto Press, 1979), 107.
38 Bernard Shaw, "The Quintessence of Ibsenism," 119–20.
39 Bernard Shaw, "The Quintessence of Ibsenism," 121, 120.
40 Bernard Shaw, "The Quintessence of Ibsenism," 232.
41 Bernard Shaw, "The Quintessence of Ibsenism," 236.

42 *Report from the Select Committee on Theatres and Places of Entertainment* (London: Her Majesty's Stationary Office, 1892), 257–8.
43 *Report from the Select Committee on Theatres and Places of Entertainment*, 328.
44 *Report from the Select Committee on Theatres and Places of Entertainment*, 333.
45 McDonald, "Continental Plays Produced by the Independent Theatre Society, 1891–8," 27–8.
46 Tracy C. Davis, "The Independent Theatre Society's Revolutionary Scheme for an Uncommercial Theatre," *Theatre Journal* 42, no. 4 (1990): 453.
47 Bernard Shaw, "The Author's Apology," *Our Theatres in the Nineties*, vol. 1 (London: Constable, 1932), v.
48 Bernard Shaw, "The Independent Theatre," *Saturday Review*, 26 January 1895. Reprinted in *Our Theatres in the Nineties*, vol. 1, 22.
49 Bernard Shaw, "The Independent Theatre," 23.
50 Bernard Shaw, "A Purified Play," *Saturday Review*, 16 February 1895. Reprinted in *Our Theatres in the Nineties*, vol. 1, 36–9.
51 For an excellent study of the politics of sexuality on the British stage, see Sos Eltis, *Acts of Desire: Women and Sex on Stage, 1800–1930* (Oxford: Oxford University Press, 2013). Eltis also shows that, at times, playwrights were rather adept at evading the censorship of the Lord Chamberlain's Office.
52 Jahan Ramazani, *Poetry of Mourning: The Modern Elegy from Hardy to Heaney* (Chicago: University of Chicago Press, 1994).
53 Bernard Shaw, "The Late Censor," *Saturday Review*, 2 March 1895. Reprinted in *Our Theatres in the Nineties*, vol. 1, 51.
54 Bernard Shaw, "The Living Pictures," *Saturday Review*, 6 April 1895. Reprinted in *Our Theatres in the Nineties*, vol. 1, 79.
55 Bernard Shaw, "The Living Pictures," 80.
56 Bernard Shaw, *The Diaries*, vol. 2, 962–3.
57 Bernard Shaw, *The Diaries*, vol. 2, 1065.
58 Bernard Shaw to R. Golding Bright, 10 June 1896, in *Bernard Shaw: Collected Letters, 1874–1897*, ed. Dan H. Laurence (London: Max Reinhardt, 1965), 632.
59 *The Incorporated Stage Society: Ten Years, 1899 to 1909* (London: Chiswick Press, 1909), 8.
60 Michael Holroyd, *Bernard Shaw: The Pursuit of Power*, vol. 2, 1898–1918 (London: Penguin, 1991), 95.
61 Bernard Shaw to R. Golding Bright, 30 November 1901, in ed. Dan H. Laurence, *Bernard Shaw: Collected Letters, 1898–1910* (New York: Viking, 1985), 243.
62 Shaw to Redford, 12 March 1898, in Laurence, *Bernard Shaw*, 13.
63 Redford to Shaw, 14 March 1898, in Laurence, *Bernard Shaw*, 14.
64 Add. Ms. 53654 H, BL.
65 "Theatrical Notes," *Pall Mall Gazette*, 28 October 1901, 1.

66 *Daily Telegraph*, 12 November 1901. VAMTP, Stage Society Files, Box 1.
67 Shaw to R Golding Bright, 4 November 1895, in Laurence, *Bernard Shaw: Collected Letters, 1874–1897*, 566.
68 Shaw to R. Golding Bright, 30 November 1901, in Laurence, *Bernard Shaw*, 242.
69 *Globe*, 7 January 1902. VAMTP, Stage Society Files, Box 1.
70 "Performances of the Stage Society," *Daily Graphic*, 7 January 1902, 5.
71 "Ms. Warren's Profession," *St. James's Gazette*, 7 January 1902, 7.
72 Bernard Shaw, preface to *Plays Pleasant and Unpleasant: Plays Unpleasant*, by Bernard Shaw (London: Constable, 1931), 147–8.
73 For an excellent discussion of Socrates's accusations and their relationship to freedom of speech and censorship, see Arlene W. Saxonhouse, *Free Speech and Democracy in Ancient Athens* (Cambridge: Cambridge University Press, 2006).
74 *Oxford English Dictionary*, s.v. "apology," accessed 28 October 2024, www.oed.com/dictionary/apology_n.
75 Shaw, preface, 150–1.
76 Shaw, preface, 152–3.
77 Shaw, preface, 157.
78 Shaw, preface, 164.
79 Shaw, preface, 165.
80 Shaw, preface, 166.
81 Shaw, preface, 159.
82 For a list of the plays produced at the Court Theatre during these years, see Dennis Kennedy, *Granville Barker and the Dream of Theatre* (Cambridge: Cambridge University Press, 1985), 208–10.
83 Bernard Shaw, "The Solution to the Censorship Problem," *Academy*, 29 June 1907. Reprinted in Bernard Shaw, *The Drama Observed*, vol. 3, ed. Bernard F. Dukore (University Park: Pennsylvania State University Press, 1993), 140–1.
84 Redford to Garnett, 5 July 1907. Edward Garnett Collection, Box 12, Folder 7, HRC.
85 Helen Smith, *An Uncommon Reader: A Life of Edward Garnett, Mentor and Editor of Literary Genius* (New York: Farrar, Straus and Giroux, 2017), 167–8.
86 Shaw to Garnett, 15 July 1907. Edward Garnett Collection, Box 13, Folder 5, HRC.
87 Archer to Garnett, 17 July 1907. Edward Garnett Collection, Box 1, Folder 9, HRC.
88 Edward Garnett, *The Breaking Point* (London: Duckworth, 1907).
89 *Globe*, 18 October 1907, 7.
90 *Western Morning News*, 19 October 1907, 4.
91 *Times*, 29 October 1907, 15.

92 Shaw to Lena Ashwell, 4 November 1907, in Laurence, *Bernard Shaw*, 718.

93 Shaw to Ashwell, 7 November 1907, in Laurence, *Bernard Shaw*, 720.

94 *Nation*, 16 November 1907. Reprinted in Shaw, *Agitations: Letters to the Press*, 93–101.

95 Barrie, Galsworthy, and Murray to Shaw, 11 February 1908. Bernard Shaw Collection, Box 47, Folder 7, HRC.

96 For a detailed account of the behind-the-scenes manoeuvring by the government, see David Thomas, David Carlton, and Anne Etienne, *Theatre Censorship: From Walpole to Wilson* (Oxford: Oxford University Press, 2007), 77–83.

97 See, for example, *Globe*, 7 April 1908, 5; *Stage*, 9 April 1908, 20; and *Standard*, 7 April 1908, 5.

98 *Hansard*, 17 December 1908, vol. 198, col. 2161.

99 *Hansard*, 22 April 1909, vol. 3, col. 1675–6.

100 See Thomas, Carlton, and Etienne, *Theatre Censorship*, 73–7, 87–8.

101 Licence for *The Shewing-up of Blanco Posnet*, 21 September 1909. Bernard Shaw Collection, Box 63, Folder 6. HRC.

102 Dawson to W. P. Byrne, 10 May 1909. LCP Corr 1916–91, *The Shewing-up of Blanco Posnet*, BL.

103 Tree to Redford, 18 May 1909; and Tree to Redford, telegram, 19 May 1909. LCP Corr 1916–91, *The Shewing-up of Blanco Posnet*, BL.

104 Redford to Whelen, 20 May 1909. LCP Corr 1916–91, *The Shewing-up of Blanco Posnet*, BL.

105 "Mr. Shaw and the Censor," *Observer*, 23 May 1909, 9.

106 *Hansard*, 26 May 1909, vol. 5, col. 1183.

107 "Dramatic Censorship," *Times*, 29 May 1909, 10.

108 The letters appeared 1–7 June; Redford's was published on 5 June.

109 "Mr. Bernard Shaw and the Censorship," *Times*, 17 June 1909, 12.

110 Redford to the Lord Chamberlain, 27 June 1909. LCP Corr. 1909/90 *Press Cuttings*, BL.

111 "The Censor's Revenge," *Times*, 26 June 1909, 8. However, the suffragette group that was producing the play withdrew it for unexplained reasons before the first performance. See Anning to Redford, 1 July 1909. LCP Corr. 1909/90 *Press Cuttings*, BL.

112 "Banned Play," *Observer*, 27 June 1909, 9.

113 This was publicly announced on 16 July. See "Stage Plays Censorship," *Times*, 16 July 1909, 8.

114 *Report from the Joint Select Committee of the House of Lords and the House of Commons on the Stage Plays (Censorship)* (London: His Majesty's Stationery Office, 1909), 127–9.

115 Shaw to Murray, 17 July 1909, in Laurence, *Bernard Shaw*, 850.

116 Shaw to Members of the Dramatists' Club, 28 July 1909. Laurence, *Bernard Shaw*, 851–3.
117 *Report from the Joint Select Committee of the House of Lords and the House of Commons on the Stage Plays*, xx.
118 Webb to Shaw, telegram, 24 July 1909, Alex C. Michalos and Deborah C. Poff, eds., *Bernard Shaw and the Webbs* (Toronto: University of Toronto Press, 2002), 93.
119 Bernard Shaw, preface to *The Shewing-up of Blanco Posnet*, 374.
120 Bernard Shaw, preface to *The Shewing-up of Blanco Posnet*, 374.
121 Bernard Shaw, preface to *The Shewing-up of Blanco Posnet*, 375.
122 Bernard Shaw, preface to *The Shewing-up of Blanco Posnet*, 375.
123 Bernard Shaw, preface to *The Shewing-up of Blanco Posnet*, 376.
124 Bernard Shaw, preface to *The Shewing-up of Blanco Posnet*, 376.
125 Bernard Shaw, preface to *The Shewing-up of Blanco Posnet*, 376.
126 Bernard Shaw, preface to *The Shewing-up of Blanco Posnet*, 377.
127 For a longer discussion of this issue and the development of Shaw's notion of "immoral" in relation to censorship, see Brad Kent, "Censorship and Immorality: Bernard Shaw's *The Devil's Disciple*," *Modern Drama* 54, no. 4 (2011): 511–33.
128 Bernard Shaw, preface to *The Shewing-up of Blanco Posnet*, 419.
129 Shaw to Samuel, 28 July 1909, in Laurence, *Bernard Shaw*, 853–5.
130 Bernard Shaw, "The Select Committee on the Censorship," *Times*, 2 August 1909, 8.
131 *Report from the Joint Select Committee of the House of Lords and the House of Commons on the Stage Plays*, 53.
132 Bernard Shaw, preface to *The Shewing-up of Blanco Posnet*, 370–1.
133 Bernard Shaw, preface to *The Shewing-up of Blanco Posnet*, 372.
134 Lady Gregory, *Our Irish Theatre: A Chapter of Autobiography* (New York: G. P. Putnam's Sons, 1913), 140.
135 Gregory to Shaw, 6 July 1909, in *Shaw, Lady Gregory and the Abbey: A Correspondence and a Record*, eds. Dan H. Laurence and Nicholas Grene (Gerrards Cross: Colin Smythe, 1993), 4–5.
136 Lady Gregory's June 1909 memoir entry, in Laurence and Grene, *Shaw, Lady Gregory and the Abbey*, 4.
137 For a detailed examination of the row, see Lucy McDiarmid, "Augusta Gregory, Bernard Shaw, and the Shewing-Up of Dublin Castle," *PMLA* 109, no. 1 (1994): 26–44.
138 Gregory to Shaw, 25–26 August 1909, in Laurence and Grene, *Shaw, Lady Gregory and the Abbey*, 49.
139 "The Production of *Blanco Posnet*," *Times*, 27 August 1909, 8.
140 "'Blanco Posnet' and the Censorship," *Times*, 11 October 1909, 10.

141 *Report from the Joint Select Committee of the House of Lords and the House of Commons on the Stage Plays*, xi.
142 Marshik, *British Modernism and Censorship*, 60, 86.
143 "Bernard Shaw Resents Action of Librarian," *New York Times*, 26 September 1905, 1. The *OED* cites this article as the source of the term.
144 Bernard Shaw, preface to *The Shewing-up of Blanco Posnet*, 368–9.
145 LCP 1917/17 *Ghosts*, BL.

3: The Scene Shifts to Ireland: James Joyce, Brinsley MacNamara, and Lennox Robinson

1 "Fighting Immoral Literature," *Limerick Leader*, 6 October 1911, 3.
2 "Pernicious Publications," *Limerick Leader*, 3 November 1911, 4.
3 "War on Bad Literature," *Limerick Leader*, 11 October 1911, 3.
4 L. M. Cullen, *Eason & Son: A History* (Dublin: Eason & Son, 1989), 253–60.
5 This strategy was also adopted by other Catholic groups. The Christian Brothers, for example, founded the nationalist Catholic magazine *Our Boys* in 1914 to counter the scores of British boys' journals that inculcated imperial values. See Michael Flanagan, "Republic of Virtue: *Our Boys*, the Campaign against Evil Literature and the Assertion of Catholic Morality in Free State Ireland," in *Ireland, Design and Visual Culture: Negotiating Modernity, 1922–1992*, eds. Linda King and Elaine Sisson (Cork: Cork University Press, 2011), 117–29.
6 John Cardinal D'Alton, *The Catholic Truth Society of Ireland: Its Origin and Purpose* (Dublin: Veritas, n.d.), 6.
7 Patrick J. Corish, "The First Fifty Years," in *Catholic Truth Society of Ireland: First Fifty Years, 1899–1949* (Dublin: Veritas, 1949), 14.
8 Corish, "The First Fifty Years," 16.
9 For a work that discusses the links between censorship and exile, see Johanna Hartmann and Hubert Zapf, eds., *Censorship and Exile* (Göttingen: V&R Unipress, 2015).
10 For Shaw's relationship with Richards, see Michel Pharand, ed., *Bernard Shaw and His Publishers* (Toronto: University of Toronto Press, 2009).
11 Joyce to Richards, 15 October 1905, in *Letters of James Joyce*, vol. 2, ed. Richard Ellmann (London: Faber and Faber, 1966), 122–3.
12 Richards to Joyce, 17 February 1906, in Ellmann, *Letters of James Joyce*, vol. 2, 130.
13 Richards to Joyce, 23 April 1906, in Ellmann, *Letters of James Joyce*, vol. 2, 132.
14 Joyce to Grant Richards, 26 April 1906, in *Letters of James Joyce*, vol. 1, ed. Stuart Gilbert (London: Faber and Faber, 1957), 60.

15 Richards to Joyce, 1 May 1906, in "Grant Richards to James Joyce," Robert Scholes, *Studies in Bibliography* 16 (1963): 145.
16 Scholes, "Grant Richards to James Joyce," 140.
17 Clare Hutton, "Chapters of Moral History: Failing to Publish *Dubliners*," *Papers of the Bibliographical Society of America* 97, no. 4 (2003): 503.
18 Joyce to Richards, 5 May 1906, in Ellmann, *Letters of James Joyce*, vol. 2, 134–5.
19 Joyce to Richards, 13 May 1906, in Ellmann, *Letters of James Joyce*, vol. 2, 137.
20 Joyce to Richards, 13 May 1906, in Ellmann, *Letters of James Joyce*, vol. 2, 137.
21 Joyce to Richards, 20 May 1906, in Gilbert, *Letters of James Joyce*, vol. 1, 62–3.
22 Joyce to Richards, 23 June 1906, in Gilbert, *Letters of James Joyce*, vol. 1, 63–4.
23 Joyce to Richards, 10 October 1906, in Ellmann, *Letters of James Joyce*, vol. 2, 177–8.
24 Richards to Joyce, 26 October 1906, in Ellmann, *Letters of James Joyce*, vol. 2, 185.
25 For accounts of Maunsel's activities, see Hutton, "Chapters of Moral History"; and Clare Hutton, "The Extraordinary History of the House of Maunsel," in *The Oxford History of the Irish Book*, ed. Clare Hutton, vol. 5, *The Irish Book in English, 1891–2000* (Oxford: Oxford University Press, 2011), 548–61. For an account of Maunsel in the larger context of publishing in modern Ireland, see Tony Farmar, *The History of Irish Book Publishing* (Stroud: The History Press, 2018). John Nash suggests that one of the effects of Joyce's dealing with Maunsel was his absence in contemporary critical accounts of Irish literature, which could be construed as another form of censorship. John Nash, "'In the Heart of the Hibernian Metropolis'? Joyce's Reception in Ireland, 1900–1940," in *A Companion to James Joyce*, ed. Richard Brown (Oxford: Blackwell, 2008), 108–22.
26 For the best account of the *Playboy* riots, see James Kilroy, *The "Playboy" Riots* (Dublin: Dolmen Press, 1971).
27 Hutton, "Chapters of Moral History," 508.
28 James Joyce, *Occasional, Critical, and Political Writings*, ed. Kevin Barry (Oxford: Oxford University Press, 2000), 153.
29 Richard Ellmann, *James Joyce: New and Revised Edition* (Oxford: Oxford University Press, 1982), 315.
30 Joyce to the Editor, 17 August 1911, in Ellmann, *Letters of James Joyce*, vol. 2, 291–3.
31 Joseph Hone, "A Recollection of James Joyce," *Envoy: An Irish Review of Literature and Art* 5, no. 17 (1951): 44.
32 Ellmann, *James Joyce*, 328.

33 Joyce to the Editor, 17 August 1911, in Ellmann, *Letters of James Joyce*, vol. 2, 291–3.
34 Ellmann, *James Joyce*, 329.
35 Lidwell to Joyce, undated, in Ellmann, *James Joyce*, 330.
36 Stephanie Rains, "'Nauseous Tides of Seductive Debauchery': Irish Story Papers and the Anti-Vice Campaigns of the Early Twentieth Century," *Irish University Review* 45, no. 2 (2015): 269.
37 "Suppression of Immoral Literature," *Irish Times*, 6 July 1912, 12.
38 Lidwell to Joyce, undated, in Ellmann, *James Joyce*, 330.
39 Lidwell to Joyce, 21 August 1912, in Ellmann, *Letters of James Joyce*, vol. 2, 309.
40 Joyce to Roberts, 21 August 1909, in Ellmann, *Letters of James Joyce*, vol. 2, 309.
41 Roberts to Joyce, 23 August 1912, in Ellmann, *Letters of James Joyce*, vol. 2, 313.
42 Roberts to Joyce, 23 August 1912, in Ellmann, *Letters of James Joyce*, vol. 2, 314.
43 James Joyce, "Gas from a Burner," *Pomes Penyeach and Other Verses* (London: Faber and Faber, 1966), 42.
44 Joyce, "Gas from a Burner," 44–5.
45 Ellmann, *James Joyce*, 337.
46 Joyce to W. B. Yeats, 19 September 1912, in Gilbert, *Letters of James Joyce*, vol. 1, 72.
47 Joyce to Yeats, 25 December 1912, in Ellmann, *Letters of James Joyce*, vol. 2, 322.
48 James Joyce, "A Curious History," *Egoist* 1, no. 2 (15 January 1914): 26–7.
49 Joyce to Richards, 16 May 1914, in Ellmann, *Letters of James Joyce*, vol. 2, 334.
50 Michael Groden, "A Textual and Publishing History," in *A Companion to Joyce Studies*, eds. Zach Bowen and James F. Carens (Westport: Greenwood, 1984), 83.
51 Paul Vanderham, *James Joyce and Censorship: The Trials of "Ulysses"* (New York: New York University Press, 1998), 1.
52 Clare Hutton, *Serial Encounters: "Ulysses" and the "Little Review"* (Oxford: Oxford University Press, 2019), 162.
53 Joseph M. Hassett, *The "Ulysses" Trials: Beauty and Truth Meet the Law* (Dublin: The Lilliput Press, 2016), 48.
54 Margaret Anderson, *My Thirty Years' War* (Westport: Greenwood Press, 1971), 175.
55 Vanderham, *James Joyce and Censorship*, 4.
56 Joyce to Frank Budgen, 16 August 1921, in *Selected Letters of James Joyce*, ed. Richard Ellmann (New York: Viking, 1975), 285.

57 See, for example, David Weir, "What Did He Know and When Did He Know It: The *Little Review*, Joyce, and *Ulysses*," *James Joyce Quarterly* 37, nos. 3–4 (2000): 389–412; Vanderham, *James Joyce and Censorship*; Hassett, *The "Ulysses" Trials*; and Hutton, *Serial Encounters*. Katherine Mullin similarly argues that Joyce provoked social purity reformers by depicting them and engaging with the subjects of their work in his oeuvre. See Katherine Mullin, *James Joyce, Sexuality and Social Purity* (Cambridge: Cambridge University Press, 2003). For a survey of Joyce's relationship with the law in a broader sense, in terms of how it functions and is depicted in his oeuvre as well as how it impacted his life, see Jonathan Goldman, ed., *Joyce and the Law* (Gainesville: University Press of Florida, 2017).

58 "Romantic Ireland's Dead and Gone," *Freeman's Journal*, 18 May 1918, 3.

59 *Irish Independent*, 6 May 1918, 5.

60 "Delvin Author's New Book," *Meath Chronicle*, 8 June 1918, 4.

61 "That 'Valley' and Those 'Squinting Windows,'" *Westmeath Examiner*, 22 June 1918, 5.

62 Padraic O'Farrell, *The Burning of Brinsley MacNamara* (Dublin: Lilliput, 1990), 29–30.

63 "Those 'Squinting Windows' and that 'Valley,'" *Westmeath Examiner*, 8 December 1923, 5.

64 "The Westmeath Boycott Case," *Irish Independent*, 6 December 1923, 5.

65 "Westmeath Case," *Freeman's Journal*, 6 December 1923, 9.

66 "'Squinting Windows' Sequel," *Irish Independent*, 7 December 1923, 9.

67 "Schoolmaster and Parish Priest," *Leitrim Observer*, 8 December 1923, 3.

68 "Attacked by a Crowd," *Irish Independent*, 5 December 1905, 4.

69 "That 'Valley' and Those 'Squinting Windows,'" *Westmeath Examiner*, 22 June 1918, 5.

70 "The Westmeath Boycott Case," *Irish Independent*, 6 December 1923, 5.

71 *Meath Chronicle*, 6 July 1918, 4.

72 "Delvin Author's New Book," *Meath Chronicle*, 8 June 1918, 4.

73 "Boycott Charge," *Freeman's Journal*, 5 December 1923, 7.

74 "Boycott Charge," *Freeman's Journal*, 5 December 1923, 7.

75 "That 'Valley' and Those 'Squinting Windows,'" *Westmeath Examiner*, 29 June 1918, 6.

76 *Meath Chronicle*, 6 July 1918, 4.

77 "'Squinting Windows' Sequel," *Irish Independent*, 7 December 1923, 9.

78 "The Valley of the Squinting Windows," *Westmeath Examiner*, 2 August 1919, 8.

79 O'Farrell, *The Burning of Brinsley MacNamara*, 43.

80 Brinsley MacNamara, "Prefatory Note," in *The Valley of the Squinting Windows* (New York: Brentano's, 1919), x.

81 MacNamara, "Prefatory Note," x.
82 MacNamara, "Prefatory Note," xii.
83 MacNamara, "Prefatory Note," xiii.
84 O'Farrell, *The Burning of Brinsley MacNamara*, 41–2.
85 "Attacked by a Crowd," *Irish Independent*, 5 December 1923, 4.
86 "Boycott Charge," *Freeman's Journal*, 5 December 1923, 7.
87 "Judge's Tribute to Parish Priest," *Freeman's Journal*, 8 December 1923, 5.
88 "'Squinting Windows' Sequel," *Irish Independent*, 7 December 1923, 9.
89 "Boycott Charge," *Freeman's Journal*, 5 December 1923, 7.
90 "Attacked by a Crowd," *Irish Independent*, 5 December 1923, 4.
91 "Attacked by a Crowd," *Irish Independent*, 5 December 1923, 4.
92 "Boys' Evidence," *Freeman's Journal*, 7 December 1923, 9.
93 "Attacked by a Crowd," *Irish Independent*, 5 December 1923, 4.
94 "The Westmeath Boycott Case," *Irish Independent*, 6 December 1923, 5.
95 "Westmeath Case," *Freeman's Journal*, 6 December 1923.
96 "The Westmeath Boycott Case," *Irish Independent*, 6 December 1923, 5.
97 "The Westmeath Boycott Case," *Irish Independent*, 6 December 1923, 5.
98 "Westmeath Case," *Freeman's Journal*, 6 December 1923.
99 "Judge's Tribute to Parish Priest," *Freeman's Journal*, 8 December 1923, 5.
100 "Judge's Tribute to Parish Priest," *Freeman's Journal*, 8 December 1923, 5.
101 "'Squinting Windows' Action," *Irish Independent*, 8 December 1923, 8.
102 "An Appeal," *Irish Statesman*, 19 January 1924, 591.
103 A. E. Malone, in O'Farrell, *The Burning of Brinsley MacNamara*, 74.
104 O'Farrell, *The Burning of Brinsley MacNamara*, 75–7.
105 MacNamara continued to satirise Delvin in other books. For more on this, see his novel *The Various Lives of Marcus Igoe* (London: S. Low, Marston & Co., 1929); and Richard T. Murphy, "Monuments of Unageing Embarrassment: Brinsley MacNamara and the Bildungsroman in the Irish Free State," *New Hibernia Review* 17, no. 4 (2013): 74–92.
106 Lennox Robinson, *Curtain Up: An Autobiography* (London: Michael Joseph, 1942), 135.
107 Robinson, *Curtain Up*, 135.
108 Lady Gregory, journal entry, 15 July 1924, in *Lady Gregory's Journals*, ed. Lennox Robinson (New York: Macmillan, 1947), 276.
109 *Irish Statesman*, 5 July 1924, 526.
110 *Irish Statesman*, 12 July 1924, 555.
111 *Irish Statesman*, 16 August 1924, 736.
112 See Oriel Prizeman, *Philanthropy and Light: Carnegie Libraries and the Advent of Transatlantic Standards for Public Space* (Farnham: Ashgate, 2012), 2–4.
113 Brendan Grimes, *Irish Carnegie Libraries: A Catalogue and Architectural History* (Dublin: Irish Academic Press, 1998), 3–5. For a more general

study of libraries in Ireland, see Mary Casteleyn, *A History of Literacy and Libraries in Ireland: The Long Traced Pedigree* (Aldershot: Gower, 1984).

114 Robinson, *Curtain Up*, 84.

115 Robinson, *Curtain Up*, 111.

116 Grimes, *Irish Carnegie Libraries*, 35.

117 Grimes, *Irish Carnegie Libraries*, 34.

118 Grimes, *Irish Carnegie Libraries*, 37.

119 Lady Gregory, 23 September 1924, in Robinson, *Lady Gregory's Journals*, 277.

120 Lady Gregory, 22 October 1924, in Robinson, *Lady Gregory's Journals*, 280.

121 Lady Gregory, 22 October 1924, in Robinson, *Lady Gregory's Journals*, 279.

122 Lady Gregory, 19 November 1924, in Robinson, *Lady Gregory's Journals*, 281.

123 Lauren Arrington, *W. B. Yeats, the Abbey Theatre, Censorship, and the Irish State: Adding the Half-Pence to the Pence* (Oxford: Oxford University Press, 2010), 64–6.

124 "Carnegie Scheme," *Nenagh Guardian*, 3 January 1925, 1.

125 See, for example, his condemnation by a Jesuit priest in "An Explanation," *Connacht Tribune*, 7 February 1925, 13.

126 Robinson, *Curtain Up*, 135.

127 Robinson, *Lady Gregory's Journals*, 272.

128 Ambrose Coleman, "Our Reading Public and the Carnegie Rural Libraries," *Irish Ecclesiastical Record* 25, no. 4 (1925), 366.

129 Coleman, "Our Reading Public and the Carnegie Rural Libraries," 369–70. Original emphases.

130 Coleman, "Our Reading Public and the Carnegie Rural Libraries," 371.

131 Frank O'Connor, *My Father's Son* (New York: Alfred A. Knopf, 1969), 34–5.

132 Hubert Butler, "*The Bell*: An Anglo-Irish View," in *Escape from the Anthill*, ed. Hubert Butler (Mullingar: The Lilliput Press, 1986), 148.

133 Robert Tobin, *The Minority Voice: Hubert Butler and Southern Irish Protestantism, 1900–1991* (Oxford: Oxford University Press, 2012), 43.

134 Benedict Kiely, "The Whores on the Half-doors: Or an Image of the Irish Writer," in *Conor Cruise O'Brien Introduces Ireland*, ed. Owen Dudley Edwards (London: Andre Deutsch, 1969), 151.

4: A Made-in-Ireland Censorship: Polemics and Institutional Formation

1 *Dáil Debates*, vol. 3, no. 9, 3 May 1923.

2 *Dáil Debates*, vol. 3, no. 12, 10 May 1923.

3 Kevin Rockett, *Irish Film Censorship: A Cultural Journey from Silent Cinema to Internet Pornography* (Dublin: Four Courts Press, 2004), 70.

4 *Dáil Debates*, vol. 3, no. 12, 10 May 1923.
5 Censorship of Films Act, 1923, art. 7.2.
6 *Dáil Debates*, vol. 10, no. 22, 3 April 1925.
7 *Dáil Debates*, vol. 11, no. 7, 1 May 1925.
8 *Dáil Debates*, vol. 11, no. 7, 1 May 1925.
9 Rev. R. S. Devane, "Indecent Literature: Some Legal Remedies," *Irish Ecclesiastical Record* 35, no. 2 (1925): 184.
10 Aidan Beatty, "Where Does the State End and the Church Begin?: The Strange Career of Richard S. Devane," *Studi Irlandesi* 9 (2019): 448. For more on Devane, see also Martin Walsh, "Richard Devane: Social Campaigner in the Free State, 1920–51," *Studies: An Irish Quarterly Review* 103, no. 41 (2014/15): 562–73.
11 Devane, "Indecent Literature," 196.
12 Devane, "Indecent Literature," 197.
13 Devane, "Indecent Literature," 198.
14 Devane, "Indecent Literature," 202–3.
15 Devane, "Indecent Literature," 204.
16 *Leader* 50, no. 12 (25 April 1925), 272. See also *Leader* 50, no. 14 (9 May 1925), 319–20; and *Leader* 50, no. 26 (1 August 1925), 621.
17 See Adams, *Censorship*, 15–21.
18 *Leader* 47, no. 24 (19 January 1924), 570.
19 *Leader* 48, no. 20 (1 June 1924), 471; and *Leader* 48, no. 23 (5 July 1924), 521–3.
20 "Irish Vigilance Association," *Leader* 49, no. 26 (24 January 1925), 613.
21 Lauren Arrington, *W. B. Yeats, the Abbey Theatre, Censorship, and the Irish State: Adding the Half-Pence to the Pence* (Oxford: Oxford University Press, 2010), 72.
22 George O'Brien to W. B. Yeats, 5 September 1925, in *A Whirlwind in Dublin: "The Plough and the Stars" Riots*, Robert G. Lowery (Westport: Greenwood Press, 1984), 11.
23 Lady Gregory, journal entry, 2 September 1925, in *Lady Gregory's Journals*, ed. Lennox Robinson (New York: Macmillan, 1947), 87.
24 W. B. Yeats to George O'Brien, 10 September 1925, in Lowery, *A Whirlwind in Dublin*, 13.
25 Lady Gregory, 20 September 1925, in Robinson, *Lady Gregory's Journals*, 87–91.
26 "Sean O'Casey's New Play 'The Plough and the Stars,'" *Irish Independent*, 9 February 1926, 9.
27 Joseph Holloway, journal entry, 8 February 1926, in *Joseph Holloway's Theatre: A Selection from His Unpublished Journal "Impressions of a Dublin Playgoer,"* eds. Robert Hogan and Michael J. O'Neill (Carbondale: Southern Illinois University Press, 1967), 251–2.

28 R. F. Foster, *W. B. Yeats: A Life, II: The Arch-Poet, 1915–1939* (Oxford: Oxford University Press, 2003), 305.
29 "Abbey Theatre Scene," *Irish Times*, 12 February 1926, 7–8.
30 Margaret Ward, *Fearless Woman: Hanna Sheehy-Skeffington, Feminism and the Irish Revolution* (Dublin: University College Dublin Press, 2019), 354.
31 "Abbey Theatre Scene," *Irish Times*, 12 February 1926, 7–8.
32 Denis Johnston, "Seán O'Casey in the Twenties," in *The O'Casey Enigma*, ed. Michael Ó hAodha (Cork: The Mercier Press, 1980), 25–6.
33 W. B. Yeats to Olivia Shakespear, 22 April 1926, in *The Letters of W. B. Yeats*, ed. Allan Wade (London: Rupert Hart-Davis, 1954), 714.
34 Sean O'Casey, *Autobiographies II: Inishfallen, Fare Thee Well, Rose and Crown, Sunset and Evening Star* (London: Macmillan, 1963), 149.
35 Hanna Sheehy-Skeffington to the *Irish Independent*, 15 February 1926, in *The Letters of Sean O'Casey, 1910–41*, vol. 1, ed. David Krause (London: Cassell, 1975), 167–8.
36 Sean O'Casey to the *Irish Independent*, 20 February 1926, in Krause, *The Letters of Sean O'Casey, 1910–41*, 169–71.
37 Joseph Holloway, 1 March 1926, in Hogan and O'Neill, *Joseph Holloway's Theatre*, 266.
38 O'Casey, *Autobiographies II*, 151.
39 Dean, *Riot and Great Anger*, 121.
40 *Report of the Committee on Evil Literature* (Dublin: The Stationery Office, 1927), 3.
41 *Report of the Committee on Evil Literature*, 4.
42 Patrick A. Brett (Honourable Secretary of the IVA) to J. P. Clare, 11 March 1926. NAI, JUS 7/2/14.
43 Judicial Proceedings (Regulation of Reports) Act 1926, 1 (1) (a).
44 "Mr. W. B. Joyce, B. A., Head Master, Central Model Schools, Marlborough Street, representative of the Dublin Branch of the Irish National Teachers' Organization, examined," 21 April 1926. NAI, JUS 7/2/12.
45 "Mr. W. B. Joyce, examined," 21 April 1926. NAI, JUS 7/2/12.
46 This low incidence of youths being corrupted by literature is supported elsewhere. For example, in his testimony, Father Quinlan noted that since being connected with a school in 1909, he had only had one case where the reading materials of a youth were of a bad nature. "Revd. M. Quinlan, S. J., President of the Catholic Headmasters' Association, examined," 21 April 1926. NAI, JUS 7/2/3.
47 "Mr. P. de Burca, of the Catholic Writers' Guild, examined," 28 April 1926. NAI, JUS 7/2/5.
48 *Report of the Committee on Evil Literature*. NAI, JUS 7/3/4.
49 Commissioner of the Garda to the Secretary of the Department of Justice, 17 May 1926. NAI, JUS 7/2/11.

50 *Report of the Committee on Evil Literature*, 7.
51 *Report of the Committee on Evil Literature*, 16.
52 *Report of the Committee on Evil Literature*, 17.
53 *Report of the Committee on Evil Literature*, 17.
54 *Report of the Committee on Evil Literature*, 18.
55 *Report of the Committee on Evil Literature*, 19.
56 *Irish Statesman*, 8 January 1927, 420.
57 *Irish Statesman*, 8 January 1927, 421.
58 "A Censorship Over Literature," *Irish Statesman*, 12 February 1927, 543.
59 "A Censorship Over Literature," 543.
60 "A Censorship Over Literature," 543.
61 Francis (Frank) O'Reilly to William Cosgrave, 6 September 1927. NAI, s5381.
62 The IVA to Patrick Shaw, 14 April 1928. NAI, s5381.
63 For Cosgrave's responses, see Department of the Taoiseach to Francis O'Reilly, 10 September 1927. NAI, s5381; and William Cosgrave to Patrick Shaw, 25 April 1928. NAI, s5381.
64 Meanwhile, the *Irish Statesman* had warned against the possibility of a zealous censorship that would make the country a cultural wasteland. The concern was that adults would be prevented access to challenging subjects because children could mistakenly become the audience. The *Irish Statesman*, 8 January 1927, 420–1. For a more complete understanding of the journal's reaction against the committee's report, see *Irish Statesman*, 12 February 1927, 542–4.
65 David Bradshaw, "James Douglas: The Sanitary Inspector of Literature," in *Prudes on the Prowl: Fiction and Obscenity in England, 1850 to the Present Day*, eds. David Bradshaw and Rachel Potter (Oxford University Press, 2013), 91.
66 Ezra Pound, in David Bradshaw, "James Douglas," 104.
67 David Bradshaw, "James Douglas," 91.
68 "Modern Sex Novelists," *Irish Rosary* 32, no. 2 (February 1928), 142.
69 Robert Kirkwood, "Unclean Literature under Innocent Guises: Indirect Methods of Campaign," *Irish Rosary* 32, no. 4 (April 1928), 281.
70 Kirkwood, "Unclean Literature under Innocent Guises," 286.
71 Kirkwood, "Unclean Literature under Innocent Guises," 287.
72 See, for example, "Evil Literature Bill," *Standard*, 18 August 1928, 10; "The Censorship Bill," *Standard*, 18 August 1928, 12; "The Censorship Bill," *Standard*, 25 August 1928, 12; "The Censorship Bill – A Flaw," *Standard*, 8 September 1928, 12; Delta, "The Evil Literature Bill," *Irish Rosary* 32, no. 9 (September 1928), 705–8; Ch. D., "Notes on the Literature Bill," *Irish Rosary* 32, no. 10 (October 1928), 797–9.
73 *Dáil Debates*, vol. 26, no. 5, 18 October 1928.

74 *Dáil Debates*, vol. 26, no. 5, 18 October 1928.
75 *Dáil Debates*, vol. 26, no. 5, 18 October 1928,
76 *Dáil Debates*, vol. 26, no. 5, 18 October 1928.
77 *Dáil Debates*, vol. 26, no. 5, 18 October 1928.
78 For Ruttledge's and de Valera's comments on the bill, see *Dáil Debates*, vol. 26, no. 5, 18 October 1928. Most surprising for observers of de Valera and his political views was his suggestion that women should be represented on the Censorship Board. This could, of course, be read in two ways: one, he had momentarily revised his famously sexist views and become more egalitarian, or two, he felt that women should be on the Censorship Board because he believed that they were more affected by evil literature owing to their weaker constitutions. If the second were the case, which it probably was, he used false logic because women, being understood as more susceptible to corruption, would therefore become corrupt censors incapable of performing their duties.
79 *Dáil Debates*, vol. 26, no. 5, 18 October 1928.
80 R. S. Devane to Michael Tierney, undated. UCD LA 30/333.
81 *Dáil Debates*, vol. 26, no. 5, 18 October 1928.
82 *Dáil Debates*, vol. 26, no. 5, 18 October 1928.
83 *Dáil Debates*, vol. 26, no. 5, 18 October 1928.
84 *Dáil Debates*, vol. 26, no. 5, 18 October 1928.
85 *Dáil Debates*, vol. 26, no. 5, 18 October 1928.
86 Holograph comments on Censorship of Publications Bill, 1928. UCD LA 30/333.
87 "Vigilance Association on Censorship Bill," *Irish Times*, 4 December 1928, 11.
88 The CTSI to all deputies, 28 November 1928. NAI, s5381.
89 Hugh P. Allen to Michael Tierney, 21 December 1928. UCD LA 30/334.
90 E. J. Gwynn to Michael Tïerney, 8 October 1928. UCD LA 30/334.
91 Irish Women Citizens' and Local Government Association to Michael Tierney, 15 October 1928. UCD LA 30/334.
92 Kilkenny Library Meeting Minutes Book, KLA.
93 "The Shewing Up of Bernard Shaw," *Kilkenny People*, 12 July 1924.
94 "Burned Books," *Connacht Sentinel*, 30 October 1928, 3.
95 See, for example, "Library Books Burned in Galway," *Irish Times*, 31 October 1928, 5.
96 *Dáil Debates*, vol. 27, no. 1, 14 November 1928.
97 Delta, "Flaws in the Censorship Bill," *Irish Rosary* 32, no. 11 (November 1928), 871–5.
98 "The Censorship Bill," *Standard*, 20 October 1928, 12; "False Alarms About the Censorship," *Standard*, 20 October 1928, 13; "Censorship Bill," *Standard*, 27 October 1928, 1; "The Censorship Bill," *Standard*, 27 October 1928, 12.

99 Nicholas Allen argues that the *Irish Statesman*'s engagement in the censorship debates on the side of freedom of expression effectively "redefined its agenda." Nicholas Allen, *George Russell (Æ) and the New Ireland, 1905–30* (Dublin: Four Courts Press, 2003), 202.
100 AE, "The Censorship Bill," *Irish Statesman*, 25 August 1928, 486.
101 G. W. Murray, "The Free State Censorship Bill," *Irish Times*, 1 September 1928, 7.
102 Henry J. Walker, "The Free State Censorship Bill," *Irish Times*, 3 September 1928, 8.
103 See W. F. Trench, "The Free State Censorship Bill," *Irish Times*, 7 September 1928, 5; Gerald Dowse, "The Free State Censorship Bill," *Irish Times*, 8 September 1928, 8; Hugh W. B. Thompson, "The Free State Censorship Bill," *Irish Times*, 7 September 1928, 8; George V. Crook, "The Free State Censorship Bill," *Irish Times*, 10 September 1928, 4.
104 T. C. Keller, "Areopagitica of Milton," *Irish Times*, 7 September 1928, 4.
105 W. B. Yeats, "The Censorship and St. Thomas Aquinas," *Irish Statesman*, 22 September 1928, 47.
106 Yeats, "The Censorship and St. Thomas Aquinas," 47.
107 W. B. Yeats, "The Irish Censorship," *Spectator*, 29 September 1928, 391–2. The fact that Yeats had retired from the Senead only the day before has led Donald R. Pearce to suggest that the article would have probably formed a speech on the subject had Yeats kept his seat. Donald R. Pearce, ed., *The Senate Speeches of W. B. Yeats* (Bloomington: Indiana University Press, 1960), 175.
108 Yeats, "The Irish Censorship," 391.
109 Yeats, "The Irish Censorship," 391.
110 Yeats, "The Irish Censorship," 392.
111 Over the next two months in the pages of the *Spectator*, Yeats's letter elicited several responses, both in agreement and in disagreement.
112 For an excellent survey of modern Irish periodicals, see Frank Shovlin, *The Irish Literary Periodical, 1923–1958* (Oxford: Clarendon Press, 2003). See also Tom Clyde, *Irish Literary Magazines: An Outline History and Descriptive Bibliography* (Dublin: Irish Academic Press, 2002). For studies of *The Bell*, see Kelly Matthews, *"The Bell" Magazine and the Representation of Irish Identity: Opening Windows* (Dublin: Four Courts Press, 2012); Niall Carson, *Rebel by Vocation: Seán O'Faoláin and the Generation of "The Bell"* (Manchester: Manchester University Press, 2016); and Bill Kirwan, "The Social Policy of *The Bell*," *Administration* 37, no. 2 (1989): 99–118.
113 For the most complete study of this subject, see Neil Miller, *Banned in Boston: The Watch and Ward Society's Crusade against Books, Burlesque, and the Social Evil* (Boston: Beacon Press, 2010).

114 Sean O'Faolain, "Censorship in America," *Irish Statesman*, 6 October 1928, 86.
115 O'Faolain, "Censorship in America," 87.
116 AE, "Notes and Comments," *Irish Statesman*, 13 October 1928, 103.
117 AE, "The Debate on the Censorship," *Irish Statesman*, 27 October 1928, 146.
118 AE, "Notes and Comments," *Irish Statesman*, 10 November 1928, 183.
119 Bernard Shaw, "The Censorship," *Irish Statesman*, 17 November 1928, 206–7. Shaw published the same article the day before in England, evidently seeking to damage the reputation of Irish censorship at home and abroad. See "Bernard Shaw Fulminates against the Irish Censorship," *Time and Tide*, 16 November 1928, 1099–1100. *Time and Tide* advertised Shaw's essay above its masthead, ensuring that it received top billing and drew more readers.
120 Shaw, "The Censorship," 207.
121 Shaw, "The Censorship," 207.
122 Shaw, "The Censorship," 208.
123 Shaw, "The Censorship," 208.
124 T. S. Eliot, "Censorship," *Time and Tide*, 23 November 1928, 1131.
125 "Mr. Shaw and the Censorship," *Standard*, 24 November 1928, 12.
126 "Amending the Censorship Bill," *Standard*, 1 December 1928; "Censorship Bogies Again," *Standard*, 19 January 1929.
127 Michael S. Howard, *Jonathan Cape, Publisher: Herbert Jonathan Cape, G. Wren Howard* (London: Jonathan Cape, 1971), 102.
128 Diana Souhami, *The Trials of Radclyffe Hall* (London: Weidenfeld and Nicholson, 1998), 168. For another account of Hall's trial in the larger context of how homosexuality was treated in Britain in her era, see Marc E. Vargo, *Scandal: Infamous Gay Controversies of the Twentieth Century* (London: Routledge, 2003).
129 *Yorkshire Post*, 18 July 1928, 4; *Times Literary Supplement*, 19 July 1928, 528.
130 Richard King, "With Silent Friends," *Tatler*, 15 August 1928, 298; and Orlo Williams, "New Novels," *Times Literary Supplement*, 2 August 1928, 557.
131 James Douglas, review of *The Well of Loneliness*, by Radclyffe Hall, *Sunday Express*, 19 August 1928. Reprinted in Vera Brittain, *Radclyffe Hall: A Case of Obscenity?* (London: Femina, 1968) 57.
132 Douglas, review of *The Well of Loneliness*, 54.
133 Douglas, review of *The Well of Loneliness*, 56.
134 He was not alone in seeing some correspondence. See letters to the editor by Clifford Bax and Hugh Walpole, "A Modern Mother," *Time and Tide*, 23 November 1928, 1131–2.
135 Douglas, review of *The Well of Loneliness*, 57.
136 "A Much-Discussed Book," *Northern Daily Mail*, 23 August 1928, 3.

137 "Ban on Novel of Sex Perversion," *Leeds Mercury*, 24 August 1928, 5.
138 "The Press Ban Battle," *Daily Herald*, 8 September 1928, 2.
139 "Shaw and Wells in Banned Book Battle," *Daily Herald*, 6 October 1928, 1.
140 Brittain, *Radclyffe Hall*, 91.
141 "*The Well of Loneliness*," *Nottingham Evening Post*, 8 October 1928, 8.
142 "'Jix,' the Silent Censor," *Daily Herald*, 1 October 1928, 5. "Jix" was the nickname of Joynson-Hicks.
143 "'Jix' Breaks His Silence," *Daily Herald*, 16 October 1928, 1.
144 See, for example, "Publication Ceased," *Cork Examiner*, 24 August 1928, 2; and "Publication Stopped," *Belfast News-Letter*, 24 August 1928, 11.
145 "*The Well of Loneliness*," *Evening Herald*, 5 October 1928, 1.
146 William O'Malley, "Book Reviews," *Independent*, 15 September 1928, 5.
147 *Dáil Debates*, vol. 26, no. 6, 19 October 1928. Byrne misidentified Flaubert's novel, referring to it as *Sappho*.
148 "*The Well of Loneliness*," *Northern Whig and Belfast Post*, 20 October, 1928, 7.
149 "Banned Book Development," *Leeds Mercury*, 25 October 1928, 7; "Book that Was Seized," *Derby Daily Telegraph*, 30 October 1928, 7.
150 "Well of Loneliness," *Midland Daily Telegraph*, 9 November 1928.
151 "Banned Book," *Northern Daily Mail*, 9 November 1928.
152 "The Banned Book," *Daily Mail*, 16 November 1928, 14.
153 "Copies to Be Destroyed," *Daily Mail*, 14 November 1928, 5.
154 See, for example, "Books Seized," *Evening Herald*, 9 November 1928; "Well of Loneliness," *Evening Herald*, 16 November 1928, 4; "*The Well of Loneliness*," *Cork Examiner*, 23 November 1928, 6; and "*The Well of Loneliness*," *Cork Examiner*, 24 November 1928, 11.
155 "Woman Novelist's Book Seized," *Liverpool Echo*, 21 February 1929, 12.
156 "Police Seize a First Novel," *Western Morning News and Mercury*, 22 February 1929, 7.
157 "*The Sleeveless Errand*," *Birmingham Gazette*, 22 February 1929, 1.
158 See, for example, "London Police Raid," *Cork Examiner*, 22 February 1929, 8; and "The Seized Novel," *Belfast News-Letter*, 25 February 1929, 11. The former also includes transcripts of the Dáil censorship debates on the same page, thereby inviting readers to draw links between the two events.
159 "Books and Manuscript (Seizure)," *Hansard*, 28 February 1929.
160 "'Degrading Muck,'" *Daily Echo*, 4 March 1929.
161 "Seized Book to Be Destroyed," *Birmingham Gazette*, 5 March 1929, 1.
162 Norah C. James, *I Lived in a Democracy* (London: Longmans, 1939), 227.
163 Eric Partridge, *The First Three Years: An Account and a Biography of the Scholartis Press* (London: Scholartis Press, 1930), 24.
164 See Neil Pearson, *Obelisk: A History of Jack Kahane and the Obelisk Press* (Liverpool: University of Liverpool Press, 2007).

165 See John de St. Jorre, *Venus Bound: The Erotic Voyage of the Olympia Press* (New York: Random House, 1996).
166 Jack Kahane, *Memoirs of a Booklegger* (London: M. Joseph, 1939), 223–4.
167 Edward Garnett, preface to *Sleeveless Errand*, by Norah C. James (Paris: Henry Babou and Jack Kahane, 1929), 3.
168 See, for example, Celia Marshik, "History's 'Abrupt Revenges': Censoring War's Perversions in *The Well of Loneliness* and *Sleeveless Errand*," *Journal of Modern Literature*, 26, no. 2 (2003): 145–59; and Angela Ingram, "'Unutterable Putrefaction' and 'Foul Stuff': Two 'Obscene' Novels of the 1920s," *Women's Studies International Forum*, 9 (1986): 341–54. Katrina Rolley argues that Hall's novel was in fact conceived as a response to censorship, in effect depicting the unmentionable in writing about homosexuality, and yet not explicitly mentioning the subject. See Katrina Rolley, "The Treatment of Homosexuality and *The Well of Loneliness*," in *Writing and Censorship in Britain*, eds. Paul Hyland and Neil Sammells (London: Routledge, 2023), 219–31.
169 *Dáil Debates*, vol. 28, no. 2, 21 February 1929.
170 *Dáil Debates*, vol. 28, no. 4, 27 February 1929.
171 *Dáil Debates*, vol. 28, no. 5, 28 February 1929.
172 *Seanad Debates*, vol. 12, no. 1, 10 April 1929.
173 *Seanad Debates*, vol. 12, no. 2, 11 April 1929.
174 *Seanad Debates*, vol. 12, no. 2, 11 April 1929.
175 For Keane's opening speech, see *Seanad Debates*, vol. 12, no. 2, 11 April 1929.
176 *Seanad Debates*, vol. 12, no. 5, 25 April 1929.
177 Delta, "The Fraud of the Censorship Bill," *Irish Rosary* 33, no. 5 (May 1929), 390–2.
178 "The Censorship Bill," *Standard*, 9 March 1929, 10; "The Censorship Bill," *Standard*, 20 April 1929, 12; "The Censorship Bill," *Standard*, 22 June 1929, 12.
179 "Amendment of the Censorship Bill," *Standard*, 2 March 1929, 10.
180 "The Censorship Act," *Standard*, 20 July 1929, 10.
181 "Notes and Comments," *Irish Statesman*, 9 February 1929, 447.
182 "Notes and Comments," *Irish Statesman*, 30 March 1929, 64.
183 "Dail and the Censorship," *Irish Statesman*, 13 July 1929, 366.
184 "Dail and the Censorship," 367.
185 Censorship of Publications Act, 1929, art. 2.
186 Censorship of Publications Act, 1929, art. 3 (1–2).
187 Censorship of Publications Act, 1929, art. 6 (1).
188 Censorship of Publications Act, 1929, art. 6 (3) a–e.
189 Censorship of Publications Act, 1929, art. 6 (6).
190 Censorship of Publications Act, 1929, art. 7 (5).

191 Censorship of Publications Act, 1929, art. 8 (1).
192 Censorship of Publications Act, 1929, arts. 10 (2), 15 (1), 16 (2), 17 (2), 18 (1).
193 Censorship of Publications Act, 1929, art. 14 (1), (2).
194 See also Andrew Murphy, *Ireland, Reading and Cultural Nationalism, 1790–1930: Bringing the Nation to Book* (Cambridge: Cambridge University Press, 2018), 172.
195 For more on this subject, see Colette Colligan, *A Publisher's Paradise: Expatriate Literary Culture in Paris, 1890–1960* (Amherst: University of Massachusetts Press, 2014).

5: A Made-in-Ireland Resistance: The Rise and Fall of the Irish Academy of Letters

1 "Decadent Literature," *Catholic Mind* 1, no. 1 (January 1930): 4.
2 Peter P. Curry, "The Thing Called Realism," *Catholic Mind* 1, no. 3 (March 1930): 68.
3 Michael Walsh, "Catholics and Literature," *Catholic Mind* 1, no. 7 (July 1930): 185.
4 "The Foreign Press Menace," *Catholic Mind* 1, no. 4 (April 1930): 92–3; "The British Press Menace," *Catholic Mind* 1, no. 4 (April 1930): 101.
5 "Working the Censorship Act," *Catholic Mind* 1, no. 5 (May 1930): 132–3.
6 Francis O'Reilly to the Minister for Justice, 8 October 1930. NAI, s2325.
7 The Department of Justice to Francis O'Reilly, 19 October 1930. NAI, s2325.
8 Francis O'Reilly to William Cosgrave, 25 October 1929. NAI, s2325.
9 James Fitzgerald-Kenney to William Cosgrave, 5 November 1929. NAI, s2325.
10 Department of Justice Internal Memorandum, 8 November 1929. NAI, s2325.
11 George Sylvester Viereck to William Cosgrave, 17 November 1930. NAI, s2323.
12 James Fitzgerald-Kenney to William Cosgrave, 11 December 1930. NAI, s2323.
13 William Cosgrave to George Sylvester Viereck, 29 January 1931. NAI, s2323.
14 George Sylvester Viereck to William Cosgrave, 10 February 1931. NAI, s2323.
15 *Annual Report of the Censorship of Publications Board for the Year Ending 31st March 1931*. NAI, s2324.
16 Register of Prohibited Publications (Books) as on the 31st March 1931. NAI, JUS 90/102/231.

17 *Annual Report of the Censorship of Publications Board for the Year Ending 31st March 1931*. NAI, s2324.
18 The numbers provided here for formal complaints are based upon those that exist in the government files kept in the National Archives of Ireland. Because of the incomplete nature of the archives, one cannot assume that these are the correct final totals, but they illustrate the point made in the Censorship of Publications Board's first annual report that the CTSI was responsible for most formal complaints.
19 Complaint form, 10 November 1930. NAI, H315/36; complaint form, 3 March 1931. NAI, H315/51; and complaint form, 4 May 1931. NAI, H315/65.
20 Complaint form, 22 July 1935. NAI, 90/102/61.
21 Complaint form, 22 July 1935. NAI, 90/102/62.
22 Complaint form, 2 November 1931. NAI, H315/88.
23 Complaint form, 11 August 1933. NAI, H315/148.
24 Complaint form, 28 March 1934. NAI, 90/102/27.
25 Complaint form, 26 March 1936. NAI, 90/102/80.
26 Complaint form, 5 April 1937. NAI, 90/102/110.
27 Complaint form, 13 August 1937. NAI, 90/102/115.
28 Complain form, 8 October 1930. NAI, H315/9.
29 O'Reilly was appointed the Congress's director of organisation in January 1930. Canon Boylan, ed., *The Book of the Congress* (Dublin: n.p., 1934), 2.
30 Complaint form, 7 March 1931. NAI, H315/57.
31 Complaint form, 11 February 1932. NAI, H315/107.
32 Complaint form, 1 December 1931. NAI, H315/90.
33 The complaint against Rearden Conner's *Shake Hands with the Devil* similarly has no comments but many cited pages. See complaint form, 4 October 1933. NAI H315/151.
34 Sean O'Faolain to the Department of Justice, 18 November 1935. NAI, H315/114.
35 Department of Justice to Sean O'Faolain, 5 December 1935. NAI, H315/114.
36 Memorandum by S. A. Roche. NAI, H315/31.
37 P. J. Melia to the Department of Justice, 11 February 1931; Department of Justice to P. J. Melia, 16 February 1931. NAI, H315/47.
38 Sean O'Faolain to Edward Garnett, n.d. (likely the end of July 1931). Garnett Collection, Box 11, Folder 6, HRC.
39 Edward Garnett, foreword to *Midsummer Night Madness*, by Sean O'Faolain (London: Jonathan Cape, 1932), 11.
40 His mother, Olivia Narney Singleton, was born in County Wexford. Helen Smith, *An Uncommon Reader: A Life of Edward Garnett, Mentor and Editor of Literary Genius* (New York: Farrar, Straus and Giroux, 2017), 4.

41 Garnett, foreword, 12.
42 Garnett, foreword, 13.
43 Garnett, foreword, 13–14.
44 Garnett, foreword, 14–15.
45 Garnett, foreword, 16.
46 Liam O'Flaherty to Edward Garnett, 29 February 1932, in *The Letters of Liam O'Flaherty*, ed. A. A. Kelly (Dublin: Wolfhound Press, 1996), 256.
47 Smith, *An Uncommon Reader*, 339.
48 T. C. Murray, "Stories of Irish Revolt," *Irish Independent*, 7 March 1932, 4.
49 For the former, see *Irish Times*, 12 March 1932, 5.
50 Austin Clarke, review of *Midsummer Night Madness*, *Times Literary Supplement*, 3 March 1932, 152.
51 Frank O'Connor, review of *Midsummer Night Madness*, *Dublin Magazine* 7, no. 2 (April–June 1932): 87.
52 The complaint form, after the twenty-fifth page is noted, simply indicates "etc.," which could mean either that more are marked in the book but not listed on the form or that the Censorship Board was invited to simply continue reading and find more problematic passages for themselves. The NAI's dossiers do not include the copies of the submitted, marked-up books.
53 For a study of the aesthetics of *Midsummer Night Madness*, see Paul Delaney, *Seán O'Faoláin: Literature, Inheritance and the 1930s* (Dublin: Irish Academic Press, 2014), 153–75.
54 The provisional council held its first meeting on 14 September 1932. W. B. Yeats to Bernard Shaw, 15 September 1932. NLI MS 30, 565.
55 "Academy of Immorality," *Catholic Mind* 3, no. 11 (November 1932): 247.
56 By the end of January 1933, Yeats had collected £700 for the Academy. W. B. Yeats to Olivia Shakespear, 29 January 1933, in *The Letters of W. B. Yeats*, ed. Allan Wade (London: Rupert Hart-Davis, 1954), 804. Yeats raised much of this money on a lecture tour of the United States in late 1932. W. B. Yeats to George Russell, 21 December 1932. NLI MS 27, 887.
57 Bernard Shaw to W. B. Yeats, 20 September 1932, in *Bernard Shaw: Collected Letters, 1926–1950*, ed. Dan H. Laurence (New York: Max Reinhardt, 1988), 308–9. Despite his protests, Shaw was unanimously elected president at the first AGM. He and Yeats were the only people to hold the offices of president and vice-president in the Academy's initial years. Shaw's final resignation as president was accepted at the AGM on 24 September 1940. At the AGM on 3 October 1945, Shaw was elected life president, a position he held until his death in 1950. See the Academy's General Meeting Minutes Book. NLI MS 33,745/1.
58 Stanley Weintraub, *Shaw's People: From Victoria to Churchill* (University Park: Pennsylvania State University Press, 1996), 112.

59 Invitation from W. B. Yeats and Bernard Shaw to potential members to join the Irish Academy of Letters. NLI MS 31,015.

60 George Russell to W. B. Yeats, 17 October 1932, in, *Letters to W. B. Yeats*, vol. 2, eds. Richard Finneran et al. (London: Macmillan, 1977), 546. Russell summarises here "a very nice letter" he had received from Hyde.

61 T. C. Murray to George Russell, 28 September 1932. NLI MS 27,888 (4).

62 T. C. Murray to George Russell, 3 October 1932. NLI MS 27,888 (4).

63 Yeats to Joyce, 2 September 1932, in Wade, *The Letters of W. B. Yeats*, 800–1.

64 Joyce to Yeats, 5 October 1932, in Gilbert, *Letters of James Joyce*, vol. 1, 325.

65 "Joyce Rejects Bid of Irish Academy," *New York Times*, 28 October 1932, 17.

66 Lord Dunsany to George Russell, 2 October 1932. NLI MS 27,888 (2).

67 The IAL to Lord Dunsany, 29 November 1934. NLI MS 27,888 (2).

68 On the Abbey's rejection of *The Silver Tassie*, see Christopher Murray, *Seán O'Casey: Writer at Work* (Montréal: McGill-Queen's University Press, 2004), 200–5. For an excellent account of O'Casey and Shaw's relationship, see Eileen O'Casey, *Cheerio, Titan: The Friendship between George Bernard Shaw and Eileen and Sean O'Casey* (New York: Charles Scribner's Sons, 1989).

69 Sean O'Casey, letter to the editor, *Irish Times*, 11 October 1932, 4. The original sent to the Academy contains some minor differences. See Sean O'Casey to the press, 4 October 1932. NLI MS 37, 976.

70 AE remarked that O'Casey "is not a person to be met in ordinary controversy. He is like one of those fighters who keep to no rules, but bite, kick in the stomach and try to gouge out the eyes of the person they fight with." George Russell to W. B. Yeats, 17 October 1932, in Finneran et al., *Letters to W. B. Yeats*, 547.

71 Murray, *Seán O'Casey*, 220.

72 Bernard Shaw, *The Adventures of the Black Girl in Her Search for God* (London: Constable, 1932), 7.

73 Shaw, *The Adventures of the Black Girl*, 57.

74 Leon Hugo, *Bernard Shaw's "The Black Girl in Search of God": The Story Behind the Story* (Gainesville: University Press of Florida, 2003), 58–9.

75 "Bee-Keepers and G. B. S.," *Irish Times*, 30 December 1932, 8.

76 "Wexford Beekeepers and George Bernard Shaw," *Free Press* (Wexford), 31 December 1932, 4.

77 "Wexford Beekeepers and George Bernard Shaw," *Free Press* (Wexford), 31 December 1932, 4.

78 "A Good Year for Honey," *Free Press* (Wexford), 31 December 1932, 5.

79 "Bee-Keepers and G. B. S.," *Irish Times*, 27 January 1933, 5.

80 "Bee-Keepers and G. B. S.," *Irish Times*, 27 January 1933, 5.

81 "Shaw the 'Prophet,'" *Times Literary Supplement*, 8 December 1932, 939.

82 John Farleigh, *Graven Image: An Autobiographical Textbook* (London: Macmillan, 1940), 369.
83 George Russell to P. J. Ruttledge, 22 May 1933. NAI, H315/43.
84 Internal memorandum from the Department of Justice to B. MacMahon, Secretary of the Censorship Board. NAI, H315/43. MacMahon's response is scrawled in the space beneath it.
85 D. de Brun to George Russell, 24 May 1933. NAI, H315/43.
86 George Russell to P. J. Ruttledge, 26 May 1933. NAI, H315/43.
87 Bernard Shaw to W. B. Yeats, 18 May 1933, in Laurence *Bernard Shaw: Collected Letters, 1926–1950*, 339–40.
88 R. F. Foster, *W. B. Yeats: A Life, II*, 452.
89 Bernard Shaw to W. B. Yeats, 4 September 1933, in Laurence, *Bernard Shaw: Collected Letters, 1926–1950*, 352–3.
90 B. MacMahon to the Department of Justice, 3 July 1933. NAI, H315/43.
91 Department of Justice to B. MacMahon, 4 July 1933. NAI, H315/43.
92 Department of Justice to B. MacMahon, 4 July 1933. NAI, H315/43.
93 C. A. Maguire to the Secretary of the Department of Justice, 24 July 1933. NAI, H315/43.
94 Internal memorandum, Department of Justice, 24 July 1933. NAI, H315/43.
95 F. R. Higgins to P. J. Ruttledge, 18 July 1933. NAI, H315/43.
96 F. R. Higgins to P. J. Ruttledge, 26 July 1933. NAI, H315/43.
97 D. de Brun to F. R. Higgins, 1 August 1933. NAI, H315/43.
98 F. R. Higgins to P. J. Ruttledge, 9 August 1933. NAI, H315/43.
99 D. de Brun to F. R. Higgins, 18 August 1933. NAI, H315/43.
100 D. de Brun to F. R. Higgins, 18 August 1933. NAI, H315/43.
101 W. B. Yeats to Bernard Shaw, 30 July 1933. NLI MS 31,020.
102 Bernard Shaw to Floryan Sobienioski, 24 July 1933, in Laurence, *Bernard Shaw: Collected Letters, 1926–1950*, 347–8.
103 Bernard Shaw to W. B. Yeats, 4 September 1933, in Laurence, *Bernard Shaw: Collected Letters, 1926–1950*, 352–3.
104 "The Academy and Censorship," *Catholic Mind* 4, no. 8 (August 1933): 145.
105 "Shaw and Yeats and Their Tribe," *Catholic Bulletin* 23, no. 9 (September 1933): 693–6.
106 Irish Academy of Letter's Annual General Meeting Minutes Book. NLI MS 33,745/1.
107 Sean O'Faolain, *Vive Moi!* (Boston: Little and Brown, 1964), 350–68.
108 Bernard Shaw to W. B. Yeats, 14 January 1934, in Laurence, *Bernard Shaw: Collected Letters, 1926–1950*, 360–1. The IAL continued to function into the 1980s, largely as an awarding body for literary merit and a social hub for writers. Sporadic records of its activities are found in the NLI MS 33,745 and NLI MS 33,746 series.

6: International Networking: Establishing Irish PEN

1 For Dawson Scott's life story, see Marjorie Watts, *Mrs Sappho: The Life of C. A. Dawson Scott, "Mother of International P.E.N."* (London: Duckworth, 1987).

2 For more on the internationalism of the League of Nations, see Ruth B. Henig, *The League of Nations* (London: Haus, 2010); and Helen McCarthy, *The British People and the League of Nations: Democracy, Citizenship and Internationalism, c. 1918–45* (Manchester: Manchester University Press, 2011).

3 R. A. Wilford, "The PEN Club, 1930–50," *Journal of Contemporary History* 14, no. 1 (January 1979): 99.

4 Marjorie Watts, *P.E.N.: The Early Years, 1921–1926* (London: Archive Press, 1971).

5 Hermon Ould, *John Galsworthy* (London: Chapman & Hall, 1934), 74.

6 See Megan Doherty, *PEN International and Its Republic of Letters, 1921–1970* (PhD diss., Columbia University, 2011).

7 Watts, *P.E.N.*, 13.

8 Watts, *Sappho*, 125–6; and Watts *P.E.N.*, 27–8

9 Watts, *Sappho*, 154.

10 Watts, *P.E.N.*, 18–20.

11 Doherty, *PEN International*, 391; and Rachel Potter, "Modernist Rights: International PEN 1921–1936," *Critical Quarterly* 55, no. 2 (July 2013): 72.

12 Ould, *John Galsworthy*, 85.

13 Doherty, *PEN International*, 385.

14 Carles Torner and Jan Martens, eds., *PEN International: An Illustrated History* (London: Thames & Hudson, 2021), 39–63. The notion of "supra-political" refers to PEN's advocacy of universal human rights.

15 Ould, *John Galsworthy*, 77.

16 Mike Nellis, "John Galsworthy's *Justice*," *British Journal of Criminology* 36, no. 1 (1996): 61–84.

17 Wilford, "The PEN Club, 1930–50," 100.

18 Ould, *John Galsworthy*, 91.

19 Michael S. Howard, *Jonathan Cape, Publisher: Herbert Jonathan Cape, G. Wren Howard* (London: Jonathan Cape, 1971), 107.

20 "P.E.N. and Censorship," *PEN News*, 4–5.

21 James Gindin suggests that Galsworthy intervened on behalf of such writers, but he offers no evidence, anecdotal or otherwise. James Gindin, *John Galsworthy's Life and Art: An Alien's Fortress* (Ann Arbor, MI: University of Michigan Press, 1987), 425.

22 Watts, *P.E.N.*, 20. In a rather hagiographic account of Irish PEN, Deirdre Brady suggests that Lady Gregory hosted informal PEN meetings at a

Dublin café, but the only evidence that she offers for this is a website that appears to have been run by the café's owners and that, as of November 2024, was inaccessible. See Deirdre Brady, "'Writers and the International Spirit': Irish PEN in the Postwar Years," *New Hibernia Review* 21.3 (2017): 117.

23 Law to Ould, 29 July 1929. Box 30, Folder 6. HRC PEN.
24 Ould to Law, 15 August 1929. Box 30, Folder 6. HRC PEN.
25 Ould to Law, 10 September, 1929. Box 50, Folder 5. HRC PEN.
26 Law to Ould, 13 September 1929. Box 30, Folder 6. HRC PEN.
27 Law to Ould, 7 December 1929. Box 50, Folder 5. HRC PEN.
28 Law to Ould, 6 April 1930. Box 50, Folder 5. HRC PEN.
29 Membership List, Dublin Centre, 1930–1. Box 78, Folder 12. HRC PEN.
30 Law to Ould, 30 April 1930. Box 50, Folder 5. HRC PEN.
31 Ould to Law, 2, 22, and 28 May 1930. Box 50, Folder 5. HRC PEN.
32 Ould to Law, 29 April 1930. Box 50, Folder 5. HRC PEN.
33 Ould to Law, 10 December 1930. Box 50, Folder 5. HRC PEN.
34 Law to Ould, 28 May 1931. Box 50, Folder 5. HRC PEN.
35 Ould to O'Faolain, 4 March 1932. Box 40, Folder 1. HRC PEN.
36 Ould to O'Faolain, 22 March 1932. Box 40, Folder 1. HRC PEN.
37 O'Faolain to Ould, 23 March 1932. Box 40, Folder 1. HRC PEN.
38 Ould to O'Faolain, 30 March 1932. Box 40, Folder 1. HRC PEN.
39 Ould to O'Faolain, 9 January 1934. Box 40, Folder 1. HRC PEN.
40 O'Faolain to Ould, 10 January 1934. Box 40, Folder 1. HRC PEN.
41 Ould to O'Faolain, 17 May 1934. Box 50, Folder 5. HRC PEN.
42 O'Faolain to Ould, Whit Monday, 21 May 1934. Box 50, Folder 5. HRC PEN.
43 Ould to O'Faolain, 25 May 1934. Box 50, Folder 5. HRC PEN.
44 O'Faolain to Ould, 23 October 1934, Irish Centre (Dublin) to PEN, 1929–34. HRC PEN.
45 O'Faolain to Ould, undated, Irish Centre (Dublin) to PEN, 1929–34. HRC PEN.
46 *Report of the General Meeting*, Dublin P.E.N. Club, Mansion House, 20 November 1935. Dublin Centre to PEN, 1935–53. HRC PEN.
47 H. G. Wells, *The Idea of a League of Nations* (Boston: The Atlantic Monthly Press, 1919). Wells is cited as the lead author; it was written in collaboration with Viscount Grey, Lionel Curtis, William Archer, H. Wickham Steed, A. E. Zimmern, J. A. Spender, Viscount Bryce, and Gilbert Murray.
48 "Editorial," *PEN News*, May 1933, 2–3.
49 Branko Matan, ed., *Speak Now or Never: The 1933 Dubrovnik PEN Club Congress* (Croatian PEN Centre: Zagreb–Dubrovnik, 1993), 28.
50 *Report of 1933 Dubrovnik Congress*. Box 82, Folder 1. HRC PEN.
51 *New York Times*, 22 May 1933. Reprinted in Matan, *Speak Now or Never*, 43.

52 "Mr. Wells's Speech at the Opening of the Jugo-Slav Congress," *PEN News*, June 1933, 2–3. See also the summary of his speech in Box 82, Folder 1. HRC PEN.
53 Minutes of the PEN Meeting, 26 May 1933. Box 82, Folder 1. HRC PEN.
54 Torner and Martens, eds., *PEN International*, 50.
55 "Editorial," *PEN News*, November 1933, 2.
56 "Provisional Committee for the Foundation of the German Library of the Burned Books," *PEN News*, March 1934, 4.
57 List of Resolutions Proposed. Box 82, Folder 3. HRC PEN.
58 Proceedings of the Edinburgh Congress. Box 82, Folder 4, 4–7. HRC PEN.
59 Proceedings of the Edinburgh Congress. Box 82, Folder 4, 29–43. HRC PEN.
60 Proceedings of the Edinburgh Congress. Box 82, Folder 4, 122–31. HRC PEN.
61 *Rules of the Dublin Centre*. Box 142, Folder 2. HRC PEN.
62 O'Faolain to Ould, 18 January 1935. Box 50, Folder 6. HRC PEN.
63 "Trials of a Humorist," *Irish Times*, 31 October 1935, 8.
64 "Censorship in the Free State," *Irish Times*, 14 November 1935, 8.
65 PEN to Irish Centre, 1935–53, Ould to Andrew Malone, 5 December 1935. Box 50, Folder 5. HRC PEN.
66 "Freedom of Expression," *PEN News*, September 1935, 4.
67 Proposition des Centres anglais et américain. Box 82, Folder 6. HRC PEN.
68 PEN Dublin Centre Minute Book, 1935–51. Irish PEN Papers. NLI MS 49143/4.
69 Frank O'Connor, "A Protest," *Irish Times*, 21 September 1936.
70 Lynn Doyle, "A Protest," *Irish Times*, 22 September 1936; and Andrew Malone, "A Protest," *Irish Times*, 24 September 1936.
71 Sean O'Faolain, "The Dangers of Censorship," *Ireland To-Day* 1.6 (November 1936): 57–63. Reprinted in Brad Kent, ed., *The Selected Essays of Sean O'Faolain* (McGill-Queen's University Press, 2016), 90–6.
72 O'Faolain, "The Dangers of Censorship," 90–1.
73 Secretary's Report, 19 November 1936. PEN Dublin Centre Minute Book, 1935–51. Irish PEN Papers. NLI MS 49143/4.
74 Meeting of 20 November 1936, Censorship of Publications Board, Minute Book 1, 1930–42, IFCO.
75 Meeting of 20 November 1936, Censorship of Publications Board, Minute Book 1, 1930-1942, IFCO. The emphasis is the Censorship Board's.
76 Meeting of 20 November 1936, Censorship of Publications Board, Minute Book 1, 1930-1942, IFCO.
77 Meeting of 20 November 1936, Censorship of Publications Board, Minute Book 1, 1930-1942, IFCO.

78 Ould to Malone, 11 January 1937. PEN to Irish Centre, 1935–53. HRC PEN. O'Faolain tendered his resignation from PEN in a letter that was read at the committee meeting on 26 November 1938. PEN Dublin Centre Minute Book, 1935–51. Irish PEN Papers. NLI MS 49143/4. I have yet to find the letter. On Hackett's resignation, see the submitted contribution for *PEN News*, 12 November 1937. Box 50, Folder 6. HRC PEN.

7: Insularity and Reform: Irish PEN in the War Years

1 Undated *PEN News* contribution. Box 50, Folder 6. HRC PEN.
2 *Report of the Honorary Secretary at the AGM*, 12 October 1940. Irish PEN Papers. NLI MS 49143/4.
3 Report for *PEN News*. Box 50, Folder 4. HRC PEN.
4 Morton to Ould, 7 November 1940. Box 50, Folder 4. HRC PEN.
5 Ould to Morton, 14 November 1940. Box 50, Folder 3. HRC PEN.
6 For a study of the effects of neutrality on life in Ireland, see Clair Wills, *That Neutral Island: A Cultural History of Ireland during the Second World War* (Cambridge, MA: Harvard University Press, 2007).
7 Ould to Harris, 30 September 1939. Box 50, Folder 5. HRC PEN.
8 My understanding of wartime censorship in Ireland – and this paragraph in particular – has been informed by the most detailed discussion of the subject: Donal Ó Drisceoil, *Censorship in Ireland, 1939–1945: Neutrality Politics and Society* (Cork: Cork University Press, 1996).
9 Ould to Harris, 14 March 1940. PEN to Irish Centre, 1935–53. HRC PEN.
10 Ould to Morton, 25 February 1941. Box 50, Folder 3. HRC PEN.
11 Morton to Ould, 17 February 1941. Box 50, Folder 4. HRC PEN.
12 For an excellent study of the effects of wartime censorship on Irish literature, see Anna Teekell, *Emergency Writing: Irish Literature, Neutrality, and the Second World War* (Evanston, IL: Northwestern University Press, 2018).
13 Dorothy Day to Ould, 8 May 1941. Box 50, Folder 6. HRC PEN.
14 Ould to Dorothy Day, 21 May 1941. PEN to Irish Centre, 1935–53. HRC PEN.
15 Harris to Ould, 23 July 1941. Box 50, Folder 6. HRC PEN.
16 Ould to Harris, 1 August 1941. Box 50, Folder 5. HRC PEN.
17 "Editorial," *P.E.N. News*, April 1940, 3.
18 These included Canada, Portugal, Poland, the USSR, Chile, China, Australia, Greece, Turkey, Switzerland, New Zealand, India, South Africa, the United States, Yugoslavia, the Netherlands, Egypt, and Ireland. List of Participants. Box 82, Folder 2. HRC PEN.

19 London PEN, Statement Arising out of the Present Situation. Box 86, Folder 2. HRC PEN. With some differences, this was originally published under the title "Statement arising out of the present situation" in the October 1939 issue of *P.E.N. News*.
20 *P.E.N. News*, January–February 1942, 17.
21 Austin Clarke to Ould, 3 March 1942, 3 March 1942. Box 50, Folder 7. HRC PEN.
22 Ould to Clarke, 9 March 1942. Box 50, Folder 5. HRC PEN.
23 Ould to Clarke, 7 April 1942. Box 50, Folder 5. HRC PEN.
24 Clarke to Ould, 11 April 1942. Box 50, Folder 7. HRC PEN.
25 Ould to Clarke, 11 May 1942. Box 50, Folder 5. HRC PEN.
26 AGM, 15 November 1941. PEN Dublin Centre Minute Book, 1935–51. Irish PEN Papers. NLI MS 49143/4.
27 Committee Meeting, 16 January 1942. PEN Dublin Centre Minute Book, 1935–51. Irish PEN Papers. NLI MS 49143/4.
28 Committee Meeting, 24 April 1942. PEN Dublin Centre Minute Book, 1935–51. Irish PEN Papers. NLI MS 49143/4.
29 "Book Censorship," *Irish Times*, 1 June 1942. 2.
30 Committee Meeting, 11 June 1942. PEN Dublin Centre Minute Book, 1935–51. Irish PEN Papers. NLI MS 49143/4.
31 Committee Meeting, 25 September 1942. PEN Dublin Centre Minute Book, 1935–51. Irish PEN Papers. NLI MS 49143/4.
32 Committee Meeting, 23 October 1942. PEN Dublin Centre Minute Book, 1935–51. Irish PEN Papers. NLI MS 49143/4.
33 Meeting Minutes, 11 December 1942. Censorship of Publications Board, Minute Book 2, 1942–51. IFCO. The letter, written by Sears, is included in its entirety.
34 Sean O'Faolain, "Letter to the Editor," *Irish Times*, 19 October 1942, 3. O'Faolain continued his attacks during the debates, which he followed closely. See Sean O'Faolain, "Letter to the Editor," *Irish Times*, 8 December 1942, 3.
35 R. Jacob, "Letter to the Editor," *Irish Times*, 21 October 1942, 3.
36 "Censorship of Books: How System Works," *Irish Times*, 28 October 1942, 2.
37 See, for example, Michael Adams, *Censorship: The Irish Experience*; Caleb Richardson, "'They are not worthy of themselves': *The Tailor and Ansty* Debates of 1942," *Eire-Ireland* 42, no. 3 & 4 (2007): 148–72; and Maryann Gialanella Valiulus, "Censorship as Freedom of Expression: *The Tailor and Ansty* Revisited," *Historical Reflections* 37, no. 2 (2011): 24–38.
38 *Seanad Debates*, vol. 27, no. 1, 18 November 1942.
39 Committee Meeting, 20 February 1942. PEN Dublin Centre Minute Book, 1935–51. Irish PEN Papers. NLI MS 49143/4.
40 *Seanad Debates*, vol. 27, no. 1, 18 November 1942.

41 *Seanad Debates*, vol. 27, no. 1, 18 November 1942.
42 *Seanad Debates*, vol. 27, no. 1, 18 November 1942.
43 "State's Best Seller," *Irish Times*, 4 December 1942, 1.
44 *Seanad Debates*, vol. 27, no. 1, 18 November 1942.
45 Keane might have pointed to the work of the influential Harvard anthropologists Conrad M. Arensberg and Solon T. Kimball, who documented that while sexual morality prevails in the country people, their conversations make constant reference to sex and breeding. See Conrad M. Arensberg and Solon T. Kimball, *Family and Community in Ireland* (Cambridge, MA: Harvard University Press, 1940), 202–31.
46 *Seanad Debates*, vol. 27, no. 1, 18 November 1942.
47 *Seanad Debates*, vol. 27, no. 1, 18 November 1942.
48 For an examination of the novel in the context of censorship, see Jana Fischerova, "The Banning and Unbanning of Kate O'Brien's *The Land of Spices*," *Irish University Review* 48, no. 1 (2018): 69–83.
49 *Seanad Debates*, vol. 27, no. 1, 18 November 1942.
50 *Seanad Debates*, vol. 27, no. 1, 18 November 1942.
51 *Seanad Debates*, vol. 27, no. 1, 18 November 1942.
52 *Seanad Debates*, vol. 27, no. 1, 18 November 1942.
53 *Seanad Debates*, vol. 27, no. 1, 18 November 1942.
54 *Seanad Debates*, vol. 27, no. 1, 18 November 1942.
55 *Seanad Debates*, vol. 27, no. 1, 18 November 1942.
56 *Seanad Debates*, vol. 27, no. 2, 2 December 1942.
57 Sean O'Faolain, "The Senate and Censorship," *Bell* 5, no. 4 (January 1943): 247–52. Reprinted in Kent, *The Selected Essays*, 187.
58 *Seanad Debates*, vol. 27, no. 3, 3 December 1942.
59 Meeting Minutes, 11 December 1942. Censorship of Publications Board, Minute Book 2, 1942–51. IFCO.
60 O'Faolain, "The Senate and Censorship," 189.
61 O'Faolain, "The Senate and Censorship," 191.
62 Harris to Ould, 2 July 1943. Box 50, Folder 7. HRC PEN.
63 O'Brennan to Ould, 2 April 1944. Box 50, Folder 7. HRC PEN.
64 *Senate Debates*, vol. 28, no. 19, 20 June 1944.
65 Ould to Rev. P. T. R. Kirk, 12 April 1944. Box, 101, Folder 1. HRC PEN.
66 Ould to Robert Atkins, 17 February 1944. Box 101, Folder 1. HRC PEN.
67 George Orwell, "Milton in Striped Trousers," *Tribune*, 12 October 1945, 12.
68 Sean O'Faolain, "The Mart of Ideas," *Bell* 4, no. 3 (June 1942): 153–7. Reprinted in Kent, *The Selected Essays*, 179.
69 O'Faolain, "The Mart of Ideas," 178.
70 O'Faolain, "The Mart of Ideas," 179.
71 Monk Gibbon, "Monk Gibbon Comments on his Commentators," *Bell* 9, no. 6 (March 1945), 533.

72 "Editors' note," *Bell* 9, no. 4 (January 1945), 313.
73 Monk Gibbon, "In Defence of Censorship," *Bell* 9, no. 4 (January 1945), 313.
74 Gibbon, "In Defence of Censorship," 316.
75 Irish Catholic journals of the post-independence period were especially vocal on this matter and made much the same argument regarding modern fiction's obsession with sexual realism to the detriment of other forms of realism, such as those that might consider the spiritual more seriously. See, for example, Peter P. Curry, "'The Thing Called 'Realism,'" *Catholic Mind* 1, no. 3 (March 1930): 68; and "Now Let the Censorship Operate," *Standard*, 15 February 1930, 10.
76 Gibbon, "In Defence of Censorship," 317.
77 Gibbon, "In Defence of Censorship," 319.
78 Sean O'Casey, "Comments by Readers," *Bell* 9, no. 5 (February 1945), 401.
79 O'Casey, "Comments by Readers," 404.
80 O'Casey, "Comments by Readers," 404–5.
81 O'Casey, "Comments by Readers," 405.
82 For his views, see T. C. Kingsmill Moore, "Comments by Readers," *Bell* 9, no. 5 (February 1945): 407–8.
83 James Hogan, "Comments by Readers," *Bell* 9, no. 5 (February 1945), 409.
84 Three unsolicited responses to Gibbon's article were published in the same issue. They did little to add to what had already been said, and the fact that they were largely against Gibbon's position is more indicative of the political leanings of the journal's readership than it is of a general consensus of Irish opinion. See "Public Opinion," *Bell* 9, no. 6 (March 1945): 528–33.
85 Monk Gibbon, "Monk Gibbon Comments on his Commentators," *Bell* 9, no. 6 (March 1945), 533.
86 Gibbon, "Monk Gibbon Comments on his Commentators," 533–4.
87 Gibbon, "Monk Gibbon Comments on his Commentators," 534.
88 The emergency censorship was ended on 11 May 1945. Ó Drisceoil, *Censorship in Ireland, 1939–1945*, 284.
89 *Dáil Debates*, vol. 98, no. 3, 17 October 1945.
90 Annual General Meeting, 27 October 1945, PEN Dublin Centre Minute Book, 1935–51. Irish PEN Papers. NLI MS 49143/4.
91 *Seanad Debates*, vol. 30, no. 10, 14 November 1945.
92 Censorship of Publications Act, 1946, 10 (1); 12 (d and e).
93 Censorship of Publications Act, 1946, 18 (2). Incredibly, this section of the act also suggests to one caught entering the country with a prohibited book that it would "be a good defence for him to prove that the book or periodical publication was imported otherwise than for sale or distribution or that it was not a prohibited book or prohibited periodical at the time he ordered it."
94 Censorship of Publications Act, 1946, 6 (2) (a).
95 O'Brennan to Ould, 19 June 1946. Dublin Centre to PEN, 1935–53. HRC PEN.

8: Equivocal Values: Irish PEN in the Age of Appeal

1 Percy Arland Ussher, *The Midnight Court and The Adventures of a Luckless Fellow: Translated from the Gaelic* (New York: Boni and Liveright, 1926).
2 Frank O'Connor, preface to *The Midnight Court: A Rhythmical Bacchanalia from the Irish of Bryan Merryman*, by Bryan Merryman, trans. Frank O'Connor (Dublin: Maurice Fridberg, 1945), 7, 6.
3 O'Connor, preface, 8–9.
4 Writing in 1929, just as the Censorship of Publications Act became law and seventeen years prior to the publication of O'Connor's translation, the conservative Catholic writer Aodh de Blácam tied himself in knots to explain that Merriman was less indecent and obscene than many of de Blácam's contemporaries. While admitting that "The Midnight Court" is "satirical and Rabelaisian," that it is written with "a boldness of language that would offend modern times," and that "Merriman wrote to shock," de Blácam claimed that Merriman "was not writing of or for a corrupt people" and that, like Chaucer, Merriman would somehow "lead no one very far wrong." Aodh de Blácam, *Gaelic Literature Surveyed* (Dublin: Talbot, 1929), 334–6. As the controversy over O'Connor's translation shows, it was thus rather easier to point to him as the one who had introduced indecent and obscene elements into Merriman's poem as opposed to confronting such material in the original.
5 Quidnunc, "An Irishman's Diary," *Irish Times*, 16 July 1946, 5.
6 Minutes of the meeting on 9 July 1946, Censorship of Publications Appeal Board Minutes Book. IFCO.
7 Minutes of the meeting on 9 July 1946, Censorship of Publications Appeal Board Minutes Book. IFCO.
8 Quidnunc, "An Irishman's Diary," *Irish Times*, 16 July 1946, 5.
9 Frank O'Connor, "Justice – How Are You?" *Irish Times*, 17 July 1946, 5.
10 Frank O'Connor, "Justice – How Are You?" *Irish Times*, 17 July 1946, 5.
11 Myles na gCopaleen, "Cruiskeen Lawn," *Irish Times*, 19 July 1946, 4.
12 The first of these, written by pseudonymous authors, were published in *Irish Times*, 20 July 1946, 5.
13 James Hogan, "The Midnight Court," *Irish Times*, 27 July 1946, 8.
14 Brian McMahon, "The Midnight Court," *Irish Times*, 27 July 1946, 8.
15 Even some people involved in the revival of the Irish language and the Irish-Ireland movement thought that O'Connor's translation was excellent and in fact surpassed the original in some respects. They also found that the decision to ban his work and to allow Merriman's poem to circulate in Irish was hypocritical. See Philip O'Leary, *Writing Beyond the Revival: Facing the Future in Gaelic Prose, 1940–1951* (Dublin: UCD Press, 2011), 275.

16 Frank O'Connor, "The Midnight Court," *Irish Times*, 29 July 1946, 5.
17 In his defence of O'Connor, Ussher said he was "a trifle aggrieved" that his own version of Merriman's poem had not received a similar advertisement in being banned and lamented the insularity of Irish life. Arland Ussher, "The Midnight Court," *Irish Times*, 12 September 1946, 7. He later claimed that his translation was not banned because there was "some oversight." Arland Ussher, *The Face and Mind of Ireland* (London: Victor Gollanz, 1949), 94.
18 Minutes of the meeting on 19 August 1946, Censorship of Publications Appeal Board Minutes Book. IFCO.
19 In fact, he wrote three letters. See Fitzroy Pyle, "The Midnight Court," *Irish Times*, 24, 26, and 27 August 1946, respectively, 7, 5, and 5.
20 Minutes, 3 June 1946. Proceedings of the 18th International Congress, Stockholm, Sweden, 2–6 June 1946. Box 86, Folder 4. HRC PEN. All quotes and information on the congress as reported in the paragraphs that follow are taken from this document.
21 Minutes, 4 June 1946. Proceedings of the 18th International Congress, Stockholm.
22 Minutes, 5 June 1946. Proceedings of the 18th International Congress, Stockholm.
23 Minutes, 5 June 1946. Proceedings of the 18th International Congress, Stockholm.
24 Those in favour were Austria, Belgium Flemish, Belgium French, Brazil, Czechoslovakia, Denmark, Finland, France, Germany émigré, Holland, Hungary, Norway, Poland, Sweden, and Venezuela, while the Yiddish centre was "strongly in favour"; the six against were Catalonia, India, Ireland, South Africa, Switzerland, and the United States; and the three abstentions were England, Iceland, and Scotland.
25 "P.E.N.," *Irish Times*, 17 June 1946, 5.
26 Morton to Ould, 7 September 1946. Box 50, Folder 4. HRC PEN.
27 *Report on the AGM*, 8 October 1946. Box 50, Folder 4. HRC PEN.
28 Morton to Ould, 1 January 1947. Box 50, Folder 4. HRC PEN.
29 Ould to O'Brennan, 22 June 1946. Box 50, Folder 5. HRC PEN.
30 This fourth article was originally proposed at the Stockholm Congress in 1946 and incorporated at the Zurich Congress in 1947. The new charter was officially ratified at the Copenhagen Congress in 1948. *PEN News*, August 1948, 6–7. See also https://pen.org/pen-charter/.
31 For a brief history of PEN's charter that brings it into the twenty-first century, see Carles Torner and Jan Martens, eds., *PEN International: An Illustrated History* (London: Thames & Hudson, 2021), 68–78.
32 Those who abstained included South Africa, Saudi Arabia, and the communist Eastern Bloc.

33 The Universal Declaration of Human Rights is accessible on the UN's website: https://www.un.org/en/universal-declaration-human-rights/.
34 Johannes Morsink, *The Universal Declaration of Human Rights* (Philadelphia: University of Pennsylvania Press, 1999), 69.
35 "Declaration of Human Rights," *PEN News*, April 1949, 4.
36 These figures are taken from the following sources: *Annual Reports of the Censorship of Publications Board and of the Censorship of Publications Appeal Board, for the years ended 31st December, 1946 and 31st December, 1947*. NAI, JUS 90/102/232; *Annual Reports of the Censorship of Publications Board and of the Censorship of Publications Appeal Board, for the years ended 31st December, 1948 and 31st December, 1949*. NAI, JUS 90/102/232; *Annual Reports of the Censorship of Publications Board and of the Censorship of Publications Appeal Board, for the years ended 31st December, 1950 and 31st December, 1951*. NAI, JUS 90/102/232; *Annual Report of the Censorship of Publications Board, for the year ended 31st December, 1952*. NAI, JUS 90/102/231; *Annual Report of the Censorship of Publications Board, for the year ended 31st December, 1953*. NAI, JUS 90/102/231; Adams, *Censorship*, 119. For the figures for the number of books examined and banned in the early years, see Adams, *Censorship*, 243.
37 Mary Flynn to Ould, 24 February 1948. Box 50, Folder 7. HRC PEN.
38 Committee Meeting, 27 February 1948. PEN Dublin Centre Minute Book, 1935–51. Irish PEN Papers. NLI MS 49143/4.
39 PEN to Sheila Pim, 26 September 1950. Box 50, Folder 5. HRC PEN.
40 Pim to Ould, 15 October 1950. Box 50, Folder 7. HRC PEN.
41 Committee Meeting, 15 December 1950. PEN Dublin Centre Minute Book, 1935–51. Irish PEN Papers. NLI MS 49143/4.
42 Pim to Ould, 27 March 1951. Box 50, Folder 7. HRC PEN.
43 Ould to Pim, 12 June 1951. Box 50, Folder 5. HRC PEN.
44 Ould to Pim, 5 July 1951. Box 50, Folder 5. HRC PEN.
45 Committee meeting, 9 November 1951. PEN Dublin Centre Minute Book, 1951–1963. Irish PEN Papers. NLI MS 49143/5.
46 Committee meeting, 30 November 1951. PEN Dublin Centre Minute Book, 1951–1963. Irish PEN Papers. NLI MS 49143/5; and Committee meeting, 15 February 1952. PEN Dublin Centre Minute Book, 1951–1963. Irish PEN Papers. NLI MS 49143/5.
47 Committee meeting, 29 February 1952. PEN Dublin Centre Minute Book, 1951–1963. Irish PEN Papers. NLI MS 49143/5.
48 Committee Meeting, 7 March 1952. PEN Dublin Centre Minute Book, 1951–1963. Irish PEN Papers. NLI MS 49143/5.
49 Committee meeting, 24 April 1953. PEN Dublin Centre Minute Book, 1951–1963. Irish PEN Papers. NLI MS 49143/5.
50 "25th P.E.N. Congress Meets in Dublin," *Irish Times*, 9 June 1953, 7; "An Irishwoman's Diary," *Irish Times*, 5 June 1953, 5.

51 "Program for the Dublin and Belfast XXVth International Congress of the P.E.N., June 8–13 1953." Box 150, Folder 1. HRC PEN.
52 See, for example, "25th P.E.N. Congress Meets in Dublin," *Irish Times*, 9 June 1953, 7; and "P.E.N. Congress in Dublin," *Irish Independent*, 9 June 1953, 6.
53 Myles na gCopaleen, "The P.E.N.," *Irish Times*, 13 June 1953, 5.
54 Wells's fears were indeed well founded. Writing in *The Bell*, John Hewitt and Roy McFadden's detailed account of the congress dwelled on the superficial by focusing on the receptions and various entertainments at the expense of showing how participants engaged with serious literary and political matters or how delegates responded to the congress's theme. John Hewitt and Roy McFadden, "International P.E.N. in Dublin," *The Bell* 18, no. 12 (Autumn 1953): 73–81.
55 "Report of the International Secretary on the Business Sessions of the XXVth International P.E.N. Congress," *The Literature of Peoples Whose Language Restricts Wide Recognition* (Dublin: The Richview Press, 1953), 74–80.
56 "Message from the XXVth International Congress of P.E.N. meeting in Dublin and Belfast." Box 159, Folder 1. HRC PEN.
57 Condensed Minutes of the Meeting of the Executive Committee of International P.E.N., 8 June 1953, Dublin. Box 159, Folder 1. HRC PEN.
58 "Report of the International Secretary on the Business Sessions of the XXVth International P.E.N. Congress," 79.
59 Giltinan to Carver, 3 May 1953. Box 159, Folder 2. HRC PEN.
60 "Report of the International Secretary on the Business Sessions of the XXVth International P.E.N. Congress," 79.
61 Committee meeting, 26 June 1953. PEN Dublin Centre Minute Book, 1951–1963. Irish PEN Papers. NLI MS 49143/5.
62 Giltinan to Carver, 11 July 1953. Box 142, Folder 1. HRC PEN.
63 Egon Larsen, "Books Banned in Eire," *Bookseller*, 13 February 1954, 695–6.
64 Donal Giltinan, "Censorship in Eire," *Bookseller*, 27 March 1954, 1026–7.
65 Committee Meeting, 30 April 1954. PEN Dublin Centre Minute Book, 1951–1963. Irish PEN Papers. NLI MS 49143/5.
66 "South African P.E.N.," *PEN News*, Spring 1954, 23–4.
67 Peter D. McDonald, *The Literature Police: Apartheid Censorship and Its Cultural Consequences* (Oxford: Oxford University Press, 2009), 22.
68 *P.E.N. Report: Report of the 26th International Congress of the P.E.N., Amsterdam 1954, June 20th-26th*, 23–4. Box 159, Folder 5. HRC PEN.
69 The official report of the congress notes that little discussion followed the reading of the resolutions. This is supported by Donal Giltinan's account: "When Reds and Exiled Countrymen Came Face to Face!" *Sunday Independent*, 4 July 1954, 8.
70 "Report on the XXVth International Congress: Amsterdam," *PEN News*, Summer 1954, 20–1.

9: Aligning with Other Intellectuals: The Irish Association for Civil Liberty and Conservative Ireland's Last Great Censorship Moral Panic

1 Conor Cruise O'Brien, foreword to *Skeff: The Life of Owen Sheehy-Sheffington*, by Andrée Sheehy-Skeffington (Dublin: Lilliput Press, 1991), vii.
2 William A. Donohue, *The Politics of the American Civil Liberties Union* (New Brunswick: Transaction Books, 1985), 17.
3 In addition to Donohue's study, see Samuel Walker, *In Defence of American Liberties: A History of the ACLU* (Oxford: Oxford University Press, 1990).
4 "ACLU History," American Civil Liberties Union, accessed 12 November 2025, www.aclu.org/about/aclu-history.
5 "Liberal Ethic Condemned by Professor," *Irish Times*, 24 January 1950, 3.
6 Owen Sheehy-Skeffington, "The Liberal Ethic," *Irish Times*, 26 January 1950, 5.
7 *The Liberal Ethic* (Dublin: Irish Times, 1950).
8 Sean O'Faolain, "The Liberal Ethic," *Bell* 16, no. 5 (February 1951): 5.
9 O'Faolain, "The Liberal Ethic," 10.
10 O'Faolain, "The Liberal Ethic," 11.
11 Sean O'Faolain, "The University Question," *Bell* 8, no. 1 (April 1944): 1–12. Reprinted in Kent, *The Selected Essays*, 257–67.
12 Sean O'Faolain, "The Dáil and the Bishops," *Bell* 17, no. 3 (June 1951): 5–13. Reprinted in Kent, *The Selected Essays*, 432–40.
13 Sean O'Faolain, "On a Recent Incident at the International Affairs Association," *Bell* 18, no. 9 (February 1953): 517–27. Reprinted in Kent, *The Selected Essays*, 444.
14 Letter from S. O'Faolain, March 1956. NAI, s2321A. The same letter, dated April 1956, and a copy of the petition were obtained by McQuaid. The petition reads:

In signing this petition, I do so exclusively for the purpose of encouraging a review of the work performed by the Censorship of Publications Board. I consider that the number of works having general literary merit that are banned is so great as to demand investigation. I am in favour of censorship being applied to pornography, but question the widespread banning of books of literary merit found acceptable in other democratic countries where the Christian Faith is practiced.

I, therefore, respectfully request the Taoiseach to initiate an investigation into the *record* and *working* of the Censorship, with a view to reconciling the protection of morals with the reading habits and interests of the educated public in Irish society. AB8/B XVIII, DDA.

15 "Flaws in Censorship Described at Meeting," *Irish Times*, 24 February 1956, 6.

16 "Meeting Hears Why We Have Censorship," *Irish Times*, 25 February 1956, 4.
17 "Newspaper Withheld by Customs," *Irish Times*, 2 April 1956, 7.
18 Quidnunc, "An Irishman's Diary," *Irish Times*, 2 April 1956, 6.
19 For their later correction, see "Censorship Did Not Withhold 'Observer,'" *Irish Times*, 5 April 1956, 1.
20 "The 'Observer,'" *Irish Times*, 4 April 1956, 5.
21 "Mystery of Withholding Newspaper Deepens," *Irish Times*, 6 April 1956, 1.
22 "Mystery of Withholding Newspaper Deepens," *Irish Times*, 6 April 1956, 1.
23 "'Observer' on Sale as Usual," *Irish Times*, 9 April 1956, 1.
24 Flyer announcing the 21 April 1956 meeting of the IACL. AB 8/B XVIII, DDA.
25 Minutes of the Irish Association for Civil Liberty, 21 April 1956. AB 8/B XXV, DDA.
26 Minutes of the Irish Association for Civil Liberty, 21 April 1956. AB 8/B XXV, DDA.
27 Minutes of the Irish Association for Civil Liberty, 21 April 1956. AB 8/B XXV, DDA.
28 E. Deale to J. Costello, 6 July 1956. NAI, s2321A.
29 "Irish Association of Civil Liberty on Censorship," July 1956. NAI, s2321A.
30 E. Deale to J. Costello, 10 August 1956. NAI, s2321A.
31 *Report of the Irish Association of Civil Liberty*, 10 August 1956. NAI, s2321A.
32 T. Coyne to J. Costello, 3 September 1956. NAI, s2321A.
33 Unsent letter from J. Costello to E. Deale, 5 September 1956. NAI, s2321A. The handwritten comments made by a civil servant at the end of the letter, dated 13 November 1956, note the taoiseach's final decision to abstain from a response.
34 Adams, *Censorship*, 246.
35 For a sympathetic treatment of the Knights, see Evelyn Bolster, *The Knights of St. Columbanus* (Dublin: Gill & Macmillan, 1979). The promotional brochure that I was given when I visited Ely House states: "The aim of the Knights is to maintain our country Christian in outlook, thought and action" and "to counteract the proliferation of non Catholic ideas in every sphere of life, local or national." *The Knights of St. Columbanus: Order of Catholic Laymen*, n.d.
36 Evelyn Bolster, *The Knights of St. Columbanus*, 51.
37 Evelyn Bolster, *The Knights of St. Columbanus*, 48.
38 See, for example, Gerard Whelan, *Spiked: Church-State Intrigue and "The Rose Tattoo"* (Dublin: New Island, 2002), 195–308.
39 M. L. Burke to the Supreme Secretary, 22 November 1945. KSC.

40 Secretary of C. K. 15 to the Worthy Supreme Secretary, 8 May 1946. KSC.
41 *Report on Evil Literature Committee Waterford Council*, 9 August 1949. KSC.
42 T. A. Buckley to E. Kavanagh, 15 September 1949. KSC.
43 E. Kavanagh to T. A. Buckley, 21 September 1949. KSC.
44 E. Kavanagh to B. F. Shields, 21 September 1949. KSC.
45 "Publishers Applications for Revocations which have come Before the Appeal Board to Date (22 September 1949)." KSC.
46 T. A. Buckley to E. Kavanagh, 24 January 1951. KSC.
47 B. MacMahon to J. J. Pigott, 19 February 1951. KSC.
48 See, for example, letter from B. MacMahon to C. O'Reilly, 26 February 1952, KSC.
49 T. A. Buckley to E. Kavanagh, 26 October 1951. KSC.
50 E. Kavanagh to T. A. Buckley, 5 December 1951. KSC.
51 C. E. Doherty to E. Kavanagh, 20 October 1950. KSC. Original emphasis.
52 E. Kavanagh to C. E. Doherty, 24 October 1950. KSC.
53 In the Knights' dossier on censorship, there are several drafts of questions to the minister for justice detailing open attacks on the Censorship Board and the Appeal Board in the early 1950s, specifically articles published in the *Irish Times*. That there is no record of these questions posed in the debates of the Oireachtas suggests that the matter was dropped, handled at the source of the attacks (the journalist in question), taken care of behind closed doors by politicians, or dismissed before being broached in the Dáil.
54 C. Russell to E. Kavanagh, 12 April 1954. KSC.
55 "Minority View Needed on Board," *Irish Times*, 7 November 1956, 7.
56 Anonymous Internal Memorandum, undated. AB 8/B XXV, DDA. Because the memorandum speaks of the late government when referring to the minister for justice, who dealt with the IACL's petition, it had to have been written after 5 March 1957, when Fianna Fáil took over from Fine Gael after the general election. That the memorandum speaks of the Censorship Board as actively working with the two factions noted means that it was written before the September resignation of the three Knights and, most likely, before their last meeting was held on May 8.
57 Anonymous Internal Memorandum, undated. AB 8/B XXV, DDA.
58 Anonymous Internal Memorandum, undated. AB 8/B XVIII, DDA.
59 Anonymous Internal Memorandum, undated. AB 8/B XXV, DDA.
60 C. Ó Suilleabháin to Éamon de Valera, 22 September 1957. NAI, s2321A. The letter was "a despairing cry from a frustrated body of Catholics" about the presence of unbanned, although purportedly obscene and indecent, publications in Ireland. Gerald Boland refused to allow a deputation of this group an audience because it had "very exaggerated notions of what was indecent and any discussions with them could not fail to be

embarrassing." Gerald Boland to Éamon de Valera, 18 November 1957. NAI, s2321A. The Conference of Convent Secondary Schools lodged a complaint similar to Ó Suịlleabháin's later the same month. Sister M. Jordana to Éamon de Valera, 27 September 1957. NAI, s2321A.

61 Memorandum written by J. Pigott for J. McQuaid, undated. AB 8/B XVIII, DDA.

62 Memorandum written by J. Pigott for J. McQuaid, undated. AB 8/B XVIII, DDA.

63 Memorandum written by J. Pigott for J. McQuaid, undated. AB 8/B XVIII, DDA. Comyn claimed that he had suggested that he would call a meeting if Pigott continued to refuse calling one himself. Oddly, a copy of his letter found its way into the censorship dossier kept in the archives of the Knights of St. Columbanus. A. Comyn to A. Fitzgerald, 15 August 1957. KSC.

64 Memorandum written by J. Pigott for J. McQuaid, undated. AB 8/B XVIII, DDA.

65 Memorandum written by J. Pigott for J. McQuaid, undated. AB 8/B XVIII, DDA.

66 Memorandum written by J. Pigott for J. McQuaid, undated. AB 8/B XVIII, DDA.

67 F. T. O'Reilly is not to be confused with Frank O'Reilly, who led the Catholic Truth Society for so many years. The latter died ten days before the appointments.

68 J. Griffin to M. Burke, 7 November 1957. KSC.

69 M. Burke to J. Griffin, 12 November 1957. KSC.

70 M. Burke to L. Browne, 29 November 1957. KSC.

71 M. Burke to all Grand Knights, 29 November 1957. KSC.

72 "Foul Books on Sale, Says Archbishop," *Irish Independent*, 4 December 1957, 9.

73 "Censorship Board: Prof. Pigott Tells Why He Resigned," *Irish Independent*, 5 December 1957, 10.

74 *Dáil Debates*, vol. 164, no. 10, 5 December 1957.

75 "Civil Liberty Association Replies to Professor Pigott," *Irish Independent*, 7 December 1957, 9; and "Civil Liberty Association Challenges Ex-Chairman," *Irish Times*, 7 December 1957, 11.

76 The following debate between Pigott and Sheehy-Skeffington occurred in the *Irish Times*. Another occurred simultaneously in the letters-to-the-editor section of the *Irish Independent*. See the letters-to-the-editor section of the *Irish Independent* on 10, 12, 13, 16, 17, 30, and 31 December 1957, and 2 and 11 January 1958.

77 Owen Sheehy-Skeffington, "The Censorship Board," *Irish Times*, 10 December 1957, 5.

78 Edgar M. Deale, "The Censorship Board," *Irish Times*, 12 December 1957, 5.
79 John J. Pigott, "The Censorship Board," *Irish Times*, 13 December 1957, 5.
80 Owen Sheehy-Skeffington, "The Censorship Board," *Irish Times*, 20 December 1957, 5.
81 Sheehy-Skeffington, "The Censorship Board," 5.
82 Sheehy-Skeffington, "The Censorship Board," 5.
83 Owen Sheehy-Skeffington, "The Censorship Board," *Irish Times*, 1 January 1958, 5.
84 K. Butterly to É. de Valera, 3 December 1957. NAI, s2321A; Father M. Troy to O. Traynor, 4 December 1957. NAI, s2321A; V. Wall to É. de Valera, 4 December 1957. NAI, s2321A; M. Cullen to É. de Valera, 11 December 1957. NAI, s2321A; D. Doyle to É. de Valera, 13 December 1957. NAI, s2321A; I. Flynn to É. de Valera, 14 December 1957. NAI, s2321A; S. Greene to É. de Valera, 20 December 1957. NAI, s2321A. Among those who protested were the Father Aloysius Girls' Club, the Catholic Youth Council (which represented the Society of St. Vincent de Paul Boys' Clubs, the Society of St. John Bosco Boys' Clubs, the Legion of Mary Boys' Clubs, and the Parish and Special Boys' Clubs), Christ the King Girls' Club, St. Philomena's Girls' Club, the Dominican College Past Pupils' Union, the Dominican Convent Cabra Past Pupils' Union, and St. Joseph's Catholic Boys' Brigade. The number of children's groups illustrates that McQuaid's argument hinged on the importance of protecting youth from corruption.
85 G. Boland to É. de Valera, 20 December 1957. NAI, s2321A.
86 Internal memorandum, 14 January 1858. NAI, s2321B.
87 E. Keane to M. Burke, 31 December 1957. KSC; T. White to M. Burke, 3 January 1958. KSC; P. Beagan to M. Burke, 9 January 1958. KSC; T. Croke to M. Burke, 4 January 1958. KSC; T. Croke to M. Burke, 18 January 1958. KSC; H. Lennon to M. Burke, 27 January 1958. KSC; T. Finn to M. Burke, 13 February 1958. KSC; M. McIntyre to M. Burke, 28 February 1958. KSC.
88 Internal Memorandum, 1 January 1958. KSC.
89 "Newsagents' Suggestion: Licensing of Book Importers," *Irish Independent*, 22 January 1958, 6.
90 Directive from M. Burke to all Grand Knights, 28 February 1958. KSC.
91 Dublin City Council to the Government, 16 January 1958. NAI, s2321B.
92 W. MacNeely and J. Fergus to É. de Valera, 30 January 1958. NAI, s2321B.
93 É. de Valera to W. MacNeely, 1 February 1958. NAI, s2321B.
94 "Bishops Warn of Peril to Young People," *Irish Press*, 1 February 1958, 7.
95 "Bishops Warn of Peril to Young People," *Irish Press*, 1 February 1958, 7.
96 "Evil Reading Matter Is Not Literature," *Irish Press*, 17 February 1958, 4.
97 "A Warning on Evil Reading," *Irish Press*, 17 February 1958, 5.
98 "A Turning from God," *Irish Press*, 17 February 1958, 5; "Indirect Attack," *Irish Press*, 17 February 1958, 5.

99 Oscar Traynor to É. de Valera, 4 February 1958. NAI, s2321B.
100 Oscar Traynor to É. de Valera, 4 February 1958. NAI, s2321B.
101 Internal Memorandum, undated. NAI, s2321B.
102 Internal Memorandum, 13 February 1958. NAI, s2321B.
103 É. de Valera to J. Fergus, 8 March 1958. AB 8/B XXV, DDA; a copy of this letter also exists in the National Archives in the file s2321B. In preparation of this letter, a report was submitted to de Valera outlining the crisis since its inception with a detailed account of how and why to respond to each point mentioned in the hierarchy's letter of January 30. Memorandum for the Government, 20 February 1958. NAI, s2321B. Bishop Fergus responded politely, thanking de Valera and noting that he would inform the hierarchy. J. Fergus to É. de Valera, 10 March 1958. NAI, s2321B.
104 *Dáil Debates*, vol. 167, no. 9, 1 May 1958.
105 *Dáil Debates*, vol. 168, no. 3, 20 May 1958.
106 *Dáil Debates*, vol. 170, no. 3, 10 July 1958.
107 M. Burke to J. Blowick, 16 May 1958. KSC.
108 For treatments of the 1958 *An Tóstal* crisis between the festival organisers and McQuaid, see Dean, *Riot and Great Anger*, 160–6; and Murray, *Seán O'Casey*, 386–404.
109 The figures for the number of books examined and banned in these years are taken from the annual reports for the Censorship Board as found in the National Archives, files JUS 90/102/231 and JUS 90/102/232.

10: Towards the Liberalisation of Censorship: John McGahern, Edna O'Brien, and the Censorship Reform Society

1 *Hansard*, vol. 597, 16 December 1958.
2 *Hansard*, vol. 560, 21 November 1956.
3 *Hansard*, vol. 567, 29 March 1957.
4 *Hansard*, vol. 595, 18 November 1958.
5 Obscene Publications Act, 1959, 4 (1) and (2).
6 For a full account of the trial, see C. H. Rudolph, ed., *The Trial of Lady Chatterley: Regina v. Penguin Books Limited* (London: Penguin, 1961).
7 "Lawrence Book in Stormont Debate?" *Irish Times*, 8 November 1960, 6.
8 "Doubts about 'Lady C.' in the North," *Irish Times*, 9 November 1960, 3.
9 "'Lady C' May Be Sold Freely in North," *Irish Times*, 25 November 1960, 5.
10 "London Letter," *Irish Times*, 11 November 1960, 7.
11 The European Economic Community was the forerunner of the European Union, into which Ireland was accepted in 1973.
12 For the effects of Vatican II on Irish Catholicism, see Louise Fuller, *Irish Catholicism Since 1950: The Undoing of a Culture* (Dublin: Gill & Macmillan,

2004), 109–23. See also Peter R. Connolly, "The Church in Ireland since Vatican II," *Furrow* 30, no. 12 (1979): 755–66; and Niall Coll, ed., *Ireland & Vatican II: Essays Theological, Pastoral and Educational* (Dublin: The Columba Press, 2015).

13 Peter R. Connolly, "Censorship and Moral Classification of Films," *Furrow* 8, no. 2 (February 1957), 113.

14 Connolly, "Censorship and Moral Classification of Films," 114.

15 Peter Connolly, "Censorship," in *No Bland Facility: Selected Writings on Literature, Religion and Censorship*, ed. James H. Murphy (Gerrards Cross: Colin Smythe, 1991), 57–85. 65. Originally published in *Christus Rex* 13, no. 3 (July 1959): 151–70.

16 Connolly, "Censorship," 69.

17 Connolly, "Censorship," 70.

18 Connolly, "Censorship," 74.

19 Connolly, "Censorship," 76.

20 For an account of McGahern's life in the decade leading up to the publication of his first novel and how it influenced his development as a writer, see Denis Sampson, *Young McGahern: Becoming a Novelist* (Oxford: Oxford University Press, 2012).

21 "Prize Fiction," *Irish Times*, 2 January 1963, 8; "George Russell Memorial Award," *Irish Times*, 20 February 1962, 7.

22 Benedict Kiely, "Life Is a Barracks," *Irish Press*, 23 February 1963, 4.

23 Bruce Arnold, "New Irish Novelist," *Irish Times*, 23 February 1963, 8.

24 John D. Sheridan, "Classic Tragedy in the Barracks," *Irish Independent*, 16 March 1963, 10.

25 "What Dublin Is Reading," *Irish Times*, 22 April 1963, 8.

26 Christopher Gore-Grimes to Faber and Faber, 31 August 1962, in Frank Shovlin, ed., *The Letters of John McGahern* (London: Faber and Faber, 2021), 67.

27 John McGahern to Charles Monteith, 11 September 1962, in Shovlin, *The Letters of John McGahern*, 67–8.

28 McGahern to Monteith, 28 November 1928, in Shovlin, *The Letters of John McGahern*, 74–5.

29 McGahern to Monteith, 3 May 1963, in Shovlin, *The Letters of John McGahern*, 86.

30 "Irish Writer's Novel Held by Customs," *Irish Times*, 6 May 1965, 1.

31 "Charity Begins ..." *Irish Times*, 7 May 1965, 11.

32 Christopher Wordsworth, "Shades of the Prison House," *Guardian*, 7 May 1965, 8.

33 Terence de Vere White, "Five to One," *Irish Times*, 8 May 1965, 8.

34 Ken Gray, "In the Dark," *Irish Times*, 10 May 1965, 9.

35 Sean Collins, "In the Dark," *Irish Times*, 10 May 1965, 9.

36 Jim Fitzgerald, "In the Dark," *Irish Times*, 17 May 1965, 7.

37 Tatler, "Book Censored," *Munster Express*, 14 May 1965, 5.
38 *Dáil Debates*, vol. 215, no. 11, 18 May 1965.
39 "The Wise Monkeys," *Irish Times*, 19 May 1965, 9.
40 John McGahern, *Memoir* (London: Faber and Faber, 2006), 250.
41 Monteith to McGahern, 10 June 1964, in Shovlin, *The Letters of John McGahern*, 120.
42 McGahern to Monteith, 22 June 1964, in Shovlin, *The Letters of John McGahern*, 121–2.
43 McGahern to Patrick Gregory, n.d. October 1964, in Shovlin, *The Letters of John McGahern*, 131.
44 "£1,000 Fellowship for Dubliner," *Irish Times*, 1 February 1964, 6.
45 "Censorship Board Bans *The Dark*," *Irish Independent*, 2 June 1965, 1.
46 See, for example, Adrian Kenny, "In the Dark," *Irish Times*, 5 June 1965, 9; Backbencher, "Straight for Home in the Senate Handicap," *Irish Times*, 5 June 1965, 10; James J. McAuley, "In the Dark," *Irish Times*, 7 June 1965, 7; R. Sharpe, "In the Dark," *Irish Times*, 9 June 1965, 7; Tracy Hill, "In the Dark," *Irish Times*, 18 June 1965, 7; and John Jordan, "In the Dark," *Irish Times*, 16 June 1965, 7. One reader, however, thought that McGahern was too negative in his depiction of Ireland and that the book was not worth banning. See Donald Braider, "In the Dark," *Irish Times*, 24 June 1965, 7.
47 "Banned," *Irish Independent*, 3 June 1965, 12.
48 Mary Kenny, "Waiting for Ginsberg," *Guardian*, 26 August 1965, 6.
49 "Novelist 'was not dismissed,'" *Irish Independent*, 5 February 1966, 11.
50 "McGahern Loses His Post as Teacher," *Irish Times*, 5 February 1966, 1.
51 Spokesman, "Novelist Had Lost I.N.T.O. Membership," *Irish Independent*, 7 February 1966, 10.
52 McGahern to Patrick Gregory, n.d., April 1965, in Shovlin, *The Letters of John McGahern*, 150.
53 McGahern to Patrick Gregory, 20 May 1965, in Shovlin, *The Letters of John McGahern*, 159.
54 McGahern, *Memoir*, 251.
55 Carlson, *Banned in Ireland*, 60.
56 McGahern, *Memoir*, 251.
57 McGahern to Michael McLaverty, 22 November 1965, in Shovlin, *The Letters of John McGahern*, 177.
58 Carlson, *Banned in Ireland*, 61.
59 *Seanad Debates*, vol. 60, no. 13, 9 February 1966.
60 John Healy, "Senate Query on McGahern Banned," *Irish Times*, 10 February 1966, 10.
61 *Seanad Debates*, vol. 27, no. 1, 18 November 1942.
62 Owen Sheehy-Skeffington, "The McGahern Affair," *Censorship: Quarterly Report on Censorship of Ideas and the Arts* 2, no. 2 (1966): 27.

63 Sheehy-Skeffington, "The McGahern Affair," 28.
64 Sheehy-Skeffington, "The McGahern Affair," 29. See also McGahern to Patrick Gregory, 12 November 1965, in Shovlin, *The Letters of John McGahern*, 176.
65 There are no documents suggesting that McQuaid had instructed Carton to act in the way he did. In fact, Carton appears to have informed McQuaid of his discussion with McGahern on 4 February 1966, just as the story was getting traction in the press. Carton told McQuaid that during his meeting with McGahern, he had told him that he could no longer employ him as a teacher. When McGahern pressed him for the reason and asked whether it was because of the book, Carton simply told him that it had caused "much discussion" but that he had not read it himself. When Carton then asked McGahern if it was true that he had married outside of the Church and McGahern confirmed that this was the case, Carton told him that he could not be reappointed at the school. Father Patrick Carton to Archbishop John McQuaid, 4 February 1966. AB8/B XXI/ b/79/2, DDA. In response, McQuaid reminded Carton that "you alone were responsible" for the decision and informed him that he was sending a lawyer to see him, to whom Carton should give all of the documents he had on the case. This demonstrates the level of interest that McQuaid had and suggests that he might have had a hand in the decision, his "reminder" perhaps being more of a command. Archbishop John McQuaid to Father Patrick Carton, 5 February 1966. AB8/B XXIV/b/79/2, DDA.
66 Sheehy-Skeffington, "The McGahern Affair," 30.
67 Edgar Deale, "Civil Liberty," *Irish Independent*, 25 March 1966, 12.
68 Canon McKevitt, "Role of Catholic Teachers," *Irish Independent*, 30 March 1966, 2.
69 Edna O'Brien, *Country Girl: A Memoir* (New York: Little, Brown, 2013), 152.
70 "'A Beacon of Brazenness and Defiance': Edna O'Brien Remembered by Anne Enright, Colm Tóibín and More," *Guardian*, 29 July 2024, accessed 2 October 2024, https://www.theguardian.com/books/article/2024/jul/29/edna-obrien-anne-enright-colm-toibin-country-girls. See, too, the witty subtitle of Maureen O'Connor's introduction to her study of O'Brien's fiction: "Edna O'Brien, Leader of the Banned." Maureen O'Connor, *Edna O'Brien and the Art of Fiction* (Lewisburg: Bucknell University Press, 2022).
71 "End of 'Thaw' in Film Censorship?" *Irish Times*, 21 November 1964, 6.
72 "Bans Don't Anger Me, Says Enda O'Brien," *Belfast Telegraph*, 7 October 1965, 14.
73 "Edna O'Brien and the Wicked Censor!" *Evening Herald*, 7 October 1965, 1.
74 Her performative sexuality is a key part of O'Brien's writerly public persona. See, for example, Maureen O'Connor, "Edna O'Brien, Irish Dandy," in *Edna O'Brien: New Critical Perspectives*, eds. Kathryn Laing, Sinéad Mooney, and Maureen O'Connor (Dublin: Carysfort Press, 2006), 38–53.

75 Tom O'Dea, "Who's Afraid of Edna O'Brien," *Irish Press*, 12 November 1966, 11.
76 "Book-Burning Investigated," *Irish Times*, 10 May 1966, 7.
77 "The Novels of Edna O'Brien," *Connacht Tribune*, 2 April 1966, 10.
78 John Horgan, "Edna O'Brien Faces Limerick Audience," *Irish Times*, 23 April 1966, 7.
79 "Edna's the Girl," *Evening Herald*, 23 April 1966, 3.
80 Horgan, "Edna O'Brien Faces Limerick Audience," 7.
81 "Edna's the Girl," *Evening Herald*, 23 April 1966, 3.
82 Horgan, "Edna O'Brien Faces Limerick Audience," 7.
83 Horgan, "Edna O'Brien Faces Limerick Audience," 7.
84 "What Have We Learned from It All," *Western People*, 30 April 1966, 11. See also "Edna's the Girl," *Evening Herald*, 23 April 1966, 3.
85 Ken Gray, "Edna O'Brien States Case," *Irish Times*, 17 November 1966, 10.
86 Gray, "Edna O'Brien States Case," 10.
87 Bruce Arnold, "Censorship and Edna O'Brien – A Special Case," *Irish Times*, 21 November 1966, 14.
88 Mary Holland, "Edna O'Brien Novel," *Irish Times*, 5 November 1966, 7.
89 Augustine Martin, "The Lonely Author," *Irish Press*, 5 November 1966, 4.
90 "Edna O'Brien Book May Be Casualty," *Evening Herald*, 14 November 1966, 3.
91 Bruce Arnold, "Edna O'Brien Book to be Banned," *Irish Times*, 14 November 1966, 1.
92 "Decision Soon on Edna O'Brien Book," *Irish Press*, 15 November 1966, 3.
93 "Journey's End for Edna O'Brien Books," *Irish Times*, 5 December 1966, 11.
94 In addition to the other articles cited here, see also "Novel Referred to Censors," *Cork Examiner*, 15 November 1966, 18.
95 See, for example, "Irish Authors May Challenge Censorship Laws," *Cork Examiner*, 28 November 1966, 14; "Will Propose Censorship Reform Body," *Irish Independent*, 3 December 1966, 14; and "Censorship Reform Society Planned," *Irish Times*, 3 December 1966, 9.
96 "Censorship Reform Society Founded," *Irish Times*, 5 December 1966, 1; and "Society to Reform Censorship Initiated," *Irish Press*, 5 December 1966, 4.
97 "Reform Society Queries Powers of Censors," *Irish Independent*, 5 December 1966, 8.
98 "Censorship Reform Society Founded," *Irish Times*, 5 December 1966, 1.
99 "Censorship Reform Society Founded," *Irish Times*, 11.
100 "Society to Reform Censorship Initiated," *Irish Press*, 5 December 1966, 4.
101 "Edna O'Brien's Latest Novel Banned by Censorship Board," *Irish Times*, 14 December 1966, 1.
102 "Banning of Book," *Irish Press*, 14 December 1966, 10.

103 "Edna O'Brien's Latest Novel Banned by Censorship Board," *Irish Times*, 14 December 1966, 1.
104 "What They Think About Her," *Irish Times*, 14 December 1966, 8.
105 "What They Think About Her," *Irish Times*, 8.
106 Connolly, "Censorship," 84.
107 *Dáil Debates*, vol. 228, no. 3, 27 April 1967.
108 Brian Lenihan, *For the Record* (Dublin: Blackwater Press, 1991), 215.
109 *Dáil Debates*, vol. 228, no. 6, 10 May 1967.
110 *Dáil Debates*, vol. 228, no. 6, 10 May 1967.
111 *Dáil Debates*, vol. 228, no. 12, 24 May 1967.
112 In a letter to the minister for justice, Bruce Arnold, representing the CRS, suggested amendments to the bill as it was introduced, including shortening the duration of bans. Bruce Arnold to Brian Lenihan, 16 May 1967. NAI, JUS/2006/140/122.
113 Memorandum for McQuaid, 12 December 1966. Censorship Files XI, DDA.
114 Liam Carey to John McQuaid, 30 January 1967. Censorship Files XI, DDA.
115 J. A. MacMahon to Roland Burke-Savage, 31 March 1967. Censorship Files XI, DDA.
116 *Seanad Debates*, vol. 63, no. 5, 7 June 1967.
117 *Seanad Debates*, vol. 63, no. 6, 14 June 1967.
118 *Seanad Debates*, vol. 63, no. 5, 7 June 1967.
119 Tomás Finn, *Tuairim, Intellectual Debate and Policy Formation: Rethinking Ireland, 1954–75* (Manchester: Manchester University Press, 2012). See especially 1–2, 16, and 210–22.
120 *Seanad Debates*, vol. 63, no. 5, 7 June 1967.
121 *Seanad Debates*, vol. 63, no. 5, 7 June 1967.
122 Bruce Arnold to Brian Lenihan, 16 May 1967. NAI, JUS/2006/140/122.
123 Memorandum, 15 May 1967. NAI, JUS/2006/140/123.
124 *Seanad Debates*, vol. 63, no. 7, 21 June 1967.
125 *Seanad Debates*, vol. 63, no. 6, 14 June 1967.
126 Although from this point on it functioned in line with more liberal views, it is important to keep in mind that censorship continued and many books remained banned. As recently as 2020, one notable scholar in Irish studies erroneously declared that the 1967 act meant the "end of literary censorship in Ireland." See Eibhear Walshe, "Censorship, Law and Literature," in *Irish Literature in Transition: 1940–1980*, ed. Eve Patten (Cambridge: Cambridge University Press, 2020), 180. In addition to the fact that many books remained censored until the twelve-year limit expired, J. P. Donleavy's *The Ginger Man* was censored again in 1969, three months after the original ban expired. See "'Ginger Man' Again Banned," *Irish Times*, 18 April 1969, 18.

127 Memorandum for the Government, 1 March 1967. NAI, TAOI 98/6/826.
128 Erskine Childers to Brian Lenhian, 3 May 1967. NAI, JUS/2006/140/122.
129 Memorandum re Censorship of Publication Acts 1929–1946, n.d. NAI, JUS/2006/140/122.

Coda

1 Peter Lennon, "The McGahern Affair," *Irish Times*, 14 February 1966, 10.
2 *Theatres Act*, 1968, 2 (1).
3 *Theatres Act*, 1968, 3 (1) and (2).
4 For discussions of the revisionist debates in Ireland, see D. G. Boyce and Alan O'Day, eds., *The Making of Modern Irish History: Revisionism and the Revisionist Controversy* (New York: Routledge, 1996); and Ciaran Brady, ed., *Interpreting Irish History: The Debate on Historical Revisionism, 1938–1994* (Dublin: Irish Academic Press, 1994).

Appendix: Books Written by Irish Writers That Were Banned in Ireland

1 This list is compiled from the six volumes of the *Register of Prohibited Publications*, which were found in the offices of the IFCO. In July 2025, the last time that I consulted the volumes, they were being catalogued in the Department of Justice's offices on St. Stephen's Green. They are being transferred to the National Archives of Ireland and will be accessible to the public by summer 2026.
2 *My Life and Loves* is the original and best-known title of Harris's autobiography.
3 In his list of books written by Irish writers that have been banned in Ireland since 1950, Donal Ó Drisceoil errs in confusing the English writer Anthony West – the son of the English authors Rebecca West and H. G. Wells – who had three of his books banned in Ireland, and the Irish writer Anthony C. West, who had two of his books banned in Ireland. However, Ó Drisceoil is right to challenge Maurice Leitch's claims to have had two of his novels banned in Ireland, as none of his books appear in the *Register of Prohibited Publications*. See Donal Ó Drisceoil, "A Dark Chapter." For Leitch's claims, see Julia Carlson, ed., *Banned in Ireland*.
4 The resubmission of Harris's *My Life and Loves* was meant to ban anew all editions of the autobiography, the prohibition orders of some past editions being revoked under the twelve-year term of the 1967 act. This was also the case for J. P. Donleavy's *The Ginger Man* some three months later.

Bibliography

Adams, Michael. *Censorship: The Irish Experience*. Dublin: Scepter Books, 1968.

Allen, Nicholas. *George Russell (Æ) and the New Ireland, 1905–30*. Dublin: Four Courts Press, 2003.

Anderson, Margaret. *My Thirty Years' War*. Westport, CT: Greenwood Press, 1971.

Antoine, André. *Le Théâtre Libre*. Paris: Ressources, 1979.

Archer, Charles. *William Archer: Life, Work and Friendships*. London: George Allen & Unwin, 1931.

Arensberg, Conrad M., and Solon T. Kimball. *Family and Community in Ireland*. Cambridge, MA: Harvard University Press, 1940.

Arrington, Lauren. "The Censorship of O'Flaherty V. C." *SHAW: The Annual of Bernard Shaw Studies* 28 (2008): 85–106.

Arrington, Lauren. *W. B. Yeats, the Abbey Theatre, Censorship, and the Irish State: Adding the Half-Pence to the Pence*. Oxford: Oxford University Press, 2010.

Asheim, Lester. "Not Censorship but Selection." *Wilson Library Bulletin* 28 (1953): 63–7.

Asheim, Lester. "Selection and Censorship: A Reappraisal." *Wilson Library Bulletin* 58 (1983): 180–4.

Astin, A. E. *Cato the Censor*. Oxford: Clarendon Press, 1978.

Atkinson, Juliette. *French Novels and the Victorians*. Oxford: Oxford University Press, 2017.

Barendt, Eric. "Copyright and Free Speech Theory." In *Copyright and Free Speech: Comparative and International Analyses*, edited by Jonathan Griffiths and Uma Suthersanen, 11–34. Oxford: Oxford UP, 2005.

Bassett, Troy J. "Circulating Morals: George Moore's Attack on Late-Victorian Literary Censorship." *Pacific Coast Philology* 40, no. 2 (2005): 73–89.

Baylen, J. O. "The 'New Journalism' in Late Victorian Britain." *Australian Journal of Politics & History* 18, no. 3 (December 1972): 367–85.

Beatty, Aidan. "Where Does the State End and the Church Begin?: The Strange Career of Richard S. Devane." *Studi Irlandesi* 9 (2019): 443–64.

Bell, Clive. *On British Freedom*. London: Chatto & Windus, 1923.

Bermeo, Nancy. "On Democratic Backsliding." *Journal of Democracy* 27, no. 1 (January 2016): 5–19.

Biever, Bruce Francis. *Religion, Culture, and Values: A Cross-Cultural Analysis of Motivational Factors in Native Irish and American Irish Catholicism*. New York: Arno Press, 1976.

Blácam, Aodh de. *Gaelic Literature Surveyed*. Dublin: Talbot, 1929.

Blackadder, Neil. "Dr. Kastan, the Freie Bühne, and Audience Resistance to Naturalism." *New Theatre Quarterly* 14 (1998): 357–65.

Blanshard, Paul. *The Irish and Catholic Power*. Boston: Beacon Press, 1953.

Bolster, Evelyn. *The Knights of St. Columbanus*. Dublin: Gill & Macmillan, 1979.

Booth, Charles. *Life and Labour of the People in London*. London: Macmillan, 1892–7.

Boyce, D. G., and Alan O'Day, eds. *The Making of Modern Irish History: Revisionism and the Revisionist Controversy*. New York: Routledge, 1996.

Boyd, Gary A. "Supernational Catholicity: Dublin and the 1932 Eucharistic Congress." *Early Popular Visual Culture* 5, no. 3 (2007): 317–33.

Boylan, Canon, ed. *The Book of the Congress*. Dublin: n.p., 1934.

Bradshaw, David. "James Douglas: The Sanitary Inspector of Literature." In *Prudes on the Prowl: Fiction and Obscenity in England, 1850 to the Present Day*, edited by David Bradshaw and Rachel Potter, 90–110. Oxford University Press, 2013.

Bradshaw, David, and Rachel Potter, eds. *Prudes on the Prowl: Fiction and Obscenity in England, 1850 to the Present Day*. Oxford University Press, 2013.

Brady, Ciaran, ed. *Interpreting Irish History: The Debate on Historical Revisionism, 1938–1994*. Dublin: Irish Academic Press, 1994.

Brady, Deirdre. "'Writers and the International Spirit': Irish PEN in the Postwar Years." *New Hibernia Review* 21, no. 3 (2017): 116–30.

Brake, Laurel. "Journalism and Modernism, Continued: The Case of W. T. Stead." In *Transatlantic Print Culture, 1880–1940: Emerging Media, Emerging Modernisms*, edited by Ann Ardis and Patrick Collier, 149–66. London: Palgrave Macmillan, 2008.

Brentford, Viscount. *Do We Need a Censor?* London: Faber and Faber, 1929.

Bristow, Edward J. *Vice and Vigilance: Purity Movements in Britain Since 1700*. Dublin: Gill and Macmillan, 1977.

Brittain, Vera. *Radclyffe Hall: A Case of Obscenity?* London: Femina, 1968.

Butler, Hubert. "The Bell: An Anglo-Irish View." In *Escape from the Anthill*, edited by Hubert Butler, 147–52. Mullingar: The Lilliput Press, 1986.

Butler, Judith. *Excitable Speech: A Politics of the Performative*. London: Routledge, 1997.

Campbell, Kate. "W. E. Gladstone, W. T. Stead, Matthew Arnold and a New Journalism: Cultural Politics in the 1880s." *Victorian Periodicals Review* 36, no. 1 (2003): 20–40.

Carlson, Julia, ed. *Banned in Ireland: Censorship and the Irish Writer*. Athens, GA: The University of Georgia Press, 1990.

Carlson, Julia. Introduction to *Banned in Ireland*. Edited by Julia Carlson, 1–18.

Carroll, Mark M. "'All for Keeping His Own Negro Wench': Birch v. Benton (1858) and the Politics of Slander and Free Speech in Antebellum Missouri." *Law and History Review* 29, no. 3 (2011): 835–97.

Carson, Niall. *Rebel by Vocation: Seán O'Faoláin and the Generation of "The Bell."* Manchester: Manchester University Press, 2016.

Casteleyn, Mary. *A History of Literacy and Libraries in Ireland: The Long Traced Pedigree*. Aldershot: Gower, 1984.

Causton, Bernard, and G. Gordon Young. *Keeping It Dark: Or, the Censor's Handbook*. London: Mandrake Press, 1930.

Cleary, Joe. *The Irish Expatriate Novel in Late Capitalist Globalization*. Cambridge: Cambridge University Press, 2021.

Cleary, Joe. *Modernism, Empire, World Literature*. Cambridge: Cambridge University Press, 2021.

Clor, Harry M. *Obscenity and Public Morality: Censorship in a Liberal Society*. Chicago: The University of Chicago Perss, 1969.

Clyde, Tom. *Irish Literary Magazines: An Outline History and Descriptive Bibliography*. Dublin: Irish Academic Press, 2002.

Cohen, Stanley. *Folk Devils and Moral Panics: The Creation of the Mods and the Rockers*, 3rd ed. London: Routledge, 2002.

Coleman, Ambrose. "Our Reading Public and the Carnegie Rural Libraries." *The Irish Ecclesiastical Record* 25, no. 4 (1925): 357–72.

Coll, Niall, ed. *Ireland & Vatican II: Essays Theological, Pastoral and Educational*. Dublin: The Columba Press, 2015.

Colligan, Colette. *A Publisher's Paradise: Expatriate Literary Culture in Paris, 1890–1960*. Amherst, MA: University of Massachusetts Press, 2014.

Collins, Aongus. *A History of Sex and Morals in Ireland*. Cork: Mercier Press, 2001.

Comyn, Andrew F. "Censorship in Ireland." *Studies: An Irish Quarterly Review* 58, no. 229 (1969): 42–50.

Connolly, Peter. "Censorship." In *No Bland Facility: Selected Writings on Literature, Religion and Censorship*, edited by Peter Connolly and James H. Murphy, 57–85. Gerrards Cross: Colin Smythe, 1991.

Conolly, L. W. *The Censorship of English Drama, 1737–1824*. San Marino, CA: Huntington Library, 1976.

Conolly, L. W. "*Mrs Warren's Profession* and the Lord Chamberlain." *SHAW: The Annual of Bernard Shaw Studies* 24 (2004): 49–95.

Coote, William Alexander, ed. *Pernicious Literature: Debate in the House of Commons, Trial and Conviction for Sale of Zola's Novels, With Opinion of the Press*. London: National Vigilance Association, 1889.

Coote, William Alexander. *A Romance of Philanthropy*. London: National Vigilance Association, 1916.

Corish, Patrick J. "The First Fifty Years." In *Catholic Truth Society of Ireland: First Fifty Years, 1899–1949*, 11–23. Dublin: Veritas, 1949.

Corkery, Daniel. *Synge and Anglo-Irish Literature*. Cork: Cork University Press, 1931.

Coustillas, Pierre. Introduction to *Literature at Nurse, or Circulating Morals*. Edited by Pierre Coustillas, 9–24.

Coustillas, Pierre, ed. *Literature at Nurse, or Circulating Morals: A Polemic on Victorian Censorship*, by George Moore. Sussex: The Harvester Press, 1976.

Craig, Alec. *The Banned Books of England and Other Countries: A Study of the Censorship of Literary Obscenity*. London: George Allen & Unwin, 1962.

Cross, Eric. *The Tailor and Ansty*. New York: Devin-Adair, 1964.

Cullen, L. M. *Eason & Son: A History*. Dublin: Eason & Son, 1989.

Cummins, Anthony. "Émile Zola's Cheap English Dress: The Vizetelly Translations, Late-Victorian Print Culture, and the Crisis of Literary Value." *Review of English Studies* 60, no. 243 (2008): 108–32.

D'Alton, John Cardinal. *The Catholic Truth Society of Ireland: Its Origin and Purpose*. Dublin: Veritas, n.d.

Davis, Tracy C. "The Independent Theatre Society's Revolutionary Scheme for an Uncommercial Theatre." *Theatre Journal* 42, no. 4 (1990): 447–54.

Dean, Joan FitzPatrick. *Riot and Great Anger: Stage Censorship in Twentieth-Century Ireland*. Madison, WI: University Wisconsin Press, 2004.

Delaney, Paul. *Seán O'Faoláin: Literature, Inheritance and the 1930s*. Dublin: Irish Academic Press, 2014.

Devane, Rev. R. S. "Indecent Literature: Some Legal Remedies." *Irish Ecclesiastical Record* 35, no. 2 (1925): 182–204.

Doherty, Megan. "PEN International and Its Republic of Letters, 1921–1970." PhD thesis, Columbia University, 2011.

Dollimore, Jonathan. *Sex, Literature and Censorship*. Cambridge: Polity Press, 2001.

Donohue, William A. *The Politics of the American Civil Liberties Union*. New Brunswick, NJ: Transaction Books, 1985.

Doyle, Tony. "Selection versus Censorship in Libraries." *Collection Management* 27, no. 1 (2002): 15–25.

Duerksen, Roland A. "Shelley and Shaw." *PMLA* 78, no. 1 (March 1963): 114–27.

Dukore, Bernard F. *Bernard Shaw and the Censors: Fights and Failures, Stage and Screen*. London: Palgrave Macmillan, 2020.

Eliot, Simon. *Some Patterns and Trends in British Publishing, 1800–1919*. London: Bibliographical Society, 1994.

Ellmann, Richard. *James Joyce: New and Revised Edition*. Oxford: Oxford University Press, 1982.

Ellmann, Richard, ed. *Letters of James Joyce*. Vol. II. London: Faber and Faber, 1966.

Ellmann, Richard, ed. *Selected Letters of James Joyce*. New York: Viking, 1975.

Eltis, Sos. *Acts of Desire: Women and Sex on Stage, 1800–1930*. Oxford: Oxford University Press, 2013.

Ernst, Morris, and Alexander Lindey. *The Censor Marches On: Recent Milestones in the Administration of the Obscenity Law in the United States*. New York: Double Day, 1940.

Ernst, Morris, and William Seagle. *To the Pure ....: A Study of Obscenity and the Censor*. New York: Viking, 1928.

Fallon, Brian. *An Age of Innocence: Irish Culture, 1930–1960*. New York: St. Martin's Press, 1998.

Farleigh, John. *Graven Image: An Autobiographical Textbook*. London: Macmillan, 1940.

Farmar, Tony. *The History of Irish Book Publishing*. Stroud: The History Press, 2018.

Fellion, Michael, and Katherine Inglis. *Censored: A Literary History of Subversion and Control*. Montréal: McGill-Queen's University Press, 2017.

Ferriter, Dermot. *Occasions of Sin: Sex and Society in Modern Ireland*. London: Profile Books, 2009.

Finn, Tomás. *Tuairim, Intellectual Debate and Policy Formation: Rethinking Ireland, 1954–75*. Manchester: Manchester University Press, 2012.

Finneran, Richard, et al., eds. *Letters to W. B. Yeats*. Vol. 2. London: Macmillan, 1977.

Fischerova, Jana. "The Banning and Unbanning of Kate O'Brien's *The Land of Spices*." *Irish University Review* 48, no. 1 (2018): 69–83.

Flanagan, Michael. "Republic of Virtue: Our Boys, the Campaign against Evil Literature and the Assertion of Catholic Morality in Free State Ireland." In *Ireland, Design and Visual Culture: Negotiating Modernity, 1922–1992*, edited by Linda King and Elaine Sisson, 117–29. Cork: Cork University Press, 2011.

Foster, R. F. *W. B. Yeats: A Life, II: The Arch-Poet, 1915–1939*. Oxford: Oxford University Press, 2003.

Foucault, Michel. *Discipline and Punish: The Birth of the Prison*. Translated by Alan Sheridan. New York: Vintage, 1995.

Frazier, Adrian. *George Moore, 1852–1933*. New Haven, CT: Yale University Press, 2000.

Fuller, Louise. *Irish Catholicism Since 1950: The Undoing of a Culture*. Dublin: Gill & Macmillan, 2004.

Galston, William A. *Anti-Pluralism: The Populist Threat to Democracy*. New Haven, CT: Yale University Press, 2018.

Gannon, P. J. "Art, Morality and Censorship." *Studies: An Irish Quarterly Review* 31, no. 124 (1942): 409–19.

Gardiner, Harold C. *Catholic Viewpoint on Censorship*, 2nd ed. Garden City, NY: Image Books, 1961.

Garnett, Edward. *The Breaking Point*. London: Duckworth, 1907.

Garnett, Edward. Foreword to *Midsummer Night Madness*, by Sean O'Faolain, 11–16. London: Jonathan Cape, 1932.

Garnett, Edward. Preface to *Sleeveless Errand*, by Norah C. James, 1–3. Paris: Henry Babou and Jack Kahane, 1929.

Gibbs, A. M. *Bernard Shaw: A Life*. Gainesville: University Press of Florida, 2005.

Gilbert, Stuart, ed. *Letters of James Joyce*. Vol. I. London: Faber and Faber, 1957.

Gindin, James. *John Galsworthy's Life and Art: An Alien's Fortress*. Ann Arbor, MI: University of Michigan Press, 1987.

Goldman, Jonathan, ed. *Joyce and the Law*. Gainesville, FL: University Press of Florida, 2017.

Grazia, Edward de. *Girls Lean Back Everywhere: The Law of Obscenity and the Assault on Genius*. New York: Random House, 1992.

Gregory, Lady. *Our Irish Theatre: A Chapter of Autobiography*. New York: G. P. Putnam's Sons, 1913.

Grene, Nicholas, and Chris Morash, eds. *The Oxford Handbook of Modern Irish Theatre*. Oxford: Oxford University Press, 2016.

Griest, Guinevere L. *Mudie's Circulating Library and the Victorian Novel*. Bloomington, IN: Indiana University Press, 1970.

Griffin, Kathi R. "The Prefaces of George Moore." In *George Moore: Spheres of Influence*, edited by Kathryn Laing and Mary Pierse, 57–78. Liverpool: Liverpool University Press, 2023.

Grimes, Brendan. *Irish Carnegie Libraries: A Catalogue and Architectural History*. Dublin: Irish Academic Press, 1998.

Groden, Michael. "A Textual and Publishing History." In *A Companion to Joyce Studies*, edited by Zach Bowen and James F. Carens, 71–128. Westport, CT: Greenwood, 1984.

Habermas, Jürgen. *The Transformation of the Public Sphere: An Inquiry into a Category of Bourgeois Society*. Translated by Thomas Burger. London: Polity Press, 1992.

Hare, Ivan, and James Weinstein, eds. *Extreme Speech and Democracy*. Oxford: Oxford University Press, 2009.

Hartmann, Johanna, and Hubert Zapf, eds. *Censorship and Exile*. Göttingen: V&R Unipress, 2015.

Hassett, Joseph M. *The "Ulysses" Trials: Beauty and Truth Meet the Law*. Dublin: The Lilliput Press, 2016.

Henig, Ruth B. *The League of Nations*. London: Haus, 2010.

Hogan, Caelainn. *Republic of Shame: Stories from Ireland's Institutions for "Fallen Women."* London: Penguin, 2019.

Hogan, Robert, and Michael J. O'Neill, eds. *Joseph Holloway's Theatre: A Selection from His Unpublished Journal "Impressions of a Dublin Playgoer."* Carbondale, IL: Southern Illinois University Press, 1967.

Holmes, David G. "The Eucharistic Congress of 1932 and Irish Identity." *New Hibernia Review* 4, no. 1 (2000): 55–78.

Holroyd, Michael. *Bernard Shaw: The Search for Love.* Vol. I, *1856–1898.* London: Penguin, 1990.

Holroyd, Michael. *Bernard Shaw: The Pursuit of Power.* Vol. II, *1898–1918.* London: Penguin, 1991.

Hone, Joseph. *The Life of George Moore.* Westport, CT: Greenwood, 1973 [1936].

Hone, Joseph. "A Recollection of James Joyce." *Envoy: An Irish Review of Literature and Art* 5, no. 17 (1951): 44–5.

Horgan, John. "Saving Us from Ourselves: Contraception, Censorship and the 'Evil Literature' Controversy of 1926," *Irish Communications Review* 5, no. 1 (1995): 61–7.

Houston, Lloyd (Meadhbh). *Irish Modernism and the Politics of Sexual Health.* Oxford: Oxford University Press, 2023.

Howard, Michael S. *Jonathan Cape, Publisher: Herbert Jonathan Cape, G. Wren Howard.* London: Jonathan Cape, 1971.

Hugo, Leon. *Bernard Shaw's The Black Girl in Search of God: The Story Behind the Story.* Gainesville, FL: University Press of Florida, 2003.

Hutton, Claire. "Chapters of Moral History: Failing to Publish *Dubliners.*" *The Papers of the Bibliographical Society of America* 97, no. 4 (2003): 495–519.

Hutton, Claire. "The Extraordinary History of the House of Maunsel." In *The Oxford History of the Irish Book*, edited by Clare Hutton. Vol. V, *The Irish Book in English, 1891–2000*, 548–61. Oxford: Oxford University Press, 2011.

Hutton, Claire. *Serial Encounters: "Ulysses" and the "Little Review."* Oxford: Oxford University Press, 2019.

Hyland, Paul, and Neil Sammells, eds. *Writing and Censorship in Britain.* London: Routledge, 2023.

Ibsen, Henrik. *Ibsen's Prose Dramas.* Translated by William Archer. London: Walter Scott, 1890–1.

Inglis, Tom. *Moral Monopoly: The Rise and Fall of the Catholic Church in Modern Ireland.* Dublin: University College Dublin Press, 1998.

Inglis, Tom. "Religion, Identity, State and Society." In *The Cambridge Companion to Modern Irish Culture*, edited by Joe Cleary and Claire Connolly, 59–77. Cambridge: Cambridge University Press, 2005.

Ingram, Angela. "'Unutterable Putrefaction' and 'Foul Stuff': Two 'Obscene' Novels of the 1920s." *Women's Studies International Forum* 9 (1986): 341–54.

Israel, Jonathan. "French Royal Censorship and the Battle to Suppress the Encyclopédie of Diderot and D'Alembert, 1751–1759." In *The Use of Censorship in the Enlightenment*, edited by Mogens Lærke, 61–74. Leiden: Brill, 2009.

Israel, Jonathan. Introduction to *Theological-Political Treatise*, by Spinoza. Edited by Jonathan Israel, viii–xxxiv. Cambridge: Cambridge University Press, 2007.

James, Norah C. *I Lived in a Democracy*. London: Longmans, 1939.

Jansen, Sue Curry. *Censorship: The Knot that Binds Power and Knowledge*. Oxford: Oxford University Press, 1991.

Johnson, R. Brimley. *Moral Poison in Modern Fiction*. London: A. M. Philpot, 1922.

Johnston, Denis. "Seán O'Casey in the Twenties." In *The O'Casey Enigma*, edited by Michael Ó hAodha. Cork: The Mercier Press, 1980, 20–33.

Jones, Francis M. *Defusing Censorship: The Librarian's Guide to Handling Censorship Conflict*. Phoenix, AZ: Oryx Press, 1983.

Jordan, Jane. "'Literature at Nurse': George Moore, Ouida, and Fin-de-siècle Literary Censorship." In *George Moore: Influence and Collaboration*, edited by Ann Heilmann and Mark Llewellyn, 69–81. Newark, DE: University of Delaware Press, 2014.

Joyce, James. "A Curious History." *Egoist* 1, no. 2 (15 January 1914): 26–7.

Joyce, James. *Dubliners*, edited by Jeri Johnson. Oxford: Oxford University Press, 2000.

Joyce, James. "Gas from a Burner." In *Pomes Penyeach and Other Verses*, 41–7. London: Faber and Faber, 1966.

Joyce, James. *Occasional, Critical, and Political Writings*, edited by Kevin Barry. Oxford: Oxford University Press, 2000.

Joyce, James. *A Portrait of the Artist as a Young Man*, edited by Jeri Johnson. Oxford: Oxford University Press, 2008.

Joyce, James. *Ulysses*, edited by Jeri Johnson. Oxford: Oxford University Press, 2008.

Kahane, Jack. *Memoirs of a Booklegger*. London: M. Joseph, 1939.

Keating, Anthony. "Censorship: The Cornerstone of Catholic Ireland." *Journal of Church and State* 57, no. 2 (2015): 289–309.

Keating, Peter. *The Haunted Study: A Social History of the English Novel, 1875–1914*. London: Secker & Warburg, 1989.

Kelly, A. A., ed. *The Letters of Liam O'Flaherty*. Dublin: Wolfhound Press, 1996.

Kennedy, Dennis. *Granville Barker and the Dream of Theatre*. Cambridge: Cambridge University Press, 1985.

Kennedy, Finola. "The Suppression of the Carrigan Report: A Historical Perspective on Child Abuse." *Studies: An Irish Quarterly Review* 89, no. 356 (2000): 354–63.

Kent, Brad. "The Banning of Bernard Shaw's *The Adventures of the Black Girl in Her Search for God* and the Decline of the Irish Academy of Letters." *Irish University Review* 39, no. 2 (2008): 271–94.

Kent, Brad. "Bernard Shaw, the British Censorship of Plays, and Modern Celebrity." *English Literature in Transition, 1880–1920* 57, no. 2 (2014): 231–53.

Kent, Brad. "Censorship." In *George Bernard Shaw in Context*, edited by Brad Kent, 199–206. Cambridge: Cambridge University Press, 2015.

Kent, Brad. "Censorship and Immorality: Bernard Shaw's *The Devil's Disciple*." *Modern Drama* 54, no. 4 (2011): 511–33.

Kent, Brad. "Shaw, *The Bell*, and Censorship in 1945." *SHAW: The Annual of Bernard Shaw Studies* 30 (2010): 161–74.

Kent, Brad, ed. *The Selected Essays of Sean O'Faolain*. McGill-Queen's University Press, 2016.

Keogh, Dermot. *The Vatican, the Bishops, and Irish Politics, 1919–39*. Cambridge: Cambridge, University Press, 1986.

Kiberd, Declan. *Inventing Ireland: The Literature of the Modern Nation*. Cambridge, MA: Harvard University Press, 1997.

Kiely, Benedict. "The Whores on the Half-Doors: Or An Image of the Irish Writer." In *Conor Cruise O'Brien Introduces Ireland*, edited by Owen Dudley Edwards, 148–61. London: Andre Deutsch, 1969.

Kilroy, James. *The "Playboy" Riots*. Dublin: Dolmen Press, 1971.

Kinservik, Matthew J. *Disciplining Satire: The Censorship of Satiric Comedy on the Eighteenth-Century London Stage*. Lewisburg, PA: Bucknell University Press, 2002.

Kirwan, Bill. "The Social Policy of *The Bell*." *Administration* 37, no. 2 (1989): 99–118.

Kiš, Danilo. *Homo Poeticus: Essays and Interviews*. New York: Farrar, Straus and Giroux, 1995.

Krause, David, ed. *The Letters of Sean O'Casey, 1910–41*. Vol. 1. London: Cassell, 1975.

Ladenson, Elizabeth. *Dirt for Dirt's Sake: Books on Trial from "Madame Bovary" to "Lolita."* Ithaca, NY: Cornell University Press, 2007.

Lærke, Mogens. Introduction to *The Use of Censorship in the Enlightenment*, by Mogens Lærke, 1–24. Leiden: Brill, 2009.

Laurence, Dan H., ed. *Bernard Shaw: Collected Letters, 1874–1897*. London: Max Reinhardt, 1965.

Laurence, Dan H., ed. *Bernard Shaw: Collected Letters, 1898–1910*. New York: Viking, 1985.

Laurence, Dan H., ed. *Bernard Shaw: Collected Letters, 1926–1950*. New York: Max Reinhardt, 1988.

Laurence, Dan H., and Nicholas Grene, eds. *Shaw, Lady Gregory and the Abbey: A Correspondence and a Record*. Gerrards Cross: Colin Smythe, 1993.

Lawrence, D. H. *Pornography and Obscenity*. London: Faber and Faber, 1929.

Lee, J. J. *Ireland 1912–1985: Politics and Society*. Cambridge: Cambridge University Press, 1989.

Lenihan, Brian. *For the Record*. Dublin: Blackwater Press, 1991.

Levmore, Saul, and Martha C. Nussbaum, eds. *The Offensive Internet: Speech, Privacy, and Reputation*. Cambridge, MA: Harvard University Press, 2011.

Llewellyn, Mark, and Ann Heilmann. "George Moore and Literary Censorship: The Textual and Sexual History of 'John Norton' and 'Hugh Monfert.'" *English Literature in Transition, 1880–1920* 50, no. 4 (2007): 371–92.

Lowery, Robert G. *A Whirlwind in Dublin: "The Plough and the Stars" Riots*. Westport, CT: Greenwood Press, 1984.

Lucey, Dr. Cornelius. "The Freedom of the Press." *Irish Ecclesiastical Record* 50, no. 840 (1937): 584–99.

Lyons, F. S. L. *Ireland Since the Famine*. Oxford: Clarendon Press, 1979.

MacNamara, Brinsley. "Prefatory Note." In *The Valley of the Squinting Windows*, edited by Brinsley MacNamara, ix–xiii. New York: Brentano's, 1919.

MacNamara, Brinsley. *The Valley of the Squinting Windows*. Dublin: Maunsel, 1918.

MacNamara, Brinsley. *The Various Lives of Marcus Igoe*. London: S. Low, Marston & Co., 1929.

Marshik, Celia. *British Modernism and Censorship*. Cambridge: Cambridge University Press, 2006.

Marshik, Celia. "History's 'Abrupt Revenges': Censoring War's Perversions in *The Well of Loneliness* and *Sleeveless Errand*." *Journal of Modern Literature* 26, no. 2 (2003): 145–59.

Martin, Peter. *Censorship in the Two Irelands, 1922–1939*. Dublin: Irish Academic Press, 2006.

Matan, Branko, ed. *Speak Now or Never: The 1933 Dubrovnik PEN Club Congress*. Croatian P.E.N. Centre: Zagreb-Dubrovnik, 1993.

Matthews, Kelly. *"The Bell" Magazine and the Representation of Irish Identity: Opening Windows*. Dublin: Four Courts Press, 2012.

Maxwell, Herbert. *Life and Times of the Right Honourable William Henry Smith, M.P.* Vol. 1. Edinburgh: William Blackwood and Sons, 1893.

McCarthy, Helen. *The British People and the League of Nations: Democracy, Citizenship and Internationalism, c. 1918–45*. Manchester: Manchester University Press, 2011.

McDiarmid, Lucy. "Augusta Gregory, Bernard Shaw, and the Shewing-Up of Dublin Castle." *PMLA* 109, no. 1 (1994): 26–44.

McDiarmid, Lucy. *The Irish Art of Controversy*. Ithaca: Cornell University Press, 2005.

McDonald, Jan. "Continental Plays Produced by the Independent Theatre Society, 1891–8." *Theatre Research International* 1, no. 1 (1975): 16–28.

McDonald, Peter D. *The Literature Police: Apartheid Censorship and Its Cultural Consequences*. Oxford: Oxford University Press, 2009.

McGahern, John. *Memoir*. London: Faber and Faber, 2006.

McGarry, Fearghal. "Independent Ireland." In *The Princeton History of Modern Ireland*, edited by Richard Bourke and Ian McBride, 109–40. Princeton: Princeton University Press, 2016.

McGowan, John. *Pragmatist Politics: Making the Case for Liberal Democracy*. Minneapolis, MN: University of Minnesota Press, 2012.

McGraw, Bryan T. *Faith in Politics: Religion and Liberal Democracy*. Cambridge: Cambridge University Press, 2010.

Merkel, Wolfgang. "Embedded and Defective Democracies." *Democratization* 11, no. 5 (2004): 33–58.

Merryman, Bryan. *The Midnight Court: A Rhythmical Bacchanalia from the Irish of Bryan Merryman*. Translated by Frank O'Connor. Dublin: Maurice Fridberg, 1945.

Michalos, Alex C., and Deborah C. Poff, eds. *Bernard Shaw and the Webbs*. Toronto: University of Toronto Press, 2002.

Mill, John Stuart. "On Liberty." In *On Liberty, Utilitarianism and Other Essays*, 2nd ed. edited by John Stuart Mill, Mark Philp, and Frederick Rosen, 1–112. Oxford: Oxford University Press, 2015.

Miller, Anna Irene. *The Independent Theatre in Europe: 1887 to the Present*. New York: Benjamin Bloom, 1931.

Miller, Elizabeth Carolyn. *Slow Print: Literary Radicalism and Late Victorian Print Culture*. Stanford, CA: Stanford University Press, 2013.

Miller, Neil. *Banned in Boston: The Watch and Ward Society's Crusade against Books, Burlesque, and the Social Evil*. Boston: Beacon Press, 2010.

Milton, John. "Areopagitica." In *The Major Works*, by John Milton. Edited by Stephen Orgel and Jonathan Goldberg, 236–73. Oxford: Oxford University Press, 2008.

Moore, George. *Avowals*. Privately published for subscribers only, 1919.

Moore, George. *A Communication to My Friends*. London: Nonesuch Press, 1933.

Moore, George. *Impressions and Opinions*. London: David Nutt, 1891.

Moore, George. *Letters of George Moore*. Bournemouth: Sydenham, 1942.

Moore, George. *Literature at Nurse, or Circulating Morals*. London: Vizetelly, 1885.

Moore, George. *A Modern Lover*. New York: Garland Publishing, 1984.

Moore, George. Preface to *Piping Hot!*, by Émile Zola, v–xviii. London: Vizetelly & Co., 1887.

Morsink, Johannes. *The Universal Declaration of Human Rights*. Philadelphia: University of Pennsylvania Press, 1999.

Mullin, Katherine. *James Joyce, Sexuality and Social Purity*. Cambridge: Cambridge University Press, 2003.

Mullin, Katherine. "Poison More Deadly than Prussic Acid: Defining Obscenity after the 1857 Obscene Publications Act (1850–1885)." In *Prudes on the Prowl: Fiction and Obscenity in England, 1850 to the Present Day*, edited by David Bradshaw and Rachel Potter, 11–29. Oxford University Press, 2013.

Mullin, Katherine. "'The Sort of Girl I'd Like to See Behind the Bar at the King's Head': Barmaids and Censorship in George Moore." In *George*

Moore: Influence and Collaboration, edited by Ann Heilmann and Mark Llewellyn, 83–97. Newark, DE: University of Delaware Press, 2014.

Murphy, Andrew. *Ireland, Reading and Cultural Nationalism, 1790–1930: Bringing the Nation to Book*. Cambridge: Cambridge University Press, 2018.

Murphy, John A. "Censorship and the Moral Community." In *Communications and Community in Ireland*, edited by Brian Farrell, 51–63. Dublin: Mercier Press, 1984.

Murphy, Richard T. "Monuments of Unageing Embarrassment: Brinsley MacNamara and the Bildungsroman in the Irish Free State." *New Hibernia Review* 17, no. 4 (2013): 74–92.

Murray, Christopher. *Seán O'Casey: Writer at Work*. Montréal: McGill-Queen's University Press, 2004.

Murray, Patrick. *Oracles of God: The Roman Catholic Church and Irish Politics, 1922–37*. Dublin: University College Dublin Press, 2000.

Nash, John. "'In the Heart of the Hibernian Metropolis'? Joyce's Reception in Ireland, 1900–1940." In *A Companion to James Joyce*, edited by Richard Brown, 108–22. Oxford: Blackwell, 2008.

Nellis, Mike. "John Galsworthy's Justice." *British Journal of Criminology* 36, no. 1 (1996): 61–84.

Newman, Stephen L. "Finding the Harm in Hate Speech: An Argument against Censorship." *Canadian Journal of Political Science* 50, no. 3 (2017): 679–97.

Nicholson, Steve. *The Censorship of British Drama, 1900*–1968. 4 vols. Exeter: University of Exeter Press, 2003–15.

Note-book of the Shelley Society. London: Reeves and Turner, 1888.

Oboler, Eli M. *Defending Intellectual Freedom: The Library and the Censor*. Westport, CT: Greenwood Press, 1980.

O'Brien, Conor Cruise. Foreword to *Skeff: The Life of Owen Sheehy-Skeffington*, by Andrée Sheehy-Skeffington, vii–xii. Dublin: Lilliput Press, 1991.

O'Brien, Edna. *Country Girl: A Memoir*. New York: Little, Brown & Company, 2013.

O'Brien, Kate. *The Land of Spices*. London: William Heinemann, 1941.

O'Casey, Eileen. *Cheerio, Titan: The Friendship between George Bernard Shaw and Eileen and Sean O'Casey*. New York: Charles Scribner's Sons, 1989.

O'Casey, Sean. *Autobiographies II: Inishfallen, Fare Thee Well, Rose and Crown, Sunset and Evening Star*. London: Macmillan, 1963.

O'Casey, Sean. *The Plough and the Stars*. London: Faber and Faber, 2001.

O'Connor, Frank. *My Father's Son*. New York: Alfred A. Knopf, 1969.

O'Connor, Frank. Preface. to *The Midnight Court: A Rhythmical Bacchanalia from the Irish of Bryan Merryman*, by Bryan Merryman. Translated by Frank O'Connor, 5–11. Dublin: Maurice Fridberg, 1945.

O'Connor, Maureen. *Edna O'Brien and the Art of Fiction*. Lewisburg, PA: Bucknell University Press, 2022.

O'Connor, Maureen. "Edna O'Brien, Irish Dandy." In *Edna O'Brien: New Critical Perspectives*, edited by Kathryn Laing, Sinéad Mooney, and Maureen O'Connor, 38–53. Dublin: Carysfort Press, 2006.

O'Donnell, Donat. *Maria Cross: Imaginative Patterns in a Group of Modern Catholic Writers*. London: Chatto & Windus, 1954.

Ó Drisceoil, Donal. *Censorship in Ireland, 1939–1945: Neutrality Politics and Society*. Cork: Cork University Press, 1996.

Ó Drisceoil, Donal. "A Dark Chapter: Censorship and the Irish Writer." In *The Oxford History of the Irish Book*. Vol. V, *The Irish Book in English, 1891–2000*, edited by Clare Hutton, 285–303. Oxford: Oxford University Press, 2011.

O'Faolain, Sean. *Bird Alone*. London: Jonathan Cape, 1936.

O'Faolain, Sean. *Midsummer Night Madness*. London: Jonathan Cape, 1932.

O'Faolain, Sean. *Vive Moi!*. Boston: Little and Brown, 1964.

O'Farrell, Padraic. *The Burning of Brinsley MacNamara*. Dublin: Lilliput, 1990.

O'Leary, Philip. *Writing Beyond the Revival: Facing the Future in Gaelic Prose, 1940–1951*. Dublin: UCD Press, 2011.

O'Shaughnessy, David, ed. *The Censorship of Eighteenth-Century Theatre: Playhouses and Prohibition, 1737–1843*. Cambridge University Press, 2023.

O'Sullivan, Michael K., and Connie J. O'Sullivan. "Selection or Censorship: Libraries and the Intelligent Design Debate." *Library Review* 56, no. 3 (2007): 200–7.

Ould, Herman. *John Galsworthy*. London: Chapman & Hall, 1934.

Parkes, Adam. *Modernism and the Theater of Censorship*. Oxford: Oxford University Press, 1996.

Partridge, Eric. *The First Three Years: An Account and a Biography of the Scholartis Press*. London: Scholartis Press, 1930.

Pašeta, Senia. "Censorship and Its Critics in the Irish Free State, 1922–1932." *Past & Present* 181 (2003): 193–218.

Pearce, Donald R., ed. *The Senate Speeches of W. B. Yeats*. Bloomington, IN: University of Indiana Press, 1960.

Pearson, Neil. *Obelisk: A History of Jack Kahane and the Obelisk Press*. Liverpool: University of Liverpool Press, 2007.

Pease, Allison. *Modernism, Mass Culture, and the Aesthetics of Obscenity*. Cambridge: Cambridge University Press, 2000.

P.E.N. *The Literature of Peoples Whose Language Restricts Wide Recognition*. Dublin: The Richview Press, 1953.

PEN Charter. "PEN International." Accessed 31 October 2024. https://pen.org/pen-charter/.

Perry, Michael J. *The Political Morality of Liberal Democracy*. Cambridge: Cambridge University Press, 2009.

Pharand, Michel, ed. *Bernard Shaw and His Publishers*. Toronto: University of Toronto Press, 2009.

Plato. *Republic*, edited by Gregory R. Crane. Perseus Digital Library, Tufts University. www.perseus.tufts.edu/hopper/.

Postlewait, Thomas, ed. *Bernard Shaw and William Archer*. Toronto: University of Toronto Press, 2017.

Potter, Rachel. Introduction to *Prudes on the Prowl: Fiction and Obscenity in England, 1850 to the Present Day*, edited by David Bradshaw and Rachel Potter, 1–10. Oxford University Press, 2013.

Potter, Rachel. "Modernist Rights: International PEN 1921–1936." *Critical Quarterly* 55, no. 2 (July 2013): 66–80.

Potter, Rachel. *Obscene Modernism: Literary Censorship and Experiment, 1900–1940*. Oxford: Oxford University Press, 2013.

Prizeman, Oriel. *Philanthropy and Light: Carnegie Libraries and the Advent of Transatlantic Standards for Public Space*. Farnham, UK: Ashgate, 2012.

Rains, Stephanie. "'Nauseous Tides of Seductive Debauchery': Irish Story Papers and the Anti-Vice Campaigns of the Early Twentieth Century." *Irish University Review* 45, no. 2 (2015): 263–80.

Ramazani, Jahan. *Poetry of Mourning: The Modern Elegy from Hardy to Heaney*. Chicago: University of Chicago Press, 1994.

Renan, Ernest. "What Is a Nation?" In *Nation and Narration*, edited by Homi Bhabha, translated by Martin Thom, 8–22. London: Routledge, 1990.

Richardson, Caleb. "'They Are Not Worthy of Themselves': *The Tailor and Ansty* Debates of 1942." *Eire-Ireland* 42, no. 3 & 4 (2007): 148–72.

Robinson, Lennox. *Curtain Up: An Autobiography*. London: Michael Joseph, 1942.

Robinson, Lennox, ed. *Lady Gregory's Journals*. New York: Macmillan, 1947.

Rockett, Kevin. *Irish Film Censorship: A Cultural Journey from Silent Cinema to Internet Pornography*. Dublin: Four Courts Press, 2004.

Rolley, Katrina. "The Treatment of Homosexuality and *The Well of Loneliness*." In *Writing and Censorship in Britain*, edited by Paul Hyland and Neil Sammells, 219–31. London: Routledge, 2023.

Rudolph, C. H., ed. *The Trial of Lady Chatterley: Regina v. Penguin Books Limited*. London: Penguin, 1961.

Ryan, Brendan. *Keeping Us in the Dark: Censorship and Freedom of Information in Ireland*. Dublin: Gill & Macmillan, 1995.

St. Jorre, John de. *Venus Bound: The Erotic Voyage of the Olympia Press*. New York: Random House, 1996.

Sampson, Denis. *Young McGahern: Becoming a Novelist*. Oxford: Oxford University Press, 2012.

Saxonhouse, Arlene W. *Free Speech and Democracy in Ancient Athens*. Cambridge: Cambridge University Press, 2006.

Schauer, Frederick. *Free Speech: A Philosophical Enquiry*. Cambridge: Cambridge University Press, 1982.

Scholes, Robert. "Grant Richards to James Joyce." *Studies in Bibliography* 16 (1963): 139–60.

Sheehy-Skeffington, Owen. "The McGahern Affair." *Censorship: Quarterly Report on Censorship of Ideas and the Arts* 2, no. 2 (1966): 27–30.

Shloss, Carol Loeb. "Privacy and the Misuse of Copyright: The Case of *Shloss v. the Estate of James Joyce*." In *Modernism and Copyright*, edited by Paul K. Saint-Amour, 243–59. Oxford: Oxford University Press, 2011.

Shaw, Bernard. *The Adventures of the Black Girl in Her Search for God*. London: Constable, 1932.

Shaw, Bernard. *Agitations: Letters to the Press, 1875–1950*, edited by Dan H. Laurence and James Rambeau. New York: Frederick Ungar, 1985.

Shaw, Bernard. "Art Corner." *The Shaw Review* 15, no. 1 (1972): 35–8.

Shaw, Bernard. *The Diaries, 1885–1897*. Edited by Stanley Weintraub. 2 vols. University Park, PA: Pennsylvania State University Press, 1986.

Shaw, Bernard. *The Doctor's Dilemma, Getting Married, and The Shewing-up of Blanco Posnet*. London: Constable, 1911.

Shaw, Bernard. *The Drama Observed*. Edited by Bernard F. Dukore. 4 vols. University Park, PA: Pennsylvania State University Press, 1993.

Shaw, Bernard. "Fragments of a Fabian Lecture 1890." In *Shaw and Ibsen: Bernard Shaw's The Quintessence of Ibsenism and Related Writings*, edited by J. L. Wisenthal, 81–96. Toronto: University of Toronto Press, 1979.

Shaw, Bernard. *Mrs Warren's Profession*. London: Grant Richards, 1902.

Shaw, Bernard. *Our Theatres in the Nineties*. 3 vols. London: Constable, 1932.

Shaw, Bernard. Preface to *Plays Pleasant and Unpleasant: Plays Unpleasant*, by Bernard Shaw, 147–75. London: Constable, 1931.

Shaw, Bernard. Preface to *The Shewing-up of Blanco Posnet*. In *The Doctor's Dilemma, Getting Married, and The Shewing-Up of Blanco Posnet*, by Bernard Shaw, 355–426. London: Constable, 1911.

Shaw, Bernard. "The Quintessence of Ibsenism." In *Shaw and Ibsen: Bernard Shaw's The Quintessence of Ibsenism and Related Writings*, edited by J. L. Wisenthal. Toronto: University of Toronto Press, 1979, 97–237.

Sheehy-Skeffington, Andrée. *Skeff: The Life of Owen Sheehy-Skeffington*. Dublin: Lilliput Press, 1991.

Shovlin, Frank. *The Irish Literary Periodical, 1923–1958*. Oxford: Clarendon Press, 2003.

Shovlin, Frank, ed. *The Letters of John McGahern*. London: Faber and Faber, 2021.

Smith, Helen. *An Uncommon Reader: A Life of Edward Garnett, Mentor and Editor of Literary Genius*. New York: Farrar, Straus and Giroux, 2017.

Smith, James M. *Ireland's Magdalen Laundries and the Nation's Architecture of Containment*. Notre Dame, IN: University of Notre Dame Press, 2007.

Smith, James M. "The Politics of Sexual Knowledge: The Origins of Ireland's Containment Culture and the Carrigan Report (1931)." *Journal of the History of Sexuality* 13, no. 2 (2004): 208–33.

Smyth, Patrick, and Ellen Hazelkorn, eds. *Let in the Light: Censorship, Secrecy and Democracy*. Dingle: Brandon, 1993.

Souhami, Diana. *The Trials of Radclyffe Hall*. London: Weidenfeld and Nicholson, 1998.

Stead, W. T. "The Future of Journalism." *The Contemporary Review* 50 (July 1886): 664.

Stead, W. T. "Government by Journalism." *Contemporary Review* 49 (January 1886): 653–74.

Stephens, John Russell. *The Censorship of English Drama, 1824–1901*. Cambridge: Cambridge University Press, 2010.

Stevas, Norman St. John. *Obscenity and the Law*. London: Secker & Warburg, 1956.

Stewart, Bruce. Ricorso. "Ricorso: A Knowledge of Irish Literature." http://www.ricorso.net/index.html.

Sutherland, Halliday. *The Laws of Life*. London: Sheed & Ward, 1935.

Sutherland, John A. *Victorian Novelists and Publishers*. Chicago: University of Chicago Press, 1976.

Teekell, Anna. *Emergency Writing: Irish Literature, Neutrality, and the Second World War*. Evanston, IL: Northwestern University Press, 2018.

Templeton, Joan. *Shaw's Ibsen: A Re-Appraisal*. London: Palgrave Macmillan, 2018.

The Liberal Ethic. Dublin: Irish Times, 1950.

Thomas, David, David Carlton, and Anne Etienne. *Theatre Censorship: From Walpole to Wilson*. Oxford: Oxford University Press, 2007.

Tobin, Robert. *The Minority Voice: Hubert Butler and Southern Irish Protestantism, 1900–1991*. Oxford: Oxford University Press, 2012.

Torner, Carles, and Jan Martens, eds. *PEN International: An Illustrated History*. London: Thames & Hudson, 2021.

Troeger, Rebecca. "'Voices of the World': National Identity and Musical Space at the 1932 Eucharistic Congress." *Éire-Ireland* 50, no. 3 & 4 (2015): 59–73.

Universal Declaration of Human Rights. "United Nations." Accessed 31 October 2024. www.un.org/en/universal-declaration-human-rights/.

Ussher, Arland. *The Face and Mind of Ireland*. London: Victor Gollanz, 1949.

Ussher, Percy Arland. *The Midnight Court and The Adventures of a Luckless Fellow: Translated from the Gaelic*. New York: Boni and Liveright, 1926.

Valiulus, Maryann Gialanella. "Censorship as Freedom of Expression: *The Tailor and Ansty* Revisited." *Historical Reflections* 37, no. 2 (2011): 24–38.

Vanderham, Paul. *James Joyce and Censorship: The Trials of "Ulysses."* New York: New York University Press, 1998.

Vargo, Marc E. *Scandal: Infamous Gay Controversies of the Twentieth Century*. London: Routledge, 2003.

Villar-Argaiz, Pilar, ed. *Literary Visions of Multicultural Ireland: The Immigrant in Contemporary Irish Literature*. Manchester: Manchester University Press, 2013.

Vizetelly, Ernest. *Émile Zola, Novelist and Reformer: An Account of His Life and Work*. London: John Lane, 1904.

Vizetelly, Henry. *Extracts Principally from English Classics: Showing That the Legal Suppression of M. Zola's Novels Would Logically Involve the Bowdlerizing of Some of the Greatest Works in English Literature*. London: Vizetelly, 1888.

Wade, Allan, ed. *The Letters of W. B. Yeats*. London: Rupert Hart-Davis, 1954.

Walker, Samuel. *In Defence of American Liberties: A History of the ACLU*. Oxford: Oxford University Press, 1990.

Walsh, Martin. "Richard Devane: Social Campaigner in the Free State, 1920–51." *Studies: An Irish Quarterly Review* 103, no. 41 (2014/15): 562–73.

Walshe, Eibhear. "Censorship, Law and Literature." In *Irish Literature in Transition, 1940–1980*, edited by Eve Patten, 169–84. Cambridge: Cambridge University Press, 2020.

Ward, Margaret. *Fearless Woman: Hanna Sheehy-Skeffington, Feminism and the Irish Revolution*. Dublin: University College Dublin Press, 2019.

Watts, Marjorie. *Mrs Sappho: The Life of C. A. Dawson Scott, "Mother of International P.E.N."* London: Duckworth, 1987.

Weintraub, Stanley. *Shaw's People: From Victoria to Churchill*. University Park, PA: Pennsylvania State University Press, 1996.

Weir, David. "What Did He Know and When Did He Know It: The *Little Review*, Joyce, and *Ulysses*." *James Joyce Quarterly* 37, no. 3–4 (2000): 389–412.

Welch, Robert. *The Concise Oxford Companion to Irish Literature* (Oxford: Oxford University Press, 2000).

Wells, H. G. *The Idea of a League of Nations*. Boston: The Atlantic Monthly Press, 1919.

Whelan, Gerard. *Spiked: Church-State Intrigue and "The Rose Tattoo."* Dublin: New Island, 2002.

Whelan, Kevin. "The Green Atlantic: Radical Reciprocities between Ireland and America in the Long Eighteenth Century." In *A New Imperial History: Culture, Identity and Modernity in Britain and the Empire, 1660–1840*, edited by Kathleen Wilson, 216–38. Cambridge: Cambridge University Press, 2004.

Whyte, J. H. *Church and State in Modern Ireland, 1923–1970*. Dublin: Gill & MacMillan, 1980.

Wilford, R. A. "The PEN Club, 1930–50." *Journal of Contemporary History* 14, no. 1 (January 1979): 99–116.

Wills, Clair. *That Neutral Island: A Cultural History of Ireland during the Second World War*. Cambridge, MA: Harvard University Press, 2007.

Wilson, Nicola. "Circulating Morals (1900–1915)." In *Prudes on the Prowl: Fiction and Obscenity in England, 1850 to the Present Day*, edited by David Bradshaw and Rachel Potter, 52–70. Oxford: Oxford University Press, 2013.

Zakaria, Fareed. "The Rise of Illiberal Democracy." *Foreign Affairs* 76, no. 6 (1997): 22–43.

Zola, Émile. *The Earth*. Translated and edited by Brian Nelson and Julie Rose. Oxford: Oxford University Press, 2016.

Zola, Émile. "Naturalism in the Theatre." In *A Sourcebook on Naturalist Theatre*, edited by Christopher Innes, translated by Albert Bermel, 47–52. London: Routledge, 2000.

Zola, Émile. *The Soil: A Realistic Novel*. London: Vizetelly, 1888.

Zola, Émile. *La Terre*. Paris: Garnier-Flammarion, 1973.

Index